Museum Learning

As museums are increasingly asked to demonstrate not only their cultural, but also their educational and social significance, the means to understand how museum visitors learn becomes ever more important. And yet, learning can be conceptualised and investigated in many ways. Coming to terms with how theories about learning interact with one another and how they relate to 'evidence-based learning' can be confusing at best.

Museum Learning attempts to make sense of multiple learning theories whilst focusing on a set of core learning topics in museums. It draws attention to the development of theory and its practical applications in museum contexts such as aquariums, zoos, botanical gardens and historical re-enactment sites, in addition to more traditional art, science, and social history museums. Importantly, it considers learning not just as a cognitive characteristic, as some perspectives propose, but also as affective, taking into consideration interests, attitudes, and emotions.

This volume will be of interest to museum studies students, practitioners and researchers working in informal learning contexts, and will help them to reflect on what it means to learn in museums and create more effective environments for learning.

Jill Hohenstein is Senior Lecturer in Psychology in Education at the School of Education, Communication and Society, King's College London. Trained as a developmental psychologist, her research examines the ways that children and adults learn in informal settings, including museums, with a particular focus on language and cognitive development.

Theano Moussouri is Senior Lecturer in Museum Studies at the Institute of Archaeology, University College London. She previously worked in museums as an audience researcher. Her current research examines motivation and meaning making in museum visitors and non-visitors; museum professionals' development and sharing of knowledge; and researcher-practitioner collaborative research.

KA 0432247 9

Museum Learning

Theory and Research as Tools
for Enhancing Practice

Jill Hohenstein and
Theano Moussouri

UNIVERSITY OF WINCHESTER
LIBRARY

 Routledge
Taylor & Francis Group

LONDON AND NEW YORK

First published 2018
by Routledge
2 Park Square, Milton Park, Abingdon, Oxon OX14 4RN

and by Routledge
711 Third Avenue, New York, NY 10017

*Routledge is an imprint of the Taylor & Francis Group, an
informa business*

© 2018 Jill Hohenstein and Theano Moussouri

The right of Jill Hohenstein and Theano Moussouri to be identified as
authors of this work has been asserted by them in accordance with
sections 77 and 78 of the Copyright, Designs and Patents Act 1988.

All rights reserved. No part of this book may be reprinted or reproduced or
utilised in any form or by any electronic, mechanical, or other means, now
known or hereafter invented, including photocopying and recording, or in any
information storage or retrieval system, without permission in writing from
the publishers.

Trademark notice: Product or corporate names may be trademarks or
registered trademarks, and are used only for identification and explanation
without intent to infringe.

British Library Cataloguing-in-Publication Data
A catalogue record for this book is available from the British Library

Library of Congress Cataloging-in-Publication Data
Names: Hohenstein, Jill, author. | Moussouri, Theano, author.
Title: Museum learning : theory and research as tools for enhancing practice /
Jill Hohenstein and Theano Moussouri.
Description: Abingdon, Oxon ; New York, NY : Routhledge, 2017. |
Includes bibliographical references and index.
Identifiers: LCCN 2017017357 (print) | LCCN 2017034080 (ebook) |
ISBN 9781315696447 (Master) | ISBN 9781317445944 (Web Pdf) |
ISBN 9781317445944 (ePub) | ISBN 9781317445937 (Mobipocket/Kindle) |
ISBN 9781138901124 (hardback : alk. paper) |
ISBN 9781138901131 (pbk. : alk. paper) | ISBN 9781315696447 (ebk)
Subjects: LCSH: Museums–Educational aspects. |
Museum techniques–Research. | Learning, Psychology of.
Classification: LCC AM7 (ebook) |
LCC AM7 .H64 2017 (print) | DDC 069.075–dc23
LC record available at https://lccn.loc.gov/2017017357

ISBN: 978-1-138-90112-4 (hbk)
ISBN: 978-1-138-90113-1 (pbk)
ISBN: 978-1-315-69644-7 (ebk)

Typeset in Sabon
by Out of House Publishing
Printed and bound by CPI Group (UK) Ltd, Croydon, CR0 4YY

UNIVERSITY OF WINCHESTER

Contents

Contributors

Chapter 4
Frances Jeens, Head of Learning, Jewish Museum London, UK. Frances contributed The Role of the Museum as a Place to Ask Anonymous Questions scenario.

Chapter 5
Sue Brunning, Curator, European Early Medieval & Sutton Hoo Collections, Department of Britain, Europe and Prehistory, the British Museum, UK. Sue wrote and contributed the Experience on Room 41 scenario.

Chapter 6
Katherine Johnson, Youth Education Programs Director at the Chicago Botanic Garden in Glencoe, IL, USA. Katherine wrote and contributed the Authentic Nature Play at the Chicago Botanic Garden scenario.

Chapter 7
Sharon Willoughby, Manager Public Programs, Cranbourne Gardens, Royal Botanic Gardens Victoria, Australia. Katherine wrote and contributed the Authentic Nature Play at the Chicago Botanic Garden scenario.

Chapter 8
The following contributors gave the authors permission to use information from the Colored Girls Museum website in order to construct The Art of Voicing Black Women's Identity as Seen Through Everyday Objects scenario.

Michael Clemmons, Curator, Colored Girls Museum, Philadelphia, PA, USA & Associate.

Vashti DuBois, Executive Director/Founder, Colored Girls Museum, Philadelphia, PA, USA.

Ian Friday, Associate Director, The Colored Girls Museum, Philadelphia PA, USA & Director-Workforce Development – CSPCD, Temple University, CSPCD, Philadelphia, PA, USA.

Chapter 9

The information for the scenario was provided in notes, interview and a paper (Davies, 2014). It was then written by the authors and further edited by Glynn Davis, Adam Corsini and Roy Stephenson.

Adam Corsini, Archaeology Collections Manager, Museum of London, London, UK. Adam wrote sections of, edited and contributed the Linking up Museums and People through Serious Pursuits scenario.

Glynn Davis, Senior Collections & Learning Curator at Colchester Museums, Colchester, UK (formerly Archaeological Collections Manager at the Museum of London's Archaeological Archive). Glynn provided original material for, edited and contributed the Linking up Museums and People through Serious Pursuits scenario.

Roy Stephenson, Head of Archaeological Collections and Archive, Museum of London, UK. Roy edited the final version of the Linking up Museums and People through Serious Pursuits scenario.

Chapter 10

Myles Russell Cook, Curator of Indigenous Art, National Gallery of Victoria, Australia & Lecturer, Design Anthropology and Indigenous Studies, University of Melbourne, Australia. Myles wrote the original paper which is used in the Aboriginal People and Museums Working Together scenario.

Acknowledgements

This book is the result of the collaborative effort and support of many people, including our colleagues at the School of Education, Communication and Society, King's College London and UCL Institute of Archaeology, museum colleagues and our students. Ideas presented in this book have been discussed with many people and have been honed by our students' questions.

Our very special thanks go to Marie Hobson. The discussions we had with her and her feedback on one of the chapters had special impact and proved to be a turning point in the development of the topic chapters in particular. We would also like to acknowledge the invaluable assistance and support of our scenario writers and/or contributors: Sue Brunning, Adam Corsini, Glynn Davis, Frances Jeens, Katherine Johnson and Sharon Willoughby. They have all been extremely generous with their time, met with us and provided feedback and ideas throughout the process, from developing the book structure and its content to sourcing photographs and reading various parts of the manuscript. Michael Clemmons, Vashti DuBois and Ian Friday have been most helpful and their ideas and vision have been a true inspiration to us. Many thanks Myles Russell Cook and Roy Stephenson for their contribution to the scenarios too.

A number of people helped us with developing the book content and its structure. In this regard, we would like to thank the Public Engagement Group of the Natural History Museum in London, and the Learning Team of the Jewish Museum London who have contributed ideas and support with great generosity. We would also like to thank the following for their ideas and support: Carol Chung, Ruth Clarke, Sally Collins, Pippa Couch, Kathryn Creed, Chris Winch, Victoria Donnellan, Sabine Doolin, Christine Gerbich, Tim Grove, Stuart Frost, Juliette Fritsch, Conny Graft, Naomi Haywood, Morna Hinton, Gina Koutsika, Effrosyni Nomikou, Emma Pegram, Juhee Park, Emily Pringle, Beth Schneider and Lucy Trench. Others helped enormously by assisting us in identifying and contacting possible scenario contributors; our thanks go to Marianna Adams, Jamie Bell, Dirk vom Lehn, Jennifer Schwarz Ballard and Asimina Vergou. Many thanks to Eleni Vomvyla, Antigonos Sochos, Paul Marshall, Pippa Couch, David Francis and Heather King for their suggestions of relevant literature.

We much appreciate the kind assistance of the following museum staff who assisted with sourcing and with copyright permissions for photographs: Iain Calderwood, the British Museum; Michael Clemmons and Ian Friday, the Colored Girls Museum; Sarah Williams, Museum of London; and Alamy Customer Service staff. We would particularly like to thank the following museums for giving us permission to use their photographs free of change: Colored Girls Museum, Chicago Botanic Garden, Jewish Museum London and Royal Botanic Gardens Victoria.

We would like to thank the two anonymous referees for their feedback and our editors at Routledge: Matthew Gibbons, Senior Editor; Lola Harre, Editorial Assistant; and Molly Marler, Editorial Assistant.

This book would not have been completed without the help of family members. Katerina Roussos has been very patient while this project was completed and she has also been the inspiration for one of the fictitious characters in our scenarios. George Roussos has been an endless source of encouragement and support.

1 Introduction

Theory can be seen as a lens through which research is filtered. As a result, the ideas that are seen to be important for use in developing evidence-based practice are all influenced by particular perspectives about learning, about research, and about museums. This is not always done in a conscious way in museum practice. As practically minded people, museum professionals are often drawn to empirical research and models that are developed in order to address pertinent questions for museum practice. We argue that, although there is nothing inherently wrong with these approaches, issues of theory-evidence gap, methodology and theoretical assumptions require attention. Similarly, models developed with practitioners in mind need to be mindful of and address these issues. This is an area where academic researchers and museum professionals can work together to develop theoretically sound and practice-relevant frameworks, through research-practice collaborations.

This book represents the culmination of multiple years of work on the part of us, and many others in the worlds of both museums and learning theory. We have been aware for some time, through literature, work experiences, and conversations with various stakeholders, that it has been difficult to formulate a way to coherently discuss theories about learning in museum contexts in a manner that is accessible but also represents theories as they are seen in the world of academia. That is, the divide between academia and practice seems to grow rather than shrink in many ways, despite the attempts to bridge gaps. We hope this book helps to provide a useful window between theory and research on the one hand and practice on the other. In this introductory chapter there are several topics we will highlight: definitions of learning, what we refer to as a museum, the purpose of considering learning theory in museums as we see it, as well as the outline of the chapters that follow.

Though on the surface it might seem rather obvious, there are many different institutions that could count as a 'museum'.

The Museums Association in the UK states that 'Museums enable people to explore collections for inspiration, learning and enjoyment. They are institutions that collect, safeguard and make accessible artefacts and specimens, which they hold in trust for society' (Museums Association, n.d.). This definition purposely includes art galleries and historical collections. We are using the term museum rather more broadly here to include both these traditional museums, containing objects of value (however that is defined), which offer a public the opportunity to see these objects so they may experience them in an authentic way. But we are also referring to science centres in which there may be very few 'objects' of value, but rather there are hands-on experiences of phenomena that the scientific community has discovered. In addition, zoos and botanical gardens which both contain living 'objects' can be thought of in ways that are similar to museums. Furthermore, heritage and archaeological sites constitute other forms of what can be thought of as open-air museums. There are also historical houses and other buildings of interest that qualify as museums in this view. Finally, newer ways of interacting with publics through dialogue events, re-enactments, and demonstrations can be considered within the auspices of museums. Gurian (2002) categorised museums into five types: object-centred, housing objects of value; narrative, including those that interpret the story of particular groups (e.g., United States Holocaust Memorial Museum); client-centred, including children's museums and science centres, many of which do not have collections but instead provide experiences and afford visitors opportunities to witness phenomena; community-centred, being of – and for – the community in which they are based; and national, which tend to attempt to represent the interests of a whole country. Though each type of museum may have specific needs and details with respect to the consideration of learning, there are undoubtedly many things that are shared by these institutional types.

Though much of the research that we present has been carried out in more 'traditional' object-centred and client-centred museums, it is important to consider the ways that other contexts may have similar or different relations to the findings of research and be able to utilise the guidance that various theories might put forth. Of course, the studies reviewed here take a specific view of museums, although this is not always explicit. Museums are often seen as social institutions for personal, social, dialogical, collective or emancipatory learning, with various degrees of reference to the ideological process of education or learning policy and mission. At the same time, we acknowledge that there is a growing use of digital technologies in museums for presentation of exhibit material as well as interactive guided tours, amongst other uses. Although we refer to studies involving digital technologies in museum learning in several places throughout the book, including a section in Chapter 6 on authenticity, we do not devote a great deal of space specifically to how learning can be enhanced (or indeed inhibited) by the use of digital technology. This may be an omission on our part. However, it was necessary to make choices about what we were able to include, due to space limitations.

We want to clarify from the outset that we think of learning as something that is cognitive, affective and psychomotor (Bloom, 1956). Whereas a very traditional view of learning would perhaps suggest that priority should to be given to the cognitive aspects of learning (e.g., knowledge for facts and 'understanding' how or why things have occurred in the way they have), we also hold dear the notion that learning is much broader than just cognitive gains. That is, learning is also emotional, attitudinal and aspirational, but bodily, too. This means that people develop and change in the ways they feel about various ideas and concepts such as impressionist art, biomedical technologies, changes in positions of power across the globe, etc. They also can sometimes become highly skilled at an activity, such as driving a car, without being able to think about or talk about the details involved in carrying out that activity. So, though there is still an emphasis on cognitive learning in various educational institutions, including museums, we think is it important to recognise the non-cognitive in learning theory and research. That being said, much of the research in museums does tend to take a cognitive focus. We try to present work in this book that goes beyond the cognitive but we are also limited by the research that has been carried out.

It is important to point out that whereas thinking of learning as memory for facts is perhaps conventional, it might not be the most useful way to capture the types of learning experiences occurring in museums. There are numerous reasons to reject mere factual learning as the standard upon which to judge museum learning. Thinking about learning as only a cognitive outcome will result in missing issues to do with conceptual development as opposed to 'information' as important elements of learning. But adding the affective and motoric types of learning to the mix will bolster arguments as to why a focus on facts as items to be learned will miss out on valuable opportunities in museums that would not count as learning facts. Moreover, whilst some theoretical perspectives about learning prioritise a notion of learning that exists within people's heads (e.g., constructivism, information processing), there are alternative views that would suggest learning and conceptual development are processes that occur in the interactional space in relationships between people (e.g., sociocultural theory). These latter types of perspectives tend to cut across cognitive and affective, or even motor, learning. There is a great deal of evidence to suggest that factual (and conceptual) cognitive learning can be connected to affective and even bodily learning (Martin & Briggs, 1986). But even this type of finding suggests that cognitive learning is somehow more important than attitudinal or emotional learning. We feel that Falk and Dierking (1997) were right, twenty years ago, to have highlighted the need to go beyond thinking about learning as memory for facts and have attempted to address this in multiple ways throughout the book.

Learning can be defined as a relatively permanent change in thought or behaviour, which might include cognition, opinions, skills or mindset as indicated above. These changes could be in areas that are of less obvious relevance to learning in museums, like firing patterns in particular neurons in the brain. But they can also appear in more observable actions, such as answers on a 'test' of knowledge. And they might also be in less tangible areas such as a vague sense of belonging to a group or feelings of being drawn to certain forms of art but not others. Illeris (2007) has pointed out that learning can be viewed as an outcome: this change in thought or behaviour mentioned above. But he notes that one could also see learning in terms of a process or even an interaction. The process of learning could be closely tied to the outcomes. That is, certain mental and emotional mechanisms might be necessary to bring about the learning outcomes that are seen. On the other hand, learning as an interaction implies that it is not an individual process, but rather involves at least two actors. The exchange between these actors can lead to different outcomes or even processes. The way one chooses to think about learning (outcome, process, or interaction) could affect the choices that are made in considering theory and research as valuable, but also how to apply the ideas from theory and research in practical settings.

It is sometimes difficult to make sense of the myriad research outcomes about a given topic. One only has to consider the news reports about the so-called benefits to our health of fats versus carbohydrates versus protein versus sugar, among other potential nutrients, to see how research does not always provide easy to follow guidelines or practical advice to the everyday consumer. We aim in this book to try to unpick some of the reasons that research findings can be at odds with one another. We think that one important element of such differences can be due to differences in theoretical perspective. Theoretical perspectives about learning (or other types of theory) are not always compatible with one another. If one buys into a particular type of learning as more important (e.g., outcome or cognitive), and this is more consistent with a particular theoretical perspective about learning, there is a good chance that the approach to research will differ from the approach taken by a different researcher with a different understanding of what learning should be seen as (e.g., interaction or affective). As covered in the next chapter on theory, sometimes theories can be built up in a way that reinforces biases about the fundamental constructs they cover, such as learning. These biases will undoubtedly influence the research that is based on these theories and any resulting guidance for practice. This may be one reason that findings from two different studies about the same topic can appear to come to varying conclusions. As such, consideration ought to be given to the theory that drove the research before trying to derive practical implications from studies.

To complicate matters, there are also disciplinary boundaries that can serve to both help and hinder understandings in the field of museum learning. For example, we draw from literature in psychology, sociology, history, philosophy and anthropology as 'primary' disciplines in this book. However, there are interdisciplinary fields that are also useful in the consideration of theories to do with learning, particularly as relevant to museums. These fields include education, women's studies, museum studies, cultural studies, tourism and leisure studies, and heritage studies, among others. Sometimes theories in two different disciplines can sound very similar to one another, and are developed in parallel to each other but only very rarely refer to each other in a cross-disciplinary way. For example, both the theory of Figured Worlds (Holland, Skinner, Lachiotte, & Cain, 2001) and the concept of 'scripts' (Schank & Abelson, 1977) relate to the ways that people come to understand expectations about how to act in particular situations. However, scripts tend to approach the idea from a very cognitive point of view, providing a way for people to act efficiently in their everyday lives; whereas Figured Worlds uses the idea about expectations as a fuzzier set of guidance, which helps people act in ways that are appropriate to their identities.

Some researchers coming from disparate fields tend to pick and choose aspects of psychological and learning science theories that suit them (or they have easy access to). This approach often results in reducing quite complex theories, constructs and principles to rather simplistic interpretations of what are, in effect, umbrella theories. One problem with this situation is that these researchers may only focus in on a small number of studies, representing particular interpretations of these theoretical perspectives whilst ignoring the complexities developed within the academic discipline by the original authors of the theories. As a result, this may lead to ignorance of what these disciplinary perspectives have to offer, which can mean that whole fields of study can miss out on meaningful dialogues. On the other hand, other researchers have made efforts to marry up different disciplinary perspectives and create more sophisticated and overarching theoretical perspectives. Beyond the theoretical level, the interaction of different disciplinary perspectives can also be useful at a methodological level. Where we have encountered potential dialogues in and between disciplines and fields, we try to point them out for the reader to help make sense of the vast array of theoretical perspectives that exist.

We feel it is important to declare our own backgrounds here in order to honestly acknowledge any biases we have. We have attempted to be inclusive in this book. But inevitably we are unable to make space for everything. We are undoubtedly influenced by our own perspectives about what is important. Given our statements about theory forming a lens with which to view research and practice, disclosure of our perspectives seems essential. One of us is a developmental psychologist who researches cognitive development and language. Hohenstein's primary theoretical perspectives stem from Piagetian, social constructivist, information processing and sociocultural backgrounds. At the same time, her research has tended to utilise quantitative methods, both observational and experimental. This research has been conducted primarily in museums and other sites of non-formal learning, like the home. Moussouri's view of learning in museums has been influenced by social constructivist and sociocultural perspectives. Having completed her first degree in education, one of the first things she noticed when working in museums was how few of the learning theories developed with formal learning settings in mind can be applied in museum settings. This shaped her approach to research, which is driven by research questions related to the value and relevance of museums in people's lives and grounded in museum practice. Her research is exploratory and qualitative in nature.

Related to the above disclosures, we are both empirical social scientists. As such, we tend to rely on empirical, rather than theoretical, research in our presentations of theory and research in this book (see Chapter 3 for more information on empirical methods). This means that our background leads us to favour studies that involve collecting data from relevant individuals or sources as opposed to those that start with an intellectual question and present analyses of exhibitions and experiences solely from the theoretical perspective of the author. We are aware that work from heritage studies often uses this technique in academic writing. As a result, we tend to draw less from that field than perhaps we could have.

This book begins with a chapter that discusses the importance of theory for both research and practice. We present the ways that theory develops over time, and how it can be difficult to change a discipline's dogmatic reliance on particular theoretical perspectives. But we also highlight the mediational role theory plays in the influence of research on practice: if theory has influenced research and research is used for evidence-based practice, then logically, theory also influences practice. At the same time, it can be difficult to make sense of the various theories about learning in museums. We emphasise the need to pay attention to what researchers mean when they align themselves with a particular theoretical perspective. Moreover, researchers might not even explicitly talk about theory in their studies, which can also introduce confusion to the issues of theory, research, and practice.

Following from this discussion of theory, Chapter 3 presents some very brief notes about methods and methodology. We think it is important to consider not just the theoretical perspectives about learning, but also the approaches that are taken to conducting empirical study. As such, we have attempted to outline some of the nuts and bolts to social science research, with a complete awareness of our inability (both due to space limitations and lack of expertise) to provide either a how-to manual for conducting research or a more thorough consideration of all of the available methods. We hope that this cursory coverage of methods and methodology will, if nothing else, help by indicating further references to follow for those who would like them.

Because we have tried in this book to ground the presentation of research and theory, we introduce our 'topic' chapters, 4–10, with a scenario that was contributed by practitioners from a number of museums around the world. The use of scenarios counterbalances the abstract nature of the theoretical discussions by grounding them in current museum practice and thinking. Hence, each topic chapter is a form of dialogue between theory, research and practice. The ensuing discussion presents our interpretations of how the practice-based scenarios relate to a variety of domain-specific theories. This is followed by the presentation of a number of either museum-based or museum-relevant empirical studies within the same domain.

We note here that the selection of topics is purposeful and yet may seem arbitrary. Each topic enabled us to look at a set of pertinent questions about learning in museums and can be approached in a cross-disciplinary way. We understand there will be overlap between topics at times; however, it seems important to separate the topics so that (a) readers can easily locate concepts they are interested in and (b) we can present the material in a more easily digestible amount of content. Attempts are made in the chapters to review learning research within each topic in a critical way, recognising that in a book of this size, it would be impossible to thoroughly cover all aspects of every topic.

Chapter 4 starts off this series of topic chapters by considering the making of meaning. This broad subject covers a number of perspectives about how different kinds of people (e.g., children, school groups, adults) have been shown to experience museum visits. A great number of theoretical perspectives are drawn upon here, including constructivism, sociocultural theory, information processing, interest, experiential learning, among others. The range of theories attempts to span cognitive and affective ways that people can make meaning in museums.

The following chapter focuses on narrative and language as tools for learning in museums. On the one hand, narrative is something that individuals use to help organise their identities, their understandings of world events and their relationships to other people. On the other hand, discourse is a bridge between people, which some theoretical perspectives (e.g., sociocultural theory, social constructivism) suggest is a key tool for learning. Chapter 5 draws together elements of narrative, discourse and communication to draw attention to the myriad research tools that can be utilised to understanding how language, storytelling and communication interact in museum learning situations.

It is often thought that one of the key attractions of museums is their ability to facilitate access to authentic objects and experiences. Chapter 6 considers how learners interpret the authenticity of what they are experiencing. We delineate the relationships between the historical, cultural and institutional contexts within which authenticity has been identified and studied and the way evidence about how people perceive authenticity has been collected and interpreted. Authenticity is not only a nebulous term but its meaning has been coloured by predominantly Western European views of the 'authentic'. This clearly has connections to learner motivations to see and be moved by 'authentic' objects or to have 'authentic experiences' in 'authentic settings'.

Chapter 7 connects learning experiences in museums to memory. We consider both personal and collective memories and their importance for setting out a learning agenda in museums. Whilst there are obvious implications from a learning agenda for personal memories, particularly as traditionally learning has been equated with memory for facts, the need to consider how a learner's previous experiences lead them to filter new experiences can be important for setting out exhibitions and activities in museums, too. Moreover, the ways that events are collectively remembered by communities will have implications for how museums approach topics they are exhibiting and organising activities around. As such, it will be important to consider not just how the majority culture views particular events, but also the views of minorities and marginalised groups.

Chapter 8 considers issues related to self and identity in museums. This chapter discusses the interrelation between the personal, social, cultural and cross-cultural dimensions of identity. We argue that theoretical and methodological approaches to studying identity in museums need to address both personal and collective identities since they mediate how people make sense of, act and reflect on their experiences in museums.

We then turn to discuss the many ways that motivation can be explored in museum settings in Chapter 9. Motivation seems an obvious element to learning and yet is still so poorly understood. Multiple theoretical (e.g., flow, serious leisure, sociocultural theory) and methodological approaches (e.g., ethnography, quasi-experimental approaches) have been proposed to help illuminate the ways that motivation interacts with other elements of learning, including cognitive outcomes, attitudinal changes, identity formation, and engagement with experiences both inside and outside school. In this central chapter we present several different theoretical perspectives drawn from multiple disciplines (e.g., anthropology, sociology, psychology) in order to try to make sense of the many connections between motivation and museum learning.

Our final topic chapter, Chapter 10, addresses a variety of issues involving culture and power in museum settings. It looks at the power relationships that exist within cultures and the role these play in shaping human experience and behaviour. It examines how particular approaches to knowledge construction and learning that have been used in museums enact and reproduce power relations. This can determine whether people choose to visit, and the ways in which they engage with and respond to the museum content, with their group members and museum staff.

In concluding this book, we draw attention to ways that we see research and practice as possibly working together. Though many have tried to create collaborations between researchers and practitioners before us (some successful, others less so), we think it is important to keep trying to forge links between research and practice. Helping to highlight the major theoretical perspectives used in museum learning research may provide tools for both groups to find common language for setting up useful partnerships. We also return to the multiple subjects in our topic chapters, hoping to synthesise some messages from each. We recognise from the outset that these topics overlap a great deal. Whilst there have been multiple cross-references within the topic chapters, some ideas about the ways the topics interact with one another are presented in this final chapter.

References

Bloom, B.S. (Ed.) (1956). *Taxonomy of educational objectives. Handbook 1: Cognitive domain.* New York: David McKay.

Falk, J. & Dierking, L. (1997). School field trips: Assessing their long-term impact. *Curator: The Museum Journal*, 40, 211–218.

Gurian, E.H. (2002). Choosing among the options: An opinion about museum definitions. *Curator: The Museum Journal*, 45, 75–88.

Holland, D., Skinner, D., Lachiotte Jr, W., & Cain, C. (2001). *Identity and agency in cultural worlds*. Cambridge, MA: Harvard University Press.

Illeris, K. (2007). *How we learn: Learning and non-learning in school and beyond*. London: Routledge.

Martin, B. & Briggs, L. (1986). *The affective and cognitive domains: Integration for instruction and research*. Englewood Cliffs, NJ: Educational Technology Publications.

Museums Association (no date). www.museumsassociation.org/about/frequently-asked-questions (last accessed 21 February, 2017).

Schank, R.C. & Abelson, R.P. (1977). *Scripts, plans, and understanding*. Hillsdale, NJ: Lawrence Erlbaum Associates.

2 Theory and museum practice

'There is nothing so practical as a good theory'
(Lewin, 1952, p. 169)

What's in a theory?

One often hears that it is important to pay attention to theory when considering options for developing a suitable learning experience, in museums and elsewhere. But why? In this chapter, we explore what theories are, how they are useful for research and for practice, and what might be useful as well as problematic about reliance on theoretical knowledge in practice. Following this discussion, we turn to the way that theories about learning can be conceptualised. And finally, we provide an in-depth exploration of a single theory, constructivism, to highlight the ways that it has been interpreted and used differently by a variety of authors across learning disciplines.

There are a number of ways of thinking about what a theory is. The common, everyday definition of 'theory' might suppose that it is conjecture or speculation that could possibly explain some phenomenon of interest. For example, one might have a theory that cats are inherently independent creatures, which helps explain why the pet cat has not managed to learn to come when called in the evening, even after bribing it with cat treats. In social sciences and natural or physical sciences, a theory is much more elaborate, built upon a multitude of previous theory and research. One definition of 'theory' appearing in the Oxford English Dictionary suggests that a theory is:

> a scheme or system of ideas or statements held as an explanation or account of a group of facts or phenomena; a hypothesis that has been confirmed or established by observation or experiment, and is propounded or accepted as accounting for the known facts; a statement of what are held to be the general laws, principles, or causes of something known or observed.
>
> (OED online)

Some researchers suspect that it is part of human nature to create and revise theories about how the world works (Gopnik & Meltzoff, 1997). However, the use of theory in a systematic way is more closely tied to the development of scientific ideas (see Kuhn, 1996; Popper, 2002). In this sense, a scientific theory is thought to be a 'comprehensive explanation of some aspect of nature that is supported by a vast body of evidence' (Ayala et al., 2008, p. 11). Theories are supported by evidence that comes from a large body of research showing findings that support the concept being purported by the theory. The ideas that are put forward in a theory should generally be testable. If there is no way to falsify a theory, some would consider it to be unscientific (Popper, 2002). For example, Popper regarded Sigmund Freud's theories about psychological development as unfalsifiable because there was no possibility of testing them. As a result, he considered them to be merely metaphysical. In addition, theories should lead to predictions about the subject of the theory. An example of such a prediction can be found in germ theory and the idea that the introduction of certain micro-organisms to otherwise uncontaminated food or living organisms could account for the appearance of some diseases. The work of scientists such as Louis Pasteur led to the testing of these principles and refutation of previous theories about the spread of infection (Pasteur, 2014).

So in short, a theory helps to explain phenomena that occur in the natural world, relying upon a large body of evidence, and leading to testable predictions of future outcomes in the same area. To further complicate matters, one can also distinguish laws from theories by saying that laws describe occurrences in the natural world without providing a broader explanation for their existence. Newton's law of universal gravitation proposes that any two bodies enact a force against one another, which is related to the mass of each of them and the distance between them. Newton referred to this exertion as 'force'. The phenomenon that he described is generally thought to be true and is used in countless situations in which it is useful to calculate the size of a pull between objects. However, his ideas about why this phenomenon occurs have been replaced by Einstein's theory of general relativity as a better explanation of the phenomenon. So whilst the law continues to play a role in the description of gravity, the theory has changed over time (Freundlich, 1920). This is to say that theory is not the same as law. Moreover, law and theory both differ from a hypothesis, which is generally thought to be more akin to the predictions that can be generated from a theory (Committee on Defining and Advancing the Conceptual Basis of Biological Sciences in the 21st Century, 2007). Together, laws, theories and hypotheses help to generate research questions and studies that help to build new theories or refine old ones in the interest of furthering understanding about the phenomena in question. Finally, it is also useful to be aware of models, which can be used to describe ways that phenomena or processes take place. A model can be used to develop theory; but it can also just show how other ideas can be perceived to fit together. For example, the contextual model of learning (Falk & Dierking, 2000) unites theories from a number of different perspectives to try to illuminate how they interact. But rather than develop new explanations for learning, it refers to previously developed explanations to apply them to the museum context.

As mentioned above, these ideas all come from work within the natural and physical sciences. How do they relate to what is done in social science and education? One might think that because the subject of study varies greatly between social and physical sciences, that the ways their study is governed by theory should also vary greatly. There are many who argue that the study of social sciences calls for different types of theories to the natural sciences (Turner, 2001). In other words, social sciences, according to such perspectives, are so different because of the complex nature of humanity and life that perhaps hypothesis testing should not be seen as an objective in social science. As such, perhaps theory itself would hold less sway over those involved in social science research. However, there are good reasons to doubt this claim. As noted by Parsons in addressing the Institute of the Society for Social Research in 1937, 'our study of fact, however little we may be aware of it, is always guided by the logical structure of a theoretical scheme, even if it is entirely implicit' (1938, p. 15). He went on to suggest that researchers only investigate the notions that they find interesting, rather than everything that is available to them, which is ultimately guided by some theoretical framework. Moreover, Suppes (1974) stated in his presidential address to the American Educational Research Association that 'a powerful theory changes our perspective on what is important and what is superficial' (p. 4). In other words, even in social science the theoretical framework one adopts will shape subsequent ideas about what matters in considerations of research and practice.

In light of these ideas about the nature of theory and how it can shape ideas in both the natural and social sciences, we set out below several of the ways in which theory can be useful in research and practice.

What are they good for?

Just because theories are 'out there' does not mean that everyone will think that it is important to find out about them. After all, if a person knows about the findings of research (which may or may not be the case), why is it necessary to know about the theoretical perspectives that helped to shape those findings? Here we explore some of the reasons why theory is important both for research and for practice. These reasons include the way that theory helps researchers both prepare for their own studies and be aware of potentially opposing perspectives. But, in a similar way, theory can help provide a lens through which to build evidence-based links to practice. As such, theory informs the work of both those conducting research and those influencing practical situations.

Theory and research

When researchers set out to conduct a study, they will often carry with them a set of biases, either implicit or explicit, that drive the types of questions they will ask about the world. Knowing something about the theoretical perspectives about that topic will help them not only to understand previous research that has been conducted but also to formulate focused questions that can be addressed using pertinent research tools. On the other hand, if they are ignorant of the theoretical perspectives, they may try to conduct a study that has been done before or may lack the insight to narrow a topic sufficiently (Greenwald, Pratkanis, Leippe, & Baumgardner, 1986).

Theory helps researchers to communicate about the perspectives they take towards a topic. When researchers publish about the research they have carried out, the declaration of a theoretical position may alert others who read the research to the reasons they conducted the research in the way they did. Likewise, when researchers have background knowledge about the theoretical perspective, they are more easily able to identify the reasoning used in an article about current research. In contrast, if the reader is less aware of the differences in theoretical perspective, she may find it difficult to understand the rationale for conducting the study.

At the same time, understanding the theory used in carrying out one study enables researchers to build upon theory, adding pieces of evidence that create a bigger picture of how the world works. That is, when deciding upon which study to carry out, researchers will often consider how the results could help paint a more complete theoretical picture in addition to how the results might be useful in a practical sense. In this way, theory can advance through an accumulation of studies that support, shape and question it (Greenwald et al., 1986).

This process by which theory is used to help guide perspectives on explanations about occurrences in the world can be thought of as a lens that can help researchers to focus on problems in ways that illuminate understandings. At the same time, theory can also be a set of blinkers that might prevent researchers from looking beyond the potential explanations allowed by the theoretical perspective they have adopted. In this way theory can be a restrictive force in the studies that are conducted. Kuhn, in his book about theoretical change, asserted that 'Further development, therefore, ordinarily calls for ... the development of esoteric vocabulary and skills ... leads ... to an immense restriction of the scientist's vision and to a considerable resistance to paradigm change' (1996, p. 64). This type of narrowing of focus can also create a tension between the findings that arise from research conducted through different theoretical paradigms.

Take as an example two researchers who are interested in child language development: one of them tends to think that children are born with an innate predisposition to learn language because of a structure in the mind or brain (nativism); the other tends to think that learning language is like learning any other material, but that language is a particularly useful thing for infants to know about (social constructivism). These two researchers are likely to approach the task of finding out how children learn about language in rather different ways. The one with a bias toward innate predisposition may focus on so-called universal tendencies that children display in the early stages of language learning. In contrast, the researcher who thinks learning language is no different from other learning may ask more questions about the linguistic environments infants are exposed to for clues about early learning. This theoretical habit formation can be seen in the practice of theory-confirming studies, which aim to test theories in such as way as to support or falsify them, as opposed to result-centred methods which set out to establish conditions under which findings are either obtained or are not (Greenwald et al., 1986). In fact, such biases correspond to the theoretical distinctions in how it is believed children learn their first language. The nativist position on language development suggests that children learn the same way regardless of the differences in environmental language (so long as the environment provides a sufficiently rich stimulus) (e.g., Pinker, 1994). On the other hand, the social constructivist position argues that children rely on the language they hear to the extent that they do not go beyond the examples they are given until they have gained enough experience to be relatively confident about creatively using language (Tomasello, 2003). In addition, the methods they use to pursue the research they carry out also quite often differ, and this usually leads to reinforcement of the differences between the theoretical perspectives.

The example about language development research shows how theory can act as a potential barrier to communication about research within the academic community. But one can imagine it might also create confusion and/or misunderstandings outside academic circles. Despite there being partial truths in each side of the argument, the general public may wonder which side is 'correct', or how to use the findings that were seemingly generated at cross-purposes.

Theory and practice

There is a substantial body of literature now to suggest that people who work in learning settings, devising, facilitating or assessing, should use research-based evidence to enable them to better fulfil the needs of the learners as well as the institutions that employ them (Hammersley, 2001). This is true in museums as well as other educational establishments (Center for Advancement of Informal Science Education, 2015). Increasingly, fundraising organisations and advocacy groups seek assurances of evidence-based approaches to teaching and learning before providing the backing that educational institutions need. Of course, theory affects research that one could try to use in a particular museum setting by virtue of it having been used to devise the research itself. That is, when people make use of research-based evidence, they are necessarily using the theory that guided the research, at least indirectly.

In addition, it could be argued that practitioners are able to more directly employ theory in the work they do. In this way, they would not only be able to more easily understand the research they might read about, but they would also be able to start from the theoretical foundations about learning (in museums) and apply that knowledge more directly to the setting in which they are working. In turn, one could then conduct one's own studies within the museum setting using one or more theoretical perspectives as a basis for the research. Some writing dealing with whether practitioners can improve their practice through the introduction of theory comes from the work on the philosophy of work-based knowledge.

There is a philosophical argument, built upon the distinction between knowing *how* and knowing *that*, which questions the merits of the use of theory in order to improve practice. According to Ryle (1945), many academics had previously equated the understanding of action (knowing *that*) with the ability to carry that action out (knowing *how*). In this case it would only be necessary to acquire the knowledge associated with a task in order to perform the task itself. What Ryle asserted in his address was that ordinary people could easily conduct highly skilled work without the need to refer to a conscious set of knowledge. A corollary of this argument is that a person can have a complete understanding of the knowledge without being able to apply the knowledge in practice. Moreover, he suggested that in order to truly have a good understanding of a topic, one must have had to make use of it in practice. Therefore, according to this idea, the best way to gain understanding is not through education of facts, but rather through hands-on experience. The claims laid out in this address were popularised in many writings, leading some to claim that practitioners do not need to know about theory in order to do their jobs well (Brown, Collins, & Duguid, 1989).

In a more recent rebuttal of this argument, Winch (2009) has provided an argument drawing upon formal logic to refute the idea that practitioners' performance will not be enhanced by a good understanding of knowledge about the topic relevant to their field. In his critique of Ryle's arguments, Winch draws upon the logic laid out in previous publications (e.g., Stanley & Williamson, 2001) to show that Ryle's (1945) ideas about knowledge and practice can be broken down into three claims: (1) If a person does something, they have knowledge about that thing; (2) if a person uses knowledge about a topic, they somehow affirm knowledge about that topic and (3) knowledge of how to do something is knowledge *that* for some idea about that thing (Winch, 2009, p. 89). Winch uses several examples of practice and judgement about practice to show that knowing *that* can be extremely useful in making decisions and evaluations about workplace situations. For instance, a surgeon who has been trained to operate with a specialism in a given aspect of anatomy will make use of theoretical knowledge about the biological constitution of a person's body when encountering new problems, rather than merely relying on a build-up of expertise through experience. The surgeon will undoubtedly gain valuable expertise through practice. But one would hope that as a patient, the knowledge *that* would be present in addition to the knowledge *how*. And Winch points out that whilst Ryle's (1949) point that learning *how* is not the same as learning *that*, this does not mean that learning *that* will not be useful for acquiring knowledge about *how* to perform in a given occupation.

In addition to the distinction between knowing *how* and knowing *that*, many have noted that thinking about one's activities is beneficial to practice. Perhaps the most well-known for this perspective is Schön (1983). Schön made popular the idea that one ought to be a 'Reflective Practitioner', though such ideas were proposed by Dewey much earlier (1938). Schön referred to a person's reflective practice as 'reflection in action', in which the person could think on their feet in order to make decisions about the best action to take in a given work situation. In contrast, one can also think about the reasons for acting in a particular way, the origins of those actions and the usefulness of them: 'reflection on action'. More recently, a distinction between 'reflectivity' and 'reflexivity' has been introduced with respect to the practice (Chilvers, 2012). Whereas reflectivity refers to Schön's reflection on action, reflexivity tends to include a sense of being open to change in addition to thinking about the influences on one's actions. One of the elements that can be included in a reflective or reflexive experience is the ways that theory or research evidence can be brought to bear on the situation. For example, are there any studies that can shed light on the learning, affect or memory of the visitor in a given museum context? In this way, individuals might also alter the course of practice through reflection on theory rather than merely being affected by previous practice.

Here we have reviewed ways that theory can be helpful (or not) to practice, both from the perspective of how theory shapes research through design and interpretation and also the way that practice can benefit from reflection on theoretical and practical experiences. We turn briefly to consider the ways that theories are developed in order to shed further light on the types of theories that have been generated within the study of learning.

Where do they come from?

Theories in a given area are generated over the course of a relatively long period of time, through the accumulation of research and problem-solving on the part of many different people. In order to try to understand better the ways that things work in the natural and social world (i.e., to be able to explain and predict occurrences), research has often begun with a set of questions that can be addressed with a systematic study of some aspect of the world. When questions are first asked, they might be extremely broad because of a lack of background information to help narrow down the scope of the question (e.g., 'Why are we here?'). Once people begin to formulate some responses to the question, then these responses can be evaluated and re-evaluated in light of further evidence that becomes available. This recurs in an iterative pattern, usually for many years. When responses to a question start to create a pattern that can be systematised to provide a set of guiding principles around a topic, the beginnings of theories start to appear. This process stems from an inductive process for the development of theory: the use of empirical data to create generalisations (Eisenhardt, 1989; Glaser & Strauss, 1967; Alvesson & Kärremon, 2011).

It is useful in thinking about the way that theories are generated to remember that research findings are not infallible (see next chapter for more detail on research methods and methodology). In other words, the findings from any given study do not equate to 'fact'. And new methods and ways of testing ideas are constantly being invented. This means that new findings (and sometimes old findings) can call into question research

findings from previous studies. When findings have been repli-
cated or confirmed multiple times, then people in the field are
more likely to think about the findings as 'true'. However, it is,
in part, the potential fragility of findings that makes the creation of new theory or editing of current theory possible. This
does not mean that findings of all types are not valuable. Quite
the contrary, findings are always valuable, especially when the
research has been well conducted. However, even the highest
quality research can be called into question with new methods
or perspectives on the topic. This is one of the reasons why
researchers continue to ask new questions, rather than just relying upon very old work: the findings and the problems that
demand investigation provide new ways of looking at natural and social phenomena. To illustrate the ways that findings
can be disregarded in favour of new research one might look
to Piaget's stage model of development. Piaget, Inhelder and
Szeminska (1960) investigated young children's ability to infer
distance in a variety of judgements about direct and indirect
distance and found that 4.5 year old children were unable to
accurately respond to ideas about length because they have a
fuzzy, or plastic, sense of how to estimate distance. In later studies, researchers such as Fabricius and Wellman (1993) devised
methods of questioning four-year-olds' understandings of distance and showed that they had much greater understanding
of length than they were previously given credit for (but see
Lourenço & Machado, 1996, for support for Piaget, even in
light of this kind of refutation). Despite the example of newer
findings overturning older ones, it is more often the case that
studies serve to add new information, often from a slightly different angle (e.g., bodily as opposed to verbal interaction; vom
Lehn, 2006), rather than knock down the results reported in
earlier research.

So theories get built up over time through the accumulation of evidence that is used to construct them. Once theories
have been proposed and accepted as credible explanations of
some phenomenon, they are, in fact, very difficult to change.
As Thomas Kuhn has noted, revolution in scientific inquiry is
relatively rare: 'In science ... novelty emerges only with difficulty, manifested by resistance, against a background provided
by expectation. Initially, only the anticipated and usual are experienced even under circumstances where anomaly is later to be
observed' (1996, p. 64). This is because theories gain momentum once researchers begin to use them. These theories then
guide the new research that is conducted. And it is only when
someone looks for new insights to explanation that new theoretical ideas are introduced. And even then, they normally take
some time to become mainstream, assuming they are accepted
at all.

That being said, there do seem to be a plethora of theories about learning and development, many of which are relevant to museum contexts. In what follows we outline some of the ways that theories have arisen as relevant to museum contexts, after which we consider the ways that one theory, Constructivism, can be interpreted in multiple ways.

Theories about learning

In order to consider how to design informal learning environments that facilitate learning effectively, it is necessary to consider what learning is and what makes learning happen. Hein (1998) has suggested that an educational paradigm requires a theory of knowledge, a theory of learning and a theory of teaching. A theory of knowledge can sometimes be referred to as an epistemology: this considers the status of knowledge in terms of its origins, its recognition and its importance. If a piece of information is not considered to be important, then there will not be much effort placed on passing it on to other people. Likewise, understanding where the information came from can help to demonstrate its importance (e.g., information that comes from highly respected sources is usually deemed more reliable than that which comes from less respected sources; Harris, 2012). Though we concern ourselves in some places with what counts as knowledge in this book (see Chapter 10, for example), we focus primarily on theories of learning and pedagogy.

Theories of learning take into consideration what types of changes take place in the minds, brains and bodies of the learners. These theories often focus on the relative role of the individual learner as compared with the people involved in the learning environment: Is learning something that is an active or a passive process? Learning theories also tend to examine processes and outcomes of learning experiences. Some time ago learning theory referred primarily to behaviourist ways of thinking about learning (e.g., stimulus-response or operant conditioning; e.g., Skinner, 1974). However, the term learning theory is used more widely now to refer to any theoretical perspective about how people learn. Another important point, which we have mentioned in the Introduction, is that though some theories may focus more closely on the cognitive (e.g., what might be tested in school as facts or 'understanding'), many theories also consider as important the ways that affect and emotion figure into the changes associated with learning. As such, we should make sure to pay attention to both attitude or affect and more traditional views on learning as measured through changes in knowledge or comprehension.

Finally, theories of teaching make use of perspectives on learning to attempt to explain the ways that learning can be facilitated most efficiently. These theories are highly applied, whereas theories of knowledge or learning might be fairly basic or academic. Without a theory of learning, it is unlikely that a theory of teaching could be developed. However, research results about learning do not automatically lead to applications for teaching. Research about pedagogy[1] should be conducted in order to determine what types of teaching experiences tend to lead to various learning outcomes. That is, just because one understands something about learning does not mean there is an intervention that can be applied to improve learning. That requires more empirical work. A great deal of the research we present in this book reports on studies about applications in practice. And some of that refers specifically to theories about learning; however, sometimes research reports do not explicitly state which theories they are based upon.

This book mainly examines different theories of learning (and some about teaching or knowledge) as identified in the research, relevant to a number of topics in research on museum learning experiences. As such, we try to focus on a variety of theories related to visitor engagement that seem important for learning in museums. We note, in an imperfect way, that these theories can often be thought of on two different spectra: social/individual and affective/cognitive. By social, we mean that learning is seen as something that is not done alone: various people, groups and the general community may be responsible for influencing the changes in any given person's learning profile. In contrast, when a theory is highly individual, it suggests that the focus is on that person's perspective in learning, whilst giving little or no acknowledgement of the learner's environment. At the same time, learning theories may tend to emphasise the affective elements of learning relative to the cognitive ones (we have not focused on theories of physical learning in this book). Figure 2.1 illustrates where we have placed many theories on these two continua. Bear in mind that we are not the final authorities on these theories and there are bound to be those who disagree with our conceptualisation of the placement of these theories, or indeed, the use of these two spectra. However, our purpose is to provide a way for people who are less familiar with the types of learning theories relevant to museums to make sense of the numerous theories that can be encountered. We also want to highlight here that there are far too many theories about learning to include all of them in this figure. We have tended to place the bigger theories and umbrella, or 'grand', theories on the figure whilst ignoring the theories that might be considered a branch of one of these larger theories. This is done merely for space limitations and ease of reading, not because of any preference for any one theory in particular.

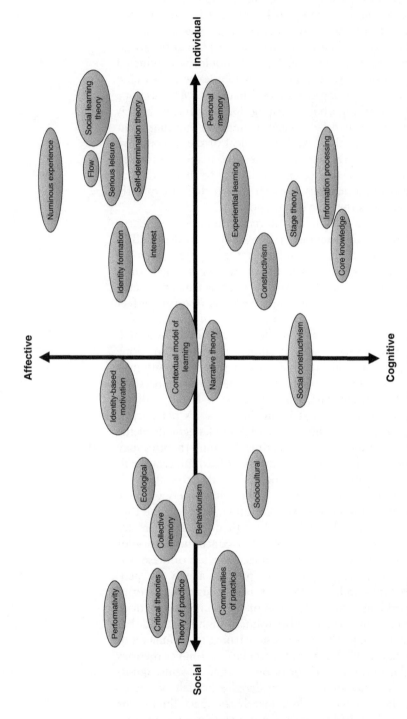

Figure 2.1 Graph illustrating many of the theories referred to in this book in relation to their position with respect to the continuum of social to individual focus and the spectrum from cognitive to affective.

Constructivism as an illustrative case

In order to show how theory can be interpreted in different ways, and how that might then influence the results one reads about in research, we will present the case of constructivism in greater detail here. But the reader should be aware that though constructivism specifically has a history of being controversial in its interpretation, any theory could be subject to similar differences in opinion.

Constructivism refers to the advancement of conceptual understanding through the agentive activity of the learner (von Glaserfeld, 1985). That is, learners learn through their own thrust towards the goals of learning, consciously or not. The idea that learners must be ready to learn stems from Piagetian and Deweyan theoretical foundations (Piaget, 1952; Dewey, 1938). Dewey (1938), through his emphasis on the development of understandings by way of experience, advocated for a democratic educative environment, facilitated by learners' autonomy in situations. Piaget (1952) is well-known for his discovery of a series of stages that people pass through on their way from infancy to adulthood. But he is also known to have proposed that learners strive for a sense of equilibrium or balance between what they sense and what they understand (an imbalance resulting in a state of confusion). In order to obtain equilibrium, learners utilise assimilation and accommodation to help make sense of the things they encounter in the world. When a new item matches a concept one already holds but is merely a new instance of that concept, the item can easily be added or assimilated to the list of items that fall under the rubric of that concept (e.g., one understands what a painting is and has a set of paintings held in memory that meet the definition – when coming across another painting, it is often the case that the new one can simply be assimilated into the same category). In contrast, when something is not easily assimilated, it may be necessary to change the concept, or accommodate that concept, in order to fit the new item in. For example, one may wonder about how to categorise a mixed-media piece of art that hangs on the wall: though it has paint as one of its materials, it also has cloth or photography or even found objects presented to the viewer. The viewer may then have to accommodate his concept of painting or even create a new concept in order to fit this new idea in. Piaget proposed that through these processes (assimilation, accommodation and equilibrium) learners come to develop conceptually. Whilst the learner is dependent upon what the learning environment is able to afford in terms of learning opportunities, the learner must also be in a suitable state or stage in order to be able to take advantage of such affordances (Piaget, 1952; Carey, 1999). Together, Piaget and

Dewey provided insights into how experience and development can be thought of as an individualistic endeavour that hinges upon the learner's ability to lead the conceptual change taking place. In other words, according to these perspectives, the learner needs to *construct* his own understanding of the subject through experience with the environment.

The way that people come to construct ideas through experience has been investigated in a number of ways. And the theory of constructivism has been interpreted in more and less 'extreme' sorts of manners. In addition to the agentive aspect to the theory, the experiential nature of it has led to the development of a number of hands-on practical experiences to help learners motivationally and conceptually become agentive rather than passive in the learning situation (Cremin, 1961; Dewey, 1938). Hands-on experiences are thought to help make ideas more tangible (Flick, 1993) but also more relevant (Kontra, Lyons, Fischer, & Beilock, 2015) and more self-directed (Duckworth, Easley, Hawkins, & Henriques, 1990). As such, a number of educational institutions, including museums, have tried to facilitate a constructivist way of learning in their offerings. Hein (1998) has notably referred to museums as ideal types of environments in which to make use of constructivist tools for learning due to their free-choice nature and access to authentic materials to learn from. However, there are also multiple ways that constructivism has been interpreted in museum settings. For instance, does the use of constructivism as a theoretical frame for a museum imply that one's questions ought not to be answered because the learner should be coming up with the answer herself? In an example from King (2009), a year four pupil incorrectly identifies a turtle case as a jellyfish and the Explainer she is interacting with does nothing to draw attention to this misconception. According to King's analysis, this was possibly because Explainers had been given the impression that constructivism – the learning theory adopted by the museum at the time – meant that learners needed to form their own impressions and as such, should not be dissuaded of ideas they raised, no matter how inaccurate scientifically.

The idea that learners should not be given any help in coming up with their own understandings has often been referred to as discovery learning (Bruner, 1961). This perspective on learning holds that it is detrimental to a learner's progression to provide information, even when the learner has asked a direct question. According to this perspective, in order to acquire deep understandings and retain motivation, a learner should have to 'discover' the properties associated with whatever topic is under focus at the time. Notice how problematic this idea would become if every person were required to learn from scratch. Each learner would have to work out on his own how to build a fire, read the written word, etc. So, really those who favour a discovery learning version of constructivism cannot possibly refer to all learners' need to reinvent the wheel for each concept acquired. Indeed, a number of studies have now demonstrated that learners in a discovery learning situation do not learn as well as those in a 'guided learning' situation where someone who is knowledgeable provides some sort of aid to help the learner understand (Klahr & Nigam, 2004; Mayer, 2004; Kirschner, Sweller, & Clark, 2006; Alfieri, Brooks, Aldrich, & Tenenbaum, 2011). As such, going so far as to not answer visitor questions in the attempt to use a constructivist philosophy is unlikely to serve learners very effectively.

To confuse matters, discovery learning itself has taken on multiple identities. Whilst many in educational and psychological literature have used the above form of discovery learning to represent an extreme form of constructivism, Hein (1998) has used this name to refer to a variety of learning that is school-like, in that there is an aim to reach a knowledge-base that is recognised by outsiders as correct. He contrasts this form of learning with what he calls constructivism, which has no clear-cut formulation of what is or is not correct (i.e., it is constructed by the learner, in a way that may or may not align with what other people's knowledge looks like).

To be clear, constructivism is a theory of 'knowing' rather than one of 'teaching'. Von Glaserfeld (1985; 1995) has suggested that there is a radical branch of constructivism that posits that 'the results of our cognitive efforts have the purpose of helping us to cope in the world of our experience, rather than the traditional goal of furnishing an "objective" representation of a world as it might "exist" apart from our experience' (1995, pp. xiv–xv). According to this perspective, real learning cannot occur without reflection. That is, new information must be acted upon, even if only mentally, in order to be transformed into understanding. To distinguish this perspective from that of, say, discovery learning, according to radical constructivism the learner may take in information in any format whatsoever. This could involve listening to someone, engaging in a hands-on activity, or pondering a combination of 'own experiences' and 'witnessed experiences'. The way new ideas are taken in is less important here than the active 'minds on' activity following the intake. So whereas with discovery learning a learner should not have help from others to arrive at an answer, with radical constructivism the learner ought to engage in thought about the ideas, regardless of how the ideas were first encountered. Even though the origin of the information is less important in radical constructivism than in discovery learning, the emphasis is still clearly on the individual and the need to reflect upon the activity.

There is also the branch of constructivism that is sometimes referred to as social constructivism (Vygotsky, 1978; Mercer & Littleton, 2007; Tomasello, 2003). Compared with other branches of constructivism, this perspective of learning places greater emphasis on the social situation in which the learners find themselves. In other words, there is an acknowledgement in social constructivism of both the individualistic nature of learning and the way that the social environment can influence the direction that a learning experience can take. Authors who work within the social constructivist perspective tend to place emphasis on the types of interactions people engage in when they enter into learning activities. This sort of emphasis, while largely based in the cognitive realm, may also focus on the affective nature of the interaction and how that could affect cognitive learning outcomes. For example, the way a group interacts to respect the voices of all its members may promote feelings of authority and also facilitate cognitive conflict, a Piagetian concept referring to an awareness of a disjunction between understanding and new ideas, which can lead to conceptual growth (Piaget, 1952; Adey, Robertson, & Venville, 2002). In contrast, when a learner is lectured at by a teacher-figure, she may not appreciate the ideas because the lecture does not take into account the level of understanding of the individuals in the audience (Hohenstein & King, 2011). Like sociocultural theoretical perspective, many who advocate for a social constructivist perspective of learning consider their theoretical roots to lie with Vygotsky (1978) and the Russian school of study; some even refer to their own work as sociocultural (see Mercer & Littleton, 2007, for example). The sociocultural school tends to focus on the group as a social unit rather than individuals learning in social situations (see Rogoff, 2003; Mai & Ash, 2012). Nonetheless, the social focus in social constructivism draws upon Vygotskian (1978) concepts such as the zone of proximal development, in which a relatively experienced person can help a less experienced person to become more capable in some skill or meaning making.

As can be seen, constructivism covers a range of perspectives with respect to the usefulness of other people in the learning situation, whilst primarily focusing on cognitive rather than affective types of learning. There is usually an emphasis on the individual as a sole learner; but others' involvement seems to fall on a spectrum from mere provider of opportunities (e.g., discovery learning) to potential sources of information or facilitation (e.g., radical constructivism) to active participants in the experience that creates an interaction that is part of the learning environment as in social constructivism. As such, it may be useful to pay attention to the precise perspective one seems to be taking when using the word 'constructivism' as it can refer to widely different meanings.

As is apparent from the above discussion, theoretical perspectives can seem to be relatively fluid, at least when considering a particular name. One person's constructivism may be another person's sociocultural theory. This does not diminish the overall importance of the roots of the theory and research on the influence on practice. However, the potential for confusion in the uninformed consumer of research can be great. Gaining an understanding of the underlying branches of learning theories and how they relate to one another provides practitioners (and researchers) with valuable tools for advancing the field of museum studies.

Note

1 Some people contrast 'pedagogy' with 'andragogy', where pedagogy refers to teaching of children. We do not make this distinction. However, we discuss aspects of theory relevant to adult learning in all of the topic chapters.

References

Adey, P., Robertson, A., & Venville, G. (2002). Effects of a cognitive stimulation program on Year 1 pupils. *British Journal of Educational Psychology*, 72, 1–25.

Alfieri, L., Brooks, P., Aldrich, N., & Tenenbaum, H. (2011). Does discovery-based instruction enhance learning? *Journal of Educational Psychology*, 103, 1–18.

Alvesson, M. & Kärremon, D. (2011). *Qualitative research and theory development: Mystery as method*. London: Sage Publications.

Ayala, F., Alberts, B., Berenbaum, M., Carvellas, B., Clegg, M., Dalrymple, G.B., Hazen, R., Horn, T., Moran, N., Omen, G., Pennock, R., Raven, P., Schaal, B., Tyson, N., & Wichman, H. (2008). *Science, evolution and creationism*. Washington, DC: National Academies Press.

Brown, J., Collins, A., & Duguid, P. (1989). Situated cognition and the culture of learning. *Educational Researcher*, 18, 32–42.

Bruner, J. (1961). The act of discovery. *Harvard Educational Review*, 31, 21–32.

Carey, S. (1999). Knowledge acquisition: Enrichment or conceptual change? In E. Margolis & S. Laurence (Eds.), *Concepts: Core readings* (pp. 459–487). Cambridge, MA: MIT Press.

Center for Advancement of Informal Science Education (2015). *Research agendas*. www.informalscience.org/research/research-agendas (accessed on 11 July 2016).

Chilvers, J. (2012). Reflexive engagement? Actors, learning, and reflexivity in public dialogue on science and technology. *Science Communication*, 35, 283–310.

Committee on Defining and Advancing the Conceptual Basis of Biological Sciences in the 21st Century (2007). *The role of theory in advancing 21st century biology: Catalyzing transformative research*. Washington, DC: National Academies Press.

Cremin, L. (1961). *The transformation of the school: Progressivism in American Education 1876–1957.* New York: Knopf.

Dewey, J. (1938). *Experience and education.* West Lafayette, IN: Kappa Delta Pi.

Duckworth, E., Easley, J., Hawkins, D., & Henriques, A. (1990). *Science education: A minds-on approach for the elementary years.* London: Routledge.

Eisenhardt, K. (1989). Building theories from case study research. *Academy of Management Review*, 14, 532–550.

Fabricius, W. & Wellman, H. (1993). Two roads diverged: Young children's ability to judge distance. *Child Development*, 64, 399–414.

Falk, J. & Dierking, L. (2000). *Learning from museums: Visitor experience and the making of meaning.* Lanham, MD: Rowman & Littlefield.

Flick, L. (1993). The meanings of hands-on science education. *Journal of Science Teacher Education*, 4, 1–8.

Freundlich, E. (1920). *The foundations of Einstein's theory of gravitation* (Brose, Trans.). Cambridge: Cambridge University Press.

Glaser, A. & Strauss, B. (1967). *The discovery of grounded theory: Strategies for qualitative research.* London: Aldine Transaction.

Gopnik, A. & Meltzoff, A. (1997). *Words, thoughts and theories: Learning, development and conceptual change.* Cambridge, MA: MIT Press.

Greenwald, A., Pratkanis, A., Leippe, M., & Baumgardner, M. (1986). Under what conditions does theory obstruct research progress? *Psychological Review*, 93, 216–229.

Hammersley, M. (2001). Some questions about evidence-based practice in education. Paper presented at the symposium on 'Evidence-based practice in education' at the Annual Conference of the British Educational Research Association, University of Leeds, England, 13–15 September.

Harris, P. (2012). *Trusting what you are told: How children learn from others.* Cambridge, MA: Harvard University Press.

Hein, G. (1998). *Learning in the museum.* London: Routledge.

Hohenstein, J. & King, H. (2011). Learning: Theoretical perspectives that go beyond context. In J. Dillon & M. Maguire (Eds.), *Becoming a teacher* (4th edition, pp. 175–184). Maidenhead: Open University Press.

King, H. (2009). Supporting natural history enquiry in an informal setting: A study of museum explainer practice. Unpublished thesis, King's College London.

Kirschner, P., Sweller, J., & Clark, R. (2006). Why minimal guidance during instruction does not work: An analysis of the failure of constructivist, discovery, problem-based, experiential, and inquiry-based teaching. *Educational Psychologist*, 41, 75–86.

Klahr, D. & Nigam, M. (2004). The equivalence of learning paths in early science instruction: Effects of direct instruction and discovery learning. *Psychological Science*, 15, 661–667.

Kontra, C., Lyons, D., Fischer, S., & Beilock, S. (2015). Physical experience enhances science learning. *Psychological Science*, 26, 737–749.

Kuhn, T. (1996). *The structure of scientific revolutions* (3rd edition). Chicago, IL: University of Chicago Press.

Lewin, K. (1952). *Field theory in social science: Selected theoretical papers*. (D. Cartwright, Ed.) London: Tavistock Publications Ltd.

Lourenço, O. & Machado, A. (1996). In defense of Piaget's theory: A reply to 10 common criticisms. *Psychological Review*, 103, 143–164.

Mai, T. & Ash, D. (2012). Tracing our methodological steps: Making meaning of diverse families' hybrid 'Figuring out' practices at science museum exhibits. In D. Ash, J. Rahm, & L. Melber (Eds.), *Putting theory into practice* (pp. 97–118). Rotterdam: Sense Publications.

Mayer, R. (2004). Should there be a three-strikes rule against pure discovery learning? The case for guided methods of instruction. *American Psychologist*, 59, 14–19.

Mercer, N. & Littleton, K. (2007). *Dialogue and the development of children's thinking: A sociocultural approach*. London: Routledge.

OED (Oxford English Dictionary) Online. www.oed.com/ (accessed 13 October, 2014).

Parsons, T. (1938). The role of theory in social research. *American Sociological Review*, 3, 13–20.

Pasteur, L. (2014). On the extension of the germ theory to the etiology of common diseases (trans. H.C. Ernst). Adelaide: University of Adelaide e-books. https://ebooks.adelaide.edu.au/p/pasteur/louis/exgerm/complete.html (accessed 23 October 2014).

Piaget, J. (1952). *The origins of intelligence in children*. New York: International Universities Press.

Piaget, J., Inhelder, B., & Szeminska, A. (1960). *The child's conception of geometry*. London: Routledge.

Pinker, S. (1994). *The language instinct*. New York: William Morrow and Co.

Popper, K. (2002). *The logic of scientific discovery*. London: Routledge.

Rogoff, B. (2003). *The cultural nature of human development*. Oxford: Oxford University Press.

Ryle, G. (1945). Knowing how and knowing that: The presidential address. *Proceedings of the Aristotelian Society*, 46, 1–16.

Ryle, G. (1949). *The concept of mind*. London: Hutchinson.

Schön, D. (1983). *The reflective practitioner: How professionals think in action*. New York: Basic Books.

Skinner, B.F. (1974). *About behaviorism*. New York: Knopf.

Stanley, J. & Williamson, T. (2001). Knowing how. *Journal of Philosophy*, 98, 411–444.

Suppes, P. (1974). The place of theory in educational research. *Educational Researcher*, 3, 3–10.

Tomasello, M. (2003). *Constructing a language*. Cambridge, MA: Harvard University Press.

Turner, J. (2001). The origins of positivism: The contributions of Auguste Comte and Herbert Spencer. In G. Ritzer & B. Smart (Eds.), *Handbook of social theory* (pp. 30–42). London: Sage Publications.

vom Lehn, D. (2006). Embodying experience: A video-based examination of visitors' conduct and interaction in museums. *European Journal of Marketing*, 40, 1340–1359.

von Glaserfeld, E. (1985). Reconstructing the concept of knowledge. *Archives de Psychologie*, 53, 91–101.

von Glaserfeld, E. (1995). *Radical constructivism: A way of knowing and learning*. London: Routledge.

Vygotsky, L. (1978). *Mind in society: The development of higher psychological processes*. Cambridge, MA: Harvard University Press.

Winch, C. (2009). Ryle on knowing how and the possibility of vocational education. *Journal of Applied Philosophy*, 26, 88–101.

3 The importance of methods and methodology for museum practice

In general, if we take seriously the question of how to connect theory and/or research with practice, we should think carefully about *how* research has been conducted in addition to the foundational theories associated with it. To really understand the usefulness of the research, it is helpful to consider issues to do with rigour of the processes, validity of the conclusions and transferability of findings. In this chapter we summarise some of the problems that can be raised to do with the nature of research, attempting to contextualise this by focusing on how research can be carried out in, or applicable to, museum settings.

The terms 'methods' and 'methodology' are often used interchangeably. However, it is often important to distinguish them because though certain types of methods (research tools or instruments) often correspond with specific methodologies (or approaches to research), there are also many studies that lack this strict adherence to these tendencies. In essence, methodology is like a further layer of theory: it is a set of theories about the use of methods.

Moreover, though this book cannot be a substitute for good research training in any discipline, it may be helpful to consider these questions of methods and methodologies if museum practitioners would like to feel more confident about becoming engaged in research that will be useful beyond the walls of their own institutions, with or without collaboration of university academics.

One of the key points of concern, and a useful bridge between theory and research, involves the ways that questions are asked in research. All systematic, empirical investigation, in social or natural science, will start with a question that should be addressed with the collection and analysis of data. Research questions are usually framed by the theoretical perspective to the situation (e.g., learning in museums) that the researcher finds most useful or is most comfortable with. That is, in research communities, people often become associated with particular theoretical perspectives and this then means they ask certain types of questions. For example, someone who uses information processing-type models of learning is likely to ask questions about the underlying cognitive mechanisms that are involved with museum-based learning, such as elements of memory capacity or analogical reasoning. In contrast, a researcher whose theoretical perspective is more closely aligned with sociocultural theory may ask questions about the conditions that tend to afford visitors access to learning opportunities, which may include scaffolding by a more knowledgeable member of a group or appropriating cultural practices by a novice member. Researchers (generally academics) who conduct basic research often focus on creating knowledge that will fit into grand schemes about 'how the world works'. As noted by Bickman and Rog (2008), applied social research differs from basic research in that applied research focuses specifically on a problem and tries to find solutions to that problem; in contrast to basic research, it tends to ask 'big' questions that involve ill-defined factors (e.g., 'how can learning on school trips to museums be improved?'); it looks for practical significance in addition to statistical or findings significance; and it tends to utilise theories in a way that combines them, rather than drawing upon them in a relatively 'pure' way. Evaluation is often seen as an investigative project that addresses a problem that is based in a particular context, the results of which can be used to improve the outcomes of the same context (Hobson, 2017). This chapter examines different approaches and paradigms to conducting research (i.e., methodologies), before highlighting a few of the methods that are most common in museum-based research on learning.

Philosophical background to research

Just as we noted in the chapter on theory that some research makes a point of describing the theory that has framed the studies that were conducted, some research makes a point of highlighting the philosophy that has helped to steer the research principles. However, a great deal of research leaves this type of information out. There may be many reasons for not being explicit with respect to research background. For the sake of allowing readers to understand when some terms are used, we shall consider some of the important perspectives on research here and in the following sections.

One idea that separates certain types of research is the ontology upon which the approach and the methods are based. Ontology refers to the way that reality is construed by someone who is interested in studying it (Ormston, Spencer, Barnard, & Snape, 2014). If one thinks that there is an objective reality that is measurable and independent of the people who study it, that person operates with a 'realism' sense of world knowledge. For example, a researcher might believe that people's intelligence is something that is available to be measured, even if it varies from day to day or week to week: it is real and it is quantifiable. In contrast, if the researcher thinks that reality is subjective, then that research will probably be working with 'idealism' as an ontology. Taking the example of intelligence again, idealists would be more likely to consider a person's intellectual ability to be something that is not only malleable and variable, but also open to interpretation, and as such, not measurable by any reliable means. Each of these two positions can be further broken down. However, due to space limitations we will not provide further distinctions in this chapter.

The different world views stemming from ontologies imply different grounds for obtaining knowledge and what type of knowledge is seen as valid, i.e., epistemology (Morgan & Smircich, 1980). An ontology that is on the realist end of the spectrum will tend to correlate with an epistemology that looks for objectivity in data collection and analysis (i.e., positivism). On the other hand, an idealist ontology will tend to correspond to ways of conducting research that will eschew objectivity, with the argument that this goal is impossible as all research is subjective regardless of intentions otherwise. As such, many social science researchers strive to find a way of ensuring rigour in a subjective type of study. In the social sciences there tends to be a divide between those on the realist and positivist (or neo-positivist) end of the spectrum and those on the idealist/subjective/interpretivist end. In effect, the ascription that this problem is only one of social science, where natural science is naturally more objective may be an illusion. Usher suggested that 'Kuhn (1970) helps us to see that the way research in the natural sciences is practised does not follow a positivist/empiricist epistemology. On the contrary, there is a significant hermeneutic/interpretative dimension' (p. 5). Table 3.1, adapted from Morgan and Smircich (1980), may help to illustrate the elements of choice involved in research methodology and the ways they tend to correspond with one another.

Approaches to research

The combination of ontology and epistemology can sometimes be referred to as an 'approach' to research, or a paradigm. That is, taking into consideration the ways that a researcher considers the nature of reality and the ways one can find out about this can lead to sympathy with a particular research approach.

There is a rather simplistic way of dividing research; and that is to suggest it is either qualitative or quantitative. That

Table 3.1. Network of assumptions that characterise the spectrum of objectivity/subjectivity in social science research (adapted from Morgan & Smirich, 1980).

	Subjectivist approaches					Objectivist approaches
Ontological Assumptions	Reality is product of mind	Reality is social construction	Reality is subject of symbolic discourse	Reality is contextual field of information	Reality is a concrete process	Reality is a concrete structure
Human Nature Assumptions	People are pure spirits	Social constructor	Actor/ Symbol user	Information processor	Adaptor	Responder
Epistemological Stance	Obtain phenomenological insight	Understand how social reality is created	Understand patterns of symbolic discourse	Map contexts	Study systems and process	Construct positivist stance

which utilises numerical ways of denoting proportions of data is deemed quantitative, and tends to use inferential statistics on data that come from questionnaires, structured interviews or experiments (see section on Methods below). That which does not is qualitative. Qualitative research tends to examine problems from the perspective of the individual participants, using methods that would be harder to quantify, such as in-depth interviews, participant observation and close analysis of 'rich' data. The problem with this delineation is that the divide denotes methods rather than methodologies. Although it may be the case that researchers who primarily use qualitative methods also tend to hold more subjective epistemologies and idealist ontologies, it is perfectly possible to conduct positivist-type interviews and analyse them quantitatively (or even quali-tatively with a relatively positivist frame of mind). Likewise, data that tend to be categorised as quantitative (e.g., a survey) may be explored in a more subjective way, albeit really getting to know the participant's feelings might be more difficult from this perspective. Conflation of research approach and method is common, but not necessarily good practice (Bryman, 1984).

There is also a set of animosities that seems to exist between researchers who tend to use particular methods and approaches. Bryman (1984) noted that those who might be called positiv-ists, or quantitative, tend not to feel the need to write about methodology. The assumption seems to be that attempts at objectivity and distance between researcher and researched are beneficial and possible. In contrast, a multitude of writ-ing about qualitative methods and methodologies appears on shelves of social science libraries. These pieces seem to deplore the false superiority of positivist methodologies and expend great efforts at disparaging the methods and mindsets of those who take a quantitative or positivist approach. One reason for this is probably the apparent default position that positivists are given as the only or best way to conduct research. Perhaps in part because of this default position, many people, including those who work in educational establishments, like schools or museums, assume that in order for research to be good quality, it must be done in a quantitative way. A good example of this can be found in a recent study of museum practitioners which investigated the participants' conceptions of research and evaluation (Hobson, 2017). Many of the participants alluded to the need for research to be quantitative in order to carry substantial weight. Sometimes policymakers and funding agencies also fall into this trap, suggesting that statistical findings provide better, more useful information than do qualitative findings. At the same time, in a battle for recognition, social scientists needed to build a force to be reckoned with because many quantitative social scientists mistakenly reject qualitative research as lacking in rigour (see Mays & Pope, 1995). That being said, quantitative research is not necessarily better than qualitative research; and it would be a mistake to assume (as do some of our students) that qualitative research will be easier than quantitative research to conduct. The placement of either qualitative or quantitative research onto a pedestal is unlikely to be helpful: good research will utilise methods that suit the research question rather than hanging dogmatically onto a particular type of method. Furthermore, it is possible for qualitative and quantitative research to be used in a collaborative way, building upon the findings of each other to lead to further studies that lend greater insight into a problem (Bryman, 1984).

In the remainder of this section we outline some approaches to research that have been written about by researchers in social science. We have drawn the selection of these particular categories from Creswell (2013), though there are other ways of grouping approaches to research.

Positivism

Positivism reflects the understanding that the world, including the social world, operates under predictable laws consisting of sets of elements, all of which can be discovered by the proper observational and measurement tools (Phillips & Burbules, 2000). There is a newer group who might be called post-positivists who still operate under the assumption that the world is discoverable, but who try to take into account the complexities that arise from the contexts in which phenomena can be observed. Positivists and post-positivists tend to try to place observations or data into discrete categories and as such, have been called reductionists. For example, they might look at conversation to identify certain words or phrases as indications of belief in or attitude toward specific things (e.g., talking about God in the context of origins of species suggests creationist reasoning rather than evolutionary reasoning). Whereas positivists may think there is 'a truth' that exists, they also tend to ascribe to the notion that it can never be found. As such, they prefer to 'show support' for hypotheses or theories rather than 'prove' them. Positivists also tend to use deductive logic to demonstrate support for or refute a theory in that they start with a theory or hypothesis and generate data that can then be analysed in light of that hypothesis, thereby helping to create consensus in the field. According to this perspective, knowledge is shaped by empirical evidence, which is, ideally, unbiased and objective. The goal in positivism is to explain relationships between variables through causal mechanisms, which further the production of theory. To follow from the previous example about origins of species, if a researcher would like to see whether talking about God can cause children to become creationist reasoners about the origins of species, he might set up a study in which one group of children is told about God's benevolent ways of looking out for humanity with another group being given an alternative, unrelated activity. After some period of time, the groups' knowledge about the origins of species is assessed to see whether the two groups differ in their advocacy of creationism. In this way, the research would be attempting to help causally explain the appearance of some creationist reasoning in children. Whilst it is acknowledged that researchers cannot themselves be completely objective, steps are taken to reduce subjectivity by introducing measures of reliability and validity (see section on Trustworthiness and Transferability).

Constructivism

In contrast to positivism, constructivists (sometimes referred to as interpretivists) believe that people engage in meaning-making activities that help to develop their sense of understandings about the world and how it works (Lincoln & Guba, 1985). In other words, all meaning is 'constructed' in social situations. In order to capture the varied ways that people view the world, constructivist researchers tend to conduct studies that aim to allow participants to fully consider and convey their own points of view. This process lends itself to inductive reasoning, rather than the deductive processes. Whilst constructivists do not ignore the theories that have come before their own research, the goal is to embed ideas within the data that have been generated in order to find patterns that lead to the development of theory. This perspective acknowledges that meaning creation is a social process, influenced by cultural and historical elements in a person's life (Crotty, 1998). As such, the development of theory should take people's interpretations into account, including acknowledgement of the researcher, him- or herself.[1]

Transformativism

The transformative perspective(s) suggest that it is not enough to take into consideration the point of view of the participants of the study. Rather, this set of perspectives champions the perspectives of marginalised people in order to improve their situations in societies in which they are relegated to lower status. Many of the so-called 'critical' theories of learning fit neatly into this approach to research. Whereas some of the other perspectives might be utilised by proponents of various theoretical positions on learning, this methodological perspective seems particularly closely aligned with critical theory (Kincheloe, McLaren, & Steinberg, 2011). The aims of these are to reduce inequalities and to promote social justice (Mertens, 2010). The various groups, amongst others, who have been identified as protagonists in this type of approach include women, people of colour, lesbian/gay/bisexual/transgender people, people with disabilities and people from lower- or working-class backgrounds. Within these approaches there is a consistent theme of resistance of oppression, asymmetric power relationships and the political systems that contribute to the associated problems.

Pragmatism

As the name may suggest, pragmatists are less dogmatic about the particular approach that is taken to a research problem and are rather more concerned about the best way of addressing whatever the problem at hand may be (Morgan, 2007). Pragmatism, as such, is not associated with any particular perspective on research, but instead is likely to use different perspectives from one problem to the next (or even multiple perspectives at once). Importantly, pragmatism tends to see truth as that which works for any given period of time (Morgan, 2007) and does not see the need to locate truth either within or outside the mind of anyone. However, pragmatists do believe that truth is contextual and influenced by social, cultural and historical events or situations. Finally, the purpose or goal of research should be to solve problems, according to this view, lending it nicely to applied research – that which sees the usefulness of research in practice as essential.

In this section we have drawn attention to four different approaches to research, any one of which might use methods that are qualitative, quantitative or both. The nature of these approaches varies with respect to where truth is presumed to lie (inside the mind or out) and the underlying purposes for conducting research. They also vary in terms of the way knowledge is generated (inductively versus deductively). It is important to bear in mind that none of these approaches is necessarily as stringent as these portrayals may sound. The degree to which each of these approaches corresponds to any particular method or set of methods also varies. We address methods in the next section.

Methods of research

We noted above the ubiquitous dichotomy of qualitative and quantitative methods (see above for why these are not really approaches). As it happens, these refer primarily to analysis, though to some extent the method of collecting data can also be categorised this way. Conducting an experiment, with the control of variables and manipulation of some 'condition' or intervention, will almost certainly involve quantitative methods. However, observation, interviews and even questionnaires can be done in a way that utilises either quantitative or qualitative analysis (or both). And then, some methods seem more 'purely' qualitative, such as ethnography. Limitations of space prevent detailing a complete range of methods, were that even possible. However, some of those that are more common in museum learning studies are described here.

Experiments and quasi-experiments

Often considered the 'gold standard' in quantitative or post-positivist studies, experiments involve changing one, independent, variable (often this could be referred to as an intervention) and measuring the effect on another, dependent, variable as a result of that change (Coolican, 1990). An example of an experimental method would be to see whether different forms of an exhibit display (independent variable) have an effect on the information learners remember about the topic (dependent variable). These types of studies are painstakingly devised, monitoring every potential measurable factor that could be considered relevant to influences on the dependent variable in order to 'control' the influences as much as possible. One element that is important to experiments is the random assignment of participants to variations (conditions) of the independent variable. Proponents of the experimental method maintain that it is necessary to be able to see how an intervention effects outcomes of the dependent variable without the influence of other variables. In naturalistic settings, it is sometimes impossible to assign people randomly so other means are utilised. For example, if one wants to see how altering a display of an exhibit will affect learning behaviours of visitors, it would be extremely difficult to alter the display on a random basis. However, it might be possible to alleviate this problem by sampling visitors on the same day of the week, but on different weeks, allowing for changes to be made to the exhibit. This quasi-experiment might involve one group of visitors to a museum on a Saturday at the beginning of the month and the next group could be visitors on the following Saturday.

In these sorts of designs, the best measurements are considered to be those that measure something before participation and then that same thing again after participation (pre-post). So, if researchers were interested in finding out how much cognitive gain occurred through visiting a particular exhibit, displayed in a given way, they might measure knowledge about the topic beforehand and then after participants saw the exhibit, measure it again. However, one can, of course, see many problems with this sort of tight research design in museum settings. If nothing else, the type of knowledge one gets out of a single display might not be measurable by a test. But also, people sometimes argue that there are too many other elements that influence learning in a museum to conduct this sort of experimental study. Despite the noted problems with designing true experiments in museums, it has been a popular method for examining learning in museums (e.g., Baum & Hughes, 2001; Doering, Bickford, Karns, & Kindlon, 1999; Pekarik, Doering, & Bickford, 1999; De Rojas & Camarero, 2006).

Action research

Like experiments, action research (AR) involves the implementation of an intervention to see whether the changes seem to have an effect on learning and/or behaviour. And whereas experiments are usually utilised by positivists, action research tends to be preferred by pragmatists (Creswell, 2013). Denscombe (2010) notes that the purpose of action research is usually to solve practical problems and form guidelines for best practice.

Initially conceptualised by Lewin (1946), action research was seen as a means to improve or transform working situations through reflection and planning, which might lead to developing new ways of acting in the workplace. This caught on in many workplaces and is now seen as a tool for improving motivation and performance in many work situations (Pasmore, 2006). Many educational institutions and programmes actively encourage staff to become proficient at the use of reflection and intervention in order to improve practice. As such, individuals can 'tinker' with elements of practice with the aim to improve the ways that learning can be facilitated. This type of research is often not recognised as making use of appropriate levels of rigour to warrant publication in academic journals. However, it is a means of research accessible to any practitioner in learning fields.

Design-based research

Design-based research (DBR) is also founded on the idea that interventions can be useful for positive change in learning (or other) environments. However, unlike AR, DBR analyses changes on a micro-level and continues to monitor the interaction between the implementation of small changes iteratively and the measurement of some outcome (Collins, 1990; Brown, 1992). The focus in DBR is on a product, like with AR. However, whereas AR might be widely utilised as a tool for professional development, DBR is recognised as a tool for improving educational instruments (Cobb, Confrey, diSessa, Lehrer, & Schauble, 2003). Some researchers have attempted to develop useful tools in museum education by implementing multiple iterations of small changes to the tool over repeated use (e.g., DeWitt & Osborne, 2007). As such, the idea behind DBR is to see whether the product does what it is intended to do. The aim of the research, therefore, is to see whether the designed element is effective, and how it might be changed to become more effective.

Interviews

On the surface, interviewing would seem a fairly straightforward element of a research process. One asks questions of someone else. However, there are multiple variants of interviews, some of which lend themselves to a more positivist way of conducting studies and others are more transformative or constructivist. In short, it is a tool used by a wide range of researchers for a variety of purposes.

Structured interviews

The most rigid version of interviews is one in which the same questions are asked of each interviewee, following the same order, without any possibility for variation in wording (Kvale & Brinkman, 2008). In order to minimise outside influences (i.e., to control variables), structured interviews should be conducted in the same way with each individual. As might be easily guessed based on the way this information has been presented, this type of interview tends to be more closely aligned with positivist research agendas.

Semi-structured interviews

Sometimes it is recognised that it is desirable to be able to gather further information from someone when it is deemed

useful. In these cases, when conducting an interview, the interviewer may ask 'probe' questions to follow up on a point of
interest or allow the interview to follow one of two different
possible paths according to the interviewee's responses (Kvale
& Brinkman, 2008). These, more flexible, interviews allow for
a somewhat more natural conversation to occur in the research
setting, while also maintaining some format to be followed. The
degree to which an interviewer is 'allowed' to go off-piste when
interviewing may depend on the goals for the research and the
overall approach to the study. As such, this type of interview
may be used with nearly any kind of approach to research, or
methodology.

Un-structured interviews
Often used in the transformative types of research, unstruc-
tured interviews are, as their name suggests, without structure
(Fontana & Frey, 1998). A researcher who uses these will sometimes send their interviewees a list of topics before the interview
is due to take place in order to help the interviewee think of
things they would like to bring up. But the job of the interviewer
in this type of interview is to keep the interviewee talking. The
data gained from this type of interview can be particularly rich
and full of latent information, like attitudes, which might not
come out if the participant is guided by questions. Interviews of
this nature tend to last a long time – well over an hour in many
cases. The difficulty in analysing this type of interview is that
the participant may go off topic or the information they provide
might not seem relevant initially. As a result, researchers can
struggle to make sense of the streams of consciousness that they
have gathered. However, if taking a relatively long view, this
type of unfettered access to a person's mind can help provide
windows into ways of thinking and points of view, particularly
when carried out over time or in combination with other methods (see Ethnography below).

Interview tools
The main tool for conducting an interview is generally the
interview schedule or guiding questions. However, there may be
times in which it is helpful to use other formats to help research
participants think about the topic of interest. Such additional
tools can either draw attention to actions that participants may
not have previously been aware of or they may provide means
for deeper contemplation that would perhaps have occurred
in their everyday lives. For example, Falk, Moussouri, and
Coulson (1998) asked their participants to create a concept
map, referred to as a personal meaning map (PMM) in their
study, about the topic of gems and minerals, which was the
topic the authors were interested in examining with respect to

the visitors' agendas for learning in the museum. In this PMM, prior to their visit, visitors started with a page that was blank aside from the words 'gems and mineral' in the centre and were asked to draw their ideas about the topic in a way that showed their understandings and connections. A short interview was used to provide clarification and elaboration of those points. Once they had completed their visit the same visitors were asked to carry out the task again and the interview questions focused on the ways that visitors constructed their PMMs and the changes from one map to another over the course of the visit. It can be seen here that the PMM served to give an initial indication of participants' ideas, which could be elaborated upon with pointed questions based on the aspects of the PMM each participant created.

Whereas the personal meaning mapping tool encourages participants to think deeply about a particular topic of study, stimulated recall attempts to focus their attention on some aspect of their behaviour as observed and recorded through photo or video documentation. Sometimes this can be something the participant has taken a photo of themselves. And other times the recording is of their actions 'from an outside perspective'. In each of these cases, the objective is to help interviewees remember or notice what they were doing at a particular point during their visit so they can tell the researcher what they were thinking about or what led them to act the way they did (Stevens & Hall, 1997). In this context, visitors are able to reflect on their actions and ideas, but may also be able to make greater sense of what they were observing in the museum at the time.

Interview formats
A final note about interviews is that not only are there multiple types and tools for conducting interviews, there are also myriad ways in which to do interviews. In the prototypical variety there is one interviewer and one interviewee and they face each other in the same physical location and can interact in real time. However, with developments in technology, it is now possible to conduct interviews with people who are not physically present, either through telephone conversations, or with video-conversations such as Skype or FaceTime. Moreover, in some cases it may be preferable to conduct an interview through an instant messaging format, whereby the interview participants do not have access to names or faces. Finally, it should be noted that it is not always desirable to conduct interviews one-on-one. Instead, there may be pairs of interviewees or focus groups, who can build on each other's ideas, constructing responses together (Willig, 2013). Each of these variations on the 'typical' interview is likely to create complications in the transcription and analysis of the interview data. That is, the greater the

technological involvement or the greater the number of people, the harder it can be to hold a clear, interpretable conversation. As such, these caveats need to be considered by researchers when designing a study.

Questionnaires

Questionnaires are ubiquitous in people's lives now. It seems that with the importance of service and social media there is an increase in the request for service users to complete surveys to evaluate their experiences. However, these are not by any means the only way to use questionnaires, nor is this use usually considered to be research. Like interviews, questionnaires can vary from the more rigid, with fixed responses (multiple-choice, Likert scale), to the very open, with questions that ask people to expound upon their ideas and reasoning (Krosnick & Presser, 2010). In fact, there would seem to be a fine line between an interview conducted by email and an open-ended questionnaire.

The advantages of using a questionnaire for research include the ease of managing responses that are fixed (Krosnick & Presser, 2010). In addition, their relatively impersonal nature can help participants to feel more anonymous than when sitting in front of a researcher. In this way, they may feel more inclined to answer honestly, or even answer at all. In addition, questionnaires are easy to distribute and cost very little to create. As a result, it is possible to collect a great deal of data in a relatively short period of time. In contrast, questionnaires are not without problems: their impersonal feel may mean that respondents do not take the same time to fill them in as they would to answer questions in person; the short, closed-ended questions also tend not to be able to provide rich insights into people's feelings and behaviours; and though they are easy to distribute, the response rate is usually quite poor so the sample may be biased to include only those who feel the research is important (see section on sampling below).

Observations

Another method that can be really useful in museum-based research is observations. It is helpful to know what people are doing while they are in the museum. As with interviews and questionnaires, there are a variety of ways that 'watching people' can be used. And there are a number of ways of actually doing the observations themselves. Beginning with the lowest tech type of observation, a person can sit and take notes to take account of what people do or say at a particular time or place. As might be surmised, there is a lot of room for error when relying on one's note-taking. When there is a great deal of activity it is extremely easy to miss something. This is especially true when thinking about language and recording what people are saying; when conversation often goes too quickly to note down in the best of situations; when there are a number of other events to get in the way of hearing accurately. One way of alleviating the pressures of having to write down everything that happens in a busy scene is to use a grid to tally types of occurrences during a given period of time (e.g., two minutes). This type of systematic observation can help to gain a sense of ways people are engaging with exhibits or materials without gathering quite as much detail (Wragg, 2012).

An aide to observation can be recordings. Audio recordings provide a way of allowing the researcher to listen to the goings on in a museum multiple times to try to make sense of what people are doing and saying. These can, of course, supplement (or be supplemented by) traditional note-taking. Further detail can be gleaned through video-recording a scene (Ash, 2014; Callanan, Valle, & Azmitia, 2014). As with audio recordings, the researcher (and their team) can view an event multiple times to try to understand how people react and experience learning. When there is more detail available it may be necessary to constrain the focus of analysis as it is impossible to analyse every little behaviour visitors will have. However, the possibilities for analysis are increased by the ability to obtain fine detail in people's engagement. Finally, there are new ways of observing behaviour in museums (and elsewhere) aided by newer technologies. For instance, it is possible either to gain permission from participants and track them through their phones, or to give them a device to carry that will allow researchers to see where they travel while they are visiting the museum (e.g., Moussouri & Roussos, 2013). The types of information gained can range from the path visitors take in the museum to the number of times they visit a particular gallery or exhibit to the amount of time they spend at each point of interest.

Like many types of method, there are numerous ways to approach the use of observation. They can inform a rich qualitative account of people's visits to the museum. Alternatively, they can be coded using classifications, which may help in a quantitative analysis of language or other behaviour. The method itself does not tie to one approach in particular.

Ethnography

Ethnography is many things to many different people. Some (Willig, 2013) consider it to be a method; whereas others (Brewer, 2000) look upon it more as a methodology. There are various types of ethnography, regardless of whether it is thought of as a method or an approach to research. As with the other methods we are presenting in this chapter, we do not have enough space to go into great depth to think about all kinds of ethnography. However, suffice it to say that this is likely to be one of the deepest forms of research because it attempts to get at the lived experience of the participants. The methods originate in early twentieth century anthropology and sociology and relate to researchers (almost always Westerners) living amongst so-called 'exotic' people either in far-off lands or in 'downtrodden' areas of Western life (e.g., Polish immigrants to the United States), getting to know how they go about their everyday lives, sometimes even participating in the various rituals and activities as if they were typical members of the group (e.g., Brewer, 2000). Current forms of ethnography, particularly those used for educational, and related, research tend to take place in much more familiar settings. Kirsten Ellenbogen (2003) has published ethnographic research in museums in which she both interviewed families to understand their perspectives about the ways that museums fit into their learning activities but also conducted close observations of their visits to museums and home life. Combining a number of means of gaining access to participant experience can provide a rich insight into people's views and understandings about particular places and practices. Often research like this will rely on only a very small group of participants, as working with more people would be both impractical and would possibly be less informative because it would begin to have a quantitative feel (grouping individuals and experiences into quantifiable categories rather than exploring the thoughts and feelings in a more holistic way). As such, the numbers of people involved as subjects of study are generally lower than in many other types of method.

Case study

The final method we are introducing here is perhaps the most narrow in that it focuses on a very small number of individuals (or institutions). The case study (which can also be thought of as either a method or a methodology (Hammersley & Gomm, 2000), like ethnography) is an extremely in-depth look at a particular person or place, the idea being that an understanding of this person/place can provide insight, at least about similar people or situations (Yin, 2003). Rather than looking at the broader picture in the way that ethnography does, the case study tends to hone in on the way a person passes through some experience by gathering as much information as possible about that experience from the person's perspective. The type of information gathered will often include documentation about the person's experiences (e.g., grades and coursework in the case of school), plus other written documents related to how the experience might have been developed (e.g., lesson plans and/or policies in the school). In addition, the person's perceptions might be examined through interviews and observations of some element of the experience (e.g., classroom behaviour). And these could even be supplemented by other people's perceptions about that person's experience (e.g., interviews with a teacher). In collecting all of this information, the researcher can then pull together a portrait of the way a person has undergone a particular experience, leading to some outcome of interest. Some studies have developed this method further by doing multiple case-studies in order to be able to compare across individual cases.

Analysis

We include here just a short note about analysis of the data that have been collected. There are a multitude of types of analysis, some fitting better with particular methods (e.g., statistical analysis and experiments) and others that might be used with a variety of methods (e.g., grounded theory and interviews, observations, ethnography, etc). The methods of analysis are as important as the methods of collecting the data. However, the data collection is more prominent and so we have provided more information about that here.

Trustworthiness and transferability

Research in academic communities will try to provide some indication that it is of high enough standard that it can be believed in, often referred to as rigour. Different approaches to research have their own standards and ways of ensuring rigour. Often in quantitative studies the terms that are used will be 'reliability' and 'validity' (Coolican, 1990). Here the idea is that if research has been done in a way that is objective and lacking in bias, a person who uses the same measures or means of collecting data should be able to get the same results as those published in research reports. Alternatively, if one were to give the same questionnaire to the same people within a reasonable period of time, the results should not differ much. These are indications of reliability. At the same time, quantitatively measured concepts ought to measure what they purport to, otherwise there is no validity to the findings. For example, if researchers want to find out whether children learn about biodiversity at an interactive, game-based museum exhibit, they should be careful they are not including measures of 'how to play the game' in their assessments of learning about biodiversity. There are various formal means of determining measures of reliability and validity. However, one corollary of the use of these concepts in research is that a study cannot have validity without also having reliability because not having a reliable measurement means that at least sometimes, the researchers are not measuring what they set out to measure.

Qualitative researchers have come up with their own ways of showing that their findings can be believable and useful. Firstly, many have noted that no matter how well-designed, no study can be completely free of bias. That is, unlike what many see experimental researchers claiming of their research (irrespective of whether they do or not), it is impossible to be entirely objective. As such, many working within a qualitative framework will attempt to acknowledge their biases rather than trying to control for them. However, even so, there is a great deal of room for unintended bias if research relies solely on the perspective of a single person (who views all data, for example). So, means to alleviate bias in analysis include member checks, in which the participant of a study looks over transcripts or analysis to ensure that the researchers have not re-framed participants' ideas into something the participants did not intend (Creswell, 2013). In addition, researchers using qualitative methods tend to use means such as triangulation of data, in which alternative types of data are collected to gain a greater sense of a useful insight to the situation. The advantages of this method of data collection is that it provides more confirmation of the types of findings that are presented and/or helps show more complexity than would have been available through a single data perspective. Alternatively, a study might rely on investigator triangulation (multiple researchers examining the same data or situation) or theory triangulation (in which more than one theoretical framework is used to interpret data).

Sample

Another aspect of empirical research that should be of concern to researchers is the sample: the people or 'things' that are being examined in order to come to some conclusion. Generally, the size of the sample will matter. When conducting quantitative research, having a sample that is big enough (but not too big) will allow researchers to generalise beyond the sample to a wider population (Creswell, 2013). For qualitative research, there is also a concern about the size of a sample but it is usually for different reasons. There is usually less desire to have findings that will generalise to the population (Miles & Huberman, 1994; Lincoln & Guba, 1985). However, there should be a big enough sample to make the analysis meaningful, with some methods of analysis suggesting that after a certain amount of data have been collected there will usually be saturation (in which no further insights can be gleaned). Rather than generalisability in these cases, researchers are often interested in transferability, a sense of the types of context for which similar patterns might be expected to be obtained.

Regardless of the size of the sample a study uses, there should be some concern for the makeup of the sample. Studies that examine the friends of the researcher are likely to be less transferable to broader contexts than those examining a sample that is more representative of a group of interest. If a researcher wants to know how women in general will react to a particular exhibition, it would be better to conduct a study with women from a variety of backgrounds, including age, education, ethnicity, birthplace, etc. Such considerations will, of course, not render a study flawless, but they will tend to help determine how far the findings can be generalised or transferred.

Ethics

A final point of note is that almost all studies must now think about the costs and benefits to knowledge in putting participants through the trouble of taking part in a piece of research. All learned societies (e.g., British Psychological Society, British Educational Research Association) have codes of conduct to emphasise the need to maintain standards of ethical conduct with research participants. Participants should be volunteers as opposed to feeling coerced to participate. They need to be informed of all of their rights as participants, which includes their right to keep their personal data confidential. That is, even if the researcher knows the participants' real names, the names should not generally be used in disseminating the findings of the investigation. As a result of these types of ethical standards, it is hoped that participants will not feel taken advantage of by researchers.

Summary

This review of methods and methodologies has necessarily been brief. We are not ourselves experts in methods and methodology. However, we feel it important to know how to find out about the use of different approaches to research and to be able to at least follow along with the language that is used in this book and elsewhere when it comes to how research has been conducted.

Tying this back in to theory, many times when research is conducted by people who ascribe to a particular theoretical perspective, they will opt for a methodology that is consistent in epistemology and ontology as their views of theory. As such, there will be many who use both sociocultural theory and constructivist methodology; or others who use a more information processing theoretical view and positivist methodology. It is important to remember, however, that these alignments are not deterministic; nor are they obligatory. As such, there will be some flexibility in the approaches different researchers take to conducting research, even within particular theoretical perspectives.

The types of questions people ask when they begin a study will have a large effect on the ways they approach and engage with research. But there is no inherently correct way to raise a question within a particular topic. What matters is the connection between theory, research question, research approach, methods of data collection and type of analysis. The more justified these connections, the more likely the research will be assessed by others in the field as meeting high standards.

Note

1 It should be noted that the learning theory constructivism and the research approach with the same name have some commonalities, such as the emphasis on the experiences of the individual as key to meaning making. However, confusing as it may be, research that takes a constructivist learning theory perspective need not use a constructivist approach (or vice versa).

References

Ash, D. (2014). Using video data to capture discontinuous science meaning making in nonschool settings. In R. Goldman, R. Pea, B. Barron, & S. Denny (Eds.), *Video research in the learning sciences* (pp. 207–226). London: Routledge.

Baum, L. & Hughes, C. (2001). Ten years of evaluating science theater at the Museum of Science, Boston. *Curator: The Museum Journal*, 44, 355–369.

Bickman, L. & Rog, D. (2008). Introduction: Why a handbook of applied social research methods?. In L. Bickman & D. Rog (Eds.), *The SAGE handbook of applied social research methods* (pp. viii–xviii). London: Sage Publications.

Brewer, J. (2000). *Ethnography*. Buckingham: Open University Press.

Brown, A.L. (1992). Design experiments: Theoretical and methodological challenges in creating complex interventions in classroom settings. *The Journal of the Learning Sciences*, 2, 141–178.

Bryman, A. (1984). The debate about qualitative and quantitative research: A question of method or epistemology? *The British Journal of Sociology*, 35, 75–92.

Callanan, M., Valle, A., & Azmitia, M. (2014). Expanding studies of family conversations about science through video analysis. In R.

Goldman, R. Pea, B. Barron, & S. Denny (Eds.), *Video research in the learning sciences* (pp. 227–238). London: Routledge.

Cobb, P., Confrey, J. diSessa, A., Lehrer, R., & Schauble, L. (2003). Design experiments in educational research. *Educational Researcher.* 32, 9–13.

Collins, A. (1990). *Toward a design science of education.* New York: Center for Technology in Education.

Coolican, H. (1990). *Research methods and statistics in psychology.* London: Hodder & Stoughton.

Creswell, R. (2013). *Research design: Qualitative, quantitative, and mixed methods approaches.* London: Sage Publications.

Crotty, M. (1998). *The foundations of social research: Meanings and perspective in the research process.* London: Sage Publications.

Denscombe M. (2010). *Good research guide: For small-scale social research projects* (4th edition). London: Open University Press.

De Rojas, M. & Camarero, M. (2006). Experience and satisfaction of visitors to museums and cultural exhibitions. *International Review on Public and Non-Profit Marketing,* 3, 49–65.

DeWitt, J. & Osborne, J. (2007). Supporting teachers on science-focused school trips: Toward an integrated framework of theory and practice. *International Journal of Science Education,* 29, 685–710.

Doering, Z., Bickford, A., Karns, D., & Kindlon, A. (1999). Communication and persuasion in a didactic exhibition: The 'Power of Maps' study. *Curator: The Museum Journal,* 42, 88–107.

Ellenbogen, K. (2003). From dioramas to the dinner table: An ethnographic case study of the role of science museums in family life. Unpublished doctoral thesis.

Falk, J., Moussouri, T., & Coulson, D. (1998). The effect of visitors' agendas on museum learning. *Curator: The Museum Journal,* 41, 107–120.

Fontana, A. & Frey, J. (1998). Interviewing: The art of science. In N. Denzin & Y. Lincoln (Eds.), *Collecting and interpreting qualitative materials* (pp. 47–78). London: Sage Publications.

Hammersley, M. & Gomm, R. (2000). Introduction. In R. Gomm, M. Hammersley, & P. Foster (Eds.), *Case study method: Key issues, key texts* (pp. 1–16). London: Sage Publications.

Hobson, M. (2017). Conceptions of research and evaluation amongst practitioners at the NHM, London. Unpublished EdD project, King's College London.

Kincheloe, J., McLaren, P., & Steinberg, S. (2011). Critical pedagogy and qualitative research: Moving to the bricolage. In N. Denzin & Y. Lincoln (Eds.), *Sage Handbook of Qualitative Research* (4th edition). Thousand Oaks, CA: Sage Publishing.

Krosnick, J. & Presser, S. (2010). Question and questionnaire design. In P. Marsden & J. Wright (Eds.), *Handbook of survey research* (pp. 263–313). Bradford: Emerald Group Publishing.

Kvale, S. & Brinkman, S. (2008). *InterViews: Learning the craft of qualitative research interviewing* (3rd edition). London: Sage Publications.

Lewin, K. (1946) Action research and minority problems. *Journal of Social Issues,* 2, 34–46.

Lincoln, Y. & Guba, E. (1985). *Naturalistic inquiry*. London: Sage Publications.

Mays, N. & Pope, C. (1995). Qualitative research: Rigour and qualitative research. *British Medical Journal*, 311, 109–112.

Mertens, D. (2010). Transformative mixed methods research. *Qualitative Inquiry*, 16, 469–474.

Miles, M. and Huberman, M. (1994) *An expanded sourcebook: Qualitative data analysis* (2nd edition). London: Sage Publications.

Morgan, G. (2007). Paradigms lost and pragmatism regained: Methodological implications of combining qualitative and quantitative methods. *Journal of Mixed Methods Research*, 1, 48–76.

Morgan, G. & Smircich, L. (1980). The case for qualitative research. *Academy of Management Review*, 5, 491–500.

Moussouri, T. & Roussos, G. (2013). Examining the effect of visitor motivation on observed visit strategies using mobile computer technologies. *Visitor Studies*, 16, 21–38.

Ormston, R., Spencer, L., Barnard, M., & Snape, D. (2014). Foundations of qualitative research. In J. Ritchie, J. Lewis, C. McNoughton Nicholls, & R. Ormston (Eds.), *Qualitative research practice: A guide for social science students and researchers* (pp. 1–25). London: Sage Publications.

Pasmore, W. (2006). Action research in the workplace: The socio-technical perspective. In P. Reason & H. Bradbury (Eds.), *Handbook of action research*. London: Sage Publications.

Pekarik, A., Doering, Z., & Bickford, A. (1999). Visitors' role in an exhibition debate: 'Science in American Life'. *Curator: The Museum Journal*, 42, 117–129.

Phillips, D. & Burbules, N. (2000). *Postpositivism and educational research*. Oxford: Roman & Littlefield Publishers, Inc.

Stevens, R. & Hall, R. (1997). Seeing tornado: How video traces mediate visitor understandings of (natural?) phenomena in a science museum. *Science Education*, 81, 735–747.

Usher, R. (1997). Introduction. In G. McKenzie, J. Powell, & R. Usher (Eds.), *Understanding social research: Perspectives on methodology and practice* (pp. 1–7). London: The Falmer Press.

Willig, C. (2013). *Introducing qualitative research in psychology* (3rd edition). Maidenhead: McGraw-Hill Education.

Wragg, T. (2012). *An introduction to classroom observation* (Classic edition). Oxford: Routledge.

Yin, R. (2003). *Case study research: Design and methods*. London: Sage Publications.

Topic chapters

The following seven chapters relate to particular topics within museum learning: meaning making, narrative and discourse, authenticity, memory, identity, motivation and culture and power. Each chapter follows a similar structure, beginning with a scenario that was contributed by practitioners in a museum context. Each topic chapter also introduces theories that are particularly relevant or heavily used in research in that topic. Some theories are referred to multiple times in different topic chapters. Others appear in only a single chapter. Following the introduction of theory, or basics, about the topic, a selection of empirical research related to learning in museums is reviewed. We then return to the scenario with a set of fictitious 'characters' to help exemplify some of the theories and research discussed in each chapter. Finally, we have posed a series of questions related to the topic at the end of each chapter to help contextualise the theories and research, particularly as some readers will not feel the scenario would pertain to their own situation, because it comes from a different type of museum or seems to relate to types of programmes or exhibition that are different to those readers tend to experience.

The scenarios that introduce each topic were not written with this topic in mind. As a result, it might be possible to match a scenario up with other topics in addition to the one we paired it with. It is not our intention to suggest that a particular scenario only illustrates a single principle. They are merely helping us to ground the topic it is paired with. The scenarios represent a single example that can be referred to throughout the topic chapter, particularly in the presentation of theory. Given that we could not possibly come up with a specific example for every possible situation or institution, we have used the questions at the end of each chapter to help readers relate the ideas about theory and research to their own practice. Principles can, of course, cut across institutions. But at times it can be difficult to see how they apply without some reflexivity. The hope is that these questions will act as a guide for thinking about the principles in one's own context. We hope, too, that together with the presentation of theory and research, the questions could be used to germinate ideas for collaborative research between museums and academics, a topic we return to in the conclusion chapter.

Finally, each of the topic chapters includes a set of marginal notes in the empirical research section. These are meant to act as a set of findings 'at-a-glance'. However, some caution is urged here. There are almost always nuances involved in research findings. Some of the studies involve highly specialised samples of participants, or particular materials. Rather than a headline that can be understood as a blanket statement about how learning functions in museums with respect to a given topic, these headlines might be better used as quick signals for readers to examine a particular piece of research more deeply. That is, it is usually the case that research – even highly rigorous studies – does not offer a one-size-fits-all solution to a problem.

4   Museums and the making of meaning

'Do Jews have a rule against gay or lesbian people?'
The role of the museum as a place to ask anonymous questions[1]

The Jewish Museum London is a centre for learning with over 16,000 student school visits every year from nursery age to eighteen years old. Whilst the informal learning programme incorporates family, young people and community programmes, the learning team mostly works with school visits, primarily adolescent pupils from a wide range of ethnic backgrounds, who attend museum-led educational sessions. The Museum is home to a number of objects representing Judaica and Jewish social history and incorporates ceremonial art, prints and drawings, objects reflecting everyday home and working life, and photographic and oral history archives. The overarching philosophy toward learning is enquiry-based, meaning that the workshops have a structure that is flexible enough to incorporate questions asked by students as the day progresses. Learning programmes for school groups tend to discuss religion and politics, which are often seen as taboo subjects. As such, the educators are well equipped to talk to students of all ages about these difficult topics.

Though the Museum normally tries to encourage open discussion of students' preconceptions about Jewish people and Judaism, they are also aware that students often want to ask questions but feel uncomfortable doing so in front of their peers. Therefore, in April 2016 the Learning Team decided to pilot a set of 'question amnesty' cards to encourage students to treat the Museum as a safe space to ask questions. These cards allow the students to ask any question they have about Jewish people and Judaism. Once completed, the cards are posted anonymously into a postbox over lunch. At the end of a day-long workshop, the facilitators endeavour to answer as many questions as possible. The team thought that these types of discussions might serve as an opportunity for students to see

Figure 4.1 A child completing a question card during a school trip to the Jewish Museum
    London. © Jewish Museum London.

that many religions are similar in addition to exhibiting and
recognising the differences.

In order to create an activity that inspired honesty in questions, helped inform students about social issues and ensured
a safe space to ask the questions, the team decided that there
would be a need to limit the number of questions they could
address at the end of the workshop. It would be impossible to
answer each question that students wrote about. As such, five
to ten questions would be addressed out of the thirty or so
that were asked by students (some of these overlapping). Some
of the concerns the team raised related to whether students
would start to ask questions that were rude or anti-Semitic
once they were granted anonymity; how not having their question answered would make students feel; educator confidence
in answering complex questions about religion and politics;
and whether the answers would actually help students to
engage and discuss topics so they could come to their own
conclusions.

Each student during the pilot was given a card during lunch
with the words 'ask us a question' on one side. On the other
side, they were reminded of the safe space for question asking and given room to provide a question. Once the questions
were submitted, educators looked through them and selected

up to ten for responding to, picking out a broad range of questions and ensuring that some of the complex questions that seemed buried beneath superficially simple questions could be addressed.

Each of the questions that was asked was recorded for future reference in the event that the team could utilise them in other ways. From over 400 question cards that were received, there was a wide range of types of questions. These questions demonstrate the ways that students processed the information from the workshops to make meaningful connections to their own experiences of the world. The categories of questions included:

1. Similarities and differences to own religion (e.g., 'Why is Jesus such an important part of Christianity when he is King of the Jews?')
2. Politics (e.g., 'What's a Zionist?')
3. How Jewish people look and behave (e.g., 'Why is Judaism so strict? What can't they just be normal?')
4. Personal questions (e.g., 'Is every staff member here Jewish?')
5. Life cycle questions (e.g., 'Can gentiles convert to Judaism and is this accepted by all branches of the Jewish faith?')
6. Equality questions (e.g., 'Do Jews have a rule against gay or lesbian people?').

The team realised upon reviewing the questions in each group that there were many complex questions, and too many to address in a full day workshop (3.5 hours).

In addition, the success of the project in getting students to anonymously ask questions that were genuine, deep and thoughtful revealed a new problem: educators also needed a safe space to be able to answer the questions. Staff did not always feel confident, sometimes because they were relatively new; other times because some of the non-Jewish staff did not know how to address questions about personal perspectives of those practising Judaism.

One of the main goals became working out how to answer all questions in a way that shows the breadth of the community. The team decided that, for the more complicated questions, the team would field them together. But additionally, the team felt it necessary to acquire more in-depth and complex subject knowledge to be able to adequately address some of the questions. Upon consulting an orthodox rabbi, who set up a series of CPD sessions, a broader set of examples were found that could be used across a range of Judaism beliefs and practices. The team also set up a series of Friday afternoon Torah study sessions led by the Head of Learning to guide the team about where to find information related to some questions in religious texts. Furthermore, a review was set up to consider a team-wide perspective about how to answer questions to ensure similarity across staff, so that anyone facilitating workshops would be equipped with similar answers.

The team valued the opportunities to think about how meaning is made through these experiences. This occurred both on the part of the staff and the students involved in asking questions. One resulting idea is that they questioned the concept of neutral space[2] in a museum that is both historical and contemporary in its collections.

Introduction

> 'The essence of the education experience is thus the making of meaning.'
>
> (Roberts, 1997, p. 133)

Modern use of the term 'meaning making' seems to stem, at least in part, from the book by Viktor Frankl, *Man's search for meaning: An introduction to logotherapy*, published in 1946. In this book, Frankl relates the tale of his own imprisonment in a Nazi concentration camp as well as his analysis of what differentiated people who were able to overcome the horrors they experienced there from those who suffered enormous psychological consequences (Frankl, 1959). Frankl noted that there is always a way to find meaning in one's life, even under conditions of atrocity and oppression. Postman and Weingartner (1969), like many others writing about psychological ideas, were inspired by Frankl's writing and appear to have coined the term 'meaning making' in an educational sense. Postman and Weingartner suggest that 'meaning making', consistent with constructivism, is preferable to the traditional conception of learning in which a person is static and the teacher is filling an empty vessel or even taking into account what the vessel already contains. Rather, their construal of learning through meaning making provides the sense that the learner is not only in charge of what will be acquired, but is also able to grow in a limitless capacity. As such, meaning making seems to imply individuality in learners, unending ability to learn, and the facility to tailor the situations in which learning occurs (Postman & Weingartner, 1969).

This emphasis on amorphous learning is naturally attractive to museums (Silverman, 1995), where it is difficult to determine exactly how or when learning occurs because of the inevitable individuality amongst visitors and the varying ways that the museum can be experienced. Of course, the fact that it is difficult to see does not mean that learning is not happening at the museum (or inspired elsewhere and acted upon in the museum, or vice versa). The idea that learning is gradual (Spock, 1999;

Siegler, 1995) and bitty is consistent with the experience of many people in observing learning that takes place in the museum. Moreover, the making of meaning, in museums and elsewhere, is ultimately a form of interpretation (Silverman, 1993). How much learners' own interpretations should be guided by those of the museum and other 'authority figures' has been the matter of much controversy in educational and museum-based literature (see Chapter 10 for more on this).

Another reason that use of the term meaning making may be favoured in museums is that it can be seen to capture not only the cognitive but also the affective, and possibly kinaesthetic aspects of learning. That is, whereas in some more formal contexts cognitive learning (e.g., getting facts or calculations correct) may take precedence, in a museum that does not have to be the primary emphasis for learning. Attitudes and inspirations can be just as important (Schauble, Leinhardt, & Martin, 1997); and the hands-on experience may further give visitors a relevant kinaesthetic reinforcement (Hein, 1998). As such, learners' interpretations of their visits involve a rich combination of emotion, cognition, sensation and reflection.

In this chapter, we review a number of theories that can be related to the construct of meaning making in museums. These range from the more psychological to those that have a sociological disciplinary foundation. We have tended to focus primarily on theories that emphasise the learner rather than theories about power relationships, which are covered in more depth in Chapter 10. Consistent with this focus on the learner, we have tended not to discuss the museum's perspective on meaning making and how museums can make meaning themselves. We also introduce some ways that research has addressed questions to do with meaning making in museums, paying attention to the theoretical perspectives that seem to be drawn upon.

The basics of meaning making

Hein (1999) made clear that, though constructivism and meaning making could be related, meaning making and constructivism are not the same thing. According to Hein, constructivism entails the making of meaning, whereas meaning making is optionally taken into consideration in other learning theories (e.g., discovery learning) and is disregarded in behaviourist perspectives. Hein's work focuses intensely on constructivism as the perspective on learning that museums ought to utilise. In contrast, sociocultural theories have grown in popularity in recent years as lenses through which to view museum-based participation. In this section, we introduce theoretical perspectives that range from the more personal or individual to the more shared or social ideas about learning; we also highlight distinctions between cognitive, affective and other theoretical perspectives.

Cognitive theories of meaning making

As noted above, constructivism is an important theory for thinking about learning and the making of meaning in museums. This has already been reviewed in Chapter 2. However, to remind the reader, the major facets of constructivism are that the learner is agentive, and must be ready and willing to engage in learning (von Glaserfeld, 1995). That is, the learner is the one to construct the knowledge that is gained in any given context. In the realm of free-choice learning, this is a highly appealing notion, in that learners who are able to think for themselves about what they want to know can pursue that interest actively. In the scenario example above, students are given the opportunity to ask questions that are truly meaningful to them, rather than relying solely on what is dictated from any staff, or even the objects in the museum. Following from Hein (1998), one of the important aspects of constructivism for the museum is that according to this perspective, learners are not passive as might be endorsed by a behaviourist point of view. Importantly, constructivism can be compared with discovery learning, in which learners are expected to learn without guidance (Lefrancois, 1997). A growing body of research points out that learners perform much better on a variety of tasks with some aid, even if the impetus for action comes from the learners themselves (Klahr & Nigam, 2004; Mayer, 2004). In other words, whereas sometimes constructivism is interpreted as a form of discovery learning in which learners ought never to be given an answer, encouraging them to find the answer themselves, most constructivists do not suggest that learners cannot learn when provided information – it is just that they must have an interest in gaining the information and be able to understand it.

Some pedagogical tools that have developed out of the concepts associated with constructivism involve the use of enquiry (inquiry in US English) to steer learners to think about problem-solving and scientific explanation (Bell, Urhahne, Schanze, & Ploetzner, 2010). The idea behind this use of enquiry for science learning entails allowing the learner to direct the experience by coming up with a problem to solve and seeking ways to solve it, with the help of knowledgeable others. Learners are encouraged to think of themselves as scientists and make use of practices that are similar to those used by scientists. In this way the experience is learner-centred and constructed. This approach to teaching science has become very popular over the last two decades. But it is not uncontroversial: Kirschner, Sweller and Clark (2006) note that constructivist-based teaching tends only

to work well for learners with sufficient background information; and as such, educators might need to be wary of just giving
learners open-ended tasks without useful guidance.

Experiential learning (Kolb, 1984) is a theory that has been
proposed to draw together ideas from a variety of well-known
theories, including those of Dewey, Piaget, Vygotsky, Kurt
Lewin, William James, Paolo Freire, among others. Its focus
is on the ways that people derive meaning through four processes associated with learning activities: experiencing, reflecting, thinking and acting. Given the name of the theory, it makes
sense that experience should form a great part of the process
of learning. In this case, it is the involvement of a variety of
senses that helps individuals to gain insight into some information or ideas. But without the process of reflecting upon
that experience, learners will only get so far. Like constructivism, experiential learning proposes that learners will attempt
to resolve conflicts between what they understand and what
they experience in the world. The process of thinking should
help to recognise where conflicts exist. Thinking, according to
this model, involves taking the reflection and applying it to
previously held ideas in order to be able to update understanding appropriately (i.e., abstraction). Finally, action according
to this theory is the process of applying what one understands
in a new situation, possibly even attempting to change the circumstances of that situation. Kolb (1984) refers to the learning spiral because each of these elements is found in a cyclical
way, but that the element has transformed by the time it is
reached again. That is, experience changes following reflection, thinking, and action; so that the next time the experience
occurs, it will have been altered by the other three learning
processes. There are obvious connections to museum learning
in this perspective. One of the ways that museums can capture
visitors' attention is by facilitating an authentic or hands-on
experience of various objects or events (more detail on authentic learning can be found in Chapter 6). As such, the experience
element can factor in greatly to a museum's plans for visitor
activity. It may be helpful to find ways to engage the other
three parts of the cycle so that the experience is truly an event
that catalyses changes in understanding. It is possible that the
question-asking programme at the Jewish Museum as exem-
plified above could give learners the opportunity to reflect on
and think about their experiences, given the ways that the children received responses to their questions from museum educators. In other words, having time to consider the ways that
the responses connect with the knowledge they have from their
own lives could help them to form abstractions about the topics, but also to see the complexities involved in the discussion
of society and culture.

It is important to draw attention here to another aspect of experiential learning theory, which is learning styles. Kolb (1984) has noted that people often perceive a better fit for themselves in a particular part of the cycle, or even more than one part (e.g., thinking and acting). Kolb has referred to this sort of pattern as a learning style. There are other types of learning styles that have been proposed, such as VAK, Visual/Auditory/ Kinaesthetic (Rundle & Dunn, 2007). It has become popular in many educational settings to interpret these ideas to mean that if someone has a preferred 'learning style', they will learn best when they receive teaching in a style that matches their learning style (International Learning Styles Network, 2006). Substantial research has now been published to show that this is unlikely to be true (e.g., Pashler, McDaniel, Rohrer, & Bjork, 2008). People, particularly children, tend to learn best when they are given multiple ways of approaching material (Goswami & Bryant, 2007). As such, it may not be a good use of resources to try to 'differentiate' material according to particular learning styles. On the other hand, conveying ideas using several methods, something museums may already be doing, given the real-life or hands-on nature of the displays, seems to enhance cognitive, and possibly affective learning.

Let us turn to another relatively individualistic perspective on cognitive learning: information processing or cognitive science. These concepts are not equivalent, yet the interdisciplinary field of cognitive science[3] tends to rely on the perspective that individuals are processing information in order to make sense of and act on it (Bender, Hutchins, & Medin, 2010). Whereas both constructivism and cognitive science perspectives have been influenced by theories like Piaget's (Piaget & Inhelder, 1969), constructivism tends to focus more on the agentive nature of learning in comparison to cognitive science. In contrast, cognitive science often examines more minute details of the mechanisms involved in learning than does constructivism. The tests and experiments that investigate what those processes are tend to involve laboratory-based experiments, neurological imaging and/or computer modelling of learning. Like constructivism, models of learning within cognitive science perspectives often focus on the way a person uses information that is available rather than the role of other people in conveying that information. As such, the focus is relatively individualistic. For example, some studies consider the use of analogy as a learning process in museum settings (Afonso & Gilbert, 2006; Gentner et al., 2016) and other studies examine the ways that memories can be triggered after a visit to a museum several years before (e.g., Hudson & Fivush, 1991) or how memories of a museum visit can be enhanced through reactivation of them using pictures (St. Jacques & Schacter, 2013). In thinking of the museum example at the start of the chapter, one could think about the processes children use to come up with questions, or how the responses become integrated in their long-term memory. Whilst these studies sometimes consider the ways that other people or things can serve to aid in the development of understanding, it is the individual's performance that is ultimately used to judge the outcome.

This brings us to some of the more socially focused theories about cognitive learning. Whilst it would be a mistake to think that all forms of constructivism only suggest that learning happens without the aid of others, the emphasis on the process of learning really is on the individual and how that person might make use of what the environment affords. Other theories tend to highlight more the relationships between learners or between the learner and a teacher figure. Here the emphasis starts to move away from how the individual navigates through the learning terrain and towards the formation of bonds between people that help learners become full-fledged members of a group. One could think of the emphasis on social versus individual responsibility on a spectrum, which is illustrated in Figure 2.1 in Chapter 2. Of course, not all authors will ascribe to the theories in the same way. But generally speaking, the spectrum from individual to social involves less or more, respectively, influence from other people in learning situations.

Moving along the continuum, the next theory about meaning making, social constructivism, seems to combine aspects of constructivism and sociocultural theory. As such, there is an acknowledgement that though individuals are the focus of study of learning, they most certainly do not engage in learning in isolation. That is, according to this theory, people are influenced by social situations, which provide environments that facilitate learning (or hinder it). This set of theories (as well as sociocultural theory) sees itself as being derived from Vygotsky's (1978) ideas about learning and development. In particular, studies have focused on the ways that peers and teachers use language that helps (or hinders) learners to improve their understandings (e.g., Mercer & Littleton, 2007) through working with the learners' zone of proximal development (Vygotsky, 1978). Often researchers taking this approach will refer to the co-construction of knowledge through common activities in informal contexts (e.g., Tenenbaum & Hohenstein, 2016; Luce, Callanan, & Smilovic, 2013; Valle & Callanan, 2006). Here there is a clear deference to the sociocultural elements of learning but the focus still tends to be on individuals and/or research foci that are broad rather than deep with respect to the learning environments. For example, a social constructivist piece of research might examine the specific elements of conversations between parents and children in a limited context (e.g., over

45 minutes while reading a book together), rather than taking into account all of the other factors that are important to the learner's making of meaning over the course of a childhood, which might be true of more socioculturally embedded projects. It may be confusing to see that some authors refer to sociocultural theory when they have an individualistic focus (see Mercer & Littleton, 2007). Despite using the language of sociocultural theory, many studies might be seen as pursuing a social constructivist agenda because of the way the learner is placed at the centre of the situation for study. At times it seems that the language of sociocultural theory is useful to some researchers for taking into consideration the social aspects of learning (which may be seen as 'fringe' in some disciplines) while still being able to communicate with research in the mainstream of these disciplines, like psychology or cognitive science. This may not make a difference to how the findings are used in practice. We merely point it out in case, when reading, people become confused about the alignment and definitions. This sort of perspective might take into account both the context that afforded a child's asking of particular questions in the Jewish Museum, but also the ways that the responses were shaped to help guide his or her developing meaning making around cultural and social identity, all the while focusing on the child as an individual, rather than emphasising the child's membership in one or more groups.

Finally, we turn to sociocultural theory. This perspective on meaning making is guided by ethnographic studies and seeks to understand the ways that communities engage in practices, and how newcomers can appropriate those practices, leading them to become fully recognised community members. There are several different branches of sociocultural theory (e.g., communities of practice, Lave & Wenger, 1991; intent participation and guided participation, Rogoff, 1990, 2003; ecological perspectives, Barron, 2006, 2015; cultural historical activity theory, Engström, 1987); all of which are united by their focus on development in relation to a group rather than solely on an individual basis. Whereas individuals may be discussed as important to the maintenance of the group, it is the group dynamics that push the movement of all of the individuals. As Barbara Rogoff has said, 'learning is ... ongoing transformation of roles and understanding in the sociocultural activities in which one participates' (1994, p. 210). Here, one can see the way that activities, and participation in them, dominate the thinking about learning. Consistent with this perspective, and expanding upon it, Stahl (2003) notes that artefacts also contribute to the context for interpretation and meaning making, 'the mediation of meaning-making by artefacts can be seen more generally than just as the transmission of personal opinions through the communication channel of a technological artifact' (p. 523). As such, this perspective on meaning making shows greater sensitivity to the processes involved in being a group member or being in a situation, which entails participating in the practices of that group (the practices, themselves, not being static entities, but rather changing over time). Using this lens to think about the question-asking activities outlined at the start of the chapter, the practice of encouraging open discussion through respectful, but honest and genuine question asking could be seen as a way of helping to ensure that young people who come to the museum become considerate, reflective members of a society that attends to the cultural perspectives of others.

Theories about affective learning and meaning making

Researchers and practitioners, both, have begun to call for studies that address outcomes of museum experience that go beyond the cognitive (e.g., Rennie & Johnston, 2004). This sort of step implies the inclusion of affective sides to learning, where affect generally refers to emotion. There is little agreement about what exactly should be included within the affective side of learning. However, Silvia (2008) notes that interest[4] ought to be considered an emotion because it has the qualities that according to Lazarus (1991) constitute emotion: physiological reactions, facial and vocal expression, subjective feelings, ways of appraising the feeling cognitively and adaptive changes over the lifetime. Silvia (2008) suggests that 'interest's function is to motivate learning and exploration' (p. 57). Interest certainly provides people with the will to pursue greater understanding of particular topics. Being able to harness or facilitate interest is a desire of many educational institutions. This is because though interest will not necessarily result in the accurate intake of information, it is likely that without interest, people will not try to make meaning in the first place. As such, museums and other institutions have an inherent interest in generating interest in their programmes and exhibitions. The children's questions at the Jewish Museum seem to stem from their own curiosity and interest in the ways that Jewish people are portrayed in popular media, and how that relates to their own ideas about the world.

Some have suggested that interests, sometimes conceptualised as likes and dislikes, can be learned by a series of evaluations. In evaluative conditioning (a form of Pavlovian or behaviourist learning), objects, events or ideas can be paired with other objects, events or ideas that have positive or negative evaluations (e.g., 'free lunch' or an aversive odour, being positive and negative respectively). Through such associations, individuals learn to associate the evaluation with the new item and form likes and dislikes (de Houwer, Thomas, & Bayens, 2001). Many psychological experiments have investigated the extent to which these pairings can lead to lasting associations. Attitudinal learning appears to be more powerful when pairings have an emotional context that is negative compared with when it is positive. And associations related to touch are generally less effective than are visual or smell pairings (de Houwer et al., 2001). However, most of these studies are done in experimental laboratories rather than in naturalistic situations. It seems that even if evaluative conditioning were playing a part in the development of likes and dislikes, there is probably more than simple association occurring. According to this perspective, if the responses to children's questions at the Jewish Museum made children feel uncomfortable, or were otherwise negatively associated, children's attitudes and interests might be curtailed, or even become antagonistic. So maintaining a positive environment in issues that deal with sensitive questions could be particularly important in this type of setting.

Another perspective on learning involves the idea of modelling and behaviour. Social learning theory posits that people can learn all sorts of things, including attitudes, through watching other people's behaviour and interactions in a particular situation (Bandura, 1971). Bandura suggested that behaviourism was an incomplete account of behaviour; rather, psychology is a 'continuous reciprocal interaction between behavior and its controlling forces' (1971, p. 2). In other words, according to this perspective, behaviour is reinforced, directly or vicariously (through paying attention to the actions and reactions of others), and it can then be repeated or adjusted according to the resulting feeling in the person. This set of evaluations can result then in feelings of efficacy, a self-rating of how good (or not) one is at a particular activity. Many studies have now verified that self-efficacy is related to people's ability to perform in any given situation (see Pajares, 1996). So, being able to 'do a museum' will have something to do with one's perception of how to do a museum. Even though Oppenheimer was apparently known to say that 'no one ever failed a museum' (Semper, 1990, p. 52), it is not necessarily the case that every visitor believes that initially. As such, a certain level of comfort with being in an informal place of learning, like a museum, might prove to be helpful in creating a positive association with both the institution and the material that is displayed. Following this line of thought, the consideration that the Jewish Museum has given as to how best to address children's questions is really important. If one of the goals is to enable broader thinking, crafting responses to their questions that help to foster openness rather than closed-mindedness seems essential.

Returning to interest, one model of interest development has been proposed by Hidi and Renninger (2006). In this they suggest that there are four main phases to the development of a passionate pursuit. These are:

1. Triggered situational interest, in which there is an environmental spark that captures one's attention, possibly leading to further uptake of the topic elsewhere.
2. Maintained situational interest, which features a prolonged engagement with material. This, however, is still task centred rather than being driven by a person's internal desire to pursue the learning.
3. Emerging individual interest refers to the beginning stages of a person's uptake of a topic as a long-term focus. This phase is more self-generated than the previous ones and is characterised by a curiosity that leads to further engagement over longer periods of time.
4. Well-developed individual interest can be identified by a person's relatively large amount of stored information about a topic. Though the focus is largely self-generated at this stage, there can still be a need for environmental support to maintain interest. A sense of perseverance to learning and resilience to setbacks is apparent in learners at this stage.

If this model is accurate, then it might be the role of museums and other educational organisations to find appropriate situational triggers to help learners find an initial hook to engage with important issues like climate change or historical interpretation. But a further role could be to provide a way for those who already have that interest, perhaps are in the emerging individual interest stage, to satisfy their needs to gain more knowledge and understanding. After considering these roles, one might come to the conclusion that there is a need to try to be all things to all people, which may not be possible. Additionally, it seems a vicious circle to suggest that once visitors see museum objects, their interpretation will lead them to be more interested; the problem of how to lure visitors to see the objects perhaps becomes even more difficult. Being a free-choice type of institution, museums tend to build upon their strengths as institutions that work with people's interests – they have, after all, sought out the location presumably with the idea in mind that they might see something they find interesting. On the other hand, in the case of school trips, whilst pupils might find things of interest at the museum, the trip was not their idea. As such, increasing their engagement through the use of responding to questions they generate could form a helpful basis for further curiosity in the area.

Theories tend to primarily focus on interpretation and meaning making from either a cognitive or an affective perspective. Few attempt to cover meaning making in a more holistic way. It is possible that some theories span the divide between cognitive and affective, even if they are not couched in those terms. We turn to some possible prospects for this holistic stance next.

Theories in which affect and cognition converge

Some might question whether the focus on either affect or cognition is helpful to considerations of meaning making. After all, one does not turn off one's emotions when trying to perform well on a test; and one does not focus one's mind solely on the happiness state resulting from successfully applying one's intelligence to a particular problem. So perhaps the divide in research terms is rather artificial. Some theories have either consciously or unconsciously spanned this chasm between emotion and cognition. Critical pedagogy, championed by Freire (1970) and developed by others, such as Giroux (2011), has been inspirational to a number of studies and practitioners. Whilst theories such as critical pedagogy and the somewhat related place-based learning (Greunewald, 2003) and indigenous pedagogy (Yunkaporta, 2009) have not targeted either the affective or cognitive sides of learning, studies that have adopted these theoretical perspectives have often focused on outcomes that include both cognitive and affective measures in their remit. Certainly the example above from the Jewish Museum involves what could be incredibly emotional topics generated by the child visitors, meaning their autonomy is acknowledged and encouraged, but they are, hopefully, also gaining conceptual understanding through the answers obtained to those questions. As such, many of the criteria associated with critical pedagogy are present in this case study. Critical pedagogy is described in much greater detail in Chapter 10; however, it seemed useful to draw attention to its transcendence across the perhaps artificial boundaries of cognition and affect for purposes of this chapter, too.

Of course, as a museum-focused depiction of learning, the contextual model of learning (Falk & Dierking, 2000; 2012) attempts to look not only at cognitive, but also at affective aspects of learning. In addition, the model tends to draw on a number of previously proposed theories, such as constructivism, sociocultural theory and experiential learning to highlight the ways that learning can be seen to occur in museum settings. Falk and Dierking note that learners occupy personal, sociocultural and physical spaces in every learning situation. More recently, they have added time as an element to the model to emphasise that learning not only occurs across a single visit to a museum, but also the process is gradual and piecemeal; and

only by examining learning over a matter of years will researchers really start to capture the nature of learning about any one
topic. These personal (interest, motivation, etc.), sociocultural
(e.g., cultural background of family and society) and physical
(e.g., size of a building, feel of the space, who one is with) contexts combine to form a unique experience that may or may
not be particularly meaningful to the learner. When the experience is meaningful, it is likely to be more memorable (Anderson,
2003) and lead to changes in cognition, affect and behaviour
(Epstein, 1994). It may be useful to point out that the contextual model of learning is not really a theory in that it does little
to try to explain how learning occurs in various learning situations, informal or otherwise. What it does is describe the learning that can be experienced, particularly in museum settings,
taking into account various perspectives on the physical, social
and personal environments involved. As such, the term model
is useful in setting out the possibilities for considering the types
of learning one can see in a museum. But some of the other
theories it is based upon do more to highlight how and why the
learning could be occurring.

One can see by considering all of the types of theory about
meaning making we have reviewed here that there is no single way of thinking about the making of meaning. Importantly,
there is research in museums that draws upon each of these
types of approaches. Next we look at some of the findings
involving meaning making in order to provide a sense of what
we know about how meaning is made, drawing attention to the
theoretical perspectives used and types of meaning making or
interpretation targeted in museums.

Meaning making in the museum

Here we turn our attention to the ways in which studies carried
out in different museum contexts have investigated meaning
making. In order to organise the section, we look at research
with children, adults and family groups. This process could seem
somewhat artificial, as it is not always easy to break results, or
studies, down in this way. And there are certainly other ways
that the body of research could be cut up. However, given some
theoretical reasons for considering learning to be stage-like
(e.g., Piaget & Inhelder, 1969), and the tendency for studies to
treat learning differently according to age, this seemed a useful
organisation here.

Children

We attend first to the studies that have been conducted to investigate children's experiences in museums. In order to further

UNIVERSITY OF WINCHESTER LIBRARY

address the ways that children make meaning in museum settings, we have divided children into younger (usually preschool to around ten) and older. What we know about older children's experiences in museums tends to come from research from school trips; whereas knowledge about younger children, though sometimes coming from school trips, often comes from laboratory or observational type studies, alone or with their parents. In comparison, studies with older children, who are often seen to be better able to judge their own understandings, may include interviews or questionnaires. Hence, there are some methodological differences between the studies on older and younger children (in addition to the age differences) that may be worth paying attention to.

Young

Young children have been studied from a variety of perspectives with a number of goals in mind. In many cases, the object is to understand how children learn and think generally. In others, the idea is to create environments that help parents and other adults facilitate children's learning behaviours in order to help them in school and other more formal situations. Sometimes the learning is domain specific; other times it is more about general learning mechanisms.

In a series of studies aimed to understand how children's play is related to their ability to make sense of science content, van Schijndel and colleagues (van Schijndel, Singer, van der Masse, & Raijmakers, 2010; van Schijndel, Franse, & Raijmakers, 2010; van Schijndel, Visser, van Bers, & Raijmakers, 2015), taking what could be seen as a social constructivist stance, have demonstrated, in museums and elsewhere, a number of features of children's environments that can be helpful for early learning. These studies were designed to assess exploratory play and the ways this play interacted with other factors, such as verbal encouragement or their ability to construct an unconfounded experiment. Using their Exploratory Play Scale, van Schijndel and colleagues were able to show that two- to three-year-old children can be coached to use play that is more exploratory, involving testing of ideas, compared with merely manipulating objects (van Schijndel, Franse, & Raijmakers, 2010; van Schijndel, Singer, et al., 2010). Preschoolers who participated in an experimental group, hearing explanations, were more likely to engage in behaviours that involved varying factors associated with the domain of focus compared to children in the control condition or scaffolding condition who tended to just manipulate the objects rather than explore them systematically. In addition, when they observed a pattern of events with presentations of apparently conflicting 'evidence', preschool-aged children were more likely to construct a design for an experiment

Young children's science learning benefits from specific guidance from adults that lacked confounding factors compared with children who had only consistent experiences (van Schijndel et al., 2015). An example of conflicting evidence was provided by placing dolls of different sizes at various distances from a light source and predicting the size of their shadows. A consistent occurrence would be to have a large doll create a large shadow. However, a bigger shadow can be created by placing a small doll closer to the light source than a large doll is placed. In this way, the evidence would conflict with the expectation. Overall, findings suggest that environments, museums and elsewhere, contain elements such as explanations that afford children opportunities for exploration, which can serve to benefit them in later interpretations about the fundamentals of science, including experimental design.

Experiences in museums may provide the types of opportunities for the development of content understanding in addition to process understanding. For example, children's understanding about buoyancy and currents can be influenced by guided experiences at museums (Tenenbaum, Rappolt-Schlictmann, & Zanger, 2004). In another study designed to examine learning in a social constructivist way, kindergarten teachers created lessons that were conducted before and after a museum visit in the experimental conditions of the study. A control group visited other galleries in the museum and did not participate in the science lessons in the classroom. Kindergartners who participated in the science intervention gained skills that helped them to articulate more complex concepts about currents and buoyancy in comparison to children in the control group.

Looking more at how children make meaning from their own perspective, studies by Anderson, Piscitelli, Weier, Everett and Tayler (2002) and Piscitelli and Anderson (2001) investigated the ways that young children experienced several museums (art, social history, science, natural history) over the course of a year. They focused primarily on groups of children (aged four to six), who visited a single institution three times. Pupils worked together in groups of four throughout their museum visits; two such groups served as the targets for observations and interviews in this study. Analyses examined recall of experiences from the trips as well as preferences and links to other experiences the children may have had. In analysing the data with a variety of theoretical lenses (constructivist, sociocultural, intrinsic motivation), it is notable that children were extremely diverse in both their memories and their preferences, suggesting that their previous experiences played a large role in the way they interpreted exhibits in the museums. On the other hand, in all settings children seemed drawn to the large-scale exhibits, which were both memorable and well-liked. Perhaps more

Young children have diverse reactions to different museums, but remember large-scale exhibits best importantly, the children's recollections included a great deal of tactile and kinaesthetic information, suggesting that these elements factored greatly into their experiences.

One study investigated the ways that sixth grade pupils in the United States perceived and talked about animals when they either visited a zoo or a natural history gallery at a museum (Birney, 1995). The research mainly examined cognitive outcomes of the visit and did not mention a theoretical perspective on learning. Although many of the same species were exhibited in the two institutions, pupils tended to pick out different animals to focus on in each location and highlighted different types of information about them in interviews following their visits. In the zoo children paid more attention to animal behaviour compared to in the museum. In contrast, children mentioned structural adaptation and background scenery more often in the museum than in the zoo. This study highlights the types of information that are easily gleaned by young visitors in different institutional settings.

Different types of institutions afford contrasting experiences for learning about similar material

It is useful to investigate children's interest in and motivation toward and understandings of animals to help assess the types of experiences that can facilitate the type of learning considered more beneficial. In a study comparing three types of school trip activity involving animals, Kimble (2014) investigated the types of expressions eight- to nine-year-old children used in natural conversation and in post-activity interviews. The three activities were a natural history specimen gallery, a live animal show and an exploration of a park (outdoors). The findings suggested that children demonstrated higher levels of motivation and emotional engagement in the park setting where animals could only be seen spontaneously rather than in a planned fashion. On the other hand, children more readily talked about species names in the natural history setting and animal behaviour in the live animal shows. When concepts from the data were divided into a conceptual framework devised for this study – Skills, Place, Emotion, Attitudes, & Knowledge (SPEAK) – the data from the park exploration fell into the S, P and E sections of the framework, whereas data from the live animal shows were concentrated in the K area and the Natural History visit data were spread fairly evenly across the different elements. As a result, it may be useful for practitioners to either capitalise on the strengths of the areas they work in, or to find ways of increasing areas they think are priorities in order to maximise the types of outcomes young students should be experiencing.

Young children are often considered not to be sophisticated enough to be able to reflect on learning. David Sobel and colleagues have found ways to measure children's understanding of their learning using a cognitive science perspective; these studies have been designed to understand what children think about their own learning, sometimes challenging the notion that young children cannot form such understandings. Importantly, metacognition and self-regulated learning (i.e., thinking about thinking) have been shown to have positive effects on learning in school and elsewhere (Schunk & Zimmerman, 1997). One recent study asked children aged four to ten years to define learning (Sobel & Letourneau, 2015). Compared with younger children, older children were much more likely to provide a definition and these definitions were more likely to describe a process as opposed to content (e.g., it is about reading) or tautologies (e.g., learning is learning), which were more prevalent in younger ages. A previous set of findings demonstrated that children tended to use a desire-based mode of thinking about learning (e.g., they wanted to learn) at four but were better able to integrate desire with ability and circumstances by the age of six (Sobel, Li, & Corriveau, 2007). To understand how children's regulation of learning might be visible in play situations, a research team at the Providence Children's Museum found that children showed intense concentration in some situations that afforded repetition or clear mastery of a task; meanwhile, in peer play children were shown to think out loud, possibly helping to provide ways of communicating their self-regulation, and that of others (Sobel, Letourneau, & Meisner, 2016).

A growing interest in children's understandings of natural history has led to a number of studies that investigate evolutionary concepts in museums and other informal contexts. Young children have been shown to be able to learn about evolutionary concepts; but the learning depends on the language that is used to frame the information (Legare, Lane, & Evans, 2012). Despite the fact that evolutionary concepts are often considered to be particularly difficult for primary school-aged children because of conceptual biases they might hold about the nature of the world (Evans & Lane, 2011), Legare and colleagues, also coming from a cognitive science perspective, demonstrated that children who were provided with language that details species variation and differential reproduction were able to endorse evolutionary concepts. In contrast, children given desire-based or need-based language endorsed concepts consistent with those linguistic patterns (e.g., animals wanted to change or had to change to survive, respectively). Further, in explaining stories about animals, the language children used in their interpretation was consistent with the language of the narratives they had heard. This pattern was stronger amongst older (eight- to twelve-year-old) children compared with younger ones (five to seven), suggesting that older children may be more ready than younger children even if both groups were able to benefit from the language of the presentation.

Young children's understandings are fairly sophisticated – perhaps more than could be expected. But children's ability to understand complex ideas may shift around six to seven years of age

Tenenbaum and Hohenstein (2016) approached the issue of children's learning about the origins of species from a social constructivist perspective, in which we regarded the way that parents and children co-constructed ideas about how species came to exist on the planet as important. In our study, parents and their children (seven or ten years old) discussed the way humans, plants and animals came to exist on earth. These conversations were coded for mentions of God and evolution and then compared with the ways that parents and children separately endorsed creationist and evolutionary perspectives on the origins of similar entities. The seven-year-old children were more likely than the ten-year-olds to endorse creationism; and ten-year-olds endorsed creationism and evolution equally, particularly for humans. However, the mention of God or evolution in the conversations predicted children's responses in the interview, even after accounting for parents' beliefs. In other words, conversations served as better predictors of the way children of both ages believed humans appeared on Earth as compared to parental beliefs. Beyond merely hearing a narrative in an experimental context, children's participation in the conversation (in which parents and children introduced God or evolution into the conversation equally) may have been more powerful than just being presented with an idea as in the Legare et al. study. The types of things that young children draw meaning from in their own interpretations may differ from those that older children are expected to benefit from. We turn now to focus on adolescents' meaning-making experiences.

Adolescents
As noted above, many of the studies on adolescents have examined school trips to museums. Whereas some of these have attempted to understand the museum experience on its own, others have compared museum experiences with classroom experiences. As an example of the former, Tal and Morag (2007) looked closely at the activities that students engaged in when they were visiting natural history galleries with their school. In particular, the authors paid attention to the interactions between students and museum practitioners using a sociocultural lens. They noted that visit guides asked questions of the students that could be answered with a 'yes' or 'no' and were relatively low-level in terms of the cognitive demand they placed on the students. Questions that engaged the students by asking them to relate the content to their own experiences were relatively infrequent. Moreover, the lessons in the museum appeared to contain a great deal of jargon that was not explained to the students, creating an experience that was potentially confusing for the inexperienced visitor. In their examination of ways that teachers

Interactions between teachers and museum educators can make a difference to the school-trip experience and museum guides collaborated, Tal and Morag found that when guides initiated interaction with teachers, it was mainly for purposes of organising the groups of pupils. However, if teachers initiated (which they did infrequently), they were more likely to attempt to co-teach, offering explanations of the ideas that the guide presented. As such, it may be that museum practitioners, in some instances, could benefit from interaction with the pupils' teachers, either setting up expectations before the visit or upon arrival, in order to inspire meaning making in their adolescent visitors.

In a relatively holistic view of the school trip, Davidson, Passmore and Anderson (2010) examined the ways that children, aged eleven to twelve, experienced a trip to a zoo in New Zealand. The study drew upon a Bourdieuian framework[5] that emphasised the cultural dialectic that influences each person's (teacher, pupil, parent, zoo staff, etc.) relationship with the various other stakeholders in the experience, a view that is also highly compatible with the sociocultural theoretical framework. They used a case study approach, gathering data from surveys, interviews, observations and written coursework, both in the classroom and on the visit, to assess the ways that the zoo trips affected learning and met expectations (or not) of the various stakeholders involved. This case study compared two classes: one that had an authoritarian and transmission-based approach to learning and one that was more constructivist in nature with a student-centred approach. Davidson et al. found that the types of things pupils seemed to learn appeared to correspond to the ways that the visits to the zoo were coordinated. The authoritarian teacher conveyed fewer expectations to the pupils about what the trip was for and the pupils noted that they learned somewhat superficial facts and funny trivia. In contrast, the constructivist teacher had expressed high hopes for the trip with her pupils and the pupils were able to articulate a great deal of information about what they learned, including causal relationships and personal connections to the animals. The zoo educators appeared to have little influence over the learning experienced by the children. And one of the main outcomes for the children was social in that they enjoyed sharing the experience with their friends on the trip. This case study highlights the ways that interpretation is dependent upon the attitudes that are set back in the classroom about the expectations and goals for the school trip. This difference is, of course, likely to not only exist in the school trip experience; the teachers no doubt differ in their approach to classroom teaching, though this was not the focus of Davidson et al.'s study. However, it is interesting to bear in mind that helping teachers to create an optimal environment for learning is likely to result in positive outcomes for pupils, teachers and museums.

School trips start at school!

Ultimately, the goal for many museum educators is to help learners gain understandings, both cognitive and affective, that enrich their ability to make informed decisions in life. Some studies aim to find out whether there is a role for the museum in enhancing learning experiences for the student. In a quasi-experiment, Sturm and Bogner (2010) examined the learning of groups of secondary pupils (aged 12.5 years) who had either worked at hands-on workstations in the classroom or in a museum. Each group engaged in activities designed to help them learn about birds in a constructivist, student-centred way. However, the pupils who participated in the museum also got to travel off-site on a 'day out'. Students who participated in the museum showed greater gains in knowledge from pre- to post-test and retained their knowledge longer compared with students participating in the classroom. In addition, the museum group scored higher on perceived competence, which may have enhanced their motivation to learn about the topic of birds as well.

Museum visits can provide additional context to school learning experiences, enriching overall learning

Spiegal et al. (2012) evaluated the ways that older children (ten to eleven), youth (twelve to fourteen) and adults think about evolution before and after a visit to a natural history gallery containing particular exhibits that emphasise the long-term nature of evolutionary change, the adaptations involving natural selection, variability and inheritance. Through both open-ended questions and questionnaires, Spiegal et al. found that visitors in all three age groups utilised explanations that were more evolutionary after their experience with the exhibits than they had before their visit. This did not mean they had abandoned their pre-visit conceptions about species change, including those that stem from religious explanations. However, the incremental influence on their conceptualisation was apparent. As such, the addition of the gallery visit seemed to increase learners' abilities to conceptualise evolution in more scientifically sound ways.

In two studies that investigated adolescents' experiences in the museum and the classroom, DeWitt and Hohenstein (2010a, 2010b) found that pupils demonstrated greater autonomy and affective engagement in the museum than when in the classroom. These studies followed students and teachers on a fairly structured project that encouraged learners to create a presentation on a topic that they researched whilst at a science museum or centre. One of these studies compared talk between children and teachers in the two settings (2010a). Here it was noted that the primary and secondary pupils tended to volunteer information more and were subject to less authoritative talk from the teacher when they were on their museum visit compared with in the classroom. This may be due to the relatively free-choice nature of the museum experience allowing the children to pursue agendas of their own making relative to when they are in the classroom. When students' conversation with each other was examined (2010b), there was a similar level of cooperative talk in both museums and classrooms. However, evidence suggested that when they were in the museum, pupils demonstrated higher levels of cognitive and affective engagement compared with the conversations that were observed in the classroom. As such, the museum experience, particularly when guided in a way that provides structure and a clear set of goals, may afford pupils on a school trip greater amounts of student-centred opportunities for interpretation and learning.

Adults

Adults are often considered in their own right as learners in museums, and rightly so. Sometimes this is because they are the 'default' visitor. In other studies, this seems to be more of a pointed effort to understand what makes an experience in a museum valuable from the adult perspective. There seems to be myriad implications for how museums might craft their programmes and exhibitions to create valuable adult as well as child experiences for making meaning. Often the focus on adult learners is about what visitors think should happen with regard to particular aspects of visits (e.g., technology). Alternatively, they may highlight relatively unusual ways of presenting ideas, other than through the presentation of objects with labels for interpretation.

In a number of studies, possibly stemming from those of McManus (1988), attempts have been made to understand more about what visitors talk about as an indication of the kinds of meaning that are created in museum visits. For example, Allen (2002) used videorecorded interactions of pairs of visitors to an exhibit about frogs to investigate the ways that people might express the making of meaning in their conversations. Some of the interesting findings include the fact that a very high proportion of what people talked about was learning-related and relevant to the exhibits (83%). She noted that there was also a high proportion of conceptual talk (37%) as well as what she called strategic talk, which incorporated aspects of procedure and meta-representation of understanding. Perhaps surprisingly, there were few utterances that showed visitors were making connections across exhibits. And when compared with a hands-on science exhibit, the live frogs exhibit seemed to elicit a greater amount of affective talk, which suggests that visitors were reacting to these (live) objects with more emotion, both positive and negative, than they might in a non-living type of science experience. This was one of the first studies to

Visitors' learning talk is conceptual and relevant, but not connected across exhibits

combine cognitive and affective learning, at least through the measurement of talk, in a museum setting.

Smith (2014) uses performativity (see Chapter 9) as a framework to discuss the reasons that people visit museums and cultural heritage sites. Rather than to necessarily obtain new information about a topic, many people, when interviewed, noted that they wanted to reinforce their sense of belonging in such places. Belonging in these contexts could refer to a sense of nationality or to a particular subculture. It is in this respect that performativity might play a role, in which visitors see their experience at the museum as helping them to perform their identities. Some visitors mentioned a specifically emotional reason for attending museums given the fact that they could easily obtain facts about the material in other ways (e.g., internet or books). As such, affective aspects of learning may be more important for many visitors than cognitive ones. The act of visiting, itself, can form a part of the meaning-making experience. The acknowledgement of this non-fact learning as important for meaning making draws attention to the importance of other affective elements of a visit. As a result, it should be important to focus not only on the information that an exhibit or gallery provides but also the way the institution as a whole sets up the identity-forming nature of a visit.

Visits are often about emotional connections with one's identity in relation to the displayed content

Consistent with this idea that part of the meaning-making experience is the visit itself, Burnham and Kai-Kee (2005) have written an essay about their experiences as museum educators in an art gallery. They draw upon experiential learning (Dewey, 1938) to help understand how teaching, what they consider to be an art form itself, can occur in museum settings. The authors see the role of (art) museum educators as facilitators of a planned, goal-directed experience that inspires visitors to use their imagination to experience and interpret for themselves the art that is displayed in the galleries. They note that emotion is crucial for the visitor experience, 'It is through emotion above all that we engage our audiences; we harness the impetus of emotion that marks encounters with works of art – interest, like, dislike, puzzlement, curiosity, passion – and strive to maintain the momentum emotion provides as we further explore the works' (p. 74). While not relying on any empirical research to support their ideas, they resonate with many studies that advocate for the use of open-ended questions to spark interest and authentic engagement (e.g., Hohenstein & Tran, 2007). In their reflection on what makes a good educator, Burnham and Kai-Kee suggest that museum educators must know their material extremely well to be able to orient the visitors without inhibiting their own interpretation of the works. This includes the history as well as the techniques involved in each of the works of art.

Hooper-Greenhill, Moussouri, Hawthorne, and Riley (2001) have also investigated visitors' meaning-making activities in an art museum through a think-aloud protocol, in which solo visitors were asked to voice their thoughts while viewing the exhibits. These audio-recorded extracts were then analysed for patterns in interpretation. Hooper-Greenhill et al. found that the adults in their study tended to both interact directly with the art and rely on museum-provided information for interpretation. In the process of interpreting the art they saw, visitors made reference to the visual aspects of the works, the socio-historical context in which they were created, and the ways in which materials were used to come up with the resulting pieces. Across the participants, there did not seem to be great differences with respect to gender or socio-economic status in the strategies used to interpret the art. Overall, visitors appeared to act in a self-directed way and felt comfortable enough within the galleries to seek out information and experience in their own ways. Another method was used to gather information about visitor interpretation of art in Serrell, Sikora and Adams' (2013) study. They asked visitors to several different galleries to take photos of exhibits or places that helped them to find meaning. For each photo they took, participants were asked to say what meaning they found in the object, probing for references to the museum's interpretive labels if not offered in their initial responses. They categorised responses in a number of ways: according to memories of personal experience, conceptual understanding of period or message, and engagement with the aesthetics. In their analysis, Serrell et al. noted that visitors often drew meaning from the information in the labels but then reflected how their own lives were related to the material. For example, when talking about an African sculpture depicting a nursing mother, some respondents either noted the universality of human experience or the message that mothering is important because of all of the potential present in an infant. The fact that visitors often spontaneously referred to the label material suggests that they actively sought out information to enhance their initial reactions to the visual aspects of the art works.

> Visitors tend to find ways to make connections to their personal experiences

In the age of ever-increasing technological advances, there often seems to be a sense that museums ought to 'keep up' with the latest fads when it comes to gadgets and digital presentation. In contrast, not everyone thinks that it is feasible or even advisable for museums to be involved with the race for technological advancement (Gilmore & Rentschler, 2002). From the adult visitor perspective, this focus on technology can be a distraction from the objects themselves and the interpretation of those objects. McIntyre (2009), coming from a tourism research background, utilised a focus group approach, consisting primarily of adult visitors to a museum in the UK. The aim

> Flashy presentation does not always equate to enhanced learning experience

was to examine the extent to which people thought that museums should update themselves technologically to become more appealing. Results suggest that these visitors tended to think that such entertaining exhibits and demonstrations, whilst good for children, usually felt cluttered and drew attention away from the ability to contemplate the material. In addition, it was felt that industries that are about entertainment do entertaining better than museums can; as such, focusing attention to quality learning would be more beneficial in attracting and maintaining adult visitors. Generally, there was a call for greater simplification of presentation whilst facilitating attention to the objects in the museum.

In contrast, Meisner et al. (2007) noted ways that digital technologies could facilitate engagement rather than hinder it. Their study, focusing on the ways that electronic interaction in exhibits can engage visitors to a gallery devoted to the scientific and socio-scientific processes associated with energy, examined individuals' performances in this gallery in light of the content and space affordances of the exhibition design. The authors' micro-analysis of visitor behaviours suggests that some types of exhibits and visitor engagement can invite others to look at what is going on, either consciously or sub-consciously. This is usually because there is a large action or a very public action associated with the exhibit. In addition, visitors are able to utilise their ability to 'work an audience', creating amusing or interesting scenarios that others can either view or join in on. The authors argue that visitors are able to share experiences at these exhibits through their actions in a way that just talking about the ideas or the experiences might not allow. In other words, the meaning created by their participation is potentially deeper through a potential for sharing interpretation than it might be in a less interactive environment. They refer to the sociocultural theoretical framework of intent participation (Rogoff, 2003; Rogoff, Paradise, Arauz, Correa-Chavez, & Angellilo, 2003) to suggest that by paying close attention to what others are doing at an exhibit, visitors can make sense of not just how to act at an exhibit, but also the nature of the exhibit itself.

In contrast to the large body of literature, both with respect to adults and children, advocating for increasing shared experiences for enhancing learning and interpretation, Packer and Ballantyne (2005) note in their study that this emphasis on shared meaning making may be somewhat overstated. Their research acknowledges the sociocultural theoretical perspective that there can be a dialogue between people, even in the absence of another person's physical presence through the ideas and interpretations of the curators and exhibit designers (see Bakhtin, 1981). They worked with single visitors and pairs, largely matched for age, sex and other factors relevant

But some technology may enhance experience if the design allows for shared engagement

to museum visiting habits at a museum of social history and geography. They observed participants during their visits and interviewed them immediately after the visit and again several weeks later (by telephone). Their findings suggest few differences between single and paired visitors with respect to the amount of time they spent reading displays or self-reports of learning either immediately or in the delayed interview. Solitary visitors seemed somewhat more likely to relate what they said they learned to their own personal past experience. But each group was equally likely to have discussed the content of the exhibition with friends or family and noted they both learned something new and were reminded of things they knew already. As such, there may not always be an added benefit to social interactions in museum visits.

Numerous museums have experimented with different types of alternative formats. Evans (2013) details an interesting way of conveying the nuances of historical interpretation. The project involves an actor who portrays a controversial historical character, inviting the audience to interact with the actor, which then gives the opportunity for reflection upon the perspective of the character within the historical context. The article is clearly relevant for collective memory as well as culture and power, given the way that it becomes apparent through the visitor responses that they did not necessarily have access to the character's perspective prior to their experiences at the museum. This is largely due to the ways that textbooks and other conventional media tend to relate history, as if it is static and factual. Yet, the museum's choice to use this programme to draw visitors into the notion of interpretation demonstrates their own ability to creatively utilise culture and power to highlight issues of societal memory and complexity of situations within a historical context. Evans notes that this type of innovation in a museum is consistent with the idea that transmission models of learning are no longer fashionable, and that engaging learners to help them think for themselves is a more desirable goal for museums.

Innovative formats may provide new ways of facilitating experiential learning through reflection

A few studies have examined other alternative formats, including some programmes that were launched in the early to mid 2000s, dialogue events: largely evening events to engage visitors with experts in socio-scientific issues. The format of these events tends to be a debate with an introduction of a perspective from experts in some topics coming from a variety of voices (e.g., in an event on smoking bans there might be a representative from a tobacco company, a medical professional, a researcher in lung cancer and the owner of an establishment that would be affected by such a ban). The aims of these events, staged at museums, were usually purported to be both to educate and to engage the public on issues but also to empower them. McCallie (2009) investigated the ways that individuals interacted at such events to coordinate their contributions to the conversation. In doing so, they (perhaps unwittingly) often together formulated the elements of a full argument around an issue. In other words, one participant might contribute a claim, which could be followed (consecutively or not) by a warrant or backing, which could later be taken up with the conclusion. The order of these might vary somewhat. What was interesting was the distributed nature of the work to construct an argument. That is, taken individually, each person's speech might seem fragmentary. But together with the other audience members, the argument became more coherent. Davies, McCallie, Simonson, Lehr and Duensing (2009) suggest that such events allow for individuals to articulate their views and learn about other perspectives in a way that is equitable and relatively safe, but authentic. They argue that the social learning occurring in these types of events is particularly valuable because of the negotiation that occurs to create meaning in these settings. As demonstrated by Lehr et al. (2007), this type of dialogue event also goes some way to overcome a transmission model of learning, in which the museum provides the learner with information to take in. Instead, the events may enable visitors to really bring their own interpretations to bear in the event that ensues.

As a major group of visitors to museums (albeit, highly diverse in terms of interests and attitudes), adults are important for consideration of the way that meaning is made in galleries and exhibitions. Many studies have examined dialogue and conversation as a window into adult learning and experience. There is general agreement that adults have a lot of experience and knowledge to bring to the table in museums. This can be seen, for instance, in their abilities to create meaningful distributed arguments (McCallie, 2009). But adults are also keen to learn new things when they visit museums on their own. They show they utilise various elements of art work to help interpret the exhibitions and the individual pieces (Hooper-Greenhill et al., 2001). Yet they may also be concerned with involving others in interaction, particularly when visiting with family members, which is the visitor group we turn to next.

Family groups

Apart from school groups, one of the major groups to visit museums is, of course, the family. A number of studies have now been conducted investigating the nature of learning in families when visiting museums. It is probably fair to say that a majority of these focus on children's learning through spending time in the family unit. However, there are some that pay attention to the family as a whole. Often these types of studies draw upon different theoretical perspectives, leading them to use different methods of research. Amongst studies that focus on the child's learning in the family context, a number pay attention to the language used by parents and children.

One such study has looked at the ways that instruction and conversation between parents and children can influence behaviour in the museum as well as children's memory of the principles of an exhibit (Benjamin, Haden, & Wilkerson, 2010). In their study with five conditional treatments, Benjamin et al. observed caregivers with their six-year-old children while they worked at an exhibit about building design. The study design crossed instruction about design with elaborative style conversational instruction (i.e., conversation that encourages child reflection through 'why' and 'how' types of questions). Dyads in the groups that received building instruction tended to build stronger constructions than did dyads in the other groups. When dyads received instruction on conversation (including the use of questions that start with 'why' or 'how') but not building, they demonstrated more responsive conversations with adults asking more questions and children responding to those questions. Children who participated in the building instruction groups were better able to identify structures that would be stable compared with the other groups. In contrast, it was the combination of building and conversation instruction that seemed to help children to remember the concepts when they were asked two weeks subsequent to their museum visit.

Combinations of instruction and conversation style lead to better learning about exhibit content in children

A similar study to the one by Benjamin et al. was conducted by Gentner et al. (2016) in that they were both about learning to build stable constructions at a museum. However, the premise in the instruction in this study involved the use of analogy to understand the way that bracing a building can make it stronger. As such, children (aged six to eight) and their caregivers participated in either a high or low alignment condition or received no training. The conditions both enabled dyads to see that the brace in the stable building helped strengthen it; but they differed in the amount that the two examples looked like each other in the other respects. When later tested about how to construct a building, children in the high alignment condition performed better than those in the low alignment and control conditions. However, when parents used language associated with the strong diagonal, children in all conditions performed better than when their parents did not use this type of language.

Valle and Callanan (2006) also investigated the ways that parents can help children to use the cultural tool of analogical reasoning. Their socioculturally informed study examined the ways that parents and children talked about science in two settings: museum and homework-like task. They found that parents used similarity comparisons to help children make connections between ideas in both settings, and that the proportion of these comparisons that were relational analogies was relatively high (about half). Parents often explicitly mapped the elements of the analogy so that children could see the relation being made. In turn, first grade children who heard analogies in the homework setting scored higher on a test of knowledge about the material than those who did not hear analogies. Parents seemed to be scaffolding their children into the use of analogies. Analogy may be a tool that becomes more useful when individuals have more knowledge about a topic. Hohenstein and Ash (in preparation) showed in their case study approach that a family with a great deal of biological background tended to analogise about the animals in a marine science centre much more than another family who had less experience with biology. For instance, the parents in the biologically grounded family compared marine snow (the detritus from animals and plants in the sea that can nourish living things closer to the bottom of the sea) with leaves that fall in the forest, which turn into fertiliser for the soil, when describing the concept for their eight-year-old son; such sophisticated comparisons were not used by the family with less biological prior knowledge.

In addition to analogies, explanations more generally have been the focus of a number of studies. Given the importance of explanation to scientific reasoning (Crowley et al., 2001), use of explanation as a tool to understanding seems a useful element of language to target in learning conversation studies. Tare, French, Frazier, Diamond, and Evans (2011) aimed to understand how parents and children would interact at a museum exhibition about evolution. In particular, they wanted to examine whether parent talk could be used to help children to interpret the content of the exhibits. The talk that resulted contained a great deal of information from the label text, suggesting that they drew heavily on the information conveyed in labels. Parents' talk exhibited both evolutionary and intuitive reasoning, which is consistent with the idea that people utilise multiple frameworks for reasoning about evolution. Parents' and children's proportion of explanation was highly correlated, suggesting that either the use of explanation by parents somehow influences that of their children or that parents and children use explanations at similar rates for some other reason, which might be firmly established prior to attending the museum.

As noted above, exploratory behaviour has been studied in relation to children's learning in the museum. van Schijndel, Franse, and Raijmakers (2010) have demonstrated that parents can influence children's exploratory behaviour while at a science-related museum exhibit. In this study, preschool-aged

Family learning talk can be facilitated with video material, through label text, and with other low-tech provisions children were observed interacting with their parents at several different hands-on learning exhibits. In one exhibit (Spinning Forces) children were shown to actively manipulate the exhibit materials more when their parents asked open questions and directed attention as compared to when they explained. In contrast, the exhibit about rolling did not show these distinctions. On the other hand, children showed more exploratory behaviour when they were exposed to minimal interaction at the rolling exhibit but more exploratory behaviour in the spinning forces exhibit when their parents explained to them. As such, exhibits do not inherently afford the same types of engagement by children, nor does the same type of interaction from parents encourage more exploration. This is consistent with findings with a variety of age groups that museum labels questioning the reasons an object was exhibited led to different types of conversation, dependent upon the nature of the object (Hohenstein & Tran, 2007). Importantly, it was possible to facilitate greater levels of exploratory behaviour through providing a short video about coaching at particular exhibits (van Schijndel, Franse, & Raijmakers, 2010).

Further studies have examined the museum's provisions to families to see whether particular types of material are better suited to facilitate children's learning. Tenenbaum, Prior, Dowling, and Frost (2010) gave families at a history museum either a booklet about the exhibitions, a backpack with materials to help facilitate engagement, or no materials at all (control condition). Booklets encouraged children to find and describe a number of objects in the galleries; backpacks contained hands-on activities in addition to information about the objects, which were designed to encourage kinaesthetic experiences to help children understand the exhibits. The researchers noted that both intervention groups spent more time at the exhibits and parents asked more historically related questions compared to families in the control condition. At the same time, children in the booklet condition used more historical talk compared to children in the other two conditions. As such, the ways families engage with exhibits can be influenced by the types of materials available to them to help make sense of the exhibits.

Crowley and Jacobs (2002) introduced the idea, using communities of practice and cognitive science frameworks, that people could develop islands of expertise that formed through capitalising on the opportunities available to them, burgeoning interest in a topic, and support networks (e.g., family members). The conversations that children have with their parents and others around them help develop the skillsets they are building in a particular area of interest, enabling them to become relative experts compared to a child who has had very different experiences and conversations. Palmquist and Crowley (2007) then

Parents are sensitive to their children's expertise

explored this phenomenon further by examining the ways that parents and children talked about dinosaurs, depending upon whether the children were already relative experts or they were novices on the topic. They looked at family conversations in a museum between six-year-old children and their parents. A brief test of dinosaur names was used to determine children's levels of expertise, with a median split to create two groups. When it came to the family conversations in the museum, parents did less talking in the expert families than they did in the novice families. This suggests that the children who were experts were able to negotiate a greater amount of the talking time and/or that parents of novices felt they should be scaffolding learning for their children more than parents of expert children. In both cases, the children's development acts as a guide for overall conversation. Perhaps building in ways for both types of child or family visitor to engage would help all families engage, even when they have different levels of expertise.

Studies that focus on the whole family as a unit for learning in the museum tend to operate under more of a sociocultural theoretical lens than those focused on children's learning (though this is not always the case). Doris Ash has used the lens of sociocultural theory to think about the zone of proximal development (Vygotsky, 1978) with regard to questioning (Ash 2004a), dialogic inquiry (Ash, 2003), joint productive activity (Ash, 2004b; Mai & Ash, 2012), with language as a marker of meaning making (Ash et al., 2007). These studies highlight the ways that parents and children work together in families of diverse backgrounds (e.g., White American and Mexican American) to find interest, discover wondrous properties, make new meaning, and reinforce old understandings. Ash's work has noted that families of various linguistic and ethnic origins often use similar mechanisms to engage with material in biological science informal settings, even though they bring resources of differing levels of canonical scientific background to the occasion. For example, an English-speaking family may have more experience in museums generally and potentially greater previous knowledge about the exhibited materials in a museum; Spanish-speaking families often have everyday experiences with materials (e.g., fishing, in the case of a marine science centre); but both working-class Spanish-speaking parents and middle-class English-speaking parents work together to scaffold learning for their children, helping them to gain new cognitive and affective experience by directing attention and asking the types of questions that are aimed at a level of understanding that is appropriate to their ability to grasp ideas developmentally and experientially in order to aid interpretation.

Like Ash, Ellenbogen has taken a longer view of learning. Her ethnographic approach to the study of how families engage

Families of all backgrounds utilise scaffolding to encourage relative novices to gain understanding in learning activities examined the patterns of both home and museum experiences to do with science (Ellenbogen, 2002, 2003). She followed families who all were regular museum visitors, but who utilised museums in different ways and had differing perspectives on what counts as education and what counts as a learning setting. In one detailed description of a family who home-schools their children, Ellenbogen (2002) offers insights into ways that museums can be seen as either informal or formal, depending on how they are used. If one is studiously taking notes of an experience, this may be considered more formal, even if the institution considers itself to be a bastion of informal opportunities. But at the same time, the formal and informal do not have to be separated in such a stark contrast, again depending on the attitudes and approaches learners take to the experiences. What seems important in her studies is the interest in the learning activity and the vigour with which learners approach the experience.

Families find different purposes for museum visits, which may vary in 'formality'

Another study that took an in-depth look at the ways families interact to interpret and make sense of concepts in a museum noted that family members all contribute to the discussion, creating a distributed network of expertise that could be drawn upon (Zimmerman, Reeve, & Bell, 2008). In their study Zimmerman et al. highlighted the ways that it was sometimes the child, sometimes the parent and sometimes the museum who provided information that helped to formulate a shared understanding of the ideas under consideration. For example, the child at one point introduced his knowledge about dinosaurs (name and properties) and the mother then provided further information, which may or may not have been supported by information in the museum label. In this case, family members were not just taking in what was transmitted by the museum, but rather critically engaging with the material and even disagreeing with it at times. The focus in this study is the family as a unit who can learn collectively, rather than the individual visitor. This view is consistent with the sociocultural perspective that learning is not an individual activity, but instead always takes place in a situated fashion, influenced by the social and material milieu.

Families can engage in collective learning, too

Whilst the studies mentioned above with a focus on whole family learning tend to utilise a sociocultural perspective on learning, Szechter and Carey (2009) also focused on the whole family but took a much more cognitive approach in their research. They mapped learning conversations and amount of time at exhibits in a comparison of exhibits designed to prolong engagement (APE) (Allen & Gutwill, 2004) and exhibits without this design function. They noted that affective talk corresponded to more time at exhibits and a higher number of exhibits visited by families. Parent educational level and frequency of museum visiting behaviour were positively related to connecting to children's prior experience in conversations,

Learning talk varies across educational levels and museum experience, but also with type of exhibit

which has been shown to be important for children's learning experiences. In addition, parent attitude to science was positively associated with the proportion of exhibits families visited in the museum. Finally, APE exhibits appeared to engage families more as evidenced by increased holding time and greater amounts of learning talk.

The majority of studies focusing on family learning tend to investigate experiences in science-related museums. One reason for this is the way that funding for research is distributed. There is a larger pool of money available for researchers in STEM (Science, Technology, Engineering, and Mathematics) learning than there is for learning in art or history. That being said, there may be lessons for all museums that can be taken from some of this family-related research. For instance, it is likely that as Szechter and Carey found, exhibits that engage families with activities to prolong their engagement will result in greater affective talk in addition to longer holding times. Children who develop interests in history are likely to have expertise in subjects that lead their parents to interact in ways that differ from how they treat history novices. As such, planning exhibitions for both parents' and children's experience levels could help to enhance overall engagement. This might be done through label text and/or through the overarching design of exhibits and galleries to help families notice similarities and differences.

A return to the Jewish Museum

Some time has passed since the Museum piloted their question cards. We are now witness to a new school group's workshop experience. This group is a bit younger – year five – than most of those who were involved in the Jewish Museum London's piloting of the question cards. But it too is a diverse group with children from a variety of ethnic and religious backgrounds, predominantly from middle and working classes. The group arrives and engages in the morning activities with enthusiasm. As with most groups, these children are encouraged to actively reflect on the topics relating to Jewish culture and religion and how they relate to their own understandings of society. The workshops utilise a number of the objects in the Museum, which are discussed by a variety of members of staff.

As lunch approaches, the students are informed about the question cards and told they should fill in the cards with their own questions about the topics they are learning about. These ten-year-olds are also told that some of their questions will be addressed in the afternoon, before leaving the Museum.

Given the varying backgrounds and experiences of the children, they are likely to have different levels of expertise on the topic of Jewish culture and Judaism; some may even have an island of expertise around this if they come from a Jewish family and have siblings or other family members who have been 'mitzvahed'. In contrast, other children may not have any awareness of Jewish culture because they come from other ethnic or religious groups. As such, the types of questions are likely to range from those arising from lack of previous knowledge to the more pointed, personal or political ones. As indicated in the scenario presented at the outset of this chapter, addressing this breadth of questions can prove challenging to staff.

Bilal and Anwar, two Muslim boys, are curious about the customs that Jewish people have and how they differ from their own. They wonder about the different holidays Jewish people celebrate and what they mean. In this respect they might be attempting to draw analogies between their own experiences and those of people whose religion is different. The research on this topic in science learning suggests that aligning different ideas as analogy to help learners understand can provide useful windows for insight into principles or ideas. In other areas, it has been demonstrated that visitors will make emotional links to their own lives when they visit museums. As such, these types of questions can show the ways that the children are contextualising the information they encounter to help them bring greater meaning.

Hannah, whose background is Anglican, considers the way people she has seen in her neighbourhood look and wants to understand the reasons behind habits of dress and hairstyle. She feels that asking this sort of question at school or 'out loud' might be discouraged because of sensitivities around differences and diversity. But here in the Museum, where there is already a sense of greater autonomy, and with the added security of anonymous questions, she builds up the courage to ask why some Jewish people 'can't just be normal'.

The Museum's staff training served them well in addressing all the students' questions. Being able to confer about the appropriate ways to respond according to multiple perspectives from Jewish culture and religion helped to instil confidence and assured the staff they could continue to facilitate the children's learning through enquiry in a way that was consistent with constructivism but also acknowledged the social relationships involved in the setting. That is, the team, through their training and growing confidence, were able to utilise the time over lunch to coordinate the ways to respond, ensuring that both Jewish and non-Jewish staff felt comfortable with helping the children to gain understandings by responding to their questions in thoughtful and complete ways, addressing not just the 'factual' answer, but also using language that models appropriate ways of speaking about people with respect. For example, in responding to the question about habits above, the team would tend to offer a group discussion about what is considered 'normal', allowing students to volunteer their thoughts and then letting the group decide whether the word 'normal' was the most appropriate. In addition, the broader question of why some Jewish people choose to live their life in a way that is visibly different to the majority (even seen as extreme or outdated by some) could also be addressed by explaining that for some Jewish people respecting their religion means making it the focus of their lives, believing everything else should revolve around it. As a result, aspects that seem abnormal to many may be the way that some groups of people can practise their faith and also take part in society in a way that feels comfortable to them.

Fortunately, Susanna, the teacher who accompanied the group, helped the class prepare for the trip by giving them some background about what to expect in the museum and the workshop. She and the chaperones asked the museum staff how they could help during the workshops. The museum staff were grateful for this offer, which helped keep students on-task throughout the day. In addition, because Susanna had been alerted to the use of questions before the trip, she was able to manage expectations about similarities and differences to children's own experiences. The next day, back in the classroom, Susanna helped the children reflect on the workshops and the question-asking experience by focusing a discussion around the topic for that week (how Jewish people express their beliefs), which helped the group to relate the ideas to their own experiences even more. In this way, she could reinforce the meaning making by working with the children's zones of proximal development, which she is more familiar with than the museum staff, and by continuing to foster the interest children expressed during the workshops that day.

Contextualising meaning making

Thinking about an exhibition you are working on in your museum, what elements of the content will be important to detail for facilitating meaning making for different aged visitors? How can text be used to enhance the interpretation for different groups (e.g., age, school versus family, solitary and social)? Is there a way to design the space for both solitary and social visitor groups? What about for groups of different types (e.g., families, schools, adult pairs)? What types of object will be most useful for making the visit meaningful? Are these particularly large objects or smaller ones? How will the visitor experience the museum's interpretation, either alone or in groups? Whose interpretation will be seen as most privileged? Are there materials that can be used to enhance the communication between visitors and the museum staff (or between different visitors)? Can there be both a cognitive and an emotional experience of meaning making?

What types of programme could be developed to engage participants about topics of interest to your museum? What sort of meaning-making perspective would be most useful in setting up this programme? Might the design of the programme depend upon the objects that are obtainable from the museum's permanent collection? Are there ways of making the programme accessible to many different types of visitor (e.g., ethnic or religious background, age group, experienced museum-visitor or not)? Should the programme be designed differently to accommodate particular groups? What types of information will staff need to facilitate the best aspects of meaning making in visitors?

How important is it for learners to be able to monitor their learning in the exhibitions at your institution? What is the relation between technology and concepts of meaning and interpretation with respect to groups and solitary visitors? What differences might be useful in considering the ways various types of groups are able to monitor their learning? How can learner autonomy be championed, both in younger and older visitors? Are there learning tools, like explanation, questioning, and analogy that can make cognitive and affective learning more meaningful? Can visitors' islands of expertise be accommodated while also catering to complete novices (of all ages)? What kinds of scaffolding, physical, textual and object-based, could help visitors make sense of the exhibition's main messages?

Notes

1 This scenario was contributed by Frances Jeens, Head of Learning, Jewish Museum London. The information was provided in notes and interview and then written in its current state by the authors.

2 The historian Randolph Starn (2005) reminds us that museums are not neutral spaces. In the process of collecting, classifying, conserving and researching objects, developing exhibitions and education, they also deliver powerful messages through selecting which stories to tell through a careful selection of objects.

3 To be sure, cognitive science is a field rather than a theory. However, there are useful ideas that can be understood by considering the idea that people process ideas and emotions to create learning. As such, we refer to this as a perspective in the same vein as a theory here. Use of the word 'cognitive' in many different ways is not intended to be misleading or confusing. However, it is important to understand that cognitive psychology is not the same as cognitive science (parts of cognitive psychology could be seen as a subset of cognitive science, which also includes other disciplines). Not all cognitive approaches come from cognitive psychology or even cognitive science.

4 Interest is also considered in Chapters 8 and 9.

5 Bourdieu's framework is covered in more detail in Chapters 8 and 10.

References

Afonso, A. & Gilbert, J. (2006). The use of memories in understanding interactive science and technology exhibits. *International Journal of Science Education*, 28, 1523–1544.

Allen, S. (2002). Looking for learning in visitor talk: A methodological exploration. In G. Leinhardt, K. Crowley, & K. Knutson (Eds.), *Learning conversations in museums* (pp. 259–303). Mahwah, NJ: Lawrence Erlbaum Associates.

Allen, S. & Gutwill, J. (2004). Designing with multiple interactives: Five common pitfalls. *Curator: The Museum Journal*, 47, 199–212.

Anderson, D. (2003). Visitors' long-term memories of World Expositions. *Curator: The Museum Journal*, 46, 401–421.

Anderson, D., Piscitelli, B., Weier, K., Everett, M., & Tayler, C. (2002). Children's museum experiences: Identifying powerful mediators of learning. *Curator*, 45, 213–231.

Ash, D. (2003). Dialogic inquiry in life science conversations of family groups in a museum. *Journal of Research in Science Teaching*, 40, 138–162.

Ash, D. (2004a). How families use questions at dioramas: Ideas for exhibit design. *Curator*, 47, 84–100.

Ash, D. (2004b). Reflective scientific sense-making dialogue in two languages: The science in the dialogue and the dialogue in the science. *Science Education*, 88, 855–884.

Ash, D., Crain, R., Brandt, C., Loomis, M., Wheaton, M., & Bennett, C. (2007). Talk, tools, and tensions: Observing biological talk over time. *International Journal of Science Education*, 29, 1581–1602.

Bakhtin, M. (1981). *The dialogic imagination: Four essays* (Ed. M. Holquist). Austin, TX: University of Texas Press.

Bandura, A. (1971). *Social learning theory*. New York: General Learning Press.

Barron, B. (2006). Interest and self-sustained learning as catalysts of development: A learning ecology perspective. *Human Development*, 49, 193–244.

Barron, B. (2015). Learning across setting and time: Catalysts for synergy. *Monograph Series II: British Journal of Educational Psychology*, 11, 7–21.

Bell, T., Urhahne, D., Schanze, S., & Ploetzner, R. (2010). Collaborative inquiry learning: Models, tools, and challenges. *International Journal of Science Education*, 32, 349–377.

Bender, A., Hutchins, E., & Medin, D. (2010). Anthropology in cognitive science. *Topics in Cognitive Science*, 2, 374–385.

Benjamin, N., Haden, C., & Wilkerson, E. (2010). Enhancing building, conversation, and learning through caregiver–child interactions in a children's museum. *Developmental Psychology*, 46, 502–515.

Birney, B. (1995). Children, animals, and leisure settings. *Society and Animals*, 3, 171–187.

Burnham, R. & Kai-Kee, E. (2005). The art of teaching in the museum. *The Journal of Aesthetic Education*, 39, 65–76.

Crowley, K., Callanan, M., Jipson, J., Galco, J., Topping, K., & Shrager, J. (2001). Shared scientific thinking in everyday parent-child activity. *Science Education*, 85, 712–732.

Crowley, K. & Jacobs, M. (2002). Building islands of expertise in everyday family activity. In G. Leinhardt, K. Crowley, & K. Knutson (Eds.), *Learning conversations in museums* (pp. 333–356). Mahwah, NJ: Lawrence Erlbaum Associates.

Davidson, S., Passmore, C. & Anderson, D. (2010). Learning on zoo field trips: The interaction of the agendas and practices of students, teachers, and zoo educators. *Science Education*, 94, 122–141.

Davies, S., McCallie, E., Simonson, E., Lehr, J., & Duensing, S. (2009). Discussing dialogue: perspectives on the value of science dialogue events that do not inform policy. *Public Understanding of Science*, 18, 338–353.

De Houwer, J., Thomas, S., & Bayens, F. (2001). Associative learning of likes and dislikes: A review of 25 years of research on human evaluative conditioning. *Psychological Bulletin*, 127, 853–869.

Dewey, J. (1938). *Experience and education.* West Lafayette, IN: Kappa Delta Pi.

DeWitt, J. & Hohenstein, J. (2010a). School trips and classroom lessons: An investigation into teacher–student talk in two settings. *Journal of Research in Science Teaching*, 47, 454–473.

DeWitt, J. & Hohenstein, J. (2010b). Supporting student learning: A comparison of student discussion in museums and classrooms. *Visitor Studies*, 13, 41–66.

Ellenbogen, K. (2002). Museums in family life: An ethnographic case study. In G. Leinhardt, K. Crowley, & K. Knutson (Eds.), *Learning conversations in museums* (pp. 81–102). Mahwah, NJ: Lawrence Erlbaum Associates.

Ellenbogen, K. (2003). From dioramas to the dinner table: An ethnographic case study of the role of science museums in family life. Unpublished doctoral thesis.

Engström, Y. (1987). *Learning by expanding: And activity-theoretical approach to developmental research*. Helsinki: Orienta-Konsultit Oy.

Epstein, S. (1994). Integration of the cognitive and psychodynamic unconscious. *American Psychologist*, 49, 709–724.

Evans, E.M. & Lane, J. (2011). Contradictory or complementary? Creationist and evolutionist explanations of the origin(s) of species. *Human Development*, 54, 144–159.

Evans, S. (2013). Personal beliefs and national stories: Theater in museums as a tool for exploring historical memory. *Curator: The Museum Journal*, 56, 189–197.

Falk, J. & Dierking, L. (2000). *Learning from museums: Visitor experiences and the making of meaning*. Lanham, MD: Altamira Press.

Falk, J. & Dierking, L. (2012). *The museum experience revisited.* Walnut Creek, CA: Left Coast Press.

Frankl, V. (1959). *Man's search for meaning: An introduction to logotherapy*. Boston, MA: Beacon Press.

Freire, P. (1970). *Pedagogy of the oppressed*. New York: Herder & Herder.

Gentner, D., Levine, S., Ping, R., Isala, A., Dhillon, S., Bradley, C., & Honke, G. (2016). Rapid learning in a children's museum via analogical comparison. *Cognitive Science*, 40, 224–240.

Gilmore A., & Rentschler R. (2002). Changes in museum management: A custodial or marketing emphasis? *Journal of Management Development*, 21, 745–760.

Giroux, H. (2011). *On critical pedagogy*. London: Bloomsbury.

Goswami, U. & Bryant, P. (2007). *Children's cognitive development and learning* (Primary Review Research Survey 2/1a), Cambridge: University of Cambridge Faculty of Education.

Greunewald, D. (2003). The best of both worlds: A critical pedagogy of place. *Educational Researcher*, 32, 3–12.

Hein, G. (1998). *Learning in the museum*. London: Routledge.

Hein, G. (1999). Is meaning making constructivism? Is constructivism meaning making? *The Exhibitionist*, 18(2), 15–18.

Hidi, S. & Renninger, K. (2006). The four-phase model of interest development. *Educational Psychologist*, 41, 111–127.

Hohenstein, J. & Ash, D. (in preparation). A window on relational shift: Families' use of analogy and comparison as a tool for learning in a museum setting.

Hohenstein, J. & Tran, L. (2007). Use of questions in exhibit labels to generate explanatory conversation among science museum visitors. *International Journal of Science Education*, 29, 1557–1580.

Hooper-Greenhill, E., Moussouri, T., Hawthorne, E., & Riley, R. (2001). *Making meaning in art museums 1: Visitors' interpretive strategies at Wolverhampton Art Gallery* [West Midlands Regional Museums Council & Research Centre for Museums and Galleries report]. Leicester: University of Leicester.

Hudson, J. & Fivush, R. (1991). As time goes by: Sixth graders remember a kindergarten experience. *Applied Cognitive Psychology*, 5, 347–360.

International Learning Styles Network. (2008). About learning styles. Retrieved 21 September, 2016, from www.learningstyles.net/en/why-join

Kimble, G. (2014). Children learning about biodiversity at an environment centre, a museum and at live animal shows. *Studies in Educational Evaluation*, 41, 48–57.

Kirschner, P., Sweller, J., & Clark, R. (2006). Why minimal guidance during instruction does not work: An analysis of the failure of constructivist, discovery, problem-based, experiential, and inquiry-based teaching. *Educational Psychologist*, 41, 75–86.

Klahr, D. & Nigam, M. (2004). The equivalence of learning paths in early science instruction: Effects of direct instruction and discovery learning. *Psychological Science*, 15, 661–667.

Kolb, D. (1984). *Experiential learning*. Englewood Cliffs, NJ: Prentice-Hall.

Lave, J. & Wenger, E. (1991). *Situated learning: Legitimate peripheral participation*. Cambridge: Cambridge University Press.

Lazarus, R. (1991). *Emotion and adaptation*. Oxford: Oxford University Press.

Lefrancois, G. (1997). *Psychology for teachers* (9th edition). Belmont, CA: Wadsworth.

Legare, C., Lane, J., & Evans, E.M. (2012). Anthropomorphizing science: How does it affect the development of evolutionary concepts? *Merrill-Palmer Quarterly*, 59, 168–197.

Lehr, J., McCallie, E., Davies, S., Caron, B., Gammon, B., & Duensing, S. (2007). The value of 'Dialogue Events' as sites of learning: An exploration of research and evaluation frameworks. *International Journal of Science Education*, 29, 1467–1487.

Luce, M., Callanan, M., & Smilovic, S. (2013). Links between parents' epistemological stance and children's evidence talk. *Developmental Psychology*, 49, 454–461.

Mai, T. & Ash, D. (2012). Tracing our methodological steps: Making meaning of diverse families' hybrid 'Figuring out' practices at science museum exhibits. In D. Ash, J. Rahm, & L. Melber (Eds.), *Putting theory into practice* (pp. 97–118). Rotterdam: Sense Publications.

Matthews, S. (2013). 'The trophies of their wars': affect and encounter at the Canadian War Museum. *Museum Management and Curatorship*, 28, 272–287.

Mayer, R. (2004). Should there be a three-strikes rule against pure Discovery Learning? The case for guided methods of instruction. *American Psychologist*, 59, 14–19.

McCallie, E. (2009). Argumentation among publics and scientists: A study of dialogue events on socio-scientific issues. Unpublished doctoral thesis. King's College London.

McIntyre, C. (2009). Museum and art gallery experience space characteristics: An entertaining show or a contemplative bathe? *International Journal of Tourism Research*, 11, 155–170.

McManus, P. (1988). Good companions: More on the social determination of learning-related behaviour in a science museum. *International Journal of Museum Management and Curatorship*, 7, 37–44.

Meisner, R., vom Lehn, D., Heath, C., Burch, A., Gammon, B., & Reisman, M. (2007). Exhibiting performance: Co-participation in science centres and museums. *International Journal of Science Education*, 29, 1531–1555.

Mercer, N. & Littleton, K. (2007). *Dialogue and the development of children's thinking: A sociocultural approach*. London: Routledge.

Packer, J. & Ballantyne, R. (2005). Shared vs. solitary: Exploring the social dimension of museum learning. *Curator*, 48, 177–192.

Pajares, F. (1996). Self-efficacy beliefs in academic settings. *Review of Educational Research*, 66, 543–578.

Palmquist, S. & Crowley, K. (2007). From teachers to testers: How parents talk to novice and expert children in a natural history museum. *Science Education*, 91, 783–804.

Pashler, H., McDaniel, M., Rohrer, D., & Bjork, R. (2008). Learning styles: Concepts and evidence. *Psychological Science in the Public Interest*, 9, 105–119.

Piaget, J. & Inhelder, B. (1969). *The psychology of the child*. New York: Basic Books.

Piscitelli, B. & Anderson, D. (2001). Young children's perspectives of museum settings and experiences. *Museum Management and Curatorship*, 19, 269–282.

Postman, N. & Weingartner, C. (1969). *Teaching as a subversive activity*. New York: Delacorte Press.

Rennie, L. & Johnston, D. (2004). The nature of learning and its implications for research on learning in museums. *Science Education*, 88, S4–S16.

Roberts, L.C. (1997). *From knowledge to narrative: Educators and the changing museum*. Washington, DC: Smithsonian Institution Press.

Rogoff, B. (1990). *Apprenticeship in thinking*. Oxford: Oxford University Press.

Rogoff, B. (1994). Developing understanding of the idea of communities of learners. *Mind, Culture, and Activity*, 1, 209–229.

Rogoff, B. (2003). *The cultural nature of human development*. Oxford: Oxford University Press.

Rogoff, B., Paradise, R., Arauz, R.M., Correa-Chavez, M., & Angellilo, C. (2003). Firsthand learning through intent participation. *Annual Review of Psychology*, 54, 175–203.

Rowe, S. (2002). The role of objects in active, distributed meaning-making. In S. Paris (Ed.), *Perspectives on object-centred learning in museums* (pp. 19–35). Mahwah, NJ: Lawrence Erlbaum Associates.

Rundle, S. & Dunn, R. (2007). The Building Excellence Survey [selfdirected learning tool]. Retrieved 21 September 2016, from www.learningstyles.net/index.php?option=com_content&task=view&id=25&Itemid=78&lang=en

Schauble, L., Leinhardt, G., & Martin, L. (1997). A framework for organizing a cumulative research agenda in informal learning contexts. *Journal of Museum Education*, 22, 3–8.

Schunk, D.H. & Zimmerman, B.J. (1997). Social origins of self-regulatory competence. *Educational Psychologist*, 32, 195–208.

Semper, R. (1990). Science museums as environments for learning. *Physics Today*, 43, 50–56.

Serrell, B., Sikora, M., & Adams, M. (2013). What do *visitors* mean by 'meaning'? *The Exhibitionist*, 33, 8–15.

Shore, L. & Stokes, L. (2006). The Exploratorium Leadership program in science education: Inquiry into discipline-specific teacher education. In B. Achinstein & S. Athanases (Eds.), *Mentors in the making* (96–108). New York: Teachers College Press.

Siegler, R.S. (1995). How does cognitive change occur? A microgenetic study of number conservation. *Cognitive Psychology*, 25, 225–273.

Silverman, L. (1993). Making meaning together. *Journal of Museum Education*, 18, 7–11.

Silverman, L. (1995). Visitor meaning-making in museums for a new age. *Curator: The Museum Journal*, 38, 161–169.

Silvia, P. (2008). Interest – The curious emotion. *Current Directions in Psychological Science*, 17, 57–60.

Smith, L. (2014). Visitor emotion, affect and registers of engagement at museums and heritage sites. *Conservation Science in Cultural Heritage*, 14, 125–132.

Sobel, D. & Letourneau, S. (2015). Children's developing understanding of what and how they learn. *Journal of Experimental Child Psychology*, 132, 221–229.

Sobel, D., Letourneau, S., & Meisner, R. (2016). Developing Mind Lab: A university–museum partnership. In D. Sobel & J. Jipson (Eds.), *Cognitive development in museums: Relating research and practice* (pp. 120–137). London: Routledge.

Sobel, D., Li, J., & Corriveau, K. (2007). 'They danced around in my head and I learned them': Children's developing conceptions of learning. *Journal of Cognition & Development*, 8, 345–369.

Spiegal, A., Evans, E.M., Frazier, B., Hazel, A., Tare, M., Gram, W., & Diamond, J. (2012). Changing museum visitors' concepts of evolution. *Evolution: Education and Outreach*, 5, 43–61.

Spock, M. (1999). The stories we tell about meaning making. *Exhibitionist*, 18, 30–34.

Stahl, G. (2003). Meaning and interpretation in collaboration. In B. Wasson, S. Ludvigsen, & U. Hoppe (Eds.), *Designing for change in networked learning environments*. New York: Springer.

Starn, R. (2005). A Historian's brief guide to new museum studies, *The American Historical Review*, 110, 68–98.

St. Jacques, P. & Schacter, D. (2013). Modifying memory: selectively enhancing and updating personal memories for a museum tour by reactivating them. *Psychological Science*, 24, 537–543.

Sturm, H. & Bogner, F. (2010). Learning at workstations in two different environments: A museum and a classroom. *Studies in Educational Evaluation*, 36, 14–19.

Szechter, L. & Carey, E. (2009). Gravitating toward science: Parent–child interactions at a gravitational-wave observatory. *Science Education*, 93, 846–858.

Tal, T. & Morag, O. (2007). School visits to natural history museums: Teaching or enriching? *Journal of Research in Science Teaching*, 44, 747–769.

Tare, M., French, J., Frazier, B., Diamond, J., & Evans, E.M. (2011). Explanatory parent–child conversation predominates at an evolution exhibit. *Science Education*, 95, 720–744.

Tenenbaum, H. & Hohenstein, J. (2016). Parent–child talk about the origins of living things. *Journal of Experimental Child Psychology*, 150, 314–329.

Tenenbaum, H., Prior, J., Dowling, C., & Frost, R. (2010). Supporting parent–child conversations in a history museum. *British Journal of Educational Psychology*, 80, 241–254.

Tenenbaum, H., Rappolt-Schlictmann, G., & Zanger, V. (2004). Children's learning about water in a museum and in the classroom. *Early Childhood Research Quarterly*, 19, 40–58.

Valle, A. & Callanan, M. (2006). Similarity comparisons and relational analogies in parent-child conversations about science topics. *Merrill-Palmer Quarterly*, 52, 96–124.

van Schijndel, T., Franse, R., & Raijmakers, M. (2010). The Exploratory Behavior Scale: Assessing young visitors' hands-on behavior in science museums. *Science Education*, 94, 794–809.

van Schijndel, T., Singer, E., van der Masse, H., & Raijmakers, M. (2010). A sciencing programme and young children's exploratory play in the sandpit. *European Journal of Developmental Psychology*, 7, 603–617.

van Schijndel, T., Visser, I., van Bers, B., & Raijmakers, M. (2015). Preschoolers perform more informative experiments after observing theory-violating evidence. *Journal of Experimental Child Psychology*, 131, 104–119.

von Glaserfeld, E. (1995). *Radical constructivism: A way of knowing and learning.* London: Routledge.

Vygotsky, L. (1978). *Mind in society: The development of higher psychological processes.* Cambridge, MA: Harvard University Press.

Yunkaporta, T. (2009). Aboriginal pedagogies at the cultural interface. Unpublished PhD thesis, James Cook University.

Zimmerman, H. Reeve, S., & Bell, P. (2008). Distributed expertise in a science center. *Journal of Museum Education*, 33, 143–152.

5 Narrative, discourse and matters of communication

Experiences on Room 41[1]

Room 41 is the British Museum's permanent home for its collections from early medieval Europe. Three major collections are displayed in the room: Late Antique and Byzantine, Continental and Insular. Combined, these collections are unparalleled in their scope and cover the entire early medieval period (c. AD 300–1100) and the whole of Europe from the Atlantic Ocean in the west to Black Sea in the east, and from the Arctic Circle in the north to North Africa in the south. Therefore they do, if we choose, give us the opportunity to take a synoptic view of this fascinating period of change and formation.

This is fantastic in many ways, but there are clearly interpretive challenges in mobilising this wealth of material and information without putting visitors off. Put bluntly, there is a lot of stuff, and a lot that can be said about that stuff. The previous version of the gallery had fallen down in this respect. Its showcases were packed with objects and information, supplemented by additional panels on walls – particularly in the Sutton Hoo section of the gallery where an entire wall was dedicated to text panels. Visitor evaluations showed that visitors tended to feel overwhelmed. When confronted with so much material, they were more likely to walk on by than be encouraged to explore and engage with the displays.

In addition, many of the peoples represented in the gallery – some probably familiar (Anglo-Saxons, Vikings, Romans) but many probably not (Vandals, Visigoths, Steppe nomads) seemed isolated from each other in the previous display. This did not reflect the reality of intense cultural interchange, influence, and movement that is a defining characteristic of the period. It was only through reading the labels carefully that this relationship would become apparent. The previous gallery, rather than working toward a united 'vision' for the entire gallery, tended to display cultural 'islands' in the room. This way of working may have resulted in the lack of visibility of the connections between sections.

Figure 5.1 The new gallery in the British Museum for Room 41. © The Trustees of the British Museum.

Our aspiration for the new gallery was to take a view of the whole room and collections, make a more coherent narrative that showed how these peoples and issues related to each other across time and space, a 'red thread' running through the gallery to help visitors negotiate and digest this complex period. We needed a strong central concept to unify these expansive collections physically and narratively. Fortunately, the collections hold the perfect vehicle for this: the Sutton Hoo ship burial.

The Sutton Hoo ship burial is an early Anglo-Saxon grave dating to the early seventh century, discovered in 1939 beneath earth mound at Sutton Hoo, Suffolk. This was a burial ground throughout the Anglo-Saxon period, and features a number of mound burials from the sixth to seventh centuries of which the big ship burial was the only one intact. The burial comprised a twenty-seven-metre long ship with central chamber packed with the famous treasures, including a helmet, which forms a central part of the display. The quality and quantity of the goods, together with the spectacular nature of the burial, strongly suggest a royal burial, perhaps even a king of East Anglia (the local Anglo-Saxon kingdom at this time). Sutton Hoo was therefore an appropriate centrepiece because it is spectacular and historically significant. But it's also an ideal *conceptual* gateway into a gallery about early medieval Europe because it contained material derived from early medieval Europe (e.g., silverware from the Byzantine Empire, coins from the Frankish kingdoms, hanging bowls from Celtic Britain). In this way it could be made to invite visitors to make connections to other regions and cultures represented in the gallery.

Our idea was to place Sutton Hoo as the physical, as well as conceptual, centre of the room. The rest of the material was then arranged around it in geographical and cultural zones, so that the relevant Sutton Hoo material was in close proximity (and conversation) with the relevant perimeter material. Our visitors would be able to see spoons and bowls in the central display that closely resembled those in the adjacent Byzantine zone of the gallery, and so on around the room.

The burial also encapsulates key themes of the period, which we used to guide our narrative and information used in the interpretation. These themes were:

- The continuing influence and legacy of Roman Empire.
- The movement of people, objects and ideas sparking meaningful cultural, social and artistic interactions.
- The importance of archaeology to understanding this period.

All in all, we hoped that using Sutton Hoo and the selected themes as unifiers would help weave these vast collections together and make the whole gallery more coherent, easier to navigate and enjoyable for our visitors. The idea was that if visitors only stop at Sutton Hoo, they would get an idea of what the gallery is all about; and if they only stop at one or two standalone displays, they will get much the same. We supported this more-engaging interpretive approach with less-stuffed showcases, more sympathetic lighting and mounting which seem to be doing a very good job of drawing visitors in to explore in more depth.

Introduction

There are many reasons to suspect that discourse and narrative are closely connected to learning both in the museum and elsewhere (e.g., Leinhardt & Knutson, 2004; Browning & Hohenstein, 2015; Vygotsky, 1978). In this respect, understanding something about both narrative and discourse, from the perspective of the learner and that of the educator, should provide a helpful window into the ways that people come to use settings such as museums for learning. According to Bruner,

> we organize our experience and our memory of human happenings mainly in the form of narrative – stories, excuses, myths, reasons for doing and not doing, and so on. Narrative is a conventional form, transmitted culturally and constrained by each individual's level of mastery and by his conglomerate of prosthetic devices, colleagues, and mentors.
>
> (1991, p. 4)

At the same time, discourse is a negotiation, between speakers, between readers and writers, or interlocutors of other types, whereby people come to find meaning in interactions (Brown & Levinson, 1987). In the words of White (1981), 'we view narrative and narrativity as the instruments by which the conflicting claims of the imaginary and real are mediated, arbitrated, or resolved in a discourse' (p. 4). This would suggest that discourse is a means of communicating narratives that somehow already exist in people (or places). There have been many reflections on the use of language and narrative in museum settings, often drawing upon a wide variety of theories and research about discourse (e.g., Roberts, 1997; Leinhardt & Knutson, 2004).

Discourse can be thought of in several different ways. At its very basic sense, it is the way that people communicate with each other; such communications can be long or fleeting. Often a narrative can be seen as a relatively long tale, perhaps interwoven with other tales, leading to a complex story that can be told about someone or something (Bruner, 1990; Roberts, 1997). For instance, the connections alluded to in the Sutton Hoo scenario above refer to interrelations of multiple tales from various geographical regions regarding cultural practices as presented through a variety of artefacts. But one can also think about narrative as smaller pieces of language, embedded in conversation, that together help form a greater whole (Bruner, 1990; Ochs, 1993). The various turns in a conversation between two people may seem disjointed if taken individually. But added together, such turns can form a set of meaningful episodes. So one might think of communication as spread across a spectrum ranging from the way ideas are expressed overall, with grand presentations through narrative, implicitly and explicitly, to the smallest elements of dialogue in groups, or even between an individual and a text. This chapter deals with the language and other rhetorical devices (e.g., pictures, symbols, body language, exhibit design) used to convey messages in museums, both from the perspective of the museum, and from the perspective of the visitor.

It is important to mention the enormous overlaps between narrative and discourse and some of the other topics covered in this book. In part, this stems from the use of narrative or discourse as a methodology to research other topics. But there are also clear theoretical links between the narratives people use to tell stories and the ways they construct identity, make meaning and form memories – topics covered in other chapters. So although this chapter attempts to locate itself in discourse especially, there are undoubtedly many ways that it will touch on the ideas that are also presented elsewhere in this book. We try to be transparent when these overlaps occur.

The basics of discourse and narrative

One of the currently popular ways that discourse has been used to understand how individuals learn about the world is through sociocultural theory, broadly speaking. There are various branches of sociocultural theory; and it will be impossible to cover each of these in a great deal of depth. However, it is potentially helpful for our purposes in this chapter to think about the ways that social constructivism compares with something like communities of practice and situated learning. In addition, it is useful to consider the perspectives from cognitive development about the ways that language can facilitate or hinder understandings from a cognitive science or information-processing perspective. We begin, however, with a look at Bruner's closely related perspective about the constructed nature of how people use stories or narrative to understand themselves and the events that occur in their lives will also be elucidated. Some of the perspectives about how museums tell stories about the objects and concepts on their premises can be considered from the point of view of narrative in practice.

Narrative theory

Much of the discussion here centres on narrative as depicted in psychological and sociolinguistic theory. It is worth noting that other disciplines have also developed ideas around narrative, including but not limited to English, history, philosophy, and anthropology.

According to Bruner (1991), narrative helps people to make sense of and communicate events that occur over time. These events are relatable because they draw upon scripts that are well-known to people[2] (Nelson, 1996; Schank & Abelson, 1977). For example, because people have script-based expectations about what happens in a museum, a narrative about how a museum visit will unfold or what is expected of people in this setting, visitors can make certain assumptions about what people will know (e.g., there is usually a series of exhibits) and can relate ideas about normal behaviour such as buying a ticket before entering or not touching the artworks. But the narrative can also distinguish itself by drawing upon people's knowledge to create memorable moments and interesting stories: when people deviate from expected behaviour, there may be reason to remark upon these events. For instance, a person who sets off alarms by reaching for a sculpture might find herself to be the centre of attention. These types of narratives both centre around and veer off from scripts that people retain from previous experiences.

In fact, Bruner (1990) has suggested that, 'the function of a story is to find an intentional state that mitigates or at least makes comprehensible a deviation from a canonical cultural pattern' (pp. 49–50). In the example above from the Sutton Hoo exhibition, one may not expect visitors to understand the connections between various groups of people and so by drawing those connections to the fore, the exhibition has highlighted what might be an unexpected relationship in this context, enabling people to encounter the displays as an interesting story.

Moreover, narrative consists of a set of parts that help to create the whole. These parts, implicit (possibly deriving from a well-known script) or explicit, help to construct a story that is greater than the sum of its parts. This can be particularly challenging in museums because of the free-choice nature of visitor behaviour (e.g., Falk & Dierking, 2000). A visitor cannot be expected to follow any particular plan and pick up all of the pieces of an exhibition, as much as any curator or museum educator may wish that were the case. The challenge here can be finding a way to convey the narrative in such a way that visitors are able to construct enough of the story, even if they visit in an unexpected order or only see some of the exhibits. One way theory might alleviate this problem can be found in Bruner's (1991) elements about narrative that help to understand the ways that narrative can be used in everyday meaning construction. He notes that narratives are embedded with intentionality on the part of the actors and the narrator, but also on the part of the 'listener', who interprets the story that is told. As such, there will necessarily be coordination between the intentional elements of the narrative, which may be out of the control of any of the actors involved! These issues become increasingly important as museums take into consideration the stories of less traditionally prominent groups in creating programmes and designing spaces (see Chapter 10). In this context, assumptions that everyone has the same reaction to an object, a text or a display become more problematic than they might have been historically, when cultural considerations were less commonplace. Bruner (1991) also mentions the need for referentiality in a narrative. That is, there must be parts of a story that the person interpreting the narrative can hang on to for grounding the story. In a museum these elements may be objects (authentic or not, see Chapter 6), common ideas or historical events, or other socially shared understandings that could be seen as the basis for an exhibition or activity. It was Bruner's contention that people learn largely through the interpretation of narrative, either as actions experienced by oneself, which are then turned into stories, or through the ability to experience someone else's reality because other people have provided the context through storytelling. Both types of learning, personal experience stories and the storytelling of others, can be construed through other theoretical lenses, some closely related, some less so; several of these are detailed in the sections that follow.

Ochs and Capp (1996) have noted that people are often confronted with what they call narrative asymmetries, events in which two or more narratives conflict in their construal of some idea or occurrence. That is, sometimes narratives tell stories that are inconsistent with one another (e.g., religious notions of the earth as less than 10,000 years old as opposed to geologists' claims that the earth's period in history began billions of years ago). When this happens, people must somehow resolve these discrepancies – they may tend to operate with either a relativistic or a fundamentalistic perspective. A relativistic perspective acknowledges that there is no one absolute 'truth'. That is, different narratives may be true for different individuals; the resolution for people then is to find ways to make sense of, or function around, the various forms of reality depicted in each narrative. In contrast, a fundamentalist perspective may deny the validity of a narrative held by another person, sometimes leading to antagonistic interactions. Like Bruner (1990), Ochs and Capp argue that people use narrative to resolve the discrepancies between their expectations and their experiences of the world, attempting to maintain a sense of consistency both within themselves and across people. When people encounter new ideas or information that is contrary to their expectations or their core beliefs, as in a 'controversial' museum display, they will need to find a way to manage that discrepancy (but see below for discussions of entrance narratives). This process is an endeavour that functions with several social partners, the visitor, the educator, the text (writer), and various 'voices' that are represented in the display. We turn now to another way of construing the social aspects of learning.

Sociocultural theory

Vygotsky (1978), as already mentioned in Chapter 4, is credited with founding a movement to consider the ways learners engage with others on a social plane. It is this repeated engagement that allows the learner to progress through a particular zone of proximal development, which enables increases in intellectual achievement and capacity: where a learner was only able to do something with the aid of someone else at one point in time, with guidance and practice that task is accomplished on one's own at some later time. The zone refers to the bounds under which a person can be helped on a particular learning task at any point in time. That is, the concepts that arise on the social plane (interpersonal) can be converted to a personal plane (intrapersonal) through habitual experience with the ideas and information originating with other people. Vygotsky proposed that one of the main cultural tools people use to conduct this communication on a social plane is language. Other tools have been described as ways of conveying information, including maps, mathematical formulae, art and music. But by far the most studied cultural tool is the language people engage in everyday, often without actively considering their discourse or narrative. Bakhtin (1981) suggested that all thought, including that in solitary situations like reading, is dialogic, as if engaged in, or preparing to engage in, discussion with someone else. From this perspective, people are constantly participating in dialogic interactions that might affect their later conceptual understandings. As such, museum experiences, by individual visitors or in groups, can be included in the multitude of learning conversations that individuals may have, given the potential for interaction between the visitor and the objects, space or text in the institution.

Many lines of work take Vygotsky and the sociocultural perspective as inspiration for their research. As noted in Chapter 2, the social constructivist approach is usually seen as drawing upon both the individualistic developmental perspective of Piaget and constructivism and the sociocultural perspective of Vygotsky (e.g., Mercer, 2000; Haden, 2010). Whilst this approach is not as grounded in the way a group functions, adopts new members and adapts to new developments in the environment as a sociocultural perspective usually is, it still places great emphasis on the way that learners are shaped by (and in turn shape) the people and environments around them. That is, social constructivists tend to take the perspective of the individual learner whilst acknowledging that the learner is not an island, interpreting and experiencing solely on his or her own. The social context is extremely important to the outcome of individual development according to this perspective. This type of work tends to focus on the details of language and conversation and how they relate to specific learning achievements in child (or learner) cognition. For instance, a study in this tradition may closely investigate the use of explanation in conversation and how children's memory for objects or facts can be related to those explanations.

In contrast, the communities of practice theory (Lave & Wenger, 1991) suggests that group tradition provides paths for learners to come to understand the ways of being or thinking associated with a particular community or culture. Viewed through the lens of this theory, changes in the ways people behave are associated with familiarisation with practices that form the basis of a community. By community, they refer to any group of people who engage in activities together with some regularity. Individuals may belong to a variety of communities: nuclear family, workplace, hobby groups, shopping circles or even museum visitors. People can establish their identities as members of these communities by taking part in the opportunities available in them, such as attending special exhibitions, forming friendship networks with other museum visitors, going to social events or lectures at museums. The more comfortable people feel within these networks, the more likely they will be to participate in the linguistic practices that are specific to these communities (Heath, 1983). On the other hand, using this theoretical lens, people who are not accustomed to the linguistic practices that are particular to a museum could feel they are relegated to the periphery, or not welcomed (Dawson, 2014). The Sutton Hoo gallery was designed with the idea that helping visitors to see the connections between the central element, the burial site, and the peripheral elements would enable them to feel comfortable with the concepts of the exhibition.

There is also a line of work that highlights particular aspects of discourse as helpful to the development of concepts. Much of this notes the benefits of explanation, both to oneself and to others (e.g., Chi et al., 1994). Some of the literature for this type of work is couched in sociocultural terms. But the focus on a measurable set of learned facts or ideas causes it to feel more socio-cognitive or 'scientific' than some of the research based in sociocultural traditions.

In what follows, we present research relevant to two different areas of visitor studies. The first examines how museums can develop narratives that help visitors' learning. The second addresses the visitors' perspective and focuses on the typology and mechanisms of discourse-related learning in museums. These are not always unrelated bodies of research. But they do, at times, draw upon very different ideas about what it means to learn.

Narrative and the museum perspective

There are a number of ways that museums participate in narrative interaction when it concerns the practices directed towards visitors. Some of these have to do with getting visitors into the museum; others relate to the interface between museum educators on the floor and groups of visitors; there is also the narrative of the objects and galleries that help tell stories designed to educate, entertain and engage the visitor. As seen in the scenario from the British Museum, their team worked to address the ways that the historical periods, geographical regions, ethnic groups and even the objects 'speak' to one another in the reconceptualisation of their gallery space. We address the different types of museum-based discourse here.

Entrance narratives[3]

In 1996 Doering and Pekarik wrote an opinion piece about the reactions visitors might have to being confronted with narratives that conflict with their own personal frameworks. They acknowledged that the amount of formal education a person has is the best predictor of whether that person would visit a museum. At the same time, they suggested that visitors only want to have their previous conceptions of the world confirmed, leaving museums open for major criticism if they attempted to deviate from the typical story the visitor expects. As such, if museums intend to educate and not just cater to the visitors' expectations, museums are challenged to both increase the number of visitors but also to engage visitors in a way that goes beyond a sense of affirmation of their world views.

A great deal of effort has gone into finding ways of expanding the typical visitor profile (Goulding, 2000; MacDonald & Fyfe, 1996; McPherson, 2006; Hayes & Slater, 2002). It is no longer acceptable to serve only the highly educated, as alluded to in Doering and Pekarik (1996). As a consequence, attempts have been made to understand visitor relationships with museums. An example of this is evident in a study by Everett and Barrett (2009) in which they utilised a narrative methodology, seeking to understand how a visitor created a story that helped to construct her identity. With this narrative inquiry, they draw upon a framework that stems from Dewey's (1938) experiential learning ideas: the focus is on experience, which is contextually and temporally based, as manifested in narrative. They provide a perspective on an atypical, female, fifty-nine-year-old visitor to art museums, noting that though she was not highly educated and did not visit museums as a child, their case study shows ways that personal connections can introduce people to museum experiences, gradually allowing them to feel comfortable through connecting with their interests, such that they become lifelong visitors. The story conveyed by the participant alludes to an ongoing relationship with one museum, which she has visited in different ways at different points in her life: as a young aspiring artist, as a mother in the company of children and as a divorced woman living on her own with more time to engage with the displays in a mature way. It might be useful for museums to consider the ways in which visitors could have different relationships with their institution over time. It may be possible, for example, to facilitate ongoing relationships by toying with the format of programming, using front-end evaluation to help target multiple age groups and people from various backgrounds. In this case, the participant of the study was attracted by her interests in art in different ways according to the needs she had at each point in her life. If museums could help to create a sense of community by anticipating the needs of a variety of types of people, there could be scope for forging this sort of lifelong relationship. Simultaneously, offering a feeling of welcome to many groups of potential visitors may help museums to construct a more complex set of narratives as an institution.

Rich narratives help diverse visitors connect with the museum in multiple ways

Museums are not strangers to the use of narrative as a tool to enhance their market positions (Wells, Butler, & Koke, 2016). The trouble can be pinpointing which narrative or how to convey a complex, yet understandable story to individuals who are considering a visit in such a way as to sway them to come. In his marketing study involving a case study participant to a heritage site, Chronis (2012) draws upon a theoretical viewpoint of visitor narrative that can help museums to streamline their story, allowing visitors to come away with a straightforward reflection on their visit. This viewpoint is derived from philosophical backgrounds such as Heidegger's (1949), which asserts that human existence takes the form of conversation involving a speaker and a listener, which could be seen as similar to Bruner's (1990) notion of learning through storytelling whereby a person is constantly relating the things around him to himself and others.

Streamlining the narrative may help visitors reflect on the visit more easily

According to Chronis' (2012) perspective, visitors engage in a cyclical process of learning that can be tapped into to promote active learning strategies through questioning and critiquing the exhibit ideas. That is, he advocates for the use of narrative in exhibitions to tell stories but also that the stories be told in such a way as to help visitors engage actively rather than passively. Chronis (2012) also suggests that assisting the visitor to form and maintain a consistent narrative will help build a narrative image for the museum itself, ultimately allowing it to attract greater numbers of visitors. Whilst the theoretical ideas are consistent with a good deal of theories about learning (e.g., constructivism, experiential learning), it should be noted that further research along these lines would be required to confirm the narrative cycle, specifically for museums as proposed here. The case study utilised may be difficult to generalise beyond the individual participant or the type of museum visited. That being said, in the Sutton Hoo exhibition scenario above, the objects themselves were able to create a particularly strong narrative about the events and the people from the time and the region(s). But the way the gallery was laid out and the inclusion of pictures and text helped provide a story to help visitors bridge the gaps that were left open in the tale, including the relation to other cultures and understandings about the actual site of the burial. These mechanisms allow a coherent narrative to be maintained throughout the gallery.

Programming, discourse and narrative

In the intervening twenty years since Doering and Pekarik's piece (1996), there has been a growing movement to try to entice visitors out of their comfort zones when it comes to stories and narratives. This can be particularly true in presenting heritage and history, as there is often a need to explore things that have happened in the past, that ancestors of current society members are responsible for (e.g., slavery) (Macdonald, 2009; Rose, 2016). Bonnell and Simon (2007) note that some exhibits or exhibitions spark controversy, a spirited discussion about the way something is presented in terms of accuracy or sentiment; exhibitions on genetically modified foods and the Enola Gay, come to mind. They suggest that dealing with 'difficult' topics is even more embroiled with emotion because of the need for visitors to face guilt or shame in a way that is unsettling because there are multiple interpretations of an event or idea. Narrative is instrumental in such cases because of the often open-endedness of the presentation, 'such exhibitions may indeed require visitors to engage in the process of confronting and dismantling their expectations and complicating their desire for a particular "way of telling" the story' (Bonnell & Simon, 2007, p. 67). This confrontation has occurred in many types of museum across a spectrum of topics relating to social justice, environmental and medical concerns, and dominant historical perspectives, to name just a few (see http://sjam.org/case-studies/using-objects/ for some examples of social justice issues that have been addressed). It is useful to note here that these issues are dealt with in slightly different ways in Chapters 8 and 10.

Some research has attempted to examine the ways visitors engage with these new programmes. One such study found that a set of dialogue events involved experts on a particular topic and museum visitors who engaged in collaborative argumentation by building on one another's statements in order to create a coherent perspective, which may have countered that of one of the expert speakers (McCallie, 2009). McCallie's findings, based on a sociocultural theoretical perspective about learning (Lave & Wenger, 1991), show that whereas what is commonly viewed as rational argument from experts and less coherent from 'laypeople', participants engaged together to formulate arguments that met rationality criteria (Toulmin, 1958). However, there is still little known about how museum narratives interact with visitors' prior knowledge and previous narrative and how resilient or malleable those narratives are when visitors encounter information that challenges their previously held notions.

A growing body of work investigates visitor reactions to exhibitions and museums through their written feedback, sometimes in the form of notes in guestbooks, and more recently through the use of 'post-it' notes. Both of these formats allow visitors to engage with the museum directly in a discursive way, as opposed to engaging with each other or in an indirect way

Visitors can engage in collaborative argumentation to get a point across with the museum. However, they differ in the amount they afford interactivity. Noy (2015) notes that texts written in visitor books are often, though not always, celebratory or congratulatory of the museum. But they are also performances, provided in a public forum in a way that is conscious that other visitors will potentially read them. In this way, Noy's work relates to the Bakhtinian (1981), sociocultural, notion that communications are always made in a context that reflects an expectation that someone might react to them. However, the writing, not unsurprisingly, also differed depending upon where the books were placed and how they were presented (e.g., at the exit, where the emphasis was on the takeaway message, or with an invitation to think about how the visitor would act in a situation that was similar to the one conveyed in the exhibition, in which the entries were often more melancholy and possibly more 'genuine' in terms of the visitors' reflections on the exhibition).

Does discourse increase authentic interaction?

Mauratonio's (2015) analysis of the use of post-it notes in a Civil War museum in the United States suggests that rather than encouraging visitors to engage with each other through the display of visitor comments about their experiences at the museum, the presentation of visitor comments instead presented a unified sense of the understandings of the Civil War. That is, the author suggested that there was a missed opportunity to engage in dialogue about the historical period. So though it appeared as though visitors participated in an interactive, discursive activity, in reality the practice merely reified the museum's own story, reinforcing its authority over the narrative it conveyed. Here, and in other places in this chapter, there are links to Chapter 10.

Museum educator discourse

Other research on narrative in the museum has investigated the ways that members of staff use language to generate stories about the experiences museums represent in order to help generate meaning making (Bruner, 1990). For instance, museum storytelling for children has been used to help create a connection between the artefacts on display and the significance behind them (Frykman, 2009). Lwin (2012) examined the way a storyteller in a history museum in Singapore drew upon narrative performance in order to contextualise the objects displayed in the galleries for her young audience members. She utilised cultural experiences to help learners create a sense of meaning with the events that the artefacts came from, naming fictional but realistic characters in the story with names that would be familiar to the children, highlighting roles the characters would have fulfilled, acting out with gestures the types of activities they would have conducted in the historical period referred to

Mediation through storytelling can enhance children's experience

in the narrative. The storyteller was thus able to convey a great deal of information, using questions and repetition, to help children make sense of the objects they would later get to see on display. Such narratives can be especially helpful to establishing a context for inexperienced visitors (Lwin, 2012).

Other work on storytelling in the museum has focused on the ways that docents convey a sense of identity through the use of narrative centred around their own experiences. Roberts (1997) has noted that storytelling can invite visitors to take another perspective, different from their own, in order to explore interpretations and feelings for later reflection. In examining the ways that docents in a Japanese-American history museum, Burdelski, Kawashima and Yamazaki (2014) use a narrative theory background to reveal both verbal and non-verbal techniques employed by the guides that afford visitor sense-making in the museum. In using gesture and intonation in speech, the docents helped visitors to gain rich details about the context of the wartime period in ways that may have been difficult to pick up through objects and labels alone. Another study of docent narrative techniques investigated the ways that Plantation Houses were portrayed (Modlin, Alderman, & Gentry, 2011). Findings in this study highlighted that the primarily white tour guides also engendered sympathy amongst the visitors, but this was largely towards the owners of the house, rather than the slaves who would have worked on the plantation. They use the concept of affective inequality to draw attention to the types of stories that are told in these tours and the silence of one of the main groups of characters in history at these sites.

Docent identity and non-linguistic cues influence visitor experience

The stories told through objects

Perhaps controversially, Sue Allen has suggested that science exhibits (particularly those that are hands-on and orientated towards scientific principle as opposed to history of science) might not be able to make use of narrative in the way that other types of museums can (2004). She noted, in her socio-cognitively focused study, that the museum itself might be able to create an overarching story but that science exhibits are much harder to create an easily perceived narrative. In her previous study (2002), Allen noted that visitors rarely made connections between exhibits in their conversation. Use of physical cordons to partition exhibits helped visitors to notice a theme across exhibits; but that still only occurred amongst half the visitors (Allen, 2003). This sort of analysis is consistent with Frykman's (2009) findings suggesting that 10/11 texts in history museums incorporated narrative, whereas only 2/3 did so in science-related museums (both natural history and science

Some material may be more conducive to narrative

centre). As such, it may be the case that science museums will find it more difficult, or unnecessary, to construct coherent narratives that their visitors will take home.

Attempts have been made to highlight ways of visually presenting narrative in science museum contexts (Dyehouse, 2011). Dyehouse's study focused on natural history and the presentation of evolution through diagrams. Through a focus on pragmatism (Dewey, 1938), the author suggests that rather than relying on a linear or ladder display to convey the evolutionary inheritances across species over time, museums would do well to incorporate displays that utilise non-linear visualisations of evolutionary changes. Of note is the author's insistence that the changes are purely in visual narrative, when they appear to be accompanied by a great deal of label text to support the visitors' understanding. So, whilst it is useful to consider not just the narrative as portrayed through language, but also other media, it is also important to remember to consider the narrative holistically, through visual, linguistic and other media.

In contrast, Scott (2007, 2014) has noticed the ways that some museums have capitalised on the sense of reverence typically conveyed in museums to enhance the messages of importance of the displays in their collections. Scott looks at both a creationist museum and displays at a Mormon temple to examine the narratives used by those institutions by 'situating visitors as participants in an educational setting' (2007, p. 202). In this type of setting, Scott argues that taking on an identity of 'museum-ness' helps reduce resistance to the messages in some settings. The creationist museum even goes so far as to discredit 'secular' scientific approaches to the natural world by enhancing the religious message through the ritual experience of the museum. Perhaps confirming Doering and Pekarik's (1996) point, visitor comments suggested that they believed the museum's narrative that the secularists and evolutionists were incorrect. It is likely that visitors already held such views rather than being converted to that opinion as a result of attending the museum (see Chapter 10 for more discussion on museum as a perceived authority); however, the appropriation of the museum identity may reinforce the messages told to visitors in these settings, a possibility that seems little explored in more traditional museum settings.

Summary

This section has drawn on research that suggests that when museums pay attention to the narratives they utilise, possibly extending the way they tell stories in new and innovative ways, they may connect with potential visitors in various points of their lives. At the same time, it will be useful to remember that visitors will arrive with their own narratives, many of which will be difficult to alter with just one short museum visit (Doering & Pekarik, 1996; Scott, 2007, 2014). Working with the materials that are available to each institution to best capture the potentials, in a multisensory way, of the storytelling capacity, which might be further enhanced by staff (live or even virtually) is no doubt the great challenge for exhibition and programme development. However, listening to both the particular voices of visitors at institutions (through public feedback or evaluation) and the more general findings of visitor research stands to enhance the learning opportunities museums can provide. We turn now from focus on the museum's narrative to visitors' experience of discourse in the museum.

Museum research drawing upon the visitor perspective

There are various ways of categorising the work that examines discourse with respect to the visitor. As noted above, discourse can be thought of as one of the elements that make up narrative, or one way of conveying narrative. Sometimes the incomplete and online nature of discourse means that a narrative is only partially evident in conversation. However, it is likely to be the case that discourse corresponds in some way to the narratives that individuals and groups use to story their lives. Here we have grouped the work into studies about visitors conversing with one another, the ways labels affect visitor conversation, space and discourse, objects and conversation and programmes or facilitation. These categories no doubt overlap a great deal, as they are likely to also be relevant to the preceding section. And there are no doubt other ways to consider discourse in museums besides those presented here.

Visitor conversation and learning

Some of the first work in museums to draw attention to visitor discourse came from Paulette McManus (1987, 1988). In a large-scale survey of museum visitor behaviour McManus outlined a series of moves that visitor groups used in conversation with one another to explore the exhibits in London's Natural History Museum. These described the ways that different types of visitor groups (e.g., families, adult peers) used expressions that involved asking for and providing information. This work, though not explicitly drawing on any learning theories itself, paved the way for future studies to try to understand more about the ways that people converse in museum settings. A note of caution is worthwhile here. Leinhardt and

Knutson (2004) mention three potential risks to equating museum conversation with learning: (1) whereas learning is an ongoing process, the conversation that is visible in the museum is a momentary occurrence (that may be part of this continued learning experience) and should be treated as such; (2) it is possible that visitors speak in an artificial way when they know they are being recorded, though the experiences of many researchers will attest to the fact that differences are unlikely to be extreme if this is the case; (3) the way that speech is broken up for purposes of analysis can result in artificially segmenting the speakers' intentions and thoughts. Different researchers will have dealt with these three problems in various ways. But readers might wish to bear them in mind when considering the following (and other) studies that relate to conversation in museum settings. These studies about visitor interaction fall into a number of different categories of topic, covered below: family sense-making, school trips, explanations, autonomy and self-monitoring.

Family sense making
Some recent studies have examined the ways that families explore museums throughout their whole visit. These types of studies tend to work with families in an in-depth way, using pre-visit and post-visit interviews, as well as audio and video recordings of the entire time a family is in the museum. Zimmerman, Reeve, & Bell (2009) and Ash (Ash, 2003, 2004; Ash et al., 2007; Mai & Ash, 2012) utilise a sociocultural lens on learning and research in order to explore the ways that families talk about science in museum settings. Much of Ash's work with her colleagues has drawn attention to the microanalytic details of family conversation, including the use of questions and inquiry in museum settings. Furthermore, her work has focused on the ways that families from different ethnic and educational backgrounds draw upon different kinds of discourse resources in their museum visits. Despite their differing educational backgrounds and, of course, the languages they speak, families from lower educated, lower income groups tend to use the same types of communicative devices, with parents working with children's zones of proximal development, for instance, to interact with each other as compared with more highly educated family groups. Zimmerman et al. (2009) focused on families who were expert museumgoers to see how they use epistemic resources, questions and statements to help make sense of the material encountered in the museum. They found that families were able to transfer understandings from prior experiences and knowledge to learn about the exhibited concepts. For instance, in their visit to an insect exhibition, one family asked questions about joints in their own bodies to draw connections to the joints of

> Families use questions, explanations and other discourse markers in their pursuit of inquiry in ways that may depend upon their background, broadly defined. These are only *sometimes* related to learning

the insects. Zimmerman et al. noted that a third of the utterances the families provided were used to describe what they saw, whereas an additional third brought in previous knowledge to contextualise the new information. Nearly 14% of the talk was categorised as comparison or analogy. Each of these techniques could be seen as ways of helping the family members to gain new perspectives on the biological specimens and exhibits they were viewing. Both of these socioculturally based sets of studies focus on the family members' relationships with one another, the long-term goals of family members and the ways people co-construct meaning during family visits to a museum.

Families have been studied using a more socio-cognitive perspective to see in what ways they discuss topics in museums when children have varying levels of prior knowledge. Crowley and Jacobs (2002) and Palmquist and Crowley (2007) investigated the ways parents and children conversed about fossils and dinosaurs. They found that parents were instrumental in helping children to form what they called 'islands of expertise'. That is, when parents mediated the conversation about fossils more, children were more likely to remember the names of the fossils later on (Crowley & Jacobs, 2002). Palmquist and Crowley (2007) noted that parents of children who were relative experts on dinosaurs contributed fewer explanations compared with parents of less knowledgeable children. Presumably this is to do with parents' sensitivity to the level of need their children have for gaining understanding. In these studies, parents and children seem to be operating within the children's zones of proximal development such that the level of information discussed is appropriate to the abilities of the children to take that information in.

Finally, other socio-cognitive research has attempted to address child learning in museums through manipulating the types of conversation that families have at an exhibit. For example, Benjamin, Haden, and Wilkerson (2010) placed parent–child dyads into groups and asked them to interact with a museum exhibit about constructing buildings. The use of elaborative talk by the parents, including explanations and wh-questions, because of its effect on other examples of child learning, was proposed to help children learn about the concepts about constructing buildings. They found that when parents were given instructions about how to build an efficient structure prior to seeing the exhibit, their children tended to learn and were able to recognise a good building two weeks later. However, when parents were instructed about using particular types of elaborative conversation, there was no improvement in children's performance. In this case, the predicted interaction between parent conversation and subject instruction did not materialise. The type of conversations between parents and children did not seem to make a difference to children's learning. As such, it may be useful to consider whether attempting to alter the means of visitors' interactions will be a useful intervention in museums. Here the instruction for working with the materials was much more helpful to learning.

School trips

A growing number of studies have investigated the ways that talk is used by pupils, school teachers and museum staff during museum visits. Given the nature of these trips as potentially being an extension of school, it is possible that the talk at a museum during such trips would differ from other types of museum activity discourse. DeWitt and Hohenstein examined the ways that teachers and students interacted with each other (2010a) or how pupils interacted with each other (2010b) in both a science museum and the classroom. These social constructivist studies indicate that teachers in both settings tend to dominate the conversation, using a high number of Initiate-Respond-Feedback (IRF; Wells, 1999) type questions with a relatively large number of open-ended questions. However, pupils exhibited a greater sense of autonomy, evidenced by their higher proportion of volunteer-type statements and the teachers' lower level of evaluations in the museum than in the classroom.

> Children's talk exhibits more autonomy in museums than in classrooms

In another study, Zhai and Dillon (2014) studied the patterns of talk used by educators in botanic gardens in communicating science to primary school students. Despite the fact that the overwhelming majority of the talk was provided by the educators (80%), more than half of their talk was coded as interactive in nature. The authors also connected the statements that pupils made, volunteering information or ideas, with educator discourse. They noted that of the three educators they followed, the pupils in the two who used a larger proportion of open-ended questions tended to volunteer their own questions and comments with greater frequency. Furthermore, these two educators also utilised storytelling in their communications of information to the pupils. These types of activities are likely to have engaged the pupils, leading to their own volunteering statements. Both DeWitt and Hohenstein (2010a, 2010b) and Zhai and Dillon (2014) take a social constructivist perspective on the ways that learning can be influenced by language in that they focus on the students' construction of knowledge as facilitated by the opportunities they have in conversation to gain support for the development of ideas and attitudes.

> Educator talk can dominate but still offer opportunity for engagement

Explanations

In the mid-1990s at the University of California, Santa Cruz, a set of studies, drawing on sociocultural and socio-cognitive perspectives on learning, was initiated investigating the use of explanations in parent–child talk in museums and other out-of-classroom environments. Maureen Callanan and Kevin Crowley started working at that point with a nearby science centre to examine how families could be seen to interact with young children in ways that might afford children opportunities to learn about the scientific exhibits in the museum. Over the years this work has branched out to many other sites and places, with varied populations, leading to a better defined understanding of explanation in conversation and its relationship to learning about science. The partnership that led to these studies is detailed in a recent chapter (Callanan, Martin & Luce, 2015).

One of the studies that got the ball rolling for this line of work was conducted by Callanan and Oakes (1992) in which the researchers invited parents to keep diary records of the causal questions their preschool aged children asked, together with the responses the parents gave to them. They demonstrated that children ask meaningful causal questions about the physical world and that parents provide useful explanations about domains of interest to four- and five-year-old children such that their knowledge base can be seen to expand, providing a foundation for further development and experience. Importantly, this work focused not just on the ways that parents helped children learn about important elements of the world, but also on the ways that children brought their own ideas (in the form of questions) to the conversational table. As such, this and following studies were really about the interactions of children's ideas and interests as well as parents' own understandings and how those interactions can lead to conceptual development in a co-constructed way.

Crowley, Callanan, Jipson et al. (2001) reported on the ways that parents and children (aged four to eight) interacted at exhibits at a science museum. In this study they noted that when children were accompanied by their parent at an exhibit, they tended to stay longer and explore the exhibit more deeply than when their parent was not present. Moreover, in this study parents often provided explanations for causal phenomena as well as connecting the museum experience to prior experiences, which could help children to better situate the information they encountered in the museum. Another related study also showed that parents explained scientific exhibits to their male children more than they did to female children (Crowley, Callanan, Tenenbaum, & Allen, 2001). After carefully planning and designing an exhibition about science content that would be more gender neutral or female friendly ('Alice's Wonderland'), another team of researchers found that this gender gap had been eliminated (Callanan, Frazier, & Gorchoff, 2015, cited in Callanan et al., 2015). Finally, whilst the studies above primarily investigated learning conversations on their own, some

Even young children can ask important questions that trigger useful explanations

Parent presence has effects on child opportunity for cognitive engagement

studies have begun to address the mechanisms involved in parent–child interactions and how this seems to matter for the ways that children develop thinking about science. In one such study, Luce, Callanan, and Smilovic (2013) found that when parent–child conversation included the use of evidence on one topic, the same four- to eight-year-old children tended to utilise evidence in making judgements about new topics, by, for example, suggesting that something they cannot see with the naked eye exists because they can see it under a microscope. As such, the children may be learning about the importance of evidence through the discourse they experience with their parents and possibly others.

Autonomy

Some research has investigated ways that interactions foster autonomy in museum settings. The above-mentioned studies by DeWitt and Hohenstein (2010a, 2010b) both examine some issues related to children's autonomy, suggesting that children in late childhood or early adolescence are more likely to engage in volunteering types of moves when they are in a museum compared with in the classroom.

In a slightly different take on autonomy, one study examines young children's interactions with respect to who leads the dialogue (Dooley & Welch, 2014). This study, conducted in a children's museum with two- to six-year-olds, asked questions about the nature of interactions that were led by either the parent or the child. Their findings indicated that when parents led the interactions, they tended to instruct children about the exhibits and activities. In contrast, children engaged in 'show and tell' types of activities and requested help quite often when they initiated interactions. As such, though the numbers of interactions led by parents and children were fairly similar, the goals of their interactions appeared to differ substantially. The types of conversations led by children were consistent with their stated goals: playing. Parents indicated that they wanted to help their children learn, which seems consistent with the ways they were seen in teacher roles in the interactions they led. The research did not specify whether there were tendencies to alternate leading and following within parent–child dyads or whether particular pairs were more parent-led versus child-led. The authors also did not indicate whether there were tensions arising due to the different goals in the dyads. Their dialogic approach, which seems closely related to sociocultural theory, emphasises the ways that dyads tend to organise their interactions within a particular type of museum setting. At this age, and within this type of environment, the focus on autonomy might have a different meaning from the research on autonomy in school trips or older children in different types of museums

The nature of an interaction changes depending on who is leading it (see above). In other words, the school trip studies highlighted where students were able to voice their opinions. Dooley and Welch were more concerned with whether children were controlling the interactions. Whilst these two ideas could be closely related, there are no doubt subtle distinctions in meaning in the term 'autonomy' beyond the age of the target individuals here.

Self-monitoring
An additional way of studying how discourse can be used to understand learning in museums is through the use of 'self-reflective talk'. Ma (2012), in her study on the ways visitors to the Exploratorium in California show learning through discourse, assessed the types of talk that appeared in a number of different types of exhibits: single-user and multiple-user, new versus old, interactive and non-interactive, and challenging compared with non-challenging. Starting from a Deweyian (1938) perspective that learning occurs through experience and reflection on that experience (Experiential Learning) and Flavell's (1979) ideas about metacognition (the ability to think about thought objectively, paying attention to how one thinks in particular situations), she followed pairs of visitors through the 'Mind' exhibition housed together in a region of the science centre. Ma was able to examine the types of reflective conversation (self-connecting, connecting the visitor to the exhibit, and self-monitoring, which referred directly to visitors' thoughts and feelings) that visitors had and found patterns between types of conversation and exhibit type. Overall, there was more talk connected to self at new exhibits, which were designed to elicit self-reflection, compared with older ones. There were also higher amounts of self-monitoring talk at exhibits with greater amounts of challenge than at exhibits with less challenge. Multiple-user exhibits, perhaps not unsurprisingly, afforded more self-reflective talk (both connections and monitoring) than did solo exhibits. In contrast and perhaps more surprisingly, there were no differences between interactive and non-interactive exhibits with regard to the amount of self-reflective talk that occurred. This type of study can help museum practitioners see the potential for a variety of learning-related interaction to take place according to the type of exhibit. There may be a great deal of planning necessary to elicit the type of learning talk that practitioners desire. However, paying attention to the qualities, like interactivity versus multiple users might be useful ways of gauging the types of talk one could expect at a given exhibit. Alternatively, it may be that exhibition developers would like to encourage a variety of different types of talk by incorporating aspects of challenge and number of users strategically.

Exhibit type makes a difference to self-reflective talk

Labels and visitor conversations

One of the perpetual questions in museum research is what the optimal layout for and information in labels ought to be. Of course, there are numerous ways of understanding the effects that labels might have on visitors, individuals and groups. Holding time, i.e., how long a visitor will stop at an exhibit, is an important factor to consider (McManus, 1989). But in addition to holding time, McManus (1989) noticed that visitors had taken in information from the labels, even though they had not mentioned the content while standing at the exhibit: often the content from label text arose in conversations at a later point in the visit.

Nearly all labels include some text, which is, of course, a form of discourse itself. Ravelli (1996) considers a range of advice for how to write a label that is accessible to visitors. She draws on Halliday's systemic-functional linguistics (1994) to discuss the elements of label text that would be suitable for average visitors to the museum. Ravelli notes that attention to *field*, *tenor* and *mode* can afford differences in label accessibility. Here, field refers to the level of technical detail in a label: it may be that a label ought to contain information that goes beyond 'common sense' but is not overly technical so that non-specialists can follow it easily. Tenor relates to the way information is translated for a label. The audience is generally expected not to be expert in the relevant field and so use of a somewhat novice-like tenor might be more appropriate than an expert-like one. Finally, mode refers to the manner in which the audience is addressed. The texts that were altered in Ravelli's study experimented with a tone that was more spoken than written, whereby the language used seemed more 'natural'. The results of visitor surveys with texts that seemed more difficult in terms of field, tenor and mode compared with some that were simplified revealed that visitors found the simplified ones easier to follow, both in terms of their preferences and their correct answers to factual questions about the material. These advisory comments seem to improve upon Devenish's (1990) taxonomic descriptions for what might entail good label script without recourse to the discourse elements of such writing. Halliday's theory will undoubtedly be only one of many ways of considering methods of improving label text. However, it is notable that use of this theoretical lens helped to create an improved learning environment for visitors in at least some instances. In addition to these theoretically based accounts about the writing of labels, there are many works about labels that may or may not directly refer to learning, conversational or otherwise (e.g., Arndt, Screven, Benusa, & Bishop, 1993; Bitgood, 2000; Serrell, 2015).

Improved label understanding follows alterations in field, tenor and mode

Beyond the writing of a label that is accessible to visitors, many have attempted to find out whether there are optimal types of labels for facilitating learning as exhibited in conversation (e.g., Borun, Chambers, Dritsas & Johnson, 1997). Roberts (1997) cites work in various museums that attempt to engage visitors through creative labelling: facilitating positive and negative emotional reactions to paintings, encouraging playful or questioning interactions with art, or providing multiple interpretations to paintings on display. The study by Borun et al. (1997) investigates a multi-pronged approach to improving family experience in science museums. One of the elements included in this approach is to provide clear, accessible labels. They examined learning behaviours such as asking and answering questions, explaining exhibits and reading text aloud. In comparison with exhibits that had not been developed to engage visitors using their research-informed enhancement techniques, families used nearly twice the amount of learning behaviours, suggesting that the exhibit developments were highly effective for promoting learning. A note of caution is warranted here because providing accessible text was only one of several elements of the exhibits that were changed so it cannot be certain that the text changes were responsible for much, if any, of the differences between control and experimental groups. However, it is likely to have been helpful, particularly as the learning behaviours included measures that were easily derived from the text of the exhibits. These methods have in common the desire to incite interest on the part of the visitor by taking a different stance toward interaction with art or science through labels.

In a study that utilised differences in knowledge as measured through a before and after test, Falk (1997) noted that when labels contained explicit information about the scientific concepts on display, both adult and child visitors tended to stay longer and to gain more knowledge compared to when the label content was less explicit. These types of findings are consistent with both a constructivist (e.g., von Glaserfeld, 1995) and a social constructivist (e.g., Mercer & Littleton, 2007) conception of learning: visitors draw upon information presented in a label, which they can make sense of through their own agency. The explicitness of the label suggests that the content matters but that visitors are ultimately responsible for understanding the material. Of course, this study was based in a science museum context; learning in different types of museums might benefit from alternative types of labels: after all, what counts as explicit in a label for a painting?

Other studies have examined the ways that visitors respond to questions that are 'planted' in the museum. Hohenstein and Tran's (2007) social constructivist study investigated visitor

Explicit information leads to greater understanding of some scientific material

conversation at three historical science exhibits at the Science Museum in London. We videotaped conversations under three conditions: with the label text that the museum had been using, the same label with an added question ('Why is this here?') and a simplified label plus question condition. Conversation was coded for explanations and questions to see whether differences arose under the three conditions. Results indicated a complex interaction between the exhibit and the condition. The conversation at one exhibit, a bowl that survived the Hiroshima bombing in World War II, did not vary at all according to condition. At another exhibit, a Mini car that had been sawed in half to reveal its compact engine and allowed visitors to sit in the seats, showed great increases in reflective questioning on the part of the visitors in both conditions involving the new question in comparison to the old label. And the final exhibit, a working model of a Victorian workshop, had a greater amount of explanations and open-ended questions in the presence of the added question in comparison to the other conditions. This analysis indicates that the relationship between content of the exhibit and labelling to promote conversation is not straightforward. Visitors reacted differently to the three different conditions at the three different exhibits.

Using a similar theoretical perspective, Gutwill and Allen (2010) also examined how visitors engaged with scientific material at a hands-on science centre (Exploratorium in San Francisco) under a variety of labelling conditions. They found that playing a game to facilitate family-generated 'juicy questions' promoted a greater amount of holding time and inquiry amongst families compared with a different game, a tour about the making of the exhibit or a control with no mediation. In the juicy question and 'hands off' game conditions, families were provided with cards to help them to follow the rules. Whilst these are not labels as such, engagement with visitors through text was important in providing the context for the game. Finally, whereas the outcomes with regard to inquiry were positive in this study, with juicy questions leading to greater amounts of collaborative inquiry, interviews with the families afterwards suggested that the families may have felt the games were somewhat artificial and 'school-like', leading to the sense that the intervention's positive outcomes came at some cost to the enjoyability of the exhibit.

Exhibit complexity interacts with learning conversations resulting from adding a question

Museum space and visitor narrative

A really interesting body of work has investigated the types of affordances available at museums (and elsewhere), which might relate to the ways that people interact in learning situations. Many of these studies utilise conversation analysis (Heritage,

2004) to examine the ways people interact in minute detail. Such analyses, admittedly, do not always focus on verbal conversation or discourse, which begs the question of what exactly 'counts' in terms of discourse. If one is thinking of the general themes of communication, non-verbal elements of interaction surely are relevant to understanding the ways people act in museums and other public places. Dirk vom Lehn and Christian Heath have painstakingly analysed interactions at a variety of exhibits to understand the precise ways that small variations in space may affect people's explanations in conversation, as mediated by such things as family members' or friends' posture (vom Lehn & Heath, 2007; vom Lehn 2006; Meisner et al., 2007). One such study has drawn attention to the ways that an exhibit that visitors often pass without taking notice when unoccupied becomes a point of interest when visitors, in this case children, are busy engaging with the topic of electricity and 'lightning' (Meisner et al., 2007). The authors note that whilst the 'open' design of the exhibit may cause it to be relatively unappealing on its own, once people have engaged with the activity through visible and audible participation, others stop to pay attention to the exhibit. Similarly, Meisner and colleagues note that when the design of the space inspires visitor 'performance', they often sustain their attention for a relatively long period of time. Often these performances are exhibitions of 'having fun' and lightheartedness.

'Open' exhibit design is linked with greater engagement once one person has already begun to use the space

Whereas some positive indications of engagement can be inferred from visitor interaction at museum exhibits, it has also been demonstrated that not all interactive design confers a sense of confidence or willingness to act. Scott and colleagues note that, in particular, shy visitors sometimes have trouble actively engaging with interactive exhibits (Scott, Hinton-Smith, Harma, & Broome, 2013). In their study, shy visitors, feeling self-conscious, would sometimes rather watch others interact with an exhibit than 'perform' the actions themselves. The script for action that can sometimes be seen in studies like that of Meisner et al. (2007) may or may not provide a sense of confidence for all visitors alike. In fact, some visitors felt they were less inhibited by being able to perform activities behind a screen, where others would not be able to see their actions (Scott et al., 2013). This is in direct contrast to the findings in which visitors were drawn to the exhibit because of people's public performance.

Not all visitors react to space in the same way

Programmes and the facilitation of visitor dialogue

Given the high regard for collaborative learning as an element of promotion of engagement through enrichment to the sociocultural environments learners have access to, several studies have experimented with tools that might enhance visitors' learning conversations. For example, Tenenbaum, Prior, Dowling and

Frost (2010) worked with a large history museum to examine whether provision of activities to families through either a backpack filled with materials or a booklet would facilitate various aspects of conversations known to benefit learning, such as explanation and questions. Their findings indicate that compared with a control condition in which there was no booklet or backpack provided to the families, parents in the two intervention conditions asked more questions and children in the booklet condition used more historical talk than did children in either the backpack or the control condition. In addition, families tended to stay longer at exhibits in the booklet and backpack conditions relative to the control condition. As such, extra programming, particularly for groups that might be anticipated to struggle with the material or signage in a section of a museum (e.g., families in a history museum), could serve to benefit the learning experiences of groups by targeting activities to make them collaborative and/or age-appropriate. However, one must remember that this is unlikely to serve an entire large museum very well as visitors may habituate to activities like this and it may be costly to run. Smaller museums might benefit more; or more targeted interventions for larger ones might work well, in contrast.

Targeted interventions can increase questions and explanations in family conversations

In another project investigating ways of enhancing visitor learning as exhibited through conversation, use of electronic guidebooks as resources for learning was investigated at a historic house (Symanski et al., 2008). In this study the authors were interested in the ways that different formats for an electronic guidebook might facilitate social learning as demonstrated through a Vygotskian situated learning framework. Their design-based study utilising conversation analysis found that when visitors engaged with an electronic guidebook that allowed them to 'eavesdrop' on their visiting partners' experiences, they were able to both explore independently and be influenced by what the other people were listening to. This eavesdropping mechanism reduced talk that was procedural in nature (e.g., about what should be listened to) in comparison to a version of the device that enabled two people to listen to the same information at the same time. In contrast, the conversational elements that related to a deeper understanding of the material of the exhibition, in this case the origins and history of the house were more prevalent in the eavesdropping condition in comparison with the open-air/simultaneous version.

Listening in on other people's guided experiences can facilitate deeper conversations in visitors

Another aspect of programming, of course, involves the facilitation of large groups of school pupils who visit. Tran (2007) investigated the ways that museum educators were able to teach science content during these short school trips. In whole group interactions, the educators in that study tended to seek opportunities to engage with the pupils creatively, facilitating their agency in the museum setting. At the same time, museum educators

Educator-centred discourse may be prevalent in museum school group interactions

often resorted to dialogic patterns reminiscent of classrooms in which there was an Initiate, Response and Evaluation pattern (IRE; Mehan, 1979). Tran noticed it was difficult for educators to move away from this teacher-centred way of talking, in part because of a perceived need to maintain control over the interactions, which seems easier in an IRE type of discourse. It is unclear that interacting in less educator-centred types of ways is possible in these fleeting meetings in which schools expect pupils to learn during what is inevitably a limited period with educators who are unfamiliar with the children.

Summary

These findings, in addition to those of McCallie reported above about dialogue events and the nature of visitor interactions, provide a window on the ways that visitors develop communications that help indicate their learning and form a vehicle to increase learning. The free-choice nature and relatively relaxed atmosphere in a museum may help younger visitors engage in learning conversations through more autonomous means. At the same time, the design of exhibits and spaces can lend itself to particular sorts of interactions, especially for some individuals. When interspersed with different types of exhibit in a planned way, exhibit design can potentially cater to a variety of different personality types and group dynamics (e.g., solo versus large group). Such claims are bolstered by reports highlighting ways that museums and other informal learning institutions can set up programmes that target multiple audiences with wide-ranging educational goals and activities. One such report focuses on Public Engagements with Science (PES) as a goal that could help museums to serve important roles in larger conversations between members of the public and other sectors (McCallie et al., 2009). Because dialogue is so well-studied in multiple contexts, there is really a high volume of studies one could refer to in the area of learning and conversation. A broad consensus tends to suggest that learning in collaboration is powerful when compared with learning on an individual basis. However, this is also likely to vary quite a lot depending upon the nature of the material, the individuals involved and the objectives of the museum.

We have covered a great deal of theoretical and empirical information in this chapter. Matters of communication are clearly important from the perspective of the museum, but also from the point of view of the visitor. Visitors engage in narrative-driven discourse amongst themselves, but also in conjunction with staff and materials in the museum. It will be impossible to always predict every narrative that each visitor will bring with them on any given day. However, because of the scripts people tend to work with, which are culturally influenced, it may be possible to consider how different types of visitors will engage with exhibitions and activities given their cultural backgrounds and educational experiences. Getting to know the communities who live in the local area may help to form new ways of connecting with non-traditional visitors, as in the study by Everett and Barrett (2009). Some reports have highlighted the need to reach out to new audiences for conducting research, but also to be creative with the ways that studies are conceptualised with respect to who designs the study and takes part, suggesting that 'citizen science' in which ordinary people get involved with the planning and execution of research might lead to greater ownership and interest in the processes (e.g., Bonney et al., 2009). There may be opportunities for this sort of innovation to also have impacts upon the ways both museums and visitors are seen in terms of their narratives and the engagement they are willing to invest in visits to museums.

At the same time, providing visitors with communications in the form of labels, or even digital information, that is clear and concise has been shown to be linked to greater amounts of learning conversations (Borun et al., 1997; Falk, 1997); whereas helping visitors to reflect on the objects or activities through questions that are appropriately aimed at the exhibit or idea can increase holding time as well as elements of conversation related to learning amongst visitors (Hohenstein & Tran, 2007; Gutwill & Allen, 2010). Attending to the ways that floor staff interact with visitors through language can also be important as Tran (2007) showed, with docents using language that echoes the type sometimes vilified in classrooms. Likewise, when there are opportunities to go beyond what might be seen as 'traditional' learning situations, it is helpful to question whether interactive 'dialogue' is helping to increase learning, or at least demonstrate it, as shown by McCallie (2009), or just reifying the museum's image or message as indicated by Mauratonio (2015). Altogether, there is a great deal to take into consideration when it comes to learning conversations. And it is understandable if museum educators find it difficult to work towards facilitation of all elements of learning all the time. But we hope that it is useful to be able to reflect on ways that learning conversation has been shown to be affected by different situational elements across museums.

A return to Room 41

Two young adults (university students of linguistics, Ellie and Tania), not regular visitors to museums of any kind, went to the British Museum to see the Rosetta Stone as part of a project on their course. They decided to see what else was in the museum as they were already there and had a couple of hours to spare. Plus, the heavy rain did not make leaving the museum particularly appealing. They wandered around the space and eventually ended up strolling into Room 41.

The layout of the gallery draws the students' attention to the centrepiece: the helmet and the description of the burial site. This is clearly impressive and they spend some time poring over the details of how the burial site was discovered and the details about the helmet. Ellie and Tania address a number of questions to each other about the ways the people lived, what sorts of occupations they might have had, and the languages they spoke. The labels provided some answers to their questions but they kept looking to see whether other displays in the gallery told them more.

Tania then wanders off to a nearby exhibit in the gallery and notices the way that the people of the time (early Anglo-Saxon England) must have been travelling a good deal. Further movement to different parts of the gallery reveals connections between the merchant travellers of the time and the similarity between the spoons and coins that are represented in the various exhibits around the gallery. Ellie is still looking at the video display in the central part of the gallery, the ship burial. Tania, now in the outer parts of the gallery, calls to Ellie, who joins her. They can then be heard to tell each other what must have happened as expressed in the labels and signage. The relative ease of interpretation is facilitated by the open space, the concrete connections through labelled information, and the similarity between objects that is highlighted both textually and geographically.

The narrative woven by the placement of the objects and the text in the signs and labels helps the pair to make sense of the connections between these geographical regions, which is consistent with theories like narrative (e.g., Bruner, 1991) and constructivism/social constructivism. That is, they have engaged with the exhibits through the powerful storytelling in the space. They rely on the storytelling of others to help them to formulate a conceptualisation of the way inhabitants of this region must have lived hundreds of years ago (narrative theory). Their own experiential learning in the space, through seeing authentic as well as reconstructed objects, watching the video and conversing with each other can then feed into the narrative they construct for themselves (social constructivism and narrative theory). Moreover, the spatial layout of the helmet and the burial construction in the centre of the gallery, with displays spaced in a radiating way containing items from various related places and peoples, helps Tania and Ellie to grasp onto the narrative that the institution has crafted about trade and cultural under-standings between peoples of widely varying backgrounds. Other visitors may be able to see their reactions to the displays and notice elements of these relationships as well, as evidenced in vom Lehn (2006).

The pair have come to the museum for reasons that have lit-tle to do with the museum itself. Their entrance narratives are likely to contain ideas about museums as 'not for them' or 'full of boring old stuff'. They were required to visit for an assess-ment; they stayed for a variety of reasons, including the way that museum was able to counter some of their apprehensions and expectations. This one visit may not transform either of them into a regular museum visitor. But it seems that each of them was surprised at their enjoyment of the space and the sensation that they gained valuable understandings of what life might have been like for the people who inhabited the area hundreds of years ago. Such narratives can feel particularly powerful to visitors, who may then go on to retell the tales on interactions on social media or in face-to-face encounters.

Contextualising discourse, narrative and communication

What cultural narratives or scripts do people tend to have about the topic of an exhibition you are developing? How can these be utilised to facilitate understanding? What types of objects do people tend to associate with those narratives? How can objects be presented collectively in the exhibition space to challenge or enhance entrance narratives? Can text be used to further manage visitor views about these objects? Thinking about these objects, how can visitor experience be enhanced by the placement and presentation of text and other visual or pictorial interpretation about the displays treating visitors as either members of a community of practice or as agentive learners whose conceptualisations can be facilitated through the application of socio-cognitive principles about elaboration and learning?

What would be appropriate language to use in developing scripts for learning activities in a programme developed in your institution? How can visitors' zones of proximal devel-opment be assessed when visits are generally so fleeting? What differences in explanation will be necessary for visitors of dif-ferent age groups? Why might certain storytelling practices on the museum floor be more (or less) useful for helping learners develop their own narratives about the topic?

How can the conversation between people in various group formations be used to facilitate further engagement amongst visitors? How might the spatial arrangements in your galleries or exhibitions create or hinder interaction between visitors? In what way can text influence visitors' engagement with the material being presented (in labels, through digital devices, printed material, etc.)?

Notes

1 This scenario was written and contributed by Dr. Sue Brunning of the British Museum. She is curator of Insular Early Medieval Collections and Sutton Hoo. Very little editing was carried out on this writing.
2 Scripts can be compared with figured worlds (Holland, Lachicotte, Skinner, & Cain, 1998 – see Chapter 8). Whereas figured worlds are developed as constructs of identity and self, leading to a sense of 'how people are' when they hold certain social positions, scripts are a set of slots that can fill in the elements of an event. As such, scripts are likely to be more concrete, albeit still relatively subconscious, as compared with figured worlds.
3 Entrance narratives are also covered as a way of understanding motivation in museum visits in Chapter 9.

References

Allen, S. (2002). Looking for learning in visitor talk: A methodological exploration. In G. Leinhardt, K. Crowley, & K. Knutson (Eds.), *Learning conversations in museums* (pp. 259–303). Mahwah, NJ: Lawrence Erlbaum.

Allen, S. (2003). To partition or not to partition: The impact of walls on visitor behavior at an exhibit cluster. Paper presented at the annual meeting of the Association of Science-Technology Centers, Minneapolis.

Allen, S. (2004). Designs for learning: Studying science museum exhibits that do more than entertain. *Science Education, 88,* S17-S33.

Arndt, M., Screven, C., Benusa, D., & Bishop, T. (1993). Behavior and learning in a zoo environment under different signage conditions. *Visitor studies: Theory, research, and practice, Vol. 5* (pp. 245–251). Jacksonville, AL: Visitor Studies Association.

Ash, D. (2003). Dialogic inquiry in life science conversations of family groups in a museum. *Journal of Research in Science Teaching, 40,* 138–162.

Ash, D. (2004). Reflective scientific sense-making dialogue in two languages: The science in the dialogue and the dialogue in the science. *Science Education, 88,* 855–884.

Ash, D., Crain, R., Brandt, C., Loomis, M., Wheaton, M., & Bennett, C. (2007). Talk, tools, and tensions: Observing biological talk over time. *International Journal of Science Education, 29,* 1581–1602.

Bakhtin, M. (1981). *The dialogic imagination: Four essays* (Ed. M. Holquist). Austin, TX: University of Texas Press.

Benjamin, N., Haden, C., & Wilkerson, E. (2010). Enhancing building, conversation, and learning through caregiver–child interactions in a children's museum. *Developmental Psychology*, 46, 502–515.

Bitgood, S. (2000). The role of attention in designing effective interpretive labels. *Journal of Interpretation Research*, 5, 31–45.

Bonnell, J. & Simon, R. (2007). 'Difficult' exhibitions and intimate encounters. *Museum and Society*, 5, 65–85.

Bonney, R., Ballard, H., Jordan, R., McCallie, E., Phillips, T., Shirk, J., & Wilderman, C.C. (2009). Public Participation in Scientific Research: Defining the Field and Assessing Its Potential for Informal Science Education. A CAISE Inquiry Group Report. Washington, DC: Center for Advancement of Informal Science Education (CAISE).

Borun, M., Chambers, M., Dritsas, J., & Johnson, J. (1997). Enhancing family learning through exhibits. *Curator*, 40, 279–295.

Brown, P. & Levinson, S. (1987). *Politeness: Some universals in language use*. Cambridge: Cambridge University Press.

Browning, E. & Hohenstein, J. (2015). The use of narrative to promote primary school children's understanding of evolution. *Education 3–13*, 43, 530–547.

Bruner, J. (1990). *Acts of meaning*. Cambridge, MA: Harvard University Press.

Bruner, J. (1991). The narrative construction of reality. *Critical Inquiry*, 18, 1–21.

Burdelski, M., Kawashima, K., & Yamazaki, K. (2014). Storytelling in guided tours: Practices, engagement, and identity at a Japanese American museum. *Narrative Inquiry*, 24, 328–346.

Callanan, M., Frazier, B., & Gorchoff, S. (2015). Closing the gender gap: Family conversations about science in an 'Alice's Wonderland' exhibit. Unpublished manuscript.

Callanan, M., Martin, J., & Luce, M. (2015). Two decades of families learning in a children's museum: A partnership of research and exhibit development. In D. Sobel & J. Jipson (Eds.), *Cognitive development in museum settings: Relating research and practice* (pp. 15–35). London: Routledge.

Callanan, M. & Oakes, L. (1992). Preschoolers' questions and parents' explanations: Causal thinking in everyday activity. *Cognitive Development*, 7, 213–233.

Chi, M., De Leewu, N, Chiu, M., & Lavancher, C. (1994) Eliciting self-explanations improves understanding. *Cognitive Science*, 18, 439–477.

Chronis, A. (2012). Tourists as story-builders: Narrative construction at a heritage museum. *Journal of Travel & Tourism Marketing*, 29, 444–459.

Crowley, K., Callanan, M., Jipson, J., Galco, J., Topping, K., & Shrager, J. (2001). Shared scientific thinking in everyday parent-child activity. *Science Education*, 85, 712–732.

Crowley, K., Callanan, M., Tenenbaum, H., & Allen, E. (2001). Parents explain more often to boys than to girls during shared scientific thinking. *Psychological Science*, 12, 258–261.

Crowley, K. & Jacobs, M. (2002). Building islands of expertise in everyday family activity. In G. Leinhardt & K. Crowley (Eds.), *Learning conversations in museums* (pp. 333–356). Mahwah, NJ: Lawrence Erlbaum Associates.

Dawson, E. (2014). 'Not designed for us': How science museums and science centers socially exclude low-income, minority ethnic groups. *Science Education*, 98, 981–1008.

Devenish, D. (1990). Labelling in museum display: A survey and practical guide. *Museum Management and Curatorship*, 9, 63–72.

Dewey, J. (1938). *Experience and education.* West Lafayette, IN: Kappa Delta Pi.

DeWitt, J. & Hohenstein, J. (2010a). A tale of two contexts: Teacher–student talk on a school trip and in the classroom. School trips and classroom lessons: An investigation into teacher–student talk in two settings. *Journal of Research in Science Teaching*, 47, 454–473.

DeWitt, J. & Hohenstein, J. (2010b). Supporting student learning: A comparison of student discussion in museums and classrooms. *Visitor Studies*, 13, 41–66.

Doering, Z. & Pekarik, A. (1996). Questioning the entrance narrative. *Journal of Museum Education*, 21, 20–23.

Dooley, C. & Welch, M. (2014). Nature of interactions among young children and adult caregivers in a children's museum. *Early Childhood Education Journal*, 42, 125–132. doi:10.1007/s10643-013-0601-x

Dyehouse, J. (2011). 'A Textbook Case Revisited': Visual rhetoric and series patterning in the American Museum of Natural History's horse evolution displays. *Technical Communication Quarterly*, 3, 327–346.

Everett, M. & Barrett, M. (2009). Investigating sustained visitor/ museum relationships: employing narrative research in the field of museum visitor studies. *Visitor Studies*, 12, 2–15.

Falk, J. (1997). Testing a museum exhibition design assumption: Effect of explicit labeling of exhibit clusters on visitor concept development. *Science Education*, 81, 679–687.

Falk, J. & Dierking, L. (2000). *Learning from museums: Visitor experiences and the making of meaning.* Plymouth: Altamira Press.

Flavell, J. (1979). Metacognition and cognitive monitoring: A new area of cognitive-developmental inquiry. *American Psychologist*, 34, 906–911.

Frykman, S. (2009). Stories to tell? Narrative tools in museum education texts. *Educational Research*, 51, 299–319.

Goulding, C. (2000). The museum environment and the visitor experience. *European Journal of Marketing*, 34, 261–278.

Gutwill, J. & Allen, S. (2010). Facilitating family group inquiry at science museum exhibits. *Science Education*, 94, 710–742.

Haden, C. (2010). Talking about science in museums. *Child Development Perspectives*, 4, 62–67.

Halliday, M.A.K. (1994). *Introduction to functional grammar.* London: Edward Arnold.

Hayes, D. & Slater, A. (2002). 'Rethinking the missionary position': The quest for sustainable audience development policies. *Managing Leisure*, 7, 1–17.

Heath, S.B. (1983). *Ways with words: Language, life, and work in communities and classrooms.* Cambridge: Cambridge University Press.

Heidegger, M. (1949). *Existence and being.* Chicago, IL: H. Regnery.

Heritage, J. (2004). Conversation analysis and institutional talk. In D. Silverman (Ed.), *Qualitative research: Theory, method and practice.* London: Sage Publications.

Hohenstein, J. & Tran, L. (2007). Use of questions in exhibit labels to generate explanatory conversation among science museum visitors. *International Journal of Science Education*, 29, 1557–1580.

Holland, D. Lachicotte, W., Jr., Skinner, D., & Cain, C. (1998). *Identity and agency in cultural worlds.* Cambridge, MA: Harvard University Press.

Lave, J. & Wenger, E. (1991). *Situated learning: Legitimate peripheral practice.* Cambridge: Cambridge University Press.

Leinhardt, G. & Knutson, K. (2004). *Listening in on museum conversations.* Walnut Creek, CA: Altamira Press.

Luce, M., Callanan, M., & Smilovic, S. (2013). Links between parents' epistemological stance and children's evidence talk. *Developmental Psychology*, 49, 454–461.

Lwin, S.M. (2012). Whose stuff is it? A museum storyteller's strategies to engage her audience. *Narrative Inquiry*, 22, 226–246.

Ma, J. (2012). Listening for self-reflective talk in visitors' conversations: A case study of the Exploratorium's Mind Collection. *Visitor Studies*, 15, 136–156.

Mai, T. & Ash, D. (2012). Tracing our methodological steps: Making meaning of diverse families' hybrid 'figuring out' practices at science museum exhibits. In D. Ash, J. Rahm, & L. Melber (Eds.), *Putting theory into practices: Tools for research in informal settings.* (pp. 97–118). Rotterdam: Sense Publishers.

Macdonald, S. (2009). Reassembling Nuremburg, reassembling heritage. *Journal of Cultural Economy*, 2, 117–134.

Macdonald, S. & Fyfe, G. (1996). *Theorizing museums: Representing identity and diversity in a changing world.* Oxford: Blackwell.

Mauratonio, M. (2015). Material rhetoric, public memory, and the post-it note. *Southern Communication Journal*, 80, 83–101.

McCallie, E. (2009). Argumentation among publics and scientists: A study of dialogue events on socio-scientific issues. Unpublished doctoral thesis. King's College London.

McCallie, E., Bell, L., Lohwater, T., Falk, J.H., Lehr, J.L., Lewenstein, B.V., Needham, C., & Wiehe, B. (2009). Many Experts, Many Audiences: Public Engagement with Science and Informal Science Education. A CAISE Inquiry Group Report. Washington, DC: Center for Advancement of Informal Science Education (CAISE). http://caise.insci.org/uploads/docs/public_engagement_with_science.pdf

McPherson, G. (2006). Public memories and private tastes: The shifting definitions of museums and their visitors in the UK. *Museum Management and Curatorship*, 21, 44–57.

McManus, P. (1987). It's the company you keep: The social determination of learning-related behaviour in a science museum. *International Journal of Museum Management and Curatorship*, 6, 263–270.

McManus, P. (1988). Good companions: More of the social determination of learning-related behaviour in a science museum. *International Journal of Museum Management and Curatorship*, 7, 37–44.

McManus, P. (1989). Oh, yes, they do: How museum visitors read labels and interact with exhibit texts. *Curator*, 32, 174–189.

Mehan, H. (1979). *Learning lessons: Social organizations in the class-room*. Cambridge, MA: Harvard University Press.

Meisner, R., vom Lehn, D., Heath, C., Burch, A., Gammon, B., & Reisman, M. (2007). Exhibiting performance: Co-participation in science centres and museums. *International Journal of Science Education*, 29, 1531–1555.

Mercer, N. (2000). *Words and minds: How we use language to think together*. London: Routledge.

Mercer, N. & Littleton, K. (2007). *Dialogue and the development of children's thinking: A sociocultural approach*. London: Routledge.

Modlin, E., Alderman, D., & Gentry, G. (2011). Tour guides as creators of empathy: The role of affective inequality in marginalizing the enslaved at plantation house museums. *Tourist Studies*, 11, 3–19.

Nelson, K. (1996). *Language in cognitive development: Emergence of the mediated mind*. Cambridge: Cambridge University Press.

Noy, C. (2015). Writing in museums: Toward a rhetoric of participation. *Written Communication*, 32, 195–219.

Ochs, E. (1993). Constructing social identity: A language socialization perspective. *Research on Language and Social Interaction*, 26, 287–306.

Ochs, E. & Capp, L. (1996). Narrating the self. *Annual Review of Anthropology*, 25, 19–43.

Palmquist, S. & Crowley, K. (2007). From teachers to testers: How parents talk to novice and expert children in a natural history museum. *Science Education*, 91, 783–804.

Piaget, J. (1952). *The origins of intelligence in the child*. New York: International University Press.

Ravelli, L. (1996). Making language accessible: Successful text writing for museum visitors. *Linguistics & Education*, 8, 367–387.

Roberts, L.C. (1997). *From knowledge to narrative: Educators and the changing museum*. Washington, DC: Smithsonian Institution Press.

Rose, J. (2016). *Interpreting difficult history at museums and historic sites*. Lanham, MD: Rowman & Littlefield.

Schank, R.C. & Abelson, R.P. (1977). *Scripts, plans, and understanding*. Hillsdale, NJ: Lawrence Erlbaum Associates.

Scott, D. (2007). Constructing sacred history: Multi-media narratives and the discourse of 'museumness' at Mormon Temple Square. *Journal of Media and Religion*, 6, 201–218.

Scott, D. (2014). Dinosaurs on Noah's Ark? Multi-media narratives and natural science museum discourse at the Creation Museum in Kentucky. *Journal of Media and Religion*, 13, 226–243.

Scott, S., Hinton-Smith, T., Harma, V., & Broome, K. (2013). Goffman in the gallery: Interactive art and visitor shyness. *Symbolic Interaction*, 36, 417–438.

Serrell, B. (2015). *Exhibit labels: An interpretive approach* (2nd edition). London: Rowman & Littlefield.

Symanski, M., Aoki, P., Grinter, R., Hurst, A., Thornton, J., & Woodruff, A. (2008). Sotto voce: Facilitating social learning in a historic house. *Computer Supported Cooperative Work*, 17, 5–34.

Tenenbaum, H., Prior, J., Dowling, C., & Frost, R. (2010). Supporting parent–child conversations in a history museum. *British Journal of Educational Psychology*, 80, 241–254.

Toulmin, S. (1958). *The uses of argument*. Cambridge: Cambridge University Press.

Tran, L.U. (2007). Teaching Science in Museums: The Pedagogy and Goals of Museum Educators. *Science Education*, 91, 278–297.

vom Lehn, D. (2006). Embodying experience: A video-based examination of visitors' conduct and interaction in museums. *European Journal of Marketing*, 40, 1340–1359.

vom Lehn, D. & Heath, C. (2007). Social interaction in museums and galleries: A note on video-based field studies. In R. Goldman, R. Pea, B. Barron & S. Derry (Eds.), *Video and the Learning Sciences*. Mahwah, NJ: Lawrence Erlbaum Associates.

von Glaserfeld, E. (1995). *Radical constructivism: A way of knowing and learning*. London: Routledge.

Vygotsky, L. (1978). *Mind in society: The development of higher psychological processes*. Cambridge, MA: Harvard University Press.

Wells, G. (1999). *Dialogic inquiry: Toward a sociocultural practice and theory of education*. Cambridge: Cambridge University Press.

Wells, M., Butler, B., & Koke, J. (2016). *Interpretive planning for museums: Integrating visitor perspectives in decision making*. London: Routledge.

White, H. (1981). The value of narrativity in the representation of reality. In W. Mitchell (Ed.), *On narrative* (pp. 1–23). Chicago, IL: The University of Chicago Press.

Zhai, J. & Dillon, J. (2014). Communicating science to students: Investigating professional botanic garden educators' talk during guided school visits. *Journal of Research in Science Teaching*, 51, 407–429.

Zimmerman, H., Reeve, S., & Bell, P. (2009). Family sense-making practices in science center conversations. *Science Education*, 94, 478–505.

6 Degrees of authenticity in museums

Authentic nature play at the Chicago Botanic Garden[1]

The Chicago Botanic Garden (CBG) is a 385-acre public garden with twenty-six display gardens and four natural areas. For years, the institution took the approach that the entire Garden offered all audiences, including families with children, a wonderful experience. This direction was reconsidered as more public gardens created special areas for children and found these gardens enable a broader range of education opportunities for young learners.

As a museum, a public garden is a collection of plants, but it is also a collection of spaces characterised by the selection and arrangement of those plants. The CBG staff recognise a range of reasons audiences visit the space. People come to enjoy the floral display, to exercise, to get ideas for planting their own gardens, for respite and relaxation, and to restore their spirituality and connection with nature. These aspects of the CBG identity are appealing to most adults, but do not fully address a child's interests and needs.

For these reasons, CBG leaders decided to convert an overflow parking lot into a Learning Campus to serve the needs of school groups, summer camps, youth and family programmes, and visitors with children. CBG staff began the planning process with many existing children's gardens serving as examples for quality control purposes.

CBG leaders decided that the Learning Campus would be a combination of several distinct features to promote learning about horticulture, plant science, ecology and conservation while providing a rich experience with nature. It would include a growing garden where children could dig, water and participate in gardening activities; a nature play space for free discovery of the natural world; a lakeside cove garden for water investigations, a live butterfly exhibition and a building with classrooms for indoor programmes.

Figure 6.1 A young girl playing with water in the Nature Play Garden area of the Learning Campus. © Chicago Botanic Garden.

The nature play space proved most challenging to design for a number of reasons. CBG staff wanted children to play, but did not want a 'playground'. They needed plants that would delight children, but also wanted to incorporate new additions to the collection, recognising that those priorities can be in conflict. They wanted to use as many native plants as possible to be authentic, but native plants are not always visually appealing and up to the display standards of CBG. They needed to create paths through the space that would be accessible to all and stroller-friendly, but wanted the space to feel natural, not constructed. Finally, they wanted children to interact with the space without destroying the plants.

As discussions proceeded, the final design emerged from these premises and it would embody the following elements: (1) the garden would be distinguished as being different from a playground in all the promotional and marketing messages and signage to manage expectations; (2) absolute minimal use of hard paved surfaces would be incorporated, using gravel and woodchips as paving materials instead; (3) rather than installing any kind of playground equipment, natural features in the landscape would be incorporated to provide the setting for play.

Drop-in programmes with interpreters would be held that teach children how to enjoy nature without destroying it; (4) a careful examination of the plant materials and their arrangement was made and, in case of a conflict, the focus would be on the child's experience in order to make the final decision, and (5) programming in the garden would promote the value of nature play, so that visitors could benefit from their experiences beyond the Garden borders.

Introduction

Authenticity has been associated with Jean-Jacques Rousseau (1712–1778) who was the first who wrote about himself as somebody who lived an authentic life in his autobiographical work *Confessions* (Lindholm, 2008). Rousseau believed that the rules of civilisation repress the expression of the authentic self. In the museum context, the concept of authenticity underlies the very notion of Western European museums and their value to society. As such, authenticity is a key topic of discussion in museums as well as in the different disciplines associated with different museum collections, such as history, archaeology or art. Yet, the way different museums and disciplines understand and conceptualise authenticity can vary widely because different types of museums and disciplines have developed their own working methods and institutional practices which has led to creating their own criteria or requirements for authenticity.

Traditionally, authenticity in museums has been seen as an attribution of an object or sets of objects and is associated with a sense of timelessness. This is not surprising, since the concept first appeared when modern museums were created in the Western world, many of which came as a reaction to mass produced replica objects during the industrial revolution as well as to dramatic changes in the natural environment and their impact on biodiversity (Roberts, 1997). Interestingly, the recent deindustrialisation in Western Europe and North America has led to a similar call to save remnants of industrial heritage (Leary & Sholes, 2000). Lindholm (2008) points out that, in the case of art works in particular, there is a parallel between the authentication process followed by curators and the official validation process of religious relics established in medieval Europe. We will return to this link between authenticity and its link to religion when we talk about numinous experience with museum objects, in Transcending reality and numinous objects below.

The disciplines of philosophy, history, art history and natural science seem to have each made a distinct contribution to the conceptualisation of authenticity. The vast majority of, at least, the early literature produced by these disciplines tends to be conceptual/theoretical in nature rather than empirically based. In contrast, anthropology and psychology have contributed to the discussion through primary research into people's understanding of the concept of authenticity. Some empirical research has also been carried out in other fields such as public history, museum and visitor studies, positive psychology, developmental psychology, management, tourism and leisure studies (Pine & Gilmore, 2007; Lowenthal, 1995 & 1992; Lipscomb, 2010). It is worth pointing out that, more recently, a Euro-centric object-focused notion of authenticity and its impact on the museum has been challenged by work carried out with different types of (tangible and intangible) heritage in other parts of the world (Byrne, 1995; Li, 2010; Alivizatou, 2012; Barber, 2013), but also by the proliferation of digital objects and user-generated digital content across different types of museums (Taylor, 2010; Bearman & Trant, 1998). As far as digital content – whether generated by the museum or users – is concerned, one of the arguments has been that it can redefine visitors' perceptions of authenticity (e.g., Russo, 2011 & 2012; Adair, Filene & Koloski, 2011). Yet, very little substantive evidence is provided that this is the case (see review of King, Stark & Cooke's (2016) work in 'Authenticity in the digital culture' below). At a theoretical level, critical theory has challenged notions of authenticity and museums as places perceived to present authentic accounts of the past (see Lowenthal, 1985 & 1998; Smith, 2006; Byrne, 1991; Hooper-Greenhill, 2000).

In addition to the different disciplinary approaches, the different meanings of authenticity seem to also be related to the historical, cultural, and institutional contexts within which it has been identified and studied. Museums are not among the physical contexts most commonly used for carrying out primary research into perceptions and attributions of authenticity. In a world where the quest for authenticity and authentic experiences touches on a wide range of human activities and experience (Lindholm, 2008; Carroll, 2014), it is remarkable the extent to which it has been taken for granted as far as museum visitors are concerned. Indeed, an interest in the perception of authenticity and authentic experiences can be seen across a number of disciplines and domains of social life, from products and services to tourism and other leisure activities, and even personal and national identity (Lindholm, 2008). By contrast, very little empirical research has examined museum visitor perceptions of and experience with authentic objects or experiences. Some really interesting work has been carried out with visitors to heritage sites, as discussed in Transcending reality and numinous objects and Authentic learning environments below. Whether implicitly present or explicitly discussed, authenticity is a very powerful concept which resonates with museum professionals and visitors alike. It can be argued that, however indirectly it might be, it has shaped the way research with visitors has been conceived and carried out, and how the collected evidence has been interpreted and applied.

Within the context of museum learning, where the focus of this book lies, the studies that have focused on visitors' encounters with objects have not explicitly examined what renders objects authentic and the impact they might have on the visitor experience. This does not diminish that fact that a large amount of research has examined the role of objects (both natural and manmade) in facilitating learning and meaning making in museums since the 1980s, in particular. Researchers have used different theoretical frameworks and different museum settings to examine how visitors encounter objects and other types of exhibits as part of their visit (Crowley & Callanan, 1997; Blud, 1990; Dierking, 1987; McManus, 1987; Falk, 1991; Hilke, 1989; Diamond, 1986; Borun et al., 1997; Ellenbogen, 2002). Furthermore, the vast majority of studies tend to be carried out in science-rich environments where two types of artefacts are typically exhibited: (1) original objects (or digitised representations of these original objects) that have served science-related purposes, and (2) low-tech interactive or digital exhibits and models where the focus is on presenting and explaining phenomena. There are only a few studies looking at tangible (or intangible) material culture and even fewer examining visitors' understanding of and relation to 'authentic' or 'real' objects in the museum environment.

Yet, authenticity is an issue that underlies many conversations, and resulting tensions, among museum professionals. As Roberts noted (1997, p. 85), two issues are of particular interest here: 'the importance of the "real" and what it means to experience it', on the one hand, and 'the value of participatory experiences' in museum settings, on the other. Both aspects of this discussion are at the core of the authenticity debate that takes into account both the object itself, but also the how and where (i.e., in which context) it is presented and, hence, the element of authenticity this context and the types of engagement it affords bring to the visitor experience. The fact that authenticity is a relative concept has also been suggested by professional bodies such as the International Council on Monuments and Sites (ICOMOS) which declared that:

> all judgements about values attributed to cultural properties as well as the credibility of related information sources may differ from culture to culture, and even within the same culture. It is thus not possible to base judgements of values and authenticity within fixed criteria.
>
> (ICOMOS, 1994, Article 11)

As Leary and Sholes (2000, p. 50) put it, presentations of objects and heritage sites are 'inherently inauthentic' since 'we may only approximate past events and experiences [...]'

The clarification of the distinction between authentic objects versus authentic experiences, debates around this distinction and their implication for museums is the main focus of this chapter. Specifically, by bringing together ideas and evidence from different disciplinary contexts, the following sections will examine how authenticity has been theorised and studied, predominantly in terms of binary oppositions: real–replica/model and original–copy/fake. It will also discuss the contextual and culturally situated nature of authenticity and argue that authenticity is not an absolute concept. Emerging evidence suggests that what we are dealing with in museum settings are degrees of authenticity as far as objects and experiences with objects are concerned.

The basics of authenticity

Drawing on work by Orvell (1989) and MacCannell (1999 [1976]), Roberts (1997) identified that two main approaches to theorising authenticity can be discerned. Orvell's (1989) approach views authenticity as an attribute inherent in the object – its materiality, form and function – while the other approach comes from semiotics and focuses on the type of experience (aesthetic, emotional and so on) museum objects can evoke in visitors (see MacCannell, 1999 [1976]). The latter approach marks a shift from examining objects and the particular qualities that render them 'authentic' to focusing on the psychological and sociocultural processes that shape how we value objects across time and space. Seen from this point of view, the concept of authenticity is produced and negotiated by the cultural context within which objects exist and are viewed as well as by the person who views them (Jones, 2010). A somewhat similar approach to authenticity has been described by Evans et al. (2002) using the terms object-based epistemology (i.e., things exist as objects and are separate to the knower) and object-based discourse (i.e., the role objects play 'in the cultural or lived history of the visitor' (Evans et al., 2002, p. 58)).

Before we turn to the presentation of the work of Evans et al. (2002), let us first examine elements of the above debate in the scenario of Learning Campus presented at the beginning of this chapter. The development of the Learning Campus in the CBG is a good example of how the different elements of the authenticity debate have been dealt with by bringing together the object and the way it is experienced. So, the Learning Campus includes the objects (i.e., plants) and what is known about them (i.e., through the perspective of horticulture, plant science, ecology and conservation), and ways of engaging with those objects in different every day contexts (such as gardening activities and free exploration of the natural world) but also in scientific contexts (i.e., water investigations and classrooms for indoor programmes). Although the guiding principles were clear, their application was more challenging. For example, native plants were seen as more authentic but they were not always the most appealing option in terms of what types of experiences and modes of participation these plants afforded a family audience. In the case of the Learning Campus, the tension between authentic (i.e., native plants) and visitor experience was resolved by making the decision to focus on the child's experience.

Going back to Evans et al.'s (2002) approach to authenticity, their work is grounded on theory of core knowledge, the theoretical roots of which are in developmental psychology. According to Evans et al. (2002, p. 61), the emphasis of naive theory is 'on causal explanation and a characterization of the body of knowledge that very young children are likely to have about the world, prior to any formal educational experiences' (this perspective is often referred to as 'core knowledge' in the psychological literature). Examining young children's 'casual intuitions' or principles (elements children draw on when they try to explain how and why something happens), how they elaborate on them when prompted, and how these principles change, develop and are assimilated into new knowledge lies at the core of the empirical research carried out within this perspective.

Evans et al. (2002, p. 57) make the point that 'an object-based epistemology provided the foundation on which the language of museums was constructed'. Their argument draws on Conn's study of the creation of American museums and the role of the newly formed field of natural history museums in the American intellectual life, and on Shapin's sociological analysis of the scientific revolution (Conn, 2000; Shapin, 1996). Based on this work, they point out that many of the American museums developed in late nineteenth and early twentieth centuries used objects to construct stories about the natural and man-made world. These stories were based on the newly formed field of natural history which was embedded in the political, religious and cultural dimensions of society. Hence, the knowledge it produced 'was invested with religious significance insofar as it was thought to reveal the handiwork of God' (Evans et al., 2002, p. 57).

The concept of object-based discourse, with its emphasis on visitor life and experience, has some similarities with MacCannell's (1999[1976]) approach (see Authenticity in tourism below) in that they both focus on the way in which objects are experienced. However, core knowledge theory focuses specifically on individual cognition and internal mental processes. What all of the approaches mentioned above have in common is that they try to address the meaning and value of objects in people's lives, albeit using different theoretical and methodological approaches. As is the case with the study of any concept or phenomenon, the theories and methods used can elucidate a concept or phenomenon and, at the same time, shape its meaning and our knowledge of it. Let us, for example, turn to developmental theory paradigms for studying authenticity, reality and fantasy among young children.

Authenticity, reality and fantasy

From a learning theory perspective, research into the understanding of authenticity, reality or fantasy can be traced back to Piaget's work looking at children's conceptions of the world. Within this paradigm, children's ability to understand what is real or not is seen as an important cognitive task. Piaget used observation and clinical interview methods to uncover and describe children's cognitive structures. This early research seemed to suggest that children confuse reality and fantasy (Piaget, 1929; Morison & Gardner, 1978). But more recent evidence suggests that children's responses were influenced by the type of tasks given and the way these were presented.

Research carried out within the same paradigm more recently has used a more nuanced approach to the categorisation tasks given to children, and has shown the importance of object properties in children's concepts. This type of research examines children's ability to distinguish between what is real and what is fantasy, which is widely reported to develop with age and to be affected by the acquisition of knowledge (e.g., Harris, 2012; Woolley & Wellman, 2004; Sharon & Woolley, 2004). Some research has also specifically looked at children's magical explanations which is treated as a sign of increased awareness of and ability to explain illusionary phenomena (such as 'magic tricks' like a colour-changing scarf; whether dogs can talk) (Woolley, 1997; Evans, Mull, & Poling, 2002).

In the section on Museums and the perception of authenticity below, we will present research into children's developing understanding of real, fake and authentic objects across settings (including museums). This research has implications for the development of spaces and resources for visitor groups that include children. However, it also has wider implications for museum learning theory and practice because it examines basic concepts such as real, original design and intentions, and object provenance all of which are relevant to our understanding of authenticity from a visitor perspective in museums. Next we turn to the concept of authentic learning environments that explores yet another dimension of authenticity.

Authentic learning environments

A rather less well-known concept that can contribute to the discussion of authenticity, especially from a learning perspective, is that of 'authentic learning environments'. Being developed from a situated learning perspective, this concept fits within an object-based discourse or the approach that views authenticity as a type of experience evoked by objects. This approach signifies a shift from the object or the visitor to the environment itself.

Brown, Collins and Duguid (1989) have examined authenticity in the context of knowledge construction and learning environments. Their position is that both learning and knowledge are situated, with the quality of learning contingent on the learning environment. According to this perspective, in traditional educational environments, such as schools, often learning and what is learned (knowledge) are seen as independent of the activity and the context in which learning takes place. They challenge this approach, citing research which shows that what is learned is an integral part of 'how it is learned and used' (Brown et al., 1989, p. 32). They advocate the use of what they call authentic activities and authentic contexts or learning environments. Authentic activities are 'defined as the ordinary practice of the culture' (Brown et al., 1989, p. 34). The term 'culture' here refers to different domains of knowledge (such as art, mathematics, history), or to social settings (such as schools, museums, workplaces). It is through their engaging in authentic activities that people develop usable, robust knowledge (knowledge that is based on the development of metacognitive skills and that it can be transferred to new situations) and this knowledge is context-dependent. Authenticity is supported when tools of a discipline are available along with the culture of those who actually use the tools. Learning is optimal when learners are exposed to the meaning and purposes of authentic domain activities. These activities are not static but are always under construction through negotiation among present and past members. It follows that authentic learning environments nurture robust knowledge.

Commenting on classroom activity, in particular, they point out that it does not provide 'students the chance to engage the relevant domain culture or "enculturation"' (Brown et al., 1989, p. 34). For Brown, Collins and Duguid, culture and community are seen as enabling or disabling for the learner and, hence, possibility or failure to learn should be assessed in relational patterns, i.e., authentic activities, tools available, the context, culture and community are interdependent. Here is an example of how these elements of an authentic learning environment were utilised in the scenario. The Learning Campus created a setting where children can learn about native plants (objects) from the CBG collection through free exploration and utilising knowledge (tools) embedded in facilitated activities such as gardening, presented in space that feels natural (context). CBG staff (community) support children's exploration, play and learning both through free exploration of the Learning Campus outdoor spaces such as rolling hills and multisensory gardens and through drop-in activities (activity).

Authenticity in tourism

MacCannell (1999 [1976]) was the first researcher who theorised tourism as a spiritual response to modernity and to the sense of inauthenticity; as a search for a long-lost authentic past. He saw tourism as a by-product of modernity, as a way for people to escape from (in-authentic) everyday life in search of authenticity in other places and times. His work examined how the tourist industry capitalises on people's desire for the authentic and he introduced the concept of 'staged authenticity' in the context of ethnic tourism (MacCannell, 1973). In order to sell a fascinating tourism package, hosts put their culture (including themselves) on sale and 'the degree that this packaging alters the nature of the product, the authenticity sought by the visitor becomes "staged authenticity" provided by the touree' (MacCannell, 1973, p. 596). The meaning of MacCannell's definition is that tourists are often provided with experiences or performances that are theatrical or orchestrated in order to meet their expectations. These experiences are usually superficial, featuring only the 'front stage' area of a culture without capturing its 'back stage'. This implies that tourists have only the illusion of being in contact with the 'real' or 'genuine' foreign culture.

MacCannell (1973) approaches the motivation of modern tourists as a type of spiritual response to the fragmentation of modern life, where people constantly feel that they are losing their attachments to elements of their lives that they called their own, such as the town, family or neighbourhood. But, at the same time, they develop a keen interest in the 'real life' of other people or in other cultures. MacCannell (1973) used six stages of authenticity which start with the overtly front stage (seen as an inauthentic experience developed specifically for tourist consumption) to the explicitly back stage (where members of a culture live their 'true lives' away from the tourist gaze). MacCannell's work has been very influential on tourism studies[2] where authenticity is perceived as a relative, socially constructed and contextually determined concept, the meaning of which changes according to the profile, expectations and prior experiences of the tourist(s). For example, Chhabra, Healy and Sills' (2003, p. 702) study revealed that a 'high perception of authenticity can be achieved when the event is staged in a place far away from the original source of the cultural tradition'.

MacCannell's (1973) work has influenced some of the studies we review in Authenticity of place and voice below. This research is especially useful to particular types of museums (such as eco-museums or open air museums), special events (such as festivals or staged drama events) and other types of cultural practices that can be described as intangible heritage (such as theatre and music performances) that have started finding their way into museum settings.

Museums and the perception of authenticity

The disciplinary perspectives briefly presented above have impacted on authenticity discourse and shaped notions of authenticity and learning in the museum context. The following sections present and discuss studies with mainly museum visitors. In the vast majority of these studies, although they use slightly different definitions of authenticity, the assumption seems to be that authenticity resides within the object. There are a few exceptions of studies that take into account the cultural or contextual significance of objects or heritage sites (e.g., Siegel & Callanan, 2007; Weidinger, 2015). Moreover, the almost exclusive focus on visitors' perceptions of objects has led to a gap in empirical work examining how people value or relate to authentic experiences. Studies by Brida, Disegna and Osti (2012) and Weidinger (2015) are rather the exception here. We have reviewed a number of relevant studies under themes that emerge from the main issues that researchers focus on when studying authenticity. Some of these research themes appear as binary pairs, while others focus on a particular aspect of people's experience of authenticity. The themes include: 'the real thing' versus replica/models, 'the real thing'/original versus fake, reality–fantasy and numinous objects, and authenticity in relation to digital objects/experiences.

'The real thing' versus replica/model

Although authenticity is often mentioned as a motivation for visiting or as an experience-enhancing element of the museum visit, it is not often the main focus of research in visitor experience. For example, in a study examining Smithsonian Institution (SI) visitors' satisfying experiences,[3] Pekarik, Doering and Karns (1999, p. 157) identified four categories of museum experiences that are satisfying (i.e., object, cognitive, introspective, and social experiences). Object experiences included: (1) 'seeing "the real thing"', (2) 'seeing rare/uncommon/valuable things', (3) 'being moved by beauty', (4) 'thinking what it would be like to own such things' and (5) 'continuing my professional development'. Visitors were asked to choose from a list of statements that described different type of experiences as they entered or left an exhibition and/or one of the SI museums. The wording of the statements derived from a combination of visitors' own words, researchers' categories and further testing with visitors. Results coming from eight studies of exhibitions in nine different SI museums seem to suggest that visitors' object experiences tended to be at the top of the most satisfying experiences in three out of the nine museums surveyed (the three museums were the Renwick Gallery with a focus on American crafts, the National Zoo and the National Museum of Natural History). Out of the five types of object experiences reported in this study, 'seeing the "real thing"' came up quite high on visitors' most satisfying museum experiences. For example, it was the second most satisfying experience at the National Museum of American History (with a total of 58% mentioning it after 'gaining information or knowledge') and at the exhibition Where Next, Columbus at the Air and Space Museum (with a total of 35% mentioning it after 'gaining information or knowledge'). 'Seeing the "real thing"' was also the most anticipated of all the object experiences amongst visitors at the National Museum of American History and Where Next, Columbus exhibition, with 18% and 16% of visitors respectively mentioning it.

Seeing real objects are among the satisfying museum experiences reported by visitors

Among the few studies with an explicit intention to examine visitor response to authentic objects in museums is that of Hampp and Schwan (2014). In their study of the criteria visitors use to evaluate authentic objects in a museum context, they used original and replica objects in a bio- and nanotechnology exhibition at the Deutsches Museum in Munich, Germany. The authors defined authentic objects 'as original objects that once served a science-related, real-world purpose and bear some significance for the history of science in museums with an emphasis on the history of science and technology' (Hampp and Schwan (2014, p. 17). Although the researchers did not discuss the theoretical underpinnings of their study explicitly, based on the overall approach used, we believe that this project is influenced by an information processing perspective.

Hampp and Schwan (2014, p. 164) set out to answer two main research questions: (1) 'How does authenticity affect the perception of objects among visitors in museums of science and technology?' and (2) 'What are other relevant factors – beyond authenticity – that affect the perception of objects among visitors in museums of science and technology?' They created two experimental situations where they presented visitors with two different display set-ups focusing on nanotechnology and medical technology. Within each display setup visitors were presented with three experimental showcases that presented different types of information about the objects: the nanotechnology display included a functional and a sociocultural perspective, while the medical display included the history of medical technology and a sociocultural perspective. The same object in each display setup was in some cases presented as original and in other cases it was presented as a replica. The adult visitors who took part in the study did not volunteer any comments on the authenticity of the objects viewed. However, when specifically asked to comment on the authenticity of the objects viewed, visitors stated that they had not paid attention to that element but that they had assumed that they were authentic since they were in the Museum. When probed further, it became apparent that visitors to a science museum do care about the authenticity of science objects and that they generally assume that museums display authentic objects. Specifically, they discussed object authenticity as facilitating their learning experience across four dimensions: (1) the ability to help them connect with *history*, (2) *charisma,* referring to 'the aura' of the object, and (3) its *rarity*, which was associated with having a special status in a particular society, (4) and the *functionality* of the object, how it worked or operated. Other elements of the objects that facilitated appreciation by visitors was: (1) their *appearance*, which was defined as 'the interplay of design and function' (Hampp & Schwan, 2014, p. 18), (2) the *intellectual insight* these objects provided as symbols of certain technological, historical and cultural significance, and (3) the *personal characteristics* of the participants referring to their prior knowledge and interest in the subject matter the objects are linked to.

Visitors believe that authentic science objects enhance their learning experience

Another study that makes a reference – albeit indirect – to museums was carried out by Frazier et al. (2009). Taking, what appears to us to be, an information-processing[4] perspective, this study examined how adults evaluate authentic objects and how their evaluation is affected by belief systems that shape people's economic and emotional judgements as well as the how they evaluate which objects are of museum-quality. They set out to examine what they call rational beliefs (such as the monetary value of objects), as well as irrational ones (such as objects' emotional value or a desire to own and touch objects) across different cultural contexts. Another point of interest from this study was whether there were any links between participants' own attachment to childhood objects (i.e., attachment objects such as soft toys) and their attitude towards authenticity in adulthood. They recruited university students from the US and the UK representing different belief systems. The researchers

(Frazier et al., 2009, p. 3) hypothesised that 'authentic objects should be rated higher than non-authentic objects on all scales', and that 'individuals who had an attachment object as a child will value authentic objects more'. The first hypothesis was confirmed by the findings since authentic objects were indeed rated higher on all scales. The higher evaluation of authentic as compared to non-authentic objects reflected their economic value but also the participants' desire to own and touch those objects. Other findings showed that women valued authentic personal objects more highly compared to men. There was also a link between those participants who had a personal attachment object as children and the monetary value they assigned to authentic objects which was generally higher as compared to the rest of the sample. This led the researchers (Frazier et al., 2009, p. 7) to conclude that: 'Attachment history may simply be a marker for individuals who are more inclined to acknowledge the unique authenticity of objects, as this is one of the characteristic features of attachment object behavior.' On a more general level, this study shows that people seem to value authentic objects as reflected by their expressed desire to own and touch them, and these attitudes and behaviours are quite widespread and embedded in everyday life. They argue that it is only a matter of degree to which each of us is inclined to exhibit those attitudes and behaviours.

People's evaluation of authentic objects is influenced by belief systems that shape how they judge the economic and emotional value of a particular object as well as which objects are museum-worthy

In another study, Frazier and Gelman (2009) explored the developmental changes in children's and adult's understanding of authenticity. This study takes a core knowledge theory perspective to examine the naive theories children have about authenticity. Participants included preschoolers, kindergarteners, grade 1 and grade 4 children, and university undergraduates. Previous research had shown that even very young children are sensitive to non-visible properties of objects. This study set out to examine whether children placed special meaning on objects based on their history rather than their appearance (the material of the object). Objects chosen fell into three categories of authentic objects: 'original creations (e.g., the very first teddy bear), famous associations (e.g., the US President's flag pin), and personal associations (e.g., one's own baby blanket)' (Frazier & Gelman 2009, p. 286). For the purposes of this study, photographs of both authentic and inauthentic objects were used. Participants were asked two questions about pairs of authentic and inauthentic objects: which object belonged in a museum and which object they would want to have. This study showed that three- and four-year-old children understood that objects have historic paths that affect the objects' nature, which moreover can be denoted as authentic through stating they belong in a museum.

Children understand that objects have historic paths that affect the objects' nature

The Frazier and Gelman (2009) study seems to make the assumption that all museum objects are authentic and that their value relates to their history and general value on a public level. It does not differentiate between different types of objects or museums. Furthermore, the study relies on prior knowledge of what a museum is (which at this age is likely to be quite limited and probably specific to a museum type that they happen to have experience with; this information is not provided in the study). Although the socioeconomic information about the children participating in this study is not detailed, they were all described as being of 'middle class' background. They also come from a particular geographical context (preschoolers from a midwestern US university town; primary school children from a school from a western US town; and the adults were undergraduate psychology students at a midwestern US university).

Following from the above points, we would like to offer a word of caution related to the applicability of the findings of these studies in the museum context. But, before we do that, we would like to emphasise that research studies tend to ask and answer specific research questions and conduct research in a rigorous way, which is what all the studies presented above have done. Although there are lessons that can be learned which are relevant to museum practice, as we have highlighted above, generalising findings and applying them in museum contexts was not within the scope of these studies. So, any practical implications that we can draw need to take that into account. What, then, do readers need to take into account? Given the controlled nature of the experiment-type of studies, their narrow socio-economic samples, their focus on a small number of objects/entities and their geographic and culture specific context, findings should be applied with caution in museum settings. First of all, museums consist of intentionally developed collections of objects rather than individual unrelated objects; this intentionality is also reflected in the way exhibitions are put together. Hence, the context within which objects are placed in an exhibition setting, and to which museum visitors respond, is a very complex system. The institutional context within which objects and collections are exhibited also play a role in the way they are presented and perceived. Since the meanings of authenticity seem to be related to the historical, cultural and institutional contexts within which it has been identified and studied, it can be argued that the way different people (learn to) value and respond to authentic objects is likely to vary across institutional settings, geographical locations and cultures.

'The real thing' or original object

The next couple of studies have also used experimental design, but these have been carried out in museum settings rather than in a laboratory environment. As highlighted by studies presented above, two of the dimensions people use to judge the authenticity of physical objects is their appearance – in particular, their design – and their provenance. For example, the use of appearance of the object as a criterion to judge its authenticity was pointed out by Hampp and Schwan's (2014) study with museum visitors. 'Original design' is another concept used by researchers from a core knowledge theory perspective to examine children's ability to understand that both natural objects and artefacts did not always exist. As mentioned in the basics of authenticity section above, original design is a key concept that directly relates to how we understand the concept of authenticity. For example, Evans et al., (2002, p. 71) report on a study they carried out with children between the ages of four and ten, according to which only children from the eight to ten age group 'had the concept of "the very first"'. Children in this age group were able to consistently recognise that: (1) animals and artefacts did not always exist, and (2) that artefacts are manmade, while animals are created by God. In contrast, some recent research has questioned whether children of this age all think animals are created by God (Evans & Poling, 2004; Tenenbaum & Hohenstein, 2016).

Original design is one of the concepts that influence how people understand object authenticity

Bunce and Harris (2014) studied children's judgements of the real/not-real status of fictional television characters in order to determine the basis for their judgements. Specifically, they started from the premise that children can base their judgement either on the ontological status of the character (i.e., 'that Harry Potter is not a real schoolboy and that Bob the Builder could not really come to mend our roof'), or on the authenticity of a representation of the character (i.e., whether somebody dressed as Father Christmas is the real one or not) (Bunce & Harris, 2014, p. 111). The researchers used photographs of the fictional characters as well as photographs of people dressed up as those characters. They (Bunce & Harris, 2014, p. 117) asked children from different age groups to examine the photograph and judge whether each figure lives in 'the real world' (ontology question) and whether each figure is 'the real' fictional character (authenticity question). Children of all age groups were able to make accurate authenticity judgement (i.e., the authenticity of the representation of the character, such as a person dressed as Father Christmas). However, when children were asked to make an ontological judgement about whether or not the figure lives in the real world, younger pre-schoolers, in particular, found this difficult. The researchers concluded that younger children's understanding that fictional characters do not live in the real world develops with age.

Young children's understanding that fictional characters do not live in the real world develops with age

In a more recent study, Bunce (2016) examined how visitors perceived natural history collections in relation to their authenticity (assessed in terms of whether it belongs to a museum) and educational value. The museum-worthiness element of this study is reminiscent of Frazier and Gelman's (2009) study presented above. The study used a taxidermied rabbit from the natural history collection of the Oxford University Museum of Natural History alongside a realistic soft toy rabbit. Family groups with children from four to ten years old (divided into age groups of four to seven and eight to ten years old and adults) were invited to take part in the study in the Museum space but as part of a specially designed activity devised for the purposes of this study. Visitors were asked to consider the taxidermied rabbit 'as a touchable [object], inside an exhibition case, or alongside a realistic soft toy rabbit' and were asked whether and why it 'belongs in a museum and could help visitors learn about rabbits' and (Bunce, 2016, p. 187). This study showed that younger children can attribute living/non-living appropriately to taxidermy, particularly when the context is facilitative, for example, when the taxidermied rabbit was presented next to the toy rabbit. While both adult and child participants (from both age groups) could recognise the educational value of taxidermied animals, judging the taxidermied rabbit as museum-worthy increased with age.

Adults and children recognise the educational value of taxidermied animals, but children's ability to judge them as museum-worthy increases with age

As is common with this type of study, the majority of the participants were from a white middle-class background and highly educated. Another limitation of this study is the fact that it made an assumption that museum professionals as well as visitors perceive authenticity as an attribute inherent in the object. This assumption led the researcher make a number of inferences about the way people encountered the taxidermied rabbit and why they responded in particular ways. For example, adult participants justified why the taxidermied rabbit was museum-worthy in terms of being able to examine it closely and study it, rather than in terms of its physical properties (e.g., having real fur).

Transcending reality and numinous objects

All of the studies presented above are based on the premise that being able to distinguish reality from fantasy is a sign of developmental maturity. However, both the conceptual and the empirical literature on authenticity are rife with examples of a special emotional state that objects or places can trigger in people, where object encounters create a sense of transcending reality. In their effort to describe or empirically examine such a state, some writers and researchers have drawn on religious studies or used spiritual references (see for example Otto, 1917/1958). Some of the terms used to describe this heightened state of mind and religious- or spiritual-like experience include: 'magical contagion' and 'sympathetic magic' (Nemeroff & Rozin,

2000), 'numen',[5] 'numinous objects/experiences' (Latham, 2013; Cameron & Gatewood, 2000 & 2003; Gatewood & Cameron, 2004; Maines & Glynn, 1993), 'reverential experience' (Graburn, 1977), 'rasa' or 'aesthetic delight' (Goswamy, 1991), 'resonance' and 'wonder' (Greenblatt, 1991), 'aesthetic experience' (Dewey, 1934), 'transaction' (Dewey & Bentley, 1949) and 'flow' (Csikszentmihalyi and Robinson, 1990). Flow theory has been the basis for the development of the theoretical framework of the studies presented in the section below. However, Flow theory is presented in the Basics of motivation in Chapter 9, so we do not repeat it here.

This section starts with Cameron and Gatewood studies, which applied the concept of numen in museum visitor research. Latham's (2013) research into numinous experiences with museum objects is based on and extends the work of Cameron and Gatewood (2000 & 2003; Gatewood & Cameron, 2004), which focuses on historic and industrial sites. The term numen, although it originally had a clear religious reference, was applied by Cameron and Gatewood (2000, p. 110) to test the hypothesis that 'sites and displays that conjure in visitors a visceral or emotional response to an earlier event or time (one that could allow them to achieve a connection with the "spirit" of times or persons past) are especially valued'. Although the methodological approaches that Latham, and Cameron and Gatewood take are quite different, their studies highlight object-visitor encounters that lead to numinous experiences.

For example, in their initial study carried out in the historic centre of Bethlehem, Pennsylvania, Cameron and Gatewood (2000 & 2003) found that visitors to historic sites expect to have 'a transcendental experience' which relates to a general interest in history. In a follow-up study carried out at the Gettysburg National Military Park in Pennsylvania, Cameron and Gatewood (2004) expanded their initial concept by describing three dimensions of the numinous experience. Unlike their initial study where predominantly quantitative data were collected, this latter study combined both quantitative and qualitative data, which enabled the researchers to delve deeper into what constitutes a numinous experience and its dimensions. These were: (1) 'deep engagement or transcendence' – this is described as a state of mind close to 'flow' the key characteristic of which is the loss of the sense of time and self; (2) 'empathy' – a state of mind where one is transported back in time and feels a strong emotional connection to those who lived then, and (3) 'awe or reverence' – described as a holy-like experience or a 'spiritual communion with something or someone' (Cameron & Gatewood, 2004, p. 208).

Studies on numinous objects and experiences take their starting point from Cameron and Gatewood's (2000, p. 109)

Objects can trigger a visceral or emotional response, known as numinous experience, which can help visitors connect to the spirit of a historic period or a person; numinous experiences are characterised by deep engagement, empathy, and a sense of awe hypothesis, as can be seen in Latham's research (2013). Latham specifically focused on instances of numen-seeking experiences with museum objects among visitors who had had deeply meaningful experiences across five US museums that included art, history as well as living and state history. This was a retrospective study that included a sample of participants who were self-selected based on their ability to provide a detailed account of a deeply moving experience with a museum object. Latham confirmed the existence of the three dimensions of numinous experience as described by Cameron and Gatewood, but also expanded on them and provided more detail. According to Latham (2013, p. 17), the contribution of this study is the 'model of the numinous encounter' it developed, which 'reveals a dynamic, transactive experience that is holistic and lived through every part of a person's senses and intellect'. It also sheds light on the salience of museum objects and the power they have to create a deeply meaningful museum experience. The study identified four essential elements of this type of experience which included: (1) *unity of the moment*, (2) *object link*, (3) *being transported* and (4) *connections bigger than self*. The *unity of the moment* element was seen as the overarching one (Latham, 2013, p. 11):

Objects that trigger numinous experiences can lead to holistic and deeply meaningful visitor experiences

> *Unity of the Moment* is the overarching whole of the numinous experience with the other three themes contributing as elements within. The tangible and symbolic object; the alterations of time, space, and body; and the deep connections – through self, spirit, and people of the past – were all wrapped up in the moment, the unity of the moment. The numinous experience ultimately is one whole swirling entity of these things, overlapping and connecting. It is the uniting of all these things – emotion, intellect, feeling, senses, imagination – that results in meaning for the experiencer.

In her interpretation of these key elements of numinous experience with museum objects, Latham (2003, p. 12) makes a direct link to Dewey's (1937) concept of *transaction* and the use of this concept in the work of Csikszentmihalyi and Rochberg-Halton (1981) – referred to as *person–object transaction* – and adapts it as *person–document transaction*. She further borrows the concept of *flow* from Csikszentmihalyi and Robinson (1990) in her interpretation of the numinous as a type of optimal experience, very much like *flow*. Finally, she also adapts William James' concept of *mystical consciousness* to highlight the spiritual character – 'the feeling of awe or reverence' – of the numinous encounter with museum objects. Findings of this study indicated that the holistic nature of the numinous experience – operating at an intellectual, emotional, imaginative and sensual level at the same time – can have a long-lasting, life-enriching impact on the visitor and those close to her, with whom the numinous experience is shared.

Authentic learning environments

The following sections examine a particular element of authentic learning environments, a concept introduced in the previous section of this chapter, that of the authenticity of place and voice.

Authenticity of place and voice

Coming from a tourism studies perspective, Brida, Disegna and Scuderi (2014) examined visitor perception of authenticity in an archaeology and a modern art museum in Italy. This was a large-scale study collecting quantitative data from 1288 questionnaires administered to visitors of the two museums (i.e., South Tyrol Museum of Archaeology in Bolzano and the Museum of Modern and Contemporary Art in Trento-Rovereto). The study identified authenticity-related factors common to both museums as well as factors particular to each museum that affected visitors' perceptions of authenticity. The authenticity elements against which both sites were evaluated included: '(a) the museum is purely a tourist attraction; (b) it is unique in the world; (c) it is a place that makes you think; (d) it describes an historical era; (e) it is a fascinating attraction' (Brida et al., 2014, p. 532). Site-specific perceptions of authenticity were also mentioned. For example, in the case of the South Tyrol Museum of Archaeology authenticity was related to the Museum's uniqueness in the world and its historical and archaeological importance.[6] In the case of the Museum of Modern and Contemporary Art, authenticity was associated with the museum's building and the perception among its visitors that it was not merely a tourist attraction. Moreover, there was an indication that specific demographic characteristics of the visitors themselves influenced their perceptions of authenticity. These included gender (with men being more likely to have higher perceptions of authenticity of both museums than women), income and place of origin (with those living in high-income families or coming from Centre-South or Islands of Italy perceiving the Contemporary Art as more authentic). Brida et al. (2014, p. 534) concluded that 'the perception of authenticity is a dynamic concept, in the sense that it changes on the basis of the audience and the phenomenon under observation'.

The next couple of studies examine places and practices beyond the museum building and/or its collections. Once again they come from a tourism studies perspective, but they too speak to people's search for the authentic and of authentic

Visitor perceptions of authenticity are affected by museum-specific factors, the visitors' socio-economic and cultural background as well as authenticity judgements common across different museum types experiences, which is often articulated in terms of a rejection of modernity, and the sense of displacement and alienation that come with it (see for example, Lindholm, 2008). The core argument here is that this sense of alienation makes people feel that living in the modern world is not 'real' and that seeking out things that are different from 'real life' (i.e., the 'real life of others') is related to the experience of things that are 'real'. This search of the authentic often leads people to searching for the authentic in a different place, culture or historical period (see MacCannell, 1999 [1976, p. 3). The next two studies examine how the search for the authentic is situated in the experience of local events, such as Christmas markets (Brida, Disegna, & Osti, 2012), and in rural localities (Weidinger, 2015). Brida et al. (2012) examined how tourists and local residents perceive their experience of the same Christmas market in Northern Italy in terms of its authenticity. This research highlighted that

Community involvement in the organisation and running of events plays a key role in the perception of a particular event as authentic by both members of the local community and visitors

the degree of community involvement in the event played a key role in both members' of the local community and visitors' perception of the event as authentic. Specifically, being able to identify themselves and local customs in the way the Christmas market was staged was associated with high support from the local community. Brida et al. (2012) suggested that the local community needs to be involved in the organisation of local events and provide opportunities for tourist and locals to interact with each other as part of the experience.

The focus on the local residents' views of authenticity of intangible heritage (such as an event like a Christmas market) is a particularly interesting line of research and one that has been explored further by Weidinger (2015). Using MacCannell's theoretical framework, Weidinger's (2015, p. 6) research examined the authentication process of rural localities (i.e., how local residents 'evaluate rural localities with regard to authenticity'). The case study was a rural tourism destination of a Bavarian forest, located in the border between Germany, Austria and the Czech Republic. It includes natural landscapes, associated activities such as skiing, hiking and biking or other offers and amenities such as wellness hotels and agritourism, and cultural (i.e., customs and local traditions) and industrial heritage (i.e., wood industry and glass manufacturing). Using a qualitative approach, the researcher interviewed representatives from the local authority, the tourism industry and heritage conservation, and also local residents. Weidinger (2015, p. 20) reported that 'the majority of both groups criticises modern architectural

Reflecting regional identity is seen as authentic by local residents and visitors to the area

styles as "in-authentic" and therefore inappropriate for the region. "Tuscan houses", especially, were seen as an effect of globalisation and would contribute to a standardisation of the views of places within the Bavarian forest, culminating in the loss of uniqueness for tourists.' In line with Brida et al.'s (2012) recommendations, Weidinger also suggested involving the locals in the process of planning and decision-making. For example, he points to tourism accommodation and how building new hotels and houses can strengthen the links between local architecture and regional identity in a way that can 'stimulate perceptions of authenticity' (Weidinger, 2015, p. 17).

Constructing reality: authenticity and the many meanings of objects

It has been theorised that museums construct 'present-day "reality"' and bring 'into focus a memory of the past that (coincidentally) supports that present' by creating 'master narratives' (Hooper-Greenhill, 2000, p. 25). To achieve this they draw on a 'network of [...] supporting material' (Hooper-Greenhill, 2000, p. 24), including authentic objects themselves and also the authentication process to which objects are subjected to determine their provenance. Objects are then brought together, they are sorted, classified and organised in collections. Although the judgement of what counts as an authentic object varies according to the nature of the object across museum types, there is little doubt that, to a large extent, the process of authentication that makes them museum-worthy shapes its possible meanings (e.g., Hooper-Greenhill, 2000; Miller, 1994). With regards to artefactual (as opposed to 'natural') objects, in particular, because they are the result of intentional human production, this is a key element of their authentic nature. The intentional design of artefacts presupposes and also shapes the intentional (or conventional) use in which artefacts will be put. Below we examine some elements that relate to the intentional design and conventional use of artefacts and how research has approached people's understanding of these elements.

Design, and in particular the original intention behind the design of objects, appears to be an important property that we take into account when assessing and categorising objects. Bloom's (1996) research looks at human artefact cognition, a branch of psychology that examines how we decide which objects are members of specific artefact categories. His research suggests that it is the designer's original intent that determines these categorisation judgements. This finding is consistent with other similar research conducted both in Western as well as in a non-Western cultural context (see for example, Barrett, Laurence and Margolis, 2008). Bloom proposes a theory of pictures according to which 'visual representations are categorized through what we infer to be the intentions of the creators' (Bloom, 1996, p. 8). This theory applies to pictures such as drawings or paintings that 'result from intentional representations', but not 'to visual representations' like photographs

> The original intention behind the design of objects determines the categories or groups into which they are subsequently classified

(Bloom, 1996, p. 8). This work can be used in art museums, in particular, where the role of drawings or paintings in the cultural life of visitors is addressed in order to show their utility as cultural artefacts.

Artefact use highlights another aspect of people's understanding of artefacts, relating to its cultural nature. This is consistent with sociocultural approaches to meaning making and learning. Siegel and Callanan's (2007) research examined the extent to which five-year-old children, seven-year-old children and adults 'would judge an artifact differently if they were told that *many* people are now using an artifact in a different way than its creator intended, as opposed to only one person' (Siegel & Callanan, 2007, p. 186). Participants were recruited and grouped according to their ethnic background and were told stories about four novel objects, using pictures of those objects and their functions. For each object, there were two conditions: they listened to stories about a novel object being used in a different way than originally designed by either one person or by many people. Both types of stories were identical, the only difference was the number of people using the novel artefact in a new way. Although there were some differences in the way the three groups reasoned about the functions of the artefacts, participants did not use only the inventor's original intention as 'the core meaning of artifacts'; they also 'focused on the everyday uses of artifacts', if they had evidence that many people used an artefact in a new way (Siegel & Callanan, 2007, p. 199). As Siegel and Callanan (2007, p. 200) state, 'children as young as 5 years old not only seem to understand that an artifact's meaning and use are largely determined by the general community, but also they seem to grasp that conventions can change'.

The categories in which objects are put and the meanings they acquire as a result are culturally determined and can change to realise the objects' potential to have multiple meanings

We believe that both of these studies have implications for the way museums can work with their communities to explore the many conventional meanings people assign to objects across time and cultures. This is particularly pertinent to co-creation projects where the authority of the museum voice and the museum-specific construction of its authenticity (largely based on the object's materiality, form and function) can appear to be able to provide the only authorised story about objects and collections.

Authenticity in the digital culture

The vast majority of the research on authenticity concerns tangible objects. What about intangible or digital objects? This is also central not only to how people relate to objects and evaluate their authentic qualities across different settings but also to the discussion of what is authentic and how we judge the authentic qualities of an object in the first place. In the last six decades, there has been a proliferation of digital technology and its application in museums (both behind the scenes enabling the management of collections and also as a means to deliver interpretation and engage visitors) (e.g., Jones-Garmil, 1997; Parry, 2007). Framed within a participatory practice and the cultural value of digital engagement framework, the existing work provides little evidence of how visitors' perceptions of authenticity change owing to the new digital reality. Referring to social media, for example, Russo (2012, p. 154) posited that they 'can extend the authenticity of collections by enabling museum professionals to establish and maintain a cultural dialogue with their audiences'. This idea seems to be widely shared in the field as King, Stark, & Cooke (2016) have found out through surveying and conducting informal group discussions with museum and heritage professionals located mainly in the UK (86%) but also in mainland Europe, Asia and Africa. The professionals who participated in this study discussed the issue of authenticity of digital tools or digital experiences in relation to whether 'real' objects and digital experiences associated with them should be integrated or presented separately. Although there was no agreement on this issue, it appears that participants who supported the separation of the two had 'an inherent respect for the objects, sites, and "real thing" in terms of engagement with history and heritage' (King et al., 2016, p. 89). Overall, participants thought that digital tools and experiences can enhance visitor engagement and add value to their visit experience. We look forward to research that will expand on these findings by adding visitor voices to those of museum professionals. This is clearly a very new and fruitful area of research.

> Researchers occasionally speculate that digital experiences can extend the authenticity of collections and enhance visitor engagement

Summary and reflections

Both the theoretical and the rather limited empirical research on authenticity in museums presented above pose more questions than provide answers, but they have been useful for providing a context for discussion. So, authenticity appears to be a rather nebulous and – as applied in museums – relatively recent concept which reflects a twentieth-century value of Western industrialised societies. Theoretical approaches to authenticity seem to have been dominated by the dichotomy between those that view it as inherent in the object and approaches that view it as a cultural construct. In an effort to go beyond this dichotomy, we looked at empirical studies that examine the concept of authenticity, its meaning and its relevance to the developing child and to everyday life contexts. A large number of these studies have been carried out from a core knowledge theory perspective within developmental psychology. Typically, researchers use different definitions of authenticity and examine different aspects and properties of the concept. Furthermore, the questions and domains of social life to which these questions apply are as diverse as the methods they use to generate data. However, the types of groups and cultural contexts in which it is studied are quite narrow. Despite the fact that some emerging research highlights the importance of the cultural context, Carroll (2014) comments on the overly restricted socioeconomic and cultural background of the participants: highly educated people in advanced market economies mainly located in the Western world. Both conceptualisations of authenticity and the way the concept has been operationalised and studied reflect a Western European perspective.

Since particular societies place high social and educational value on museums, one also needs to take into account relations of power involved in what counts as knowledge, and how museums privilege certain types of knowledge that is shared about particular objects, and how they provide access to certain type of learning resources (including objects). As Hampp and Schwan's (2014) study demonstrated, visitors operate on the assumption that museum objects are authentic by virtue of the fact that they are in a museum. It seems that participants in this study only reacted to 'inauthentic objects' when told that, according to the evaluation system of a particular community, they were deemed as inauthentic. On the other hand, the concept of authentic learning environments develops a different approach to authenticity by focusing on the environment instead. It takes a more holistic approach and examines the relationship between authentic activities and authentic tools/knowledge situated in the context of the community of people who develop and use them. Authenticity is not something that resides in an object or part of an experience but an integral part of the practice of a community.

Another important point in the discussion of authenticity and approaches to knowledge is that, whether viewed as being centred on an object-based epistemology or an object-based discourse, neither of them is static; they keep evolving and so does the meaning and our understanding of authenticity. Although current approaches to authenticity across disciplines represented in museums have been shaped by the early history of both these disciplines and the museum as an institution, to hang on to the 'original' meaning of authenticity as something that resides only within the object is to deny recent developments within disciplinary perspectives, and museum theory and practice. These developments acknowledge that meaning from objects is derived from both their physical and/or biological as well as their social and intellectual dimensions. This becomes even more important nowadays as museums try to attract and be relevant to new, under-represented audiences, retain traditional audiences, maintain high standards in research with collections, and develop content for exhibitions, programmes and resources that respect its integrity.

A return to the Learning Campus at CBG

We will now revisit the Learning Campus at CBG and follow two girls, Cara and Lily, who are here to take part in the summer camp. Cara and Lily don't know each other but they arrived early and they sat next to each other waiting for the other kids to arrive.

Cara, a nine-year-old girl and Lily, an eight-year-old girl and her brother, Sam, have just arrived at the CBG for their first day of the summer camp, or Camp CBG as one of the ladies who greeted them at the entrance called it. Cara cannot wait for the camp to start! She has always liked nature and being outdoors. She likes climbing trees and hiking in the woods, in particular, and she knows that they will do some hiking later on. She watched a video clip about the camp on the Garden's website and saw a group of kids going into the woods. Lily, on the other hand, is not very enthusiastic about this year's summer camp. She does not like being outdoors with new kids she does not know. This year it was her brother Sam's turn to choose which camp they would go to. He has liked animals and nature since he was very little. Lily feels nervous and lonely. She glances at the girl sitting next to her who grins back at her and says 'Hi, my name is Cara. What's your name?' Lily is very shy but there is something about Cara that she really likes.

All the kids have now arrived and the instructors tell them what they will be doing for the rest of the day. There will be arts activities, they will do gardening, look at plants, play games, have lunch, make flower pots out of clay, birdwatching, catch bugs, make their own snacks and lots more. The instructors go through the 'codes of conduct' and tell everybody to make sure they have their water bottles with them and drink water regularly. It's going to be a hot day so they will do some gardening first and then come back indoors for a snack, rest and to keep out of the sun. The group sets off for the growing garden where they are asked to go around the growing beds. Cara and Lily go to one of the growing beds, while Sam joins a group of younger boys around his age. The kids get into pairs and take turns to water the plants using a watering bucket. Cara and Lily will take care of a plant called 'Tara' which, their instructor tells them, is a prairie dropseed plant native to North America. Cara tells Lily that she sees this plant a lot when she goes hiking with her family and that she likes it because it sounds a bit like her name: 'Cara-Tara, don't you think it rhymes?' Lily readily agrees and looks at the plant again. At closer inspection it looks so beautiful; she likes its fine texture and emerald-green leaves. The instructor shows them a bunch of weeds and asks them to very carefully take them out of the growing beds and put them in a bag. He explains that plants need space to grow and that weeds grow very quickly and don't let other plants grow. Another instructor-helper goes around and helps children with their tasks. Cara and Lily ask her about their plant, 'Tara', and instructor-helper tells them that it is a very special plant because it can survive long periods of drought. It is also a favourite plant with many birds that eat its seeds. They also learn that you can make a very tasty flour from its seeds. Native Americans ground the seeds of Tara to make flour. This aspect of the camp CBG programme values both the importance of the 'real' object (i.e., native prairie dropseed plant) and the 'object-based epistemology' (i.e., the natural history of the object), and of the participatory experience that Cara and Lily have as they take care of the plant. It also values the 'object-based discourse' by associating Tara to its cultural history and the role it plays in the food heritage of Native Americans. Presented in this context, Tara encouraged Cara, Lily and the instructor-helper to engage in a dialogue about the plant.

Now the instructor tells them about how important soil is for the survival of plants. He asks all of the kids if they know how many different types of soils there are. A few kids have a guess but nobody really knows. The instructor tells them about different types of soil like sandy soils, clay soils and loamy soils and brings some samples for them to see and touch. Cara goes right in there and feels the different types of soil. Lily is worried that she will get dirty but she is really enjoying gardening and seeing Cara touch the soil encouraged her to join in. The sandy soil feels so smooth and light. It reminds her of last year's summer holiday in North Carolina's Outer Banks where she played on the sand dunes with her brother. Now the instructor tells them that the darker loamy soils are more fertile because they have more organic matter in them, which helps plants grow. 'Did you know that soil is a living system?', he asks. He says that, apart from organic matter, soil also has minerals, moisture and air. All of those things make a good home for plants and animals. The girls are surprised to find out that soil has air in it. That makes them go back to the soil samples and touch the different types of soil again. While they are doing that, the instructor tells them that soil is very good at filtering water. At some point, Lily notices a fresh earthy smell that comes off the soil they watered a few minutes ago. Almost simultaneously Cara says that she really likes how wet soil smells. The instructor overhears the conversation and asks everyone to try and smell the ground. He then asks if anybody knows why wet soil has that fragrant smell, but nobody does.

He tells them that many micro, tiny-tiny, organisms live in soil. They like it when it is damp and warm. As the soil dries out, like now because it is getting hot, the bacteria creates spores in the soil which start 'flying' in the air. It is the spore that makes that earthy smell, not the water. 'Wow, that is amazing!', Lily thinks. Cara tells Lily that she really enjoys weeding and watering plants. Taking care of plants feels like she is their mum. Lily had never thought about gardening in that way before but she thinks that Cara is right. She will ask her mum to buy a plant for her room. Maybe she can have a lily; she would like a plant named after her. She feels confident that she knows how to take good care of a plant now, but she needs to find out more about lilies. She wonders whether lilies are native flowers. She remembers seeing some gardening books for children in the Learning Campus when they first came in. She will have a look at them when they have a break later today. From a theoretical perspective, we can also see that the whole set-up of the programme so far is consistent with sociocultural learning theory and fits the characteristics of an authentic learning environment. The part of the programme we have observed so far involves children in the ordinary activity of gardening, working collaboratively and using the tools gardeners use in their practice, while making the activity relevant to children's worlds, interests and priorities. This process makes children, rather than abstract knowledge, central to their own learning, enabling them to take ownership over their learning. This example of deep learning experience can help children use the knowledge they acquired during this programme and apply it in other contexts.

It is now getting really hot and the sun is very strong. The instructor tells the kids to finish what they are doing, collect all the tools and put them away; it is time to go back indoors and have their snack. Lily and Cara feel thirsty and a bit tired, but happy at the same time. Gardening is hard work but really fun!

Contextualising authenticity

What does authenticity mean for your museum, in relation to objects, events, visitor experiences, exhibition spaces and other designed environments? Do all members of staff (curatorial, conservation, interpretation and learning, digital media) understand authenticity in the same way? Do members of staff involved in the marketing of your museum and its activities understand the important of authenticity as defined by your museum? How can you bridge different understandings of authenticity and go beyond simplistic binary oppositions, such as object vs experience?

How can you create authentic learning environments that are framed by the culture of the domain of practice they represent (e.g., gardening, ecology, medicine, mathematics, history)? How can you involve members of the community whose culture, history, heritage or objects are used in the creation and delivery of an exhibition or a programme? What meanings do objects in your collection have across different cultures and times? Which communities do you need to involve in exploring the multiple meanings of the objects in your collection? What possibilities for creating different narratives do these other meanings objects have afford? How can you represent these narratives in an exhibition?

How can you present tangible or intangible objects from different cultures in a culturally appropriate way? What do you know about how your visitors perceive authenticity in relation to the objects, resources, environments and experiences your museum offers? How does social class, gender, age and ethnicity affect those perceptions? How can you use this knowledge to offer visitors different authentic learning environments? How can authentic learning environments facilitate learning experiences of groups of visitors as well as lone visitors?

Which objects from your collections are likely to trigger strong emotional connections? What meanings can you facilitate through these strong emotional connections to objects? How is this type of object connection different to a content knowledge-based approach?

Notes

1 This scenario was written and contributed entirely by Katherine Johnson – Youth Education Programs Director at the Chicago Botanic. We did only minimal editing/formatting in order to maintain the integrity of the original text.
2 For a discussion of different conceptualisations of authenticity in tourist studies see Yang, L. & Wall, G. (2014). *Planning for ethnic tourism.* Farnham: Ashgate.
3 Using exit surveys at particular exhibitions and/or SI museum exits, the studies were carried out at the American Crafts exhibition at the Renwick Gallery; the Amazonia Habitat & Science Gallery at the National Zoological Park; the Geology, Gems and Minerals, and the Mammals exhibitions at the National Museum of Natural History; the Where Next, Columbus exhibition at the National Air and Space Museum; the Puja: Expressions of Hindu Devotion and the Twelve Centuries of Japanese Art from the Imperial Collection exhibitions at the Arthur M. Sackler Gallery; the National Museum of American Art & the National Portrait Gallery, and the National Museum of American History.
4 This is based on our reading of the theory and methodology of this study as the researchers have not been explicit about its theoretical underpinnings.

5 Term originally used by Rudolf Otto (first published in German in 1917 and translated into English in 1958) to refer to God or deity.
6 The Museum hosts a permanent exhibition of Ötzi, 'the iceman', a mummy from the Neolithic period of a man living in the region more than 5,000 years ago, discovered accidently by two hikers on Ötzal Alps.

References

Adair, B., Filene, B., & Koloski, L. (Eds). (2011). *Letting go? Sharing historical authority in a user-generated world*. Philadelphia, PA: Pew Center for Arts and Heritage.

Alivizatou, M. (2012). Debating heritage authenticity: kastom and development at the Vanuatu Cultural Centre, *International Journal of Heritage Studies*, 18(2), 124–143.

Barber, K. (2013). Shared authority in the context of tribal sovereignty: Building capacity for partnerships with indigenous nations. *The Public Historian*, 35(4), 20–39. doi:10.1525/tph.2013.35.4.20

Barrett, H.C., Laurence, S., & Margolis, E. (2008). Artifacts and original intent: A cross-cultural perspective on the design stance. *Journal of Cognition and Culture*, 8, 1–22.

Bearman, D. & Trant, J. (1998). Authenticity of digital resources: Towards a statement of requirements in the research process. *D-Lib Magazine*. [Accessed online, 26 February 2017: www.dlib.org/dlib/june98/06bearman.html].

Bloom, P. (1996). Intention, history and artifact concepts. *Cognition*, 60, 1–29.

Blud, L. (1990). Social interaction and learning among family groups visiting a museum. *Museum Management and Curatorship*, 9, 43–51.

Borun, M., Chambers, M.B., Dritsas J., & Johnson, J.I. (1997). Enhancing family learning through exhibits, *Curator*, 40(4), 279–295.

Brown, J.S., Collins, A., & Duguid, P. (1989). Situated cognition and the culture of learning. *Educational Researcher*, 18(1), 32–42.

Brida, J.G., Disegna, M, & Osti, L., (2012). Perceptions of authenticity of cultural events: A host-tourist analysis. *Tourism, Culture and Communication*, 12(2), 85–96.

Brida J.G., Disegna M., & Scuderi R. (2013). Visitors of two types of museums: Do expenditure patterns differ? *Tourism Economics*, 19(5), 1027–1047.

Brida, J.G., Disegna, M., & Scuderi, R. (2014). The visitors' perception of authenticity at the museums: Archaeology versus modern art. *Current Issues in Tourism*, 17(6), 518–538.

Bunce, L. (2016). Dead ringer? Visitors' understanding of taxidermy as authentic and educational museum exhibits, *Visitor Studies*, 19(2), 178–192. doi:10.1080/10645578. 2016.1220189

Bunce, L. & Harris, P.L. (2014). Is it real? The development of judgments about authenticity and ontological status. *Cognitive Development*, 32, 110–119. doi:10.1016/j.cogdev.2014.10.001

Byrne, D. (1991). Western hegemony in archaeological heritage management. *History and Anthropology*, 5, 269–276.

Byrne, D. (1995). Buddhist stupa and Thai social practice. *World Archaeology*, 27(2), 266–281.

Cameron, C. & Gatewood, J. (2000). Excursions into the un-remembered past: What people want from visits to historical sites. *The Public Historian*, 22(3), 107–127. doi:10.2307/3379582

Cameron, C.A. & Gatewood, J.B. (2003). Seeking numinous experiences in the unremembered past. *Ethnology*, 42, 55–71.

Carroll, G.R. (2015). Authenticity: Attribution, value, and meaning. In R.A. Scott & M.C. Buchmann (Eds.), *Emerging trends in the social and behavioral sciences: An interdisciplinary, searchable, and linkable resource*. New York: John Wiley & Sons.

Chhabra, D., Healy, R., & Erin S. (2003). Staged authenticity and heritage tourism. *Annals of Tourism Research* 30(3), 702–719.

Chhabra, D. (2005). Defining authenticity and its determinants: Toward an authenticity flow model. *Journal of Travel Research*, 44(1), 64–68.

Conn, S. (2000). *Museums and American intellectual life, 1876–1926*. Chicago, IL: University of Chicago Press, 1998; paperback edition.

Crowley, K. & Callanan, M. (1997). Describing and supporting collaborative scientific thinking in parent–child interactions. *Journal of Museum Education* 23, 12–17.

Csikszentmihalyi, M. & Robinson, R. (1990). *The art of seeing: An interpretation of the aesthetic encounter*. Los Angeles: J. Paul Getty Trust.

Csikszentmihalyi, M. & Rochberg-Halton, E. (1981). *The meaning of things: Domestic symbols and the self*. New York: Cambridge University Press.

Dewey, J. (1934). *Art as experience*. New York: Capricorn Books.

Dewey, J. & Bentley, A.F. (1949). *Knowing and the known*. Boston, MA: Beacon.

Diamond, J. (1986). The behaviour of family groups in science museums. *Curator*, 29(2), 39–154.

Dierking, L.D. (1987). Parent-child interactions in free-choice learning settings: An examination of attention-directing behaviors. *Dissertation Abstracts International*, 49(4), 778A.

Ellenbogen, K. (2002). Museums in family life: An ethnographic case study. In G. Leinhardt, K. Crowley, & K. Knutson (Eds.), *Learning Conversations in Museums* (pp. 81–102). Mahwah, NJ: Lawrence Erlbaum Associates.

Ellenbogen, K., Luke, J., & Dierking, L.D. (2004). Family learning research in museums: An emerging disciplinary matrix? *Science Education*, 88, 48–58.

Evans, M., Mull, M.S., & Poling, D.A. (2002). The authentic object? A child's-eye view. In S.G. Paris (Ed.), *Perspectives on object-centered learning in museums* (pp. 55–77). Mahwah, NJ: Lawrence Erlbaum Associates.

Falk, J. (1991). Analysis of the behavior of family visitors in natural history museums. *Curator*, 34, 44–50.

Frazier, B.N. & Gelman, S.A. (2009). Developmental changes in judgments of authentic objects. *Cognitive Development*, 24, 284–292.

Frazier, B.N., Gelman, S.A., Wilson, A., & Hood, B. (2009). Picasso paintings, moon rocks, and hand-written Beatles lyrics: Adults' evaluations of authentic objects. *Journal of Cognition and Culture*, 9, 1–14.

Gatewood, J.B. & Cameron, C.A. (2004). Battlefield pilgrims at Gettysburg National Military Park. *Ethnology*, 43, 193–216.

Goswamy, R. (1991). Another past, another context: Exhibiting Indian art abroad. In I. Karp & S.D. Lavine (Eds.), *Exhibiting cultures: The poetics and politics of museum display* (pp. 68–78). Washington, DC: Smithsonian Institution Press.

Graburn, N. (1977). The museum and the visitor experience. In L. Draper (Ed.), *The visitor and the museum* (pp. 5–26). Seattle, WA: Museum Educators of the American Association of Museums.

Greenblatt, S. (1991). Resonance and wonder. In I. Karp & S.D. Lavine (Eds.), *Exhibiting cultures: The poetics and politics of museum display* (pp. 42–56). Washington, DC: Smithsonian Institution Press.

Hampp, C. & Schwan, S. (2014). Perception and evaluation of authentic objects: findings from a visitor study. *Museum Management and Curatorship*, 29(4), 349–367.

Harris, P.L. (2013). Fairy tales, history and religion. In M. Taylor (Ed.), *Oxford handbook of the development of imagination*. New York: Oxford University Press.

Hilke, D.D. (1989). The family as a learning system: an observational study of families in museums. In B.H. Butler & M.B. Sussman (Eds.), *Museum visits and activities for family life enrichment* (pp. 101–129). New York: Haworth Press.

Hooper-Greenhill, E. (2000). *Museums and the interpretation of visual culture*. London: Routledge.

ICOMOS (1994). The Nara Document on Authenticity. Available: www.icomos.org/charters/nara-e.pdf [Accessed: 25 February 2017].

Jones, S. (2010). Negotiating authentic objects and authentic selves: beyond the deconstruction of authenticity, *Journal of Material Culture*. 15(12), 181–203.

Jones-Garmil, K. (1997). Laying the foundation: Three decades of computer technology in the museum. In K. Jones-Garmil (Ed.), *The wired museum: Emerging technology and changing paradigms* (pp. 35–62). Arlington, VA: American Association of Museums.

King, L., Stark, J.F., & Cooke, P. (2016). Experiencing the digital world: The cultural value of digital engagement with heritage. *Heritage & Society*, 9(1), 76–101.

Latham, K.F. (2013). Numinous experiences with museum objects. *Visitor Studies* 16(1), 3–20.

Leary, T. & Sholes, E. (2000). Authenticity of place and voice: Examples of industrial heritage preservation and interpretation in the U.S. and Europe. *The Public Historian*, 22(3), 49–66. doi:10.2307/3379578

Li, N. (2010). Preserving urban landscapes as public history: The Chinese context. *The Public Historian*, 32(4), 51–61. doi:10.1525/tph.2010.32.4.51

Lindholm, C. (2007). *Culture and authenticity*. Oxford: Blackwell.

Linhein Muller, K.A. (2013). Crafting the past: theory and practice of museums. *EXARC Journal*, 2013(1), http://journal.exarc.net/issue-2013-1/aoam/crafting-past-theory-and-practice-museums

Lipscomb, S. (2010). Historical authenticity and interpretative strategy at Hampton Court Palace. *The Public Historian*, 32(3), 98–119. doi:10.1525/tph.2010.32.3.98

Lowenthal, D. (1992). Authenticity? The dogma of self-delusion. In M. Jones (Ed.), *Why fakes matter: Essays on the problem of authenticity* (pp. 184–192). London: British Museum Press.

Lowenthal, D. (1995). Changing criteria of authenticity. In K.E. Larsen (Ed.), *NARA conference on authenticity in relation to the World Heritage Convention* (pp. 121–135). Paris: ICOMOS.

Lowenthal, D. (1998). Fabricating heritage, *History and Memory*, 10(1), 5–24.

MacCannell, D. (1973). Staged authenticity. *American Journal of Sociology* 79, 589–603.

MacCannell, D. (1976). *The tourist: A new theory of the leisure class.* New York: Schocken.

Maines, R.P. & Glynn, J.J. (1993). Numinous objects. *The Public Historian*, 15(1), 9–25.

McManus, P. (1987). 'It's the company you keep...: The social determination of learning-related behaviour in a science museum' *The International Journal of Museum Management and Curatorship*, 6, 263–270.

Morison, P. & Gardner, H. (1978). Dragons and dinosaurs: The child's capacity to differentiate fantasy from reality. *Child Development*, 49, 642–648.

Nemeroff, C. & Rozin, P. (2000). The makings of the magical mind. In K.S. Rosengren, C.N. Johnson, & P.L. Harris (Eds.), *Imagining the impossible: Magical, scientific, and religious thinking in children* (pp. 1–34). New York: Cambridge University Press.

Orvell, M. (1989). *The real thing: Imitation and authenticity in American culture. 1880–1940.* Chapel Hill, NC and London: University of North Carolina Press.

Otto, R. (1917/1958). *The idea of the holy: An inquiry into the non-rational factor in the idea of the divine and its relation to the rational* (2nd edition) [J.W. Harvey, Trans.] London: Oxford University Press.

Pekarik, A.J., Doering, Z.D, & Karns, D.A. (1999). Exploring satisfying experiences in museums. *Curator: The Museum Journal*, 42(2), 152–173.

Piaget, J. (1929). *The child's conception of the world.* London: Routledge & Kegan Paul.

Pine, J. II. & Gilmore, J.H. (2007). *Authenticity.* Boston, MA: Harvard Business School Press.

Roberts, L.C. (1997). *From knowledge to narrative: Educators and the changing museum*, Washington, DC: Smithsonian Institution Press.

Rozin, P. & Nemeroff, C. (2002). Sympathetic magical thinking: The contagion and similarity 'heuristics'. In T. Gilovich, D. Griffin, & D. Kahneman (Eds.), *Heuristics and biases: The psychology of intuitive judgment* (pp. 201–216). Cambridge: Cambridge University Press.

Russo, A. (2012). The rise of the 'media museum'. In E. Giaccardi (Ed.), *Heritage and social media: Understanding heritage in a participatory culture* (pp. 145–157). London and New York: Routledge.

Shapin, S. (1996). *The scientific revolution.* Chicago, IL and London: University of Chicago Press.

Sharon, T. & Woolley, J.D. (2004). Do monsters dream? Children's understanding of the fantasy/reality distinction. *British Journal of Developmental Psychology*, 22, 293–310.

Siegel, D. & Callanan, M. (2007). Artifacts as conventional objects. *Journal of Cognition & Development*, 8, 183–203.

Smith, L. (2006). *The uses of heritage*, London and New York: Routledge.

Taylor, B. (2010). 'Reconsidering digital surrogates: Towards a viewer-orientated model of the galley experience'. In S. Dudley (Ed.), *Museum materialities: Objects, engagements, interpretations* (pp. 175–184). London: Routledge.

Tenenbaum, H. & Hohenstein, J.M. (2016). 'Parent-child talk about the origins of living things'. *Journal of Experimental Child Psychology*, 150, 314–329.

Weidinger, T. (2015). Encountering local inhabitants' perspectives in terms of authenticity: The example of rural tourism in Southern Germany. *Dos Algarves: A Multidisciplinary e-Journal*, no. 25. [Accessed on 26 February 2017: www.dosalgarves.com/rev/N25/1rev25.pdf].

Woolley, J.D. (1997). Thinking about fantasy: Are children fundamentally different thinkers and believers from adults? *Child Development*, 68(6), 991–1011.

Woolley, J.D. & Wellman, H.M. (1990). Young children's understanding of realities, nonrealities, and appearances. *Child Development*, 61, 946–961.

7   Remembering, reminding and reminiscing in museums

Build your own bush bark hut[1]

The Australian Garden, set within the Cranbourne Gardens of the Royal Botanic Gardens Victoria in Melbourne, Australia, is an inspiring and immersive contemporary display of the Australian flora, landscapes, art and architecture. Set in fifteen hectares, the Australian Garden design follows a conceptual journey of water from the arid inland landscapes of central Australia, along dry riverbeds and down mighty rivers to the coastal fringes of the continent. Within this striking landscape, display gardens explore the beauty and diversity of Australian plants and the evolving connections between people, plants and place. The Australian Garden is also a place where visitors can discover inspiration and information about how to use Australian plants in their own gardens.

Evaluations of the site indicated that visitors were enjoying the new garden, but also that visitors exploring this new and highly designed landscape might need extra clues as to how to physically explore or inhabit this highly stylised landscape. In particular, families were often missing the furthest Northern Display Gardens – this pointed to the need to animate this area in some way with an activity or displays that might encourage families to explore further and stay a little longer in this area. Garden staff also wanted to work within a seasonal theme to build a temporary outdoor discovery project. They created a space in which families could play together with found material from the garden and surrounding bushland to build their own bark huts. This activity has strong cultural resonance and societal memory in an Australian context relating to both traditional indigenous shelters in this area of Victoria and the early bark slab houses created by Europeans.

The Garden itself is situated in an area in which many new homes are being built each week. This means that the community is literally growing and surrounding the Gardens. As

Figure 7.1 Example of a bush bark hut built by visitors to the Royal
Botanic Gardens. Photo provided courtesy of the Royal
Botanic Gardens Victoria.

a consequence this area has lots of young families with small
children. Engaging these families at the Gardens with nature
play and gardening activities are important objectives aimed at
increasing the plant literacy and eco-citizenry of the Garden's
local community.

The Public Programs branch (the team responsible for
Customer Service, Interpretation and Education) of the institution managed the design and implementation of this project.
They attested that the notion of place-based education (Sobel,
2004) as well as the need to provide children with learning and
developmental opportunities in the natural world served as theoretical background to the design of the project. They also draw
attention to connections between learning opportunities, collective memory and personal memory development.

Some of the outcomes of the project were surprising, even to
the project managers at the Gardens: families needed much less
prompting to build the bark huts than expected; and the ways
in which the huts morphed and were remade each day by different families were unexpected. Perhaps less surprisingly, staff
noticed that parents were discussing the connections between

indigenous and settler structures whilst helping their children participate in the building experiences. Furthermore, parents were sharing their own memories of playing in the bush and the shape of huts they had created as children, sharing tips on how to form hut shapes like they did.

Additionally, at the urging of the family visitors, staff began to promote families taking photos of their creations and sharing them on Instagram. By placing a blackboard sign in the Garden, families were supported in this spontaneous activity with a couple of hashtags that made these images easier to find online. In this way, families helped to create a sense of community in which to build and reinforce their memories of the experience beyond the visit to the Gardens.

Overall, the team felt it was a great activity to run during the nature play season – it certainly ticked the boxes of animating the Northern Display Gardens, engaging the target family audience and creating connections between children and the natural world.

Introduction

When thinking about how memory is relevant to working in a museum environment, it seems there are at least two main reasons museum professionals would want to take memory into account. The first is so that exhibits, programmes and activities can be designed that will both build upon visitors' previous memories but also create experiences that are memorable. After all, for a long time, theoretical perspectives on learning were largely equated with memory for facts (see Falk & Dierking, 1997, for discussion of why this is not helpful). In the example above, the use of photographs to enhance families' experiences of their visits beyond the boundaries of the Royal Botanical Gardens Victoria might be seen as tools for increasing memory in ways that accentuate activities and experiences as cues for concepts, facts and even just the events themselves. There are now ways of investigating the complexities of memory as related to learning that can be used to help people understand what will be remembered and why; some of these are explored in this chapter.

The second reason that memory is a useful concept in museums has to do with the ways that visitors can be reminded of their own relations to history, art and culture through their experiences with the artefacts presented in museums. This sort of perspective has links to studies of memory from a history or material culture point of view. From this perspective, memory can be reified or passed on from one generation to the next through institutional messages; alternatively, institutions may choose to find ways to question collective memory as it is conventionally known (e.g., Witcomb, 2013). As museums undoubtedly convey particular cultural and historical meanings to their visitors (consciously or unconsciously), it is helpful to consider the ways that collective memories can be built and passed on through museum experiences. For instance, conducting formative evaluation to understand how audiences will relate to and react to the messages being developed in an exhibition could be helpful to successfully challenging commonly held views, if that is the intention in a programme or exhibition. The bush bark building activity at the Royal Botanic Gardens Victoria in Australia consciously considered how collective memory of this sort of construction would have an impact on the families' activities.

Traditionally, memory has been thought of, like learning, as something people have. Recent work has sought to challenge this notion and instead proposes that memory is something people do (e.g., Smith, 2006; Wertsch, 2009). In this chapter we first discuss the ways that memory has been theorised to cover the basic elements of psychological memory in addition to ways that research has shown memory processes to operate on an individual or personal basis. Next, we cover some tenets of collective memory, which usually has a sociological foundation but also has some basis in psychological research. We will then turn to research in museums, with some additions from non-museum settings that might be relevant, to discuss how theory about memory can be applied in the museum context. As with the rest of our topic chapters, there will be room towards the end for a return to the opening scenario and contextualising theory and research in practical settings.

Basics of personal constructs of memory

Models of the structure of human memory have not changed significantly for more than forty-five years. Most people who work within the field of memory research tend to agree that there are certain processes for memory and various types of memory. In this section, we outline Atkinson and Shiffrin's (1968) highly influential model of memory storage in addition to several important distinctions in types of memory that have been proposed to provide a backdrop to memory research in practical settings. Whilst this model remains powerful in terms of the architecture of memory, where disagreement occurs is in formulations about how different types of memory relate to one another and the processes that can be invoked to improve one's remembering capabilities. There has been adjustment to the relative size of the role of social and situational influences that have been applied to the study of memory. Whereas in previous decades the emphasis was primarily on the individual, current studies often give greater credence and acknowledgement to

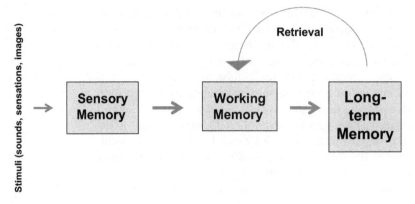

Figure 7.2 Model of memory storage (adapted from Atkinson & Shiffrin, 1968).

situated memory, influenced by social circumstances, as well as dialogue and conversation (covered in Chapter 5).

The foundational model to do with how memory works comes from Atkinson and Shiffrin (1968). This model (pictured in Figure 7.2) proposes that information about the world first enters the mind through the largely unconscious (or preconscious) process, sensory memory. This type of memory takes in information in an 'unfiltered' way, not discriminating for any particular type of information. Prior to reading this sentence, you may or may not have been aware of the feeling of the seat against your legs underneath you (or the air coming into your lungs, or the cars driving by outside). Nonetheless, your body was taking all of that information in. Any sensory information that is not deemed useful is not processed any further and as such, only lasts up to one second in duration. However, information that is useful attracts conscious attention and moves to short-term or working memory. Here is where the main work of 'thinking' happens. People are able to keep information in the working memory store by focusing attention through a variety of mechanisms, including rehearsal (repetition of information, verbally or otherwise). Working memory is known to be able to store 7 ± 2 pieces of information at any one time (Miller, 1956). That is, the average person is able to keep between five and nine items in memory at once. And without rehearsal, it will decay within about thirty seconds. From working memory, when information is processed meaningfully, it is likely to be passed to long-term memory, which is what matches most closely to what the everyday term 'memory' refers to. This is where people store memories that can be held for a relatively short time (a few minutes) up to a lifetime.

There are also some useful distinctions made to the mechanisms for storage in long-term memory (LTM). Most broadly, LTM can be divided into declarative and non-declarative.

Non-declarative memory is often thought of as implicit (Squire, 1992). This is a somewhat misleading name because though the name 'implicit' suggests that it is unavailable (unconscious) to the learner, most of what it consists of can be brought to awareness. However, what is placed in non-declarative memory stores are primarily things that people are not conscious of. Major categories of non-declarative memory include procedural memory (i.e., knowing how to carry out a skill like ride a bicycle), and emotional memory, namely, emotions attached in an unreflective way to events and information (e.g., an association between the smell of Mexican food and joy). This phenomenon of non-declarative memory may sound a lot like a potentially more familiar reference to involuntary memory, made by Proust (1983), in which a bite into a tea-soaked madeleine brought back a childhood memory in incredible vividness of imagery and emotion. This example of non-declarative memory shows the ways that memories can be triggered non-cognitively and usually lack conscious control.

The type of memory that educators typically try to influence is called declarative memory, which can be broken down into semantic (stuff that is known generally, e.g., 'The capital of the United Kingdom is London') and episodic (memory relevant to particular events, like 'the first time I went to London it was raining') (Tulving, 1972). It is often suggested (e.g., Clark & Paivio, 1991) that semantic memory is more valued than episodic memory in educational contexts because semantic memory tends to be shared by societies and communities, (i.e., it consists of 'facts' as opposed to idiosyncratic knowledge). As will be discussed below, it may be the case that episodic memory can be *converted* to semantic memory over time in a process called 'semantic shift', a process we will return to later. A pictorial model for LTM can be seen in Figure 7.3.

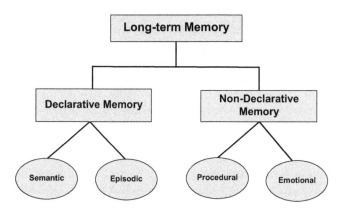

Figure 7.3 A graphic model of long-term memory storage.

Some studies have suggested that the area of the brain that is most responsible for memory is the hippocampus (Skinner & Fernandes, 2007). Some research also indicates that this region is activated in both familiarity and recollection exercises, depending upon the strength of the memory (Smith, Wixted, & Squire, 2011), suggesting that these are potentially related processes even if recognising and recalling involve slightly different cognitive skills.

A visitor's prior knowledge is surely something that is stored in LTM. The way that prior knowledge interacts with current experiences has proven to be something of a mystery. That is, there are differences of opinion as to the extent to which a person's prior knowledge acts as a facilitator or a hindrance for future learning (Roschelle, 1995). By most accounts, without prior experience or knowledge, it will be impossible to develop more sophisticated understandings (Driver, Asoko, Leach, Mortimer, & Scott, 1994; Piaget, 1970). One cannot teach a toddler about particle physics. In contrast, many accounts suggest that prior knowledge can get in the way of understanding in a more advanced way (Sinatra, Heddy, & Lombardi, 2015; Vosniadou & Brewer, 1992). It may even be the case that some types of knowledge are not attainable because of conflicts between different cultural beliefs. For example, certain religious beliefs suggest that beliefs about the evolution of life forms are myths – the two belief systems are incompatible. If prior knowledge is both necessary and problematic, how can learning occur at all? The answer is bound to lie in the gradual nature of learning. Whereas there are some instances, deemed 'aha moments', that seem to indicate a learner has suddenly dawned upon a new way of thinking, most of the time people do not come to new ideas in an abrupt way (Brown, Collins, & Duguid, 1989). As Roschelle (1995) has advocated, it may be more useful to think about altering or adjusting prior knowledge, rather than replacing it. Some pedagogical models based on constructivism as a theory of learning are founded upon the idea that the learner's prior experience is key for the basis of future learning. For example, with inquiry-based learning (e.g., Papert, 1980), the educator tries to facilitate learning by helping the learner to come up with questions that can be addressed by working from learners' current knowledge base, helping them to formulate new constructs. Additionally, some problem-based learning ideas, popular in some classroom teaching, in which pupils work toward a goal and in doing so must make use of a variety of learning concepts and tools, utilise learners' own initiatives for projects to help them to go from current understandings to build new ones (Hmelo-Silver, 2004). Drawing on constructivist notions of learning, the agentive nature of these activities forces learners to pay attention in order to make sense of the ideas, which helps them to retain the concepts in LTM. The bush bark building activity could be facilitating memory through its encouragement of problem-solving and active, hands-on experience.

It is important to point out that memory is a construction and is never an exact replica of real occurrences, both in terms of episodic and semantic memory (Fischbach & Coyle, 1997); and this applies equally to personal memory as to collective memory (Schacter, 1997). As such, it is important to consider relationships between how memory is construed in preparation of exhibits and programmes, but also in terms of what individuals are likely to remember from prior experiences and the ones they have whilst visiting a museum. In the example above from the Royal Botanic Gardens Victoria, the team there note that they often try to evoke memories in their visitors through sensory stimulation and hands-on activities. The parents' memories of their childhood experiences are no doubt recalled through the smells, sensations and the kinaesthetic experience of building the huts. Studies have drawn upon various aspects of memory when investigating what people remember about their visits to museums and how such memories are instrumental in their motivation to visit again (or not), and whether they help to learn about the exhibited material.

Basics of constructs about collective memory

The idea behind collective memory is that communities share a history that helps to form their identity. Such communities might consist of just a few individuals (e.g., a nuclear family or a school class). Alternatively, a community might be made up of thousands, or even millions, of people with shared backgrounds and narratives (e.g., members of a large museum, even if they do not see themselves that way, or citizens of a particular country). Some of the concepts that the theories about collaborative remembering will grapple with include the ways that thoughts are passed from one set of individuals to another, or how events become memorialised in the eyes of residents. Museums need to take the constructs associated with collective memory into account because they are related to the ways exhibits, galleries and whole museums are presented to the public, and how the public interpret them. Importantly, as emphasised by Smith (2006), it is not just the positive things from a community that need remembering. What gets remembered is no doubt a result of the power hierarchies in a group as well as the broad cultural trends at a particular time (see Chapter 10 for a more in-depth discussion of these issues). It seems natural that some museum environments, such as the heritage industry, might tend to portray collective memory in a rosy light. However,

UNIVERSITY OF WINCHESTER LIBRARY

various conflicting versions of memory undoubtedly exist and within museum dialogues 'there is a greater sense of active negotiation occurring over the values, meanings, and ideologies represented in the links individuals and groups establish with the past, and the sense of continuity and identity that is drawn from those links' (Smith, 2006, p. 63). This sense of negotiation is surely present in the ongoing, everyday work that museum staff engage in, bringing with them their own conscious and unconscious collective memories to the constructions of events, exhibitions, activities.

As Wertsch (2009) has pointed out, collective memory is usually studied in natural environments, taking into account the types of interactions various community members engage in leading to particular accounts of memory. Through this process, the accuracy of memory is less important than it might be in the study of individual memory. Wertsch suggests that cultures identify with largely implicit sets of stories that make up a community's histories. For example, the thoughts and feelings various people visiting the Botanic Garden in Victoria might have towards bush bark huts stem from what they know already based on the attitudes and ideas about the people who used those huts originally, either indigenous or colonisers. Such narratives can send powerful, yet unvoiced messages about how members of a group interpret future events as well as remember events from the past. In this way, collective memory forms on the basis of cultural tools, such as narrative (e.g., Bruner, 1990) and calendars or art (e.g., Connerton, 1989), or other traditions associated with memory (Zerubavel, 1996). According to Zerubavel (1996), there are implicit rules about what gets remembered, which leave some communities 'forgotten' while others are seen as victors whose histories are remembered. That is, communities have unspoken ways of 'knowing' what becomes memorialised over time. Examples of this include the 'discoveries' of places, like the American continent, which was inhabited long before Christopher Columbus ever arrived, though many history books and cultural practices in the United States have traditionally treated his arrival as the start of history there.

Connerton (1989) notes that what gets remembered or commemorated can often be traced to the formation of habit in a ritualisation of action that takes place in social situations. For example, some rituals like certain Christian communities greeting each other by saying 'God be with you' is now commemorated by our use of words like 'Goodbye' in situations in which individuals part company. Such habits are passed on from one generation to another, often without explicit reference to where they derive from or even that they exist. It is these sorts of implicit practices that become embedded in the minds

of individuals as a collective memory, leading to shared understandings about expectations and history.

How do events in the world become memorialised as important? In their chapter on memorialisation, Pennebaker and
Gonzales (2009) have suggested that it has a lot to do with the
attitudes a community has to the nature of the event and the
age at which people tend to be affected by major events. They
draw on examples and research that illustrate that, particularly
for events that have negative connotations towards a community, there is often a lapse of time of about twenty-five years
before memorialisation occurs. For example, though there were
memorials soon after John F. Kennedy was assassinated in the
rest of the United States, none was created in Dallas, the place
of his murder, until much later. Similarly, Memphis, Tennessee
did not dedicate a memorial to Martin Luther King for many
years after his death, even though many other cities did so right
away; coincidentally (or not), Memphis was the city in which
King was assassinated. In contrast, rates of violent crime and
high blood pressure went up in each of those locations, relative
to the rest of the country, in the year after the assassinations.
This suggests that these communities were struggling with the
knowledge that they were somehow related to these negative
incidents in US history (Pennebaker & Gonzales, 2009).

In addition, Pennebaker and Gonzales (2009) note the
twenty- to thirty-year gap between major events and other
forms of 'retelling', including major motion pictures. This
might be attributable to the cohort effect (Conway, 1990)
whereby events that are memorialised by a community tend to
affect those between the ages of thirteen and twenty-five at the
time of their occurrence the most. This group may be affected
more than other groups due to the period of identity formation
coinciding with such an event (Erikson, 1950). The reasoning
then behind the long delay in commemoration could be related
to the relative lack of power young people have (those who are
13–25 at the time of an event) compared with those who tend
to have more power and resources with which to create ways
of memorialising events (middle-aged adults; Pennebaker &
Gonzales, 2009). Taken together, these suggestions would predict that the set-up and maintenance of museum programmes
and exhibitions might also be affected by the way the community has reacted to events and the age of those involved in
putting forward the ideas. As an example, in 2004 a memorial museum for the Killing Fields in Cambodia was opened
by a survivor of this period in Seattle, Washington, USA, some
twenty-five years after the atrocities in Southeast Asia. One
possibility for thinking about dealing with more contemporary
events in museums would be to work with the age groups who
would tend to be more affected at the time of the event, though

specific museum-based research has not seemed to address the effectiveness of this tactic thus far.

One of the more recently proposed perspectives on learning that is relevant to collective memory is that of place-based education (PBE, Greunewald, 2003; Sobel, 2004). PBE advocates motivating pupils to engage with the local environment while participating in learning that is experiential in nature (Dewey, 1938). As such, PBE tends to appear in educational settings that utilise real-life problems situated in real communities that pupils can help to solve. Until recently, PBE tended to be concerned with projects that were more relevant to rural education. However, consistent with the suggestions of Greunewald (2003) that critical pedagogy (also addressed in Chapter 10), which appears more frequently in urban environments and PBE have a great deal in common, some PBE projects have also appeared in cities. Important to the principles of PBE is the notion of place. A connection to place affords a relevance of local projects, which creates a sense of urgency, leading to the solving of local problems. For example, students might create a project based around water quality in the local river and find that it has high levels of contaminants, which leads them to seek out means to inform local businesses and involve them in coming up with ways to clean up the river. Such connections to place might also tie in nicely to projects associated with history of place as evident in the example from the Botanical Gardens at the start of this chapter in which the connection to hut building constructions takes on a very local significance. In other words, the ways that people feel about the local community and the collective memories associated with it can help to create a need to be active citizens, becoming involved in ways to improve the community.

Altogether then, the study of collective memory considers what is remembered by a community of any size (e.g., family, neighbourhood, nation), placing emphasis on the types of information that gets passed down from one generation to the next and the mechanisms involved in remembering as a group. In what follows we examine what research has to say about personal and collective remembering in museum contexts.

Museums and memory studies

In this section we draw attention to studies that are relevant to learning in museums as related to memory. In some cases it is clear that visitor memories of past events and understandings can be utilised to build connections to new (or nostalgic) objects or activities. At other times, the ways that memories have been shown to develop as a result of museum experiences will be brought to bear.

Personal narratives as links to museum content

Of course, visitors bring memories with them to museums. Importantly, there is little research that explicitly addresses the way personal memories interact with visitors' experiences in museums. However, some studies (e.g., Smith, 2014) have shown that one of the benefits visitors may have is the ability to commemorate one's own connections to the issues involved in an exhibition, sometimes even reinforcing ideals and values from one's past experiences. Rowe, Wertsch and Kosyaeva (2002) note that visitors' personal narratives can be linked to those of a larger group in places such as history museum settings. However, even in other types of museums, people's memories and previous experiences can be helpful in relating to the museum's activities. Afonso and Gilbert (2006) examined whether visitors used their own memories to help make sense of scientific topics at exhibits. They asked adult visitors to an interactive science centre to say what exhibits reminded them of. Quite often visitors recalled episodic and semantic memories associated with the topic of the exhibit. Many times these memories were not linked to understanding the exhibit itself, but instead were related to an interest in the exhibit. For example, people remarked on the ways that the physical science topics of the exhibits related to things experienced by their friends or family, such as noting the way that sperm whales communicate could be linked with the way that their own young children learn language, but seldom connected their memories to explanations of the science underpinning the exhibits. As such, it is likely that visitors are constantly inserting their own narratives for purposes of interpreting the material they are encountering at the museum, even if those memories are used more in the interest of affective as opposed to cognitive learning.

> Visitors more often associate exhibits with emotionally related compared with content-related memories

Episodic memory creation

Much of what occurs in terms of memory creation will take the form of episodic memories. Several studies have shown that people tend to remember the event of visiting the museum more than they might the actual content (e.g., Anderson, 2003; Falk & Dierking, 1997). An early study of the way people remember museum exhibits investigated how child and adult visitors at Launch Pad, an interactive science gallery at the Science Museum, London, recalled information about the exhibits after a period of six months (Stevenson, 1991). A fair proportion of exhibits were spontaneously recalled in elaborate detail (24%) and a further 24% were recalled in detail after being prompted by a photograph or another person. A photographic prompt of the exhibit elicited a mention (e.g., 'I remember that one') of an

> Content of museum exhibits appears to be memorable, at least when visitors are asked to recall

additional 27% of the exhibits. So altogether, visitors tended to recall a majority of the exhibits present. Similarly, McManus (1993) found that half of all of the memories provided in her self-report recollection study were about the objects that were seen on a museum visit. In contrast, Anderson (2003), in his study on very long-term memories (30 years) from the World Exposition, found that visitors tended to remember things that were important to them at the time: young children remembered the trip to McDonald's, adolescents, the opportunity for social activity and mothers remembered the availability of changing facilities. His study pointed out that those who remembered the content best were enthusiasts of topics the particular exhibits were about. These findings speak to the idea that the working memory encoded the events according to what the visitors tended to focus on at the time, which then remained in long-term memory for a sustained period. Falk and Dierking (1990) noted that adults subsequently remembered more detail about their visits if they were infrequent museum visitors as children, compared with those who visited more often. This type of finding is consistent with the idea that the more distinctive an event is, the more likely it will be retained in long-term memory.

Interest is related to long-term memory formation

Distinctiveness has been suggested to be an important factor in the creation of new memories, particularly those that are autobiographical (some episodic memories are purely about the self and as such, can be considered a special form of episodic memory) in nature. Distinctiveness, or the level at which something can be thought of as different from the normal, seems to provide something an individual can use to store and retain memories for later recollection (Hunt, 2006). When something is unusual, it becomes more memorable because it stands out from the typical experience. The commute during which one observes an accident in the road is likely to be better remembered than the one in which one merely passes along the route without incident. This heightened memorability is available in both adults (Hunt, 2006) and in children (Howe, 2006) and has been shown in several domains like memory for words (e.g., Schmidt, 1985), as well as less tangible memories like smell (Herz, 1997). Perhaps it would be natural then, to conjecture that for those who have not visited museums before, the first time they go is likely to be remembered rather well, given its distinctiveness; comparatively, if one is a regular museum visitor, any one visit may not be easily recalled.

Unusual experiences can lead to better retention because the event 'stands out' in memory

As has been discussed more thoroughly in the chapter on authenticity (Chapter 6), the idea of numinous experiences (Gatewood & Cameron, 2004; Latham, 2013) can also be associated with the distinctiveness of a memory. An example might be an up-close view of a dinosaur's skeleton, or that of a blue whale, which can give the visitor a sense of awe at the size and/or age of the animal. Here the recognition that one is encountering an object that has special significance leads to a sense of wonder and near spiritual connection to history or the world more broadly. These types of occurrence are probably relatively rare and seem to be elusive or difficult to predict. However, when such impressive exhibits in museums inspire an experience that has these qualities of numinousness, they may facilitate further reflection, leading to enhanced episodic and semantic memory.

Some would suggest that the distinctiveness is increased when the material to be remembered is autobiographical or at least self-generated (e.g., Howe, 2006; Pathman, Samson, Dugas, Cabeza & Bauer, 2011; Schacter, Gutchess, & Kensinger, 2009; St. Jacques & Schacter, 2013). That is, when people have come up with the information or episodes themselves, they are more likely to accurately recall it later. For instance, compared with pictures of exhibits they had visited but not photographed themselves, museum visitors (children and adults) were better able to identify photographs of exhibits they had taken themselves (Pathman et al., 2011). Such results might have implications for whether museums decide to allow visitors to photograph the exhibits on display: research suggests taking their own photographs would allow visitors to retain content better in comparison to viewing similar photographs later. A fair amount of neurological evidence has supported the idea that an individual's memory for material that is self-generated is stored separately to information that is not obtained in this way. This research suggests that a region known as the medial pre-frontal cortex is activated when people encode and recall material that was self-generated (MacRae, Moran, Heatherton, Banfield, & Kelly, 2004).

> Self-generated information may help the distinctiveness of memories, leading to better retention

Semantic shift

It is perhaps understandable that visitors would develop episodic memories as a result of a trip to a museum. It might be hoped that people would also develop greater semantic knowledge or conceptual developments as a result of such trips. In this way, museums might be able to show what is sometimes thought of as 'real' learning (i.e., cognitive and fact-based), stemming from museum engagement. This sort of memory will be particularly difficult to show evidence for, as research will not be able to easily tell what a visitor knows already when entering the museum, and will find it hard to measure using a post-test what information is acquired (see Chapter 3 for more detail). In addition, the short period of time in which a visit to a museum occurs can make it difficult to do more than acquire episodic memories. The suggestion is that in order for semantic memory to be created, reinforcement of the learning taking place at museums would be required (Afonso & Gilbert, 2006; Stevenson, 1991). On the other hand, experiences that create rich episodic memories may be retained and converted into semantic memories later (Herbert & Burt, 2004). In a university setting, Herbert and Burt exposed students to information about statistics that was either rich in detail, or did not include much detail. Those who participated in the rich detail group had higher recall of the experience immediately and better knowledge of the statistical principles five weeks afterwards. As such, the richness appears to have contributed to both the creation of episodic memories and the shift to semantic knowledge as opposed to merely episodic information. Afonso and Gilbert (2006) suggest as an implication of their study of science centre visitors that episodic rich experiences with exhibits can potentially lead to greater interest in a topic. This would imply that those experiences would need to lead to either emotionally positive episodic memories, or at least ones that inspired further action on the part of the visitor (e.g., an exhibit that elicited anger about the state of the environment might be a negative memory that could spark interest in environmental activism).

Greater detail in episodic memories may help a shift to semantic memory

There is other evidence about the way that episodic memories can be converted into semantic knowledge. Adelman, Falk and James (2000) investigated visitor understanding following a visit to the National Aquarium in Baltimore, a museum devoted to the local area's conservation with a mission to help visitors become more aware of the pressing need to preserve the natural environment. Adelman et al. found that up to six weeks after the visit participants were better able to articulate some of the ideas conveyed in the museum compared with just after their visit. Participants also espoused positive attitudes towards conservation and had gained awareness of the local conservation issues. In contrast, there was little evidence that this knowledge of the need to conserve had transformed itself into new actions to conserve. As such, the place-based messages in the institution were successful in that visitors appeared to gain knowledge. However, assuming that one visit can make a difference to people who were already relatively aware of conservation issues, it may have been that six weeks was not enough time after the visit to see any change in behaviour as a result of a visit.

Some episodic memories from museum visits can appear to shift to semantic memories, but possibly not immediately following the visit

Emotion and the construction of long-term memory

Studies have often demonstrated that visitors to museums remember emotion associated with their visits (e.g., Falk & Dierking, 1990). David Anderson (2003) has suggested that there is a reciprocal relationship between affect or interest and memory. In other words, the things that interested a visitor were those that were remembered best; and the memorable experiences tended to reinforce previously held interests and affects towards the material on display at the World Expo. More theoretical and research information about interest can be found in Chapter 4. These findings are consistent with the idea that experiences that are encoded with positive or negative affect are better remembered than those which are more neutral in emotion (Reisberg & Heuer, 2004).

Anderson and Shimizu (2007) have analysed factors that seem to influence the vividness of visitors' long-term memory of the 1970 World Expo in Japan. In terms of vividness, memories were considered to be more vivid when they were recalled with more rich description and more passionate appearing body language and tone. They noted that memories that were encoded as either highly negative or highly positive had the greatest amount of vividness associated with them. Memories that were neutral in terms of affect were less vividly recalled. A similar pattern was also reported with respect to agenda fulfilment. In other words, events seemed to be recalled with more vividness when they had either been extremely positive or negative in terms of obtaining the intended objectives of the visit or the affective experience, rather than when there was nothing unusual with respect to affect or agenda. Note that affect and agenda can often coincide: upset agendas may be highly related to negative affect. These ideas are consistent with the idea discussed above that distinctiveness is related to greater memory retention.

> Both positive and negative emotions can lead to vivid memories, which are better recalled after a very long time

In addition to its effects on personal memory, the ways that emotion interacts with collective memory can be important in the preparation and presentation of exhibitions and galleries in museums. Crowshaw (2007) calls attention to the ways that photography can be used to focus visitor emotion on the horror of the Holocaust in World War II. He notes that in this case, pictures of the events may promote the intergenerational memorialisation of the terror of those who lived through the experiences. Similarly, Evans (2013) explores the use of theatrical presentation of history to engage visitors in an interactive experience to question the canonical memories of the portrayal of historical personage. By eliciting emotional reactions in the participants, it may be possible to enter into further dialogue about the nature of collective memories of historical events. The literature on collective memory in museums tends to centre on historically focused institutions; however, as with the Adelman et al. (2000) article cited above, a museum may utilise or be affected by the collective memory associated with the objects it displays and the programmes it organises in such a way as to help visitors turn episodic memories into semantic ones.

> Emotion can act as a catalyst for effective museum installations

Memory and connections to other knowledge

As indicated previously, memories from visits to museums are likely to be episodic in nature. The likelihood of creating a semantic memory is increased when experiences are connected to other memories or knowledge (Adelman et al., 2000; Ellenbogen, 2002; Falk, Scott, Dierking, Rennie, & Jones, 2004). As Anderson, Piscitelli, Weier, Everett and Tayler (2002) have stressed, museum environments that help children to identify with the objects and activities through a sense of their own cultures and contexts will be better remembered compared with those that are more abstract. In their study of several types of museums in Australia, Anderson and colleagues followed children's schools over their repeated trips to a single museum. The four- to six-year-olds in their study were observed and interviewed and readily recalled exhibits and concepts that were conveyed using stories or theatre. The researchers noticed that children identified fewer conceptual memories in the science and art museums compared with the natural history and social history museums. They conjectured that compared with the former, the latter contained a greater number of objects that were familiar to the children and could be connected to their experiences with books, toys and other experiences.

Follow-up conversation also has been shown to lead to memory for museum experiences. There are a number of reasons for this. Saying something aloud or explaining to someone else can act as a form of rehearsal of events and so reinforces the experience of the museum itself (Chi, De Leew, Chiu, & Levancher, 1994). In addition, the conversation may draw attention to ideas or ways of synthesis that were not considered during the visit to the museum itself. Visits that spark conversations have indeed been shown to be more memorable (Stevenson, 1991; Medved & Oatley, 2000). This is consistent with the previously reported results on the long-view with respect to learning (Brown et al., 1989). As such, encouraging visitors to engage with their websites after a visit may help reinforce the episodic memories and perhaps convert those memories to semantic ones.

It is also important to recognise the bi-directional nature of the constitution of memory and other factors. As was noted above, events that are more affectively charged have been shown to be better remembered; and memory, motivation and affect are mutually reinforcing (Anderson & Shimizu, 2007; Medved & Oatley, 2000; Spock, 2000). In other words, memories are enhanced through affect and motivation, but motivation and affect are in turn facilitated through memory. Furthermore, these circular connections are likely to be sustained through experiences outside the museum, such as conversation with others, thinking about the exhibits or even changing one's

---

Marginal notes:

Concretising concepts through connections to local culture or context may help visitors, at least young children, to recall information

Content from visits that inspire follow-up conversations may be more memorable

behaviour as a result of the museum encounter (Medved & Oatley, 2000). Thus, in thinking about the Botanical Gardens example above, the creation of photographs of visitor bush bark huts that can be shared online forms a means of revisiting the experience through networks, conversation, emotion and reflection on the connections people have with their heritage and the local environment.

Another useful way of considering the relation between memory and museum experience is to examine whether memories are, in fact, helpful in promoting learning from the exhibits. As noted above, Afonso and Gilbert showed that in their visit to the science centre visitors were reminded of a variety of unrelated experiences. These were often useful in terms of the affective enhancement of the visit. However, the study also suggested that memories that linked exhibits with visitor knowledge in only a superficial way (as in by means of what something looks or sounds like or what it does) might actually obstruct the development of understanding of the scientific phenomena that were presented in the exhibition. In their study, when visitors made an analogical link (which is seen to show a deep connection between how two systems work) between previous experience or knowledge and the exhibits, they were more likely to display understanding of the scientific ideas than if they merely made superficial connections. For example, in one instance a visitor connected the memory of a record player to an explanation of how a tape-recording might work. In this case, the connections between the functions of the tape recorder and the record player hindered the ability to correctly understand the mechanics of a tape recorder.

> Deep connections in memories to personal experiences inspire better understandings of the exhibits than do surface connections

Memory retrieval

As has already been described, it can be difficult to estimate just what is recalled from a museum visit. It is nearly impossible to accurately conduct a pre-post visit enquiry into what people 'know' about an exhibition's topic because of the nature of museum visitation and the nature of what people know. That is, it can be extremely difficult to tap into what a potential visitor knows about a topic because there are bound to be pieces of information that are important to their knowledge that either researchers do not think to ask about or that the visitor does not realise is important. As such, visitors may know a great deal more than what they are able to say at the time of a questionnaire or interview. However, it may be useful to take into consideration the ways that memory can be called upon by the visitor. In a now classic study of children's memories of a museum visit from their US kindergarten school trip, Hudson and Fivush (1991) explored the ways that memories of the trip

> Although memory for a visit decreases over time, cues can serve to help recall even several years later

were affected by the lapse of time. Interestingly, there is little evidence that the ability to recall accurately from LTM changes very much with age, particularly for episodic memories, though working memory capacity may grow over time (Demetriou, Christou, Spanoudis, & Platsidou, 2002). Whilst people get better at organising information so that it can be recalled later in semantic memory situations (like exams), the long-term memory capacity seems to change little. Hudson and Fivush interviewed pupils on the same day as a school trip, six weeks later, one year later and six years later. When asked what they were able to remember from their trip to the Jewish museum, children in the same day and six weeks post-visit interviews were generally able to recall a great deal, with children remembering less one year and six years later. However, when they were prompted with clues about one of the activities they undertook (playing in the sandbox) and photographs from the venue, their ability to recollect experiences at the museum increased dramatically. These findings are reminiscent of those from Stevenson's (1991) study, but the period of recollection is longer and the children younger. Even six years later, children were able to provide details about the visit to the museum from their kindergarten experience. Such evidence indicates that there may be ways to trigger memories of a museum experience, even large spans of time after the fact. Even so, the types of things that these children did recall were those that might be seen as 'less typical' of a museum visit (e.g., making artefacts, using archaeological tools), which is consistent with the idea of distinctiveness discussed earlier (e.g., Howe, 2006). Here the bush bark hut-making experience in the example from the Botanical Gardens may form the basis of a distinctive activity that becomes highly memorable. Combined with the conversational reinforcement from their parents, encouragement to take photos, post them online, and revisit the experience, these types of activities are likely to be encoded in memory more than activities that do not share these elements of distinctiveness and revisitation.

At the same time, there is also potential for the distortion of memory when attempting to facilitate recollection of a museum visit. A great deal has been made of false memories and their occurrence (or not) in cases of child abuse (see Goodman et al., 2003). However, given that memory is itself an amorphous and flexible phenomenon, it may be that sometimes 'normal' events are mis-remembered or distorted in memory. A case in point appears in the work of St. Jacques and Schacter (2013). Participants in this study wore cameras during a visit to a natural history museum and then two days later were given a 'reactivation experience' in which they were shown slide shows of photos from the exhibits at the museum, either their own photos (perspective match) or photos of the same locations taken

Memories can be easily 'falsified' in some people

from a different angle (perspective mismatch). Two days subsequent to reactivation participants were asked to judge photos to see whether their memories of the events were affected by the reactivation experience (match or mismatch). The test photographs showed (1) sites that were experienced by the visitors (target) or (2) sites that were not experienced (lure). They were also asked to indicate to what extent the slideshow caused them to 'relive' their museum experience. For those who had a high rating for reliving their museum experience, the reactivation mismatch tended to cause them to misremember lure photographs as sites they had been to; this was less true for people who did not report a high reliving experience in the slideshow. As a result, St. Jacques and Schacter suggest, 'reactivation can selectively affect subsequent retrieval of individual memories, and that such reactivation may consequently enhance and distort later memory' (p. 542). That is, the way questions are asked about previous experiences may in fact change the ways that people are able to recall those experiences.

A return to the bush bark huts

Let us now imagine what might happen when a family of five, two parents (Sandy, an engineer and Pat, a primary school teacher) in their thirties, their young children, Sam (eight) and Jo (six), with a grandparent (Emily), come to visit the bush bark hut building activity in the Royal Botanic Gardens. Like many of the visitors, they are a young family who live locally. They belong to the nearby community and visit the Gardens occasionally. Sam has also been on a visit with classmates on a school trip.

Upon entering the new area of the Gardens, Sam remarks about not remembering this part of the Gardens from the last visit. Indeed, none of the family members had been here before. They look at the examples, the pictures and the materials to learn a bit about what is expected in this area. Once they realise they should get involved and create a hut themselves, the children get excited and begin sorting through the wooden materials. The children, themselves, have no memory of the huts. However, their parents and Emily all have some memory of such huts, either through previous building experiences, or through reading about them in school. At the same time, both children bring experiences of building smaller constructions (with toys and found objects) with them to the site. While the members of the party have different memories that are relevant to the huts, none of them is a blank slate, consistent with most models of personal memory (e.g., constructivism, information processing).

As the children start putting pieces of bark together, Sandy is helping to create a stable construction, drawing upon stored declarative memories about how stable structures are formed, but also probably pulling out particular episodic memories from when building something similar in the past. Meanwhile, Emily and Pat find that this project is allowing them to recall memories from their long-term memory banks; and they begin to discuss a time that they built a similar hut when Pat was a bit older than Sam. Emily can remember a time when the sight of these types of huts was more common near towns and cities. Pat, Sandy, and Emily all carry with them slightly different attitudes towards the huts, which have historical significance for the area, as might be expected with such differing experiences. Each of them is affected by a collective memory about the way this type of hut was used by the people in the area, both indigenous and settler. The connotations these types of huts carry perhaps vary between generations. Older generations may tend to see them as a sign of a past that included lower levels of technology, was simpler and perhaps more dangerous. Pat, however, may feel they symbolise the way that indigenous peoples were oppressed by the settlers to Australia. Despite this somewhat negative opinion, Pat has positive emotional connections to past experiences of building the huts. That is, sometimes the personal and the collective memories conflict; and there is nothing a museum practitioner can do to avoid that. However, anticipating such conflicts could make an experience like this at the Gardens more pleasant for all members of the party.

For Sam, this experience becomes potentially distinctive because later that day the family goes out to purchase a tent for an upcoming camping trip. Tents are obviously quite different to the huts, particularly in material, but sometimes have a similar shape and function to the huts. This is Sam's first experience of tents and so is likely to form an association between the bush bark hut activity and tents. Despite being relatively young, Sam may be able to look back at this experience and have things brought to light by things that trigger the memory, such as pictures of bush bark huts or a new encounter with the bush bark material, or even future experiences with tents.

As they leave, the family notices that there is an Instagram tag for this activity. In the car on the way home, the children go on to upload pictures of their huts and begin to view pictures of huts posted by other families. Some have different constructions, less stable than their own or taller. Sandy is able to help provide explanations about the way different structures will withstand (or not) various climates and weather circumstances. As they drive, their conversation revisits the huts they saw in pictures and the history of the area, with Emily able to contribute further information from her memories as a girl in the region. This sort of collaborative reminiscing about their experience will probably help each person rework the experiences of the day in their working memory, to create a relatively stable episodic memory in LTM. At the same time, the pieces of information about the historical context provided by the signs at the Gardens, and reinforced by Emily and Pat, may pass through the semantic shift and help form semantic memory, facts and concepts, about the way people used the huts, both historically and in contemporary times.

Contextualising memory

In what ways can visitors to your museum be encouraged to create memory-aiding devices such as conversations, references to photographs, websites and social media? Will the age of the visitor make a difference to what type of device would be most helpful? Would the use of multiple devices create more opportunities for remembering the experiences they have had? Are there spatial arrangements in the museum that might facilitate messages to encourage the use of these devices?

How could you trigger people's memories from a visit to your museum from long ago? Are there ways to help visitors recall their visits some time after they have been to the museum? Has your museum tended to rely on evaluations taken from what people recall only just after they have been to an exhibition? How would evaluations differ if they were done several weeks or months later? Might there be possibilities for tapping into a longer-term type of learning or shifts from episodic to semantic memory?

How can connections be made between visitors' previous knowledge and the ideas expressed in the gallery or exhibit you are working on? How can different visitors' varying levels of background information about a topic be catered for? What would make a visit to your museum distinctive? Would that still be distinctive after multiple visits to your museum? Are there items in your museum that generate strong emotions? Could connections to these emotions help to create long-term memories for your visitors? Are there ways to overcome findings that children find social history and natural history more memorable than science and art?

What sorts of connections could there be between visitors' collective memories about the topic of an exhibition or programme you are working on and the way the topic framed by the museum? How aware are museum staff of collective memory about this topic? What alternative collective memories should be considered? Are there ways of developing learning outcomes that take into account collective memory (or memories)? Should only people 'of a certain age' be key in developing exhibitions about a topic due to the cohort effect in relation to particular events?

Note

1 This scenario was contributed by Sharon Willoughby, Manager, Public Programs, Royal Botanic Gardens, Victoria, Australia, with minimal editing by the authors.

References

Adelman, M., Falk, J., & James, S. (2000). Impact of National Aquarium in Baltimore on visitors' conservation attitudes, behavior, and knowledge. *Curator: The Museum Journal*, 43, 33–61.

Afonso, A. & Gilbert, J. (2006). The use of memories in understanding interactive science and technology exhibits. *International Journal of Science Education*, 28, 1523–1544.

Anderson, D. (2003). Visitors' long-term memories of World Expositions. *Curator: The Museum Journal*, 46, 401–421.

Anderson, D., Piscitelli, B., Weier, K., Everett, M., & Tayler, C. (2002). Children's museum experiences: Identifying powerful mediators of learning. *Curator: The Museum Journal*, 45, 213–231.

Anderson, D. & Shimizu, H. (2007). Factors shaping vividness of memory episodes: visitors' long-term memories of the 1970 Japan World Exposition. *Memory*, 15, 177–191.

Atkinson, R. & Shiffrin, R. (1968). Human memory: A proposed system and its control processes. In K. Spence & J. Spence (Eds.), *The psychology of learning and motivation: Advances in research and theory* (Vol. 2, pp. 89–195). New York: Academic Press.

Brown, J.S., Collins, A., & Duguid, P. (1989). Situated cognition and the culture of learning. *Educational Researcher*, 18, 32–42.

Bruner, J. (1990). *Acts of meaning*. Cambridge, MA: Harvard University Press.

Chi, M., De Leeuw, N., Chui, M., & Levancher, C. (1994). Eliciting self-explanations improves understanding. *Cognitive Science*, 18, 439–477.

Clark, J. & Paivio, A. (1991). Dual coding theory and education. *Educational Psychology Review*, 3, 149–210.

Connerton, P. (1989). *How societies remember*. Cambridge: Cambridge University Press.

Conway, M. (1990). *Autobiographical memory: An introduction*. Philadelphia, PA: Open University Press.

Crowshaw, R. (2007). Photography and memory in Holocaust museums. *Mortality: Promoting the interdisciplinary study of death and dying*, 12, 176–192.

Demetrious, A., Christou, C., Spanoudis, G., & Platsidou, M. (2002). The development of mental processing: Efficiency, working memory, and thinking. *Monographs of the Society for Research in Child Development*, 67, 1–167.

Dewey, J. (1938). *Experience and education*. New York: Kappa Delta Pi.

Driver, R., Asoko, H., Leach, R., Mortimer, E., & Scott, P. (1994). Constructing scientific knowledge in the classroom. *Educational Researcher*, 23, 5–12.

Ellenbogen, K. (2002). Museums in family life: An ethnographic case study. In G. Leinhardt, K. Crowley, & K. Knutson (Eds.), *Learning conversations in museums* (pp. 81–101). London: Taylor & Francis.

Erikson, E. (1950). *Childhood and society*. New York: Norton.

Evans, S. (2013). Personal beliefs and national stories: Theater in museums as a tool for exploring historical memory. *Curator: The Museum Journal*, 56, 189–197.

Falk, J. & Dierking, L. (1990). The effect of visitation frequency on long-term recollection. *Visitor Studies: Proceedings of the 3rd Annual Visitor Studies Conference* (pp. 94–104).

Falk, J. & Dierking, L. (1997). School field trips: Assessing their long-term impact. *Curator: The Museum Journal*, 40, 211–218.

Falk, J., Scott, C., Dierking, L., Rennie, L., & Jones, M.C. (2004). Interactives and visitor learning. *Curator: The Museum Journal*, 47, 171–198.

Fischbach, G. & Coyle, J. (1997). Preface. In D. Schacter (Ed.), *Memory distortion: How minds, brains and societies reconstruct the past* (pp. ix–xi). Cambridge, MA: Harvard University Press.

Gatewood, J. & Cameron, C. (2004). Battlefield pilgrims at Gettysburg National Military Park. *Ethnology*, 43, 193–216.

Goodman, G., Ghetti, S., Quas, J., Edelstein, R., Alexander, K., Redlich, A., Cordon, I., & Jones, D. (2003). A prospective study for memory of child sexual abuse: New findings relevant to the repressed-memory controversy. *Psychological Science*, 14, 113–118.

Greunewald, D. (2003). The best of both worlds: A critical pedagogy of place. *Educational Researcher*, 32, 3–12.

Herbert, D. & Burt, J. (2004). What do students remember? Episodic memory and the development of schematization. *Applied Cognitive Psychology*, 18, 77–88.

Herz, R. (1997). The effects of cue-distinctiveness on odor-based context-dependent memory. *Memory & Cognition*, 25, 375–380.

Hmelo-Silver, C. (2004). Problem-based learning: What and how do students learn? *Educational Psychology Review*, 16, 235–266.

Howe, M. (2006). Developmental invariance in distinctiveness effects in memory. *Developmental Psychology*, 42, 1193–1205.

Hudson, J. & Fivush, R. (1991). As time goes by: Sixth graders remember a kindergarten experience. *Applied Cognitive Psychology*, 5, 347–360.

Hunt, R. (2006). What is the meaning of distinctiveness for memory research? In R. Hunt & J. Worthen (Eds.), *Distinctiveness and memory* (pp. 3–25). Oxford: Oxford University Press.

Latham, K. (2013). Numinous experiences with museum objects. *Visitor Studies*, 16, 3–20.

MacRae, C., Moran, J., Heatherton, T., Banfield, J., & Kelly, W. (2004). Medial prefrontal activity predicts memory for self. *Cerebral Cortex*, 14, 647–654.

McManus, P. (1993). Memories as indicators of the impact of museum visits. *Museum Management & Curatorship*, 12, 367–380.

Medved, M. & Oatley, K. (2000). Memories and scientific literacy: remembering exhibits from a science centre. *International Journal of Science Education*, 22, 1117–1132.

Miller, G. (1956). The magical number seven, plus or minus two: Some limits on our capacity for processing information. *Psychological Review*, 63, 81–97.

Papert, S. (1980). *Mindstorms: Children, computers, and powerful ideas*. New York: Basic Books.

Pathman, T., Samson, Z., Dugas, K., Cabeza, R., & Bauer, P. (2011). A 'snapshot' of declarative memory: Differing developmental trajectories in episodic and autobiographical memory. *Memory*, 19, 825–835.

Pennebaker, J. & Gonzales, A. (2009). Making history: Social and psychological processes underlying collective memory. In P. Boyer & J. Wertsch (Eds.), *Memory in mind and culture: Cognitive predispositions and cultural transmission* (pp. 171–193). Cambridge: Cambridge University Press.

Piaget, J. (1970). *Genetic epistemology*. New York: Columbia University Press.

Proust, M. (1983). *Remembrance of things past* (trans. by C.K. Scott Moncrieff). London: Penguin.

Reisberg, D. & Heuer, F. (2004). Memory for emotional events. In D. Reisberg & P. Hertel (Eds.), *Memory and emotion* (pp. 3–41). New York: Oxford University Press.

Roschelle, J. (1995). Learning in interactive environments: Prior knowledge and new experience. In J.H. Falk & L.D. Dierking (Eds.), *Public institutions for personal learning: Establishing a research agenda* (pp. 27–51). Washington, DC: American Association of Museums.

Rowe, S., Wertsch, J., & Kosyaeva, T. (2002). Linking little narratives to big ones: narrative and public memory in history museums. *Culture & Psychology*, 8, 96–112.

Schacter, D. (1997). Memory distortion: History and current status. In D. Schacter (Ed.), *Memory distortion: How minds, brains and societies reconstruct the past* (pp. 1–43). Cambridge, MA: Harvard University Press.

Schacter, D., Gutchess, A., & Kensinger, E. (2009). Specificity of memory: Implications for individual and collective remembering. In P. Boyer & J. Wertsch (Eds.), *Memory in mind and culture* (pp. 83–111). Cambridge: Cambridge University Press.

Schmidt, S. (1985). Encoding and retrieval processes in the memory for conceptually distinctive events. *Journal of Experimental Psychology: Learning, Memory & Cognition*, 11, 565–578.

Sinatra, G., Heddy, B., & Lombardi, D. (2015). The challenges of defining and measuring student engagement in science. *Educational Psychologist*, 50, 1–13.

Skinner, E. & Fernandes, M. (2007). Neural correlates of recollection and familiarity: A review of neuroimaging and patient data. *Neuropsychologia*, 45, 2163–2179.

Smith, C., Wixted, J., & Squire, L., (2011). The hippocampus supports both recollection and familiarity when memories are strong. *The Journal of Neuroscience*, 31, 15693–15702.

Smith, L. (2006). *Uses of heritage*. London: Routledge.

Smith, L. (2014). Visitor emotion, affect and registers of engagements at museums and heritage sites. *Conservation Science in Cultural Heritage*, 14, 125–132.

Sobel, D. (2004). *Place-based education: Connecting classrooms and communities*. Great Barrington, MA: The Orion Society.

Spock, M. (2000). 'When I grow up I'd like to work in a place like this': Museum professionals' narratives of early interest in museums. *Curator: The Museum Journal*, 43, 19–31.

Squire, L. (1992). Declarative and non-declarative memory: Multiple brain systems supporting learning and memory. *Journal of Cognitive Neuroscience*, 4, 232–243.

St. Jacques, P. & Schacter, D. (2013). Modifying memory: selectively enhancing and updating personal memories for a museum tour by reactivating them. *Psychological Science*, 24, 527–543.

Stevenson, J. (1991). The long-term impact of interactive exhibits. *International Journal of Science Education*, 13, 521–531.

Tulving, E. (1972). Episodic and semantic memory. In E. Tulving & W. Donaldson (Eds.), *Organization of memory* (pp. 381–403). New York: Academic Press.

Vosniadou, S. & Brewer, W. (1992). Mental models of the earth: A study of conceptual change in childhood. *Cognitive Psychology*, 24, 535–585.

Wertsch, J. (2009). Collective memory. In P. Boyer & J. Wertsch (Eds.), *Memory in mind and culture: Cognitive predispositions and cultural transmission* (pp. 117–137). Cambridge: Cambridge University Press.

Witcomb, A. (2013). Understanding the role of affect in producing a critical pedagogy for history museums. *Museum Management and Curatorship*, 28, 255–271.

Zerubavel, E. (1996). Social memories: Steps to a sociology of the past. *Qualitative Sociology*, 19, 283–299.

8 The role of self and identity in learning

The art of voicing black women's identity as seen through everyday objects[1]

The Colored Girls Museum tells the story of black girls and women in the United States, using tangible objects, such as lace doilies, wooden statues, original art work and photographs, and intangible objects such as music and storytelling. Housed in the home of the Director and founder of the Museum in Germantown in Philadelphia, the Colored Girls Museum has ten rooms, looking at different aspects of the history of black girls and women. For example, the bedroom represents adult relationships; the Colored Boys room explores ideas that shape those adults' relationships later in black women's lives; the laundry room represents the concept of laundrywoman; the kitchen exhibits ceramics and beading created by black woman artists; the living room presents art works created by more than twenty black women; the upper room has been transformed into a place of prayer and meditation; the toolshed focuses on female factory workers through photographic material mainly.

DuBois, who still lives in the house, thinks of the Colored Girls Museum as her roommate, and believes that both the Museum's name and the fact that it is a living house makes it accessible and inclusive. DuBois' concept behind the Colored Girls Museum gives a new meaning to a living museum – a living space and place that makes its visitors feel at home with their surroundings. She conceived the Museum as a place where the history of black girls and women is being built and archived but also co-constructed and shared.

DuBois' vision and strong idea, the Colored Girls Museum, found a lot of support with local communities – many of whom donated objects – and local artists alike. In fact, it is a collective of artists who worked together to bring the concept of the Museum to fruition. Different artists curated each of the ten rooms using objects that have a special meaning and place in

Figure 8.1 A view of the living room towards the fireplace where artwork of black artists can be seen. Photographed by Debbie Lerman. © The Colored Girls Museum and Debbie Lerman.

the life of the black women who donated them. Blending art, social history and social commentary, each room uses objects that are meaningful to the life experiences of the black girls and women who donated them and, at the same time, reflect the collective experiences of black women growing up in the United States.

For example, the tool shed has a focus on black women as factory workers; there is a laundry room dedicated to washer-women; there is even a Colored Boys room which aims to create a dialogue between black women and boys, where black women can reflect on how black boys have shaped their sense of self and their identity. These rooms are filled with everyday objects donated by black women, including vases, wooden figurines, tables, chairs, posters, paintings, old photographs, clocks, bed sheets, needlework, handcrafted dolls, dresses and a wooden ironing board. Art work and art installations also have a distinct place in the Museum, owing to the generative power of art. DuBois believes that art can play a central role in the lives of black women as it can help them process and make sense of their everyday experiences.

The ideas that the Colored Girls Museum embodies were so powerful that it has attracted growing interest and support from across the United States. The story of black women is intertwined with the creation of the United States as a nation, as black women have shaped and have been shaped by it. As stated on the Museum's website: 'Colored Girls have a unique and complex history – it is a history formed by great tragedy and great triumph – a history which intersects and overlaps with other histories but remains distinct as colored women navigate their dual circumstances as "colored and female" [...]'

Introduction

Learning and identity are strongly related and both develop through the practices people adopt in their life experiences. In the museum context, self and identity play a key role in learning in at least two ways. The way identities are represented in an exhibition, for example, influences how visitors make sense of these representations of identity, as it can reinforce or challenge stereotypes about a theme or group of people. Visitors' sense of self and identity shape and are shaped by what people choose to engage with and learn in an exhibition. The representation and enactment of identity in museums are two sides of the same coin. Take the scenario above as an example. It demonstrates how personal and collective identities mediate how people make sense of, act and reflect on their experiences in and with the world around them: objects – such as lace doilies or old photographs of female factory workers – talk to the experience and personal identity of individual women. At the same time, they also resonate with the experiences of girls and young black women who, as a social group, may identify with this particular community and their experience of growing up, working and living in the US. The Colored Girls Museum has chosen to display everyday objects and the experience of black women with them as an art installation, thereby providing an arts lens (the generative power of art) to explore women's sense of personal and collective identity.

Self and identity are central to understanding how the human mind works in addition to the relationship between individuals (personal identity), on the one hand, and society and culture (collective identities), on the other. Self and identity are at the core of the questions: 'What about us is consistent? What is malleable? What does it mean to be an individual and also a member of a community?' (Lindholm, 2001, p. vii). They have played a central role in our effort 'to understand how people live in the world, make choices, and make meaning of their experiences', across different social and cultural contexts (Oyserman et al., 2012, p. 71), including museums. For example, in Chapter 9, we discuss that even the choice to visit or not is influenced by people's identity.

In the twenty-first century, in particular, the quest for identity has become even more important because of the impact and influence of modernisation and globalisation. As the world becomes more globalised and interconnected, identities become more fragmented and fluid, leading to different ways of constructing and practising identities. According to Bauman (2000), this multiplicity of identities that co-exist within every person is the result of a shift that took place in the latter half of the twentieth century when there was an increased emphasis on freedom (to live and enjoy life, to consume, to purchase). This shift has created opportunities for new life pursuits and self-realisation, but has also brought about unique challenges: people need to be flexible and adaptable, and to pursue new opportunities as and when these present themselves. This has created uncertainty and insecurity. While traditional societies provided its members with examples of types of identity, in post-traditional societies, identity and its formation is a work in progress. In this context, how identities and the meaning of these identities are negotiated become important (Côté & Levine, 2002; Holland et al., 1998). For example, the Colored Girls Museum has actively sought to provide a voice to black women who have historically been oppressed and had their experiences and voices silenced. Through their collection of personal, everyday objects the Museum gives black women both a personal and a collective voice and representation.

What is starting to become clear from the discussion so far is that self and identity are a major thematic area in social science theory and research from the disciplines of psychology (Côté & Levine, 2002; Simon, 2008), sociology (House, 1977), anthropology (Holland et al., 1998; Sökefeld, 1999), and cultural studies (Hall, 1996; Redman, 2000). Conceptualisations of identity can be traced back in a long tradition of – by and large – Western debate on the nature of self, which goes back to Plato's theory of agency, which was then spiritualised in Christianity and transformed by St. Augustine (AD 354–430) in his autobiography (see Lindholm, 2001). Our own research in the identity literature has shown that, across all disciplines, the study of self and identity tends to locate identity either in the context of individual experience or in collective patterns within and across societies and cultures. What differentiates these two umbrella approaches to self and identity is how they account for difference. Approaches to personal identity tend to view identity as self-constituted and emphasise the uniqueness and individuality which make a person different from others. Approaches to collective identities emphasise the social and cultural dimensions that shape identity, and focus on things such as social group membership or positionality (gender, class, religion, ethnicity or sexual orientation), which are linked to power and status in society. The issue of positionality is further discussed in Chapter 10.

The latter direction of studying identity as socially patterned has been further strengthened through interdisciplinary sharing and more conscious efforts to coalesce disciplinary perspectives. These tend to emphasise the 'multidimensionality' of identity (see, for example, the model by Côté & Levine, 2002, pp. 131–139) and often strive to develop frameworks that can offer a more comprehensive understanding of identity through drawing on interdisciplinary perspectives. Of particular interest, for example, are approaches from the psychology of culture and the way they conceptualise and study self, identity, or agency, and the cultural differentiation of the functioning of the self (Markus & Kitayama, 1991, 2010; Miller, 2001; Oyserman et al., 2012). The unique insights that such multidisciplinary frameworks can bring to our understanding of multiple dimensions of self and identity, and the fact that they can answer more complex, real-life questions makes them particularly relevant to museums with respect to both how identities are represented in exhibitions or programmes, for example, and also how they are enacted by visitors.[2]

In order to put this in the museum context, let us briefly turn our attention to how identity has been studied in museums. Identity has been used as a lens to study other phenomena such as how museums construct narratives (as discussed in Chapter 5) that reflect particular national or cultural identities (Macdonald, 2003); and how identity mediates visitor learning and shapes visitor museum experiences both during and after the actual visit (Stainton, 2002; Paris & Mercer, 2002) or through digital resources (Walker, 2006). Research carried out in informal learning contexts highlights the role that personal and/or collective identities play in filtering the museum experience and, at the same time, in being shaped by the museum experience (Falk, 2006; Falk et al., 2008; Falk, 2009; Fienberg & Leinhardt, 2002; Latchem, 2006; Leinhardt & Knutson, 2004; Rounds, 2006). More recently, some research has examined how gender identity intersects with other categories of identity (such as ethnicity and class), and is performed in the museum space in a way that includes or excludes other members of the visiting group and the degree to which it leads to learning (Archer et al., 2016). So far, it can be argued that, in museum research, only some dimensions or types of identity have been used as an analytical lens in order to examine questions such as why people visit museums, how they make meaning of their experiences or how their visit is remembered. In museum practice, on the other hand, both personal and collective identities come into play – consciously or unconsciously –

when planning for exhibition spaces (as the scenario aptly demonstrates) and programmes, but also when people choose to visit museums, interact with exhibit features and with other visitors and staff. This gap between the proliferation of theory about identity and limited operationalisation and empirical evidence of the role of identity in learning is one of the key points this chapter addresses.

We will start by critically discussing particular disciplinary views on personal, social, cultural and cross-cultural dimensions of identity. We then bridge those views and discuss emerging frameworks that bring new insights into the personal and social production of identity and difference. The chapter concludes by discussing how these frameworks have been used in the museum context.

The basics of identity

This section will examine a rather large number of seemingly disparate theories coming from different theoretical perspectives. This is mainly for two reasons. Firstly, despite the central role identity plays in both the development of exhibitions or programmes as well as how these are perceived or filtered through visitors' identities, there is very little empirical support for the assumption that many theories make about the role of self and identity. This is particularly evident in naturalistic contexts (see for example, Altschul, Oyserman, & Bynee, 2006). In the museum context, for example, evidence of inherited and emergent identities has been considered in the development of many museum projects, and also collected in many audience studies often using particular disciplinary theories. However, more often than not, they have been used in an unconscious manner where the assumptions made are not transparent. The critical museum studies literature is full of such examples. Despite the problems that this approach entails, what museum professionals find problematic is exploring yet another theory of identity, the application of which is usually not immediately apparent – at best – or its meaning is impenetrable and its particular focus does not lend itself to a direct application across contexts – at worst. This brings us to the second reason why the presentation below includes a number of diverse theories. We hope that we can make them more accessible and show their potential in thinking about and researching the role of identity in museum learning.

Overview and key concepts

Definitions of identity tend to address different aspects or dimensions of the concept, ranging from those that examine individual and self-identity to those that explore collectively shared identities such as national, social or cultural identity. The extent to which people are capable of acting or whether their ability to act is constrained by social structures is also a matter of debate across different disciplines. In the sociological literature, this is often referred to as the 'structure–agency debate' which refers to the relative importance of agency (i.e., whether people are capable of intentional (agentic) behaviour/actions) over structure (i.e., whether human behaviour is constrained by social structures (such as family, religion, education, media, law, politics, and economy)). Both the terms and definitions reflect not just disciplinary perspectives but also particular theoretical and methodological approaches within and across disciplines. Mainstream social and developmental psychology tends to view identity as the individual's exclusive 'property'. Hence, the focus is on the individual's uniqueness (Côté & Levine, 2002; Heider, 1958).

More recently, however, a renewed interest in approaches to the psychology of culture – cultural psychology[3] (sometimes known as psychological anthropology), cross-cultural psychology, and indigenous psychology – has produced research that examines the relationships between personal and collective identity by bringing together psychological, sociological and anthropological views of the self (Lindholm, 2001; Greenfield, 2000; Miller, 2001; Markus & Kitayama, 1991, 2010). Within these approaches, a considerable amount of research has been conducted at the interface of self and culture, with attempts to connect the self and its social and cultural environment. These approaches have demonstrated the cultural grounding of the self as well as of psychological theory itself (Miller, 2001), and have shed light on the cultural basis of the functioning of the self. The latter includes two different senses of self or agency: the independent (a self-contained and autonomous entity) and the interdependent self (viewing self in relation to others in the social context), and the degree to which these elements of self – although they coexist – are prioritised in different cultures (Geertz, 1975, Markus & Kitayama, 1991; Lindholm, 2001, pp. 210–213). Indeed, the current view is that conformity and a concern for the opinion of others as well as values of autonomy and self-expression exist in both sociocentric (where social norms and expectations shape the actions of the individual; interdependent self) and egocentric societies (where the individual becomes independent from others and her actions are a consequence of her own thoughts and feelings; see independent self above) (Lindholm, 2001, pp. 213–217).

According to Oyserman et al. (2012), the latter line of research, where both the independent and interdependent self are taken into account, is of particular importance as it suggests that, within and across cultures, people have an array of self-concepts (e.g., personal 'me' or individualistic concepts, and social 'us' or collectivistic concepts) which are activated by cues, and are dynamically developed as people respond to cues or situations in different contexts as well as in the moment and over time. These self-concepts affect decision-making and behaviour, and shape the way people make sense of the world. This means that although people experience self and identity as stable, they are also dynamically constructed in context. For example, the scenario demonstrates how objects have the ability to represent individual experiences of black girls and women and also how they act as cues that can activate 'me' concepts. At the same time, they can create and represent a collection of experiences of black women growing up in the United States, acting as cues for social 'us' concepts. Furthermore, when seen as art objects/installations, they can provide the means for black women to make sense of and contextualise their everyday experiences.

The boundaries between autonomy and interdependence, identified as the relation between the individualistic and the collectivistic self, have also been one of the central themes in anthropology and cultural studies. Taking a wider focus, these two disciplines place more emphasis on relationships of domination, for example, in the way knowledge is organised and in the way the dominant culture and ideology is psychologically internalised and shapes one's personality (Lindholm, 2001, pp. 217–218). Lindholm (2001) comments that much of anthropological and sociological work has been influenced by Antonio Gramsci's notion of cultural hegemony which refers to 'an emotionally charged image of what is right and good' (2001, p. 218). This work examines the way in which this image of what is right and good is normalised and is psychologically internalised by the oppressed. In other words, people who are marginalised because of their social class, ethnicity or gender and so on passively accept having their personalities shaped by the outside world. This then leads to them accepting their inferior position as inevitable, as also discussed in Chapter 10. For example, the concept of the washerwomen discussed in one of the rooms of the Colored Girls Museum explores the very limited employment opportunities available to black women in the United States up until two generations ago.

If we accept that social reproduction is inevitable, then how can social change be explained? In other words, to what extent can this socialisation process can be resisted by individuals? Indeed, there is theoretical and empirical work that focuses on acts of resistance – most of which are often unconscious – by members of lower ranking groups. One such example is the work by Holland et al. (1998). In their review of relevant anthropological and cultural psychological literature on the relation between culture and self, Holland et al. (1998) note that a critical turn in anthropology (as well as in other disciplines) has enabled anthropologists to ask questions that address issues of power, agency and activity. Following this line of thought, Holland et al. examined questions such as, 'how specific, often socially powerful, cultural discourses and practices both position people and provide them with the resources to respond to the problematic situations in which they find themselves' (1998, p. 32). This theoretical framework – which is explained in more detail below in 'Sociological and anthropological perspectives on identity' – pays attention to hidden or sometimes unconscious acts of resistance by oppressed groups. The scenario in this chapter offers a good example of particular cultural discourses and practices: the laundry room with its objects which are associated with the racial inequalities in employment that black women face in the US are now placed in an art context providing its visitors with alternative stories and images detailing different forms of cultural expression available to them. As Holland et al. (1998, p. 5) comment, identities 'are important bases from which people create new activities, new worlds and new ways of being'. They locate the formation and maintenance of identity in social practice, and view them as the result of 'considerable social work' and as 'unfinished and in process' (Holland et al., 1998, p. vii).

Defining self, identity and agency

Although the study of self, identity and agency has been the focus of different disciplines, the terms are still somewhat nebulous. Discussing identity-related terminology and its purpose, Oyserman et al. (2012, p. 94) note that, '[...] while self and identity are often used interchangeably, some clarity can be attained by considering them as a series of nested constructs, with self as the most encompassing term, self-concept being embedded within the self, and identities being embedded within self-concepts.' Oyserman (2015, pp. 1–14) notes that self is temporal (it has many past and current identities as well as possible future ones) and has motivational power (it suggests possibilities for actions that make certain future identities accessible, that may or may not be compatible with desired future selves in the extent to which these are conscious) (see Figure 8.2). Referring to the concept of agency, in particular, Markus and Kitayama (2010, p. 421) comment that it 'is the most general or global term and refers to acting in the world', while Sökefeld (1999) adds that agency does indeed refer to 'the ability to act on one's own account' but this is always done 'with reference

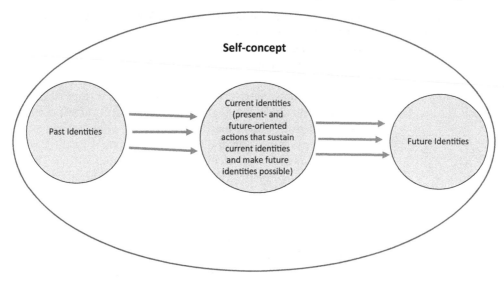

Figure 8.2 Diagram describing the relationship between past, current and future identities as embedded within the self-concept.

to others'. We are reminded here of the idea of positionality or group membership referred to above.

The idea put forward by Oyserman et al. (2012) of the self being a superordinate category to the plurality of identities it can assume is also highlighted in anthropological conceptualisations of self and identity (Sökefeld, 1999). For example, in the scenario one's self can assume the identity of belonging to the group of African Americans, while at the same time assuming other identities not shared with this group such as sexual orientation or religious identity or as a bilingual English and French speaker. Self-concept (the collection of beliefs about one's self) relates to the identities embraced by the self, and is at play whenever the self negotiates all those identities (for an example of what these terms mean and how they might play out in practice in a museum context see A return to the Colored Girls Museum below). Still, the concepts of self, identity and agency are difficult to define and there is no agreement on their definition. Referring to the variety of terms used, how they are defined and operationalised across disciplines, Oyserman et al. (2012) comment that these can cause a great deal of confusion.

Social and cultural psychological perspectives on identity

The subjective aspects of identity are also of particular importance 'because the subjective streamlike quality of consciousness seems to play an important role in grounding a person's sense of self or identity' (Simon, 2008, p. 5). Simon refers to the work of philosophers and psychologists like Erik Erikson, William James and Owen Flanagan (see Simon, 2008, pp. 4–10). This work takes a phenomenological orientation and tries to describe how identity is mediated in a social world, according to which both identity experiences and self-consciousness feed into the construction of self-reflexive stories about one's self (Simon, 2008, p. 19). Simon (2008) highlights the role activity and self-control play in focusing our attention and setting goals in line with our interests. Simon's work was very influential in the development of ideas about identity-related visit motivations (Falk, 2009), presented below. Also the link between identity, interest and motivation is referred to in Chapter 9. Identity, interest and motivation can also be seen in the context of participation in different communities. In Chapter 10 we discuss how memberships in particular communities enable its members to pursue socially and culturally meaningful activities afforded by any given society (or not). Chapter 10 specifically examines how certain people and groups are excluded from accessing social organisations and cultural resources.

Learning identity

In the context of formal and informal learning, some cultural psychological work has focused on the role that a sense of self, identity and agency play in driving learning. Here the term 'learning identity' has been used to refer to how individuals view themselves as learners and how they experience their agency in relation to activities within any domain of knowledge such as art or literature (Hull & Greeno, 2006; Renninger, 2009). Learning identity has been conceptualised in different ways: as an embodied experience developed though one's interactions with material resources and with other people (Wenger, 1998); as personal beliefs and attitudes reflected in the learner's personal narratives (Hull & Greeno, 2006; Kelly, 2007; Sfard & Prusak, 2005); or as roles and statuses, that is, by tracking moment-to-moment interactions that position learners on certain roles and statuses in relation to learning (Holland et al., 1998).

A common element across these different conceptualisations is that identity development is closely related to participation and learning in a given domain. In this context, domain-specific terms such as 'science identity' have been used to refer to a sense of being competent at science as demonstrated by an individual's performance in varying contexts, and the extent to which this performance is recognised by significant others as being a science person (Carlone & Johnson, 2007). Carlone and Johnson (2007) note that the components of competence, performance and recognition can be affected by race, ethnicity and gender. More broadly speaking, developing science identity is viewed as concurrent with and contingent on developing other deeply held cultural identities such as ethnicity, gender or social networks (Bell et al., 2009), an interest in science and age-related identities (Renninger, 2009).

Hull and Greeno's (2006) work, which considers after-school programmes as an important setting for identity formation, also deals with learning identity in a participatory sense. In their work, learning identity is conceptualised as having three aspects: interpersonal, epistemic and discursive (Hull & Greeno, 2006, p. 83). Firstly, identity is cultivated as people interact with others and also with the content of activities they participate in. People develop epistemic identity as their expertise and understanding related to subject matter content of activities increases through learning. They develop discursive identity as one tells stories about who one was, is and wants to become through the process of learning (2006, p. 84). The link between identity and discourse is also examined in Chapter 5. What is important to point out here is that learning identity can be seen as a 'positional identity' that enables learners to develop agentive identities in practice. This view resonates with Sfard and Prusak (2005), and Holland et al. (1998), whose works link identity to the activity of communication. In their works, identity is conceptualised as 'stories' in which 'people tell others who they are, but even more importantly, they tell themselves, and they try to act as though they are who they say they are' (Holland et al., 1998, p. 3). Identity is seen as discursive, and can be defined as collections of stories about persons or narratives about individuals that are reifying, significant, and endorsable (Sfard & Prusak, 2005, p. 16). In brief, a person develops a learning identity not only by engaging in an activity and negotiating himself in relation to a domain, but also by communicating stories about himself to others, through which he becomes the person he wants to become. This idea that a person communicates stories about himself to others resonates with Bruner's work which is presented in Chapter 5.

Accepting that identity and agency are positional means that they may change on the basis of participating in practices, rather than being something given or static. Practice can, after all, change and transform as people interact with available resources and their expectations (Hull & Greeno, 2006), and as people's activity intersects with their expectations of 'what has happened, is happening and might happen' (Lave, 1988, p. 185) during the activity. This further supports the point raised above that it is possible for visitor identities to shift from one already existing identity to another through activity (e.g., during a museum visit). The issue that arises here is how museum professionals can facilitate such possibilities. Furthermore, the positional nature of identity means that it can develop in different contexts. This leads us to another interesting question: how do these identities intersect and interact with each other during the museum visit? Museums, owing to the open-ended nature of their collections, could potentially enable the mediation of connections between different identities developed in different contexts. This can be particularly important in emotive exhibitions and those that deal with controversial or difficult subjects, where challenging preconceptions or presenting alternative knowledge about the subject matter might be important. Here the concept of positional identity – that may change on the basis of participating in practices – becomes important as it allows for a change in preconception and for self-growth to happen. This process of self-growth and development is at the core of understanding one's own identity as a learner. Museums can play a major role in developing this possibility for their visitors.

In museums in particular, the concept of learning identity has been introduced relatively recently (Bell et al., 2009). Research by Archer et al. (2016) carried out at a science museum, and which is presented in the next section, shows how science identity plays out in practice. There are also some links to the school context, albeit indirect. Both learning identity and more domain-specific identities (such as science identity) have also been closely linked to motivation, as discussed in Chapter 9.

Sociological and anthropological perspectives on identity

Sociology, anthropology and cultural studies tend to explore the social and cultural contexts that influence identity, which can be similar to some of the work done from a social or cultural psychological perspective. Debates about identity in sociology tend to revolve around the 'structure–agency' question (Côté & Levine, 2002) and ask questions such as: Is human self-definition determined by external (social), political, cultural and economic forces, or by internal forces and individual potentials (agency)? More recently, sociological perspectives about identity formation have tried to move away from the external–internal dichotomy by ascribing both 'internal' and 'external' qualities of the concept (Jenkins, 2008, 2000). For example, Jenkins (2000, p. 7) explains that self-identification emerges in interactions between relationships of similarity and difference between a social group and ourselves. The identification process is also influenced by 'external' comparison: an individual's self-consciousness is shaped and influenced by 'objective' social circumstances manifested in day-to-day interactions, social roles, cultural institutions and social structures.

The dialectic between social structure and individual agency which was introduced above is at the core of Bourdieu's theory of practice (1977). Key concepts used in the theory of practice include habitus, capital and field (the concept of field will be discussed in Chapter 10). Of particular importance in this chapter is the concept of habitus that he used to describe 'the permanent internalisation of the social order in the human body' (Eriksen & Nielsen, 2001, p. 130) that happens through osmosis or immersion rather than formal learning. The importance of habitus lies in the insights it can give us into how bodies are cultured, and the impact this has for individuals/agents, institutions and societies. Specifically, habitus operates as a structuring force for individual actions and differentiation from other individuals. This process of internalising social order in the human body – which manifests itself in postures, gestures, the way individuals carry themselves – forms 'permanent dispositions'. Dispositions[4] in this context refers to deeply ingrained habits and skills that one develops through life experiences available to them, and can include – among other things – aesthetic orientations to culture, and tastes orientated towards particular leisure and cultural spheres of activity.

These dispositions are important because they incline individuals to act in particular ways. For example, individuals' positive predisposition towards museums is developed very early in their lives, often in the family, and evolves into 'permanent disposition' which can predict their patterns of cultural participation and quality of engagement with cultural institutions (Bourdieu & Darbel, 1991). These patterns of participation and engagement can be discerned by the way people engage with cultural resources physically and intellectually (see, for example, how boys engage with science in Archer et al.'s study (2016) discussed below). Habitus helps explain how interest in cultural engagement is initiated and how it evolves by linking it to internalised, embodied experiences that are socially determined. In this context, family becomes the connection between class trajectory and individual trajectory: for those borne into a privileged class, its habitus is like a second nature to them, while for those newly arrived, cultural capital is something they continuously need to strive for and work at (Wilkes, 1990). In this process, class habitus creates social difference. It is worth mentioning that, in the context of museums and other cultural organisations,[5] the concept of cultural capital has been viewed positively (i.e., as a way to explore how audiences value and engage (or do not engage) with museums) or negatively (as reproducing disadvantage and contributing to social reproduction).

The concepts of habitus and cultural capital have been used and adapted by researchers across different disciplines. For example, Holland et al. (1998) examined how identities mediate between predetermined social positions and agency. We will come back to the idea of social positions in the next section of this chapter when we examine the identity-related visit motivations (Falk, 2009). But, first, let us examine Holland et al.'s (1998) work. Drawing on Bourdieu's, Vygotsky's and Bakhtin's theoretical contributions, Holland et al. (1998) developed a theory of self-formation which explores how identities mediate between predetermined social positions and agency. They postulate that the social categories within which people are positioned (e.g., student, patient, police officer) are associated with certain patterns of expectations, which help us understand each other, but also to understand ourselves in relation to these worlds. This is what the authors refer to as figured worlds. These social categories are 'socially and culturally constructed realms of interpretation' that shape expectations of how people should behave (Holland et al., 1998, p. 52). They also shape which outcomes are more valued in such figured worlds. An important distinction is that figured worlds do not relate to the concept of a group's culture; instead the focus is on activity (i.e., people being actively engaged with their environment). 'Each [figured world] is a simplified world populated by a set of agents (in the world of romance: attractive women, boyfriends, Lovers, fiancés) who engage in a limited range of meaningful acts or change of state (flirting with, falling in love, dumping, having sex with) as moved by a specific set of forces (attractiveness, love, lust)' (Holland et al., 1998, p. 52). Through continual participation in a figured world, it becomes embodied (i.e., we are able to feel, hear, see, touch, taste it), it can be played out, and also reproduced.

The concept of figured world brings together social position as it is experienced and acted out in different contexts, and also our ability to figure or craft alternative identities for ourselves. 'Identities are our ways of figuring the interface among these dimensions of collective life; our ways of naming the places where society organizes persons and persons in turn reorganize, albeit in modest steps, societies; the pivots of our lived worlds' (Holland et al., 1998, p. 287). This reference to 'modest steps' suggests that identity (personal and collective) formation takes time and figuring ways of being and acting in the world cannot be devised and practised in short periods of time. This is an important point to keep in mind for the way we develop exhibitions or programmes and the impact we expect to have to visitors' lives. Let us look at how the Colored Girls Museum helps its visitors contextualise black women's social position historically in the United States, while at the same time allowing them to explore alternative identities. We have established the role of social position, in particular, of the older generation of black women in US society. For a large number of them manual unskilled work (i.e., factory worker or 'washerwoman') was the only line of work available to them. This meant that particular positions were afforded them in society. What the Colored Girls Museum is actively trying to support and sustain is providing black women new means of figuring their identities through the medium of art. By enabling them to engage in art activities that link up different identities of women of colour across time, the Museum encourages women to think critically about their personal and collective identities, expand or reinvent them. This can lead to them creating positions that they can actively choose.

Summary

The discussion in this section mainly focused on attempts to bridge psychological, sociological and anthropological approaches to identity, where the concept of identity is approached from different perspectives. Although this work is very diverse, what it has in common is a focus on the qualitative aspect of identity – that is the qualities with which an individual or a group associates – and on the process of identity formation and maintenance, viewed as the dialogue between the personal and collective identity. According to Oyserman et al. (2012, p. 70):

> self and identity theories assume that people care about themselves, want to know who they are, and can use this knowledge to make sense of the world. Self and identity are predicted to influence what people are motivated to do, how they think and make sense of themselves and others, the actions they take, and their feelings and ability to control or regulate themselves.

As pointed out above, empirical support for the assumption that many theories make that self and identity matter is limited, especially in naturalistic contexts. Oyserman et al. (2012, p. 82) have discussed the limited available evidence for whether self and identity play a role in making choices and behaviour, and highlight the 'theory–evidence gap' that exists and the failure on the part of a large number of publications to acknowledge this. They (Oyserman et al., 2012) also point out that it is important to gather evidence about how and when context influences self and identity and shapes behaviour. The following section focuses on the identity research that has gathered a limited amount of relevant evidence in the museum context.

Self and identity in the museum context

Two key terms are discussed in relation to visiting and engaging with museums in this section: different elements of 'identity' and 'learning identity'. The role of 'agency' is discussed much less – at least explicitly – in the museum audience research literature, with the exception of the sociologically informed research (see

Bourdieu & Darbel, 1991; Archer et al., 2016). Visitor identity has not been an explicit focus of mainstream museum learning research and practice. However, a lot of applied audience research has used easily identifiable aspects of visitor identity – namely, socio-economic characteristics – mainly for marketing purposes. Identity has also become more prominent in museum policy, practice and applied research, especially in relation to impact and to debates about the value of museums (Newman & McLean, 2004; Bunting, 2007; Burns Owens Partnership, 2005; Hooper-Greenhill, 2007; Matarasso, 1997). This makes it more important to bridge the theory–evidence gap, mentioned above. The discussion that follows examines both direct and indirect references to identity in museum audience research, starting with social identity.

From demographics to identity formation and change

Early audience research in museums tended to focus almost exclusively on the demographic characteristics (such as age, gender and socio-economic background) of museum visitors as a way of understanding who they are, how they behave and how to best attract them (Lindauer, 2005; 1996). The focus was overwhelmingly on using demographic characteristics as static individual variables. It also took a particular view of collective identity: it was not seen as situated but as permanent and generic or universal, and they refer to particular societal roles (i.e., man or woman) and structural differentiations (i.e., social class). Taking the view that demographic characteristics are solid and fixed, they were used to predict participation (i.e., frequency of attendance and number of people in the party), and engagement patterns with educational provision across a range of types of museums (Davis, 1994, 2005).[6]

These types of studies were followed by research, which, although not explicitly referring to identity, examined visitor motivation and cultural frames of reference (e.g., Doering & Pekarik, 1996) with the aim to better understand the visitor museum experience. It was not until the early 2000s when research conducted from a predominantly, but not exclusively, sociocultural perspective (e.g., Leinhardt et al., 2002) introduced the concept of identity explicitly in relation to learning in museums. This early research has gradually influenced more mainstream museum learning research, which in the past was conducted within a constructivist framework (Falk & Dierking, 1992), and which has now produced work informed by concepts borrowed from a social constructivist approach to learning (Falk, 2006).

Yet, the term identity is not always explicitly defined and this seems to be the case particularly in edited books. For example, in the Leinhardt et al. (2002) volume, identity is specifically mentioned or alluded to in eight out of a total of thirteen chapters, and it is defined in four of those eight chapters (Leinhardt & Gregg 2002; Fienberg & Leinhardt, 2002; Stainton, 2002; Paris & Mercer, 2002). Definitions of identity across this book's chapters may include authors' own definition or a theoretically driven definition. The varied approaches to theoretically driven identity definitions (or lack thereof) demonstrates the difficulty in operationalising and empirically studying identity and its role in learning and meaning making in museums.

Because identity and learning are closely interlinked, the aspects of identity researchers choose to consider is central to how they approach learning, as Leinhardt and Knutson (2004) have pointed out. This makes the need to be explicit about how identity is defined and how it is operationalised central to learning research. For Leinhardt and Knutson (2004, p.18), learning in a museum is influenced by and measured across several dimensions or factors, one of which is the identity of the visitor group in relation to the exhibition content. With respect to identity, Leinhardt and Knutson (2004) and Fienberg and Leinhardt (2002) focus on two dimensions of identity: motivation and prior knowledge. Although these two aspects of identity are clearly important within a sociocultural approach to learning, it is not clear why only these two aspects of identity have been chosen. The idea that identity is a motivating factor is consistent with Oyserman's (2015) definition of identity that we have adopted here (see Defining self, identity and agency above).

> Personal and collective identity influences learning

Enacting identity in the museum context and beyond: motivation, prior knowledge, experience and visit memories

Leinhardt and Gregg (2002) worked with preservice student teachers who visited Birmingham Civil Rights Institute in Alabama as part of their teacher training course. The visit involved a series of activities that afforded both individual and group experiences coupled with small and large group discussions. The activities were designed to use a museum as a unique learning environment in order to get preservice teachers to engage in conversations about race and the Civil Rights Movement within an emotionally charged exhibition. Comparison of the pre- and post-visit data showed that within a very short period of time preservice teachers not only increased their knowledge, but they were also able to critically engage in more nuanced and elaborate conversations around issues of race, and to appropriate part of the Civil Rights Movement into their own identity. Preservice teachers acquired a considerable amount of knowledge and understanding of the Civil

> Higher engagement with museum resources can increase knowledge and expertise, and deepen understanding

Rights Movement, as shown by their discussions after the visit which contained more analysis and synthesis of information rather than lists of unconnected information. This high level of engagement is seen as an essential aspect of the development of teaching expertise that preservice teachers acquire as they move from the periphery to the centre of their practice. For example, they were able to design lesson plans and activities that took advantage of elements of the museum display that are not accessible within a typical school environment, while at the same time taking into account the time constraints and type of resources available to a school. Furthermore, their knowledge about civil rights was constructed based on their own sense of identity as well as the tools they had acquired as part of their professional training, that is, their professional identity. This can also be relevant for other museum visitors – particularly organised educational groups – who will be drawing on different aspects of their identity to make sense of the museum content. The high level of engagement recorded in this study reflects the type of focused attention and interest as well as reflection on the visit experience that well designed pre- and post-visit as well as in-setting activities can trigger. This can be true of the learning experiences that school groups can have when their museum trip is planned and carefully designed. It also highlights how students' prior knowledge and experiences can shape their response to emotionally charged exhibitions, in particular. How can the activities be designed to take students through a learning journey, part of which may make them feel uncomfortable or require them to deal with material and questions that are unfamiliar or related to taboo subjects, like race for example?

Deeper understanding can be cultivated by well-designed pre- and post-visit and in-museum activities

How does identity play out in less emotive exhibitions? Fienberg and Leinhardt (2002) examined the relation between visitors' identities and their conversations in the museum as a measure of connectedness to museum content using interviews and audiotaped conversations among visitor groups in a history museum. The focus was on the Glass: Shattering Notions exhibition, which presents the history of glass making in Western Pennsylvania. They used multiple identity characteristics, including background knowledge and/or interests related to the content of the exhibition (i.e., glass), levels of museum experience and ties to Pittsburgh or Western Pennsylvania where the exhibition was located (Fienberg & Leinhardt, 2002). Fienberg and Leinhardt (2002, p. 209) found that the identity of the visitors influenced the nature of their conversations during the visit. So, groups who had high knowledge and interest in glass 'tended to engage in more expanded "explanation level" talk than did others' (ibid, p. 209). It was also reported that 'the presence of certain social roles, such as those in a parent/child relationship, were likely to be associated with an increased level of explanatory talk within groups that did not necessarily possess high levels of content knowledge' (Fienberg & Leinhardt, 2002, p. 209). Visitor conversations do not just reflect visitor identities. It was also argued that they support a sense of connectedness to the museum content and to other group members (Fienberg & Leinhardt, 2002). In this way, they both reflect, sustain, and build personal and social identity.

> Elements of personal identity influence the nature and length of conversations which, in turn, connect visitors to the museum content and other group members

We now turn our attention to memories of museum visits and the role that past identities play in the way these are remembered fifteen to thirty years after the actual visit. David Anderson and his colleagues (Anderson, 2003; Anderson & Shimizu, 2007) carried out a series of studies examining people's recollections from World Expo exhibitions. Although the main focus of these studies was on memory – as reported in Chapter 7[7] – some of the findings relate to identity. Anderson (2003) found that people's sociocultural identity at the time of their visit shaped the way the visit was experienced at the time, and also how the visit was then remembered. He defined sociocultural identity as '[...] the inherent set of interests, attitudes, beliefs, social roles, stage of life and behaviours that collectively define the participants at the time of their Expo experiences' (Anderson, 2003, p. 406). Specifically, he found that the social dimension of a person's sociocultural identity elicited the strongest memories of their experiences, more so than specific exhibitions and displays. However, he noted that, not only what a person remembered, but how they reflected on their experiences through the 'frame' of their identity and their role in the visit, were important. Anderson concluded that 'memories were overwhelmingly dominated and mediated by the sociocultural identity of the individual at the time of the visit' (Anderson, 2003, p. 409). How can museums understand and utilise people's sociocultural identities in the development of exhibitions or events? To date, museum visitors have arbitrarily been put in certain groups because they share certain characteristics, such as social role or age (i.e., family groups, adults or young adults). These characteristics fit some of the criteria of the sociocultural identities as defined by Anderson but certainly not all of them. In fact, being in a family group does not say anything about the interests, attitudes or beliefs of its members. This issue is discussed in Chapter 9 from a slightly different perspective. We next examine two studies that have tried to explore what types of identities are at play when people visit museums.

> The strongest and more lasting museum visit memories are associated with visitors' sociocultural identities (see also Chapter 7)

Identity as a motivator and as a 'filter'

Falk (2009, p. 158) focuses on small 'i' identities (i.e., personal identity as opposed to collective identities) and, in particular, those aspects of identity that change before each visit. He views visitor experience as consisting of ephemeral and constructed relationships that uniquely occur at any given visit. Hence, in this model a visitor could go to the same museum many times on different days and, each time, enter with a different identity. Falk (2009) argues that these small 'i' identities are formed through the confluence of two streams of thought on the part of the visitor. The idea of the stream of thought comes from Simon's (2008) analysis of the 'subjective stream-like quality of consciousness', mentioned in the theory section. Simon's work, coming from social psychology, has been a key influence in the development of Falk's conceptualisation of identity. The first stream includes the needs the individual wishes to satisfy through some kind of leisure time activity. The second stream of thought is the 'specific mental models of various leisure settings, including museums, that individually and collectively support various leisure-related activities' (Falk, 2009, p. 158). When these two streams of thought come together when an individual makes a decision to visit a specific museum, this decision-making process results in the formation of one of five 'identity-related museum motivations'. These are: explorers, facilitators, experience seekers, professional/hobbyists and rechargers. Explorers are driven by curiosity and they visit museums because they value the intellectual experiences these offer. Facilitators correspond to socially motivated groups of visitors and their main motivation is to satisfy the needs and desires of other members of their group. Family groups may fall in this category, although it would be wrong to assume that all family members are facilitators. Experience seekers correspond to people seeking type of experiences that could be classified as sightseeing. Professional/hobbyists correspond to experts. Rechargers correspond to art lovers seeking a 'spiritual' type of experience, indicated by Falk's previous name for them 'spiritual pilgrims' (Falk & Storksdieck, 2005). Falk (2009) sees the individual's entering motivations creating a basic trajectory for the visit which can predict how visitors will interact with their setting. He argues that although the general patterns of a visit are predictable, the details of each visitor's experience is highly personalised and unique. According to Falk (2009, p. 160), the visitor museum experience is satisfying if the marriage of perceived identity-related needs and museum affordances proves to be well-matched, and he does not think that the visitor's motivation-based identity changes as part of a visit. This, for example, is contrary to some of the sociocultural approaches to identity presented above (see for example Oyserman et al., 2012). This approach to identity also ignores the role identities have in mediating between predetermined social positions and agency (Holland et al., 1998).

Personal identities can shape the general patterns of a visit

The concept of identity-related museum motivations has attracted a lot of attention from museum practitioners, but it has also attracted a lot of criticism from researchers who use the concept of identity in their research. The criticism seems to focus on two main issues. Firstly, in an effort to simplify and operationalise very complex theoretical concepts, it is argued that the analytical framework used has ended up being reductionist. Secondly, theoretical concepts used have not been applied as initially intended. Here, the concept of positionality (borrowed from Holland et al., 1998) is given as an example. Positionality refers to an individual's social position as defined by gender, sexuality, social class and so on (i.e., what Falk calls 'big "I" identities'), and shapes the action of the individual and his or her perspective. For example, Dawson and Jensen (2011) argue that Falk's use of small 'i' identities problematically de-emphasises the role of demographic factors in identity construction. Dawson and Jensen (2011) discuss research carried out by other researchers who emphasise the importance of the role of class (see Willis, 1977), educational attainment (see Bourdieu & Darbel, 1991), social exclusion (see Bourman, 1996; Jensen 2010) and other sociocultural factors in their decision to attend or not, and the ultimate value of cultural institution visits for particular individuals.

Dawson and Jensen (2011) also argue that visitors' initial expectations can change as they encounter new ideas and experiences and that Falk's model does not take this into account. This is a disputed point within visitor studies, with Doering and Pekarik (1996) and Falk (2009) both arguing that it is very difficult for visitors' identities or entrance narratives to be changed by a museum, while Wagoner and Jensen (2010) argue that they can be changed. Further support for the role that adjustment or improvisation that happens during the museum visit activity can play in changing (or indeed preserving) identity comes from Holland et al.'s (1998) research.

Identities can shift during the visit

Another criticism to Falk's conceptualisation of identity and its role in museum visiting comes from Rounds (2006) who treats the subject from an intellectual standpoint rather than empirical one. He approaches museum-going as a type of experience where visitors engage in 'identity work'. 'Identity work' – defined as 'the processes through which we construct, maintain, and adapt our sense of personal identity, and persuade other people to believe in the identity' (Rounds 2006: 133) – is used as a concept to describe the browsing behaviour so commonly observed in museum environments and supports the legitimacy of visitors' partial use of the museum exhibition content. Importantly, Rounds acknowledges the role of structure (the external world, with its limitations and affordances; see also theory section above) in providing a place, way and reason for identity to emerge. Beyond their value in linking identity to museum visiting and opening up new areas for research, the above approaches signal a shift in museum learning theory and practice.

A different way of conceptualising identity and its role in museum visiting comes from research carried out in art museums. In her study of how people – both visitors and non-visitors – perceive art museums and how these perceptions shape visitation patterns, Stylianou-Lambert (2009) used self-identity (i.e., personal identity) as a dimension that shapes the ways people perceive museums. The study was carried out exclusively in Cyprus using semi-structured interviews with sixty people. Stylianou-Lambert (2009) identified a series of different 'filters' (referred to as 'museum perceptual filters') which were shaped by people's sense of personal identity at the time of the interview. The 'museum perceptual filters' affect people's perceptions of the art museum and also their decisions to visit. These filters include: 'the professional', 'art-loving', 'self-exploration', 'cultural tourism', 'social visitation', 'romantic', 'rejection' and 'indifference'. Personal identity appeared to vary across visitors who use different museum perceptual filters, with people using the professional and self-exploration filter reporting high connection, while those using the art-loving and cultural tourism filters reported high to moderate connection. Finally, those using the social visitation filter reported low connection to personal identity.

> Personal identity acts as a filter through which the museum is perceived and affects levels of engagement

Enacting gender and class identity

Shifting focus slightly, the following studies use concepts and theories coming from anthropology and cultural studies. These studies emphasise relationships of domination, for example, in the way knowledge is organised and in the way the dominant culture and ideology is psychologically internalised and shapes one's personality. Following this line of thought, for example, Paul Willis (1977) examined how social reproduction is experienced by white working-class boys failing school. Willis studied groups of boys placed in the bottom sets of bands and how they developed an anti-school subculture (similar to the laddish behaviour described by Archer et al. (2016) below), which was seen as a conscious act of resistance (i.e., working-class boys choosing to fail themselves by rejecting all school values). In the museum context, this would be the equivalent of choosing not to visit museums, or museums not being part of one's life (either because one is not aware that they exist or because it is not the kind of activity they and their community would engage in). In the first case, they actively choose to reject museums, while the second case is more of a passive rejection of museums.

> Fear of being stereotyped or judged (e.g., not knowing how to navigate the museum, or how to behave in the museum environment) leads to racial and ethnic discrimination

Going back to studies carried out in other contexts, some work has focused on how this socialisation process can be resisted, either consciously or unconsciously. The focus here is on acts of resistance – most of which are often unconscious – by members of subordinate groups. These type of studies are reminiscent of Holland et al.'s (1998) work.

Although carried out in school settings, it is also worth mentioning Claude Steele and his colleagues' (Steel, 1997; 2003; Steel & Aronson, 1995) influential studies of the academic performance of African American and Latino American students, who have historically been marginalised both in formal education and in society more generally. Steel's (1997, 2003) research focuses on what he calls 'identity threats' – such as the fear of being stereotyped or the fear of being judged based on gender, race or age – that exist in different contexts and can help explain racial and ethnic achievement gaps in formal education or disadvantage in the wider society. Of particular interest is his focus on situational or contextual cues, for example, in situations where the curriculum does not represent the experiences of black students and, in effect, marginalises them. For example, evidence collected from both white and black students suggests that, when they were told that a test would measure their cognitive ability, black students tended to underperform as compared to the white students due to fear that they would confirm the stereotype that black students are less intelligent (Steel, 2003; Steel & Aronson, 1995). Although taking a different approach, Steel's reference to situational cues is reminiscent of the idea put forward by Oyserman et al. (2012) that certain self-concepts can be activated by cues that are embedded in different contexts. This would be an interesting concept to explore in the museum context which includes many intentionally designed cues (i.e., wayfinding systems, visuals that attract and direct the attention or textual interpretation and other interpretive devices that help visitors make sense of objects). But, it also includes many unintentional cues, such as lack of images of women, children or people from different cultural backgrounds, which could lead to their alienation from the museum setting.

Gender identities can encourage engagement or disengagement with the museum content

We now turn our attention to a study carried out in a science museum targeting groups of boys on a visit with their school. This study, carried out by Archer et al. (2016), is one of the few ethnographic studies that focuses on the construction and performance of identity, tracking moment-to-moment interactions as well as reflections of participants in a museum context. It makes clear reference to its theoretical underpinnings: it uses both sociological and cultural studies approaches to conceptualise social and cultural identities (notably the work of Bourdieu presented in the previous section of this chapter, and also to more specific conceptualisations of gender and ethnicity[8]).

Identity performances were seen as 'combining talk, gestures, embodiment, and behaviors' (Archer et al., 2016, p. 450) and the analytical framework used reflected this theoretical position. The study focused on performances of masculinity enacted by a group of thirty-six boys during a field trip to a science museum with their school. Students came from urban schools, a range of ethnic backgrounds and from a predominantly working-class background. Data sources included ethnographic field notes, photographs and audio recordings of students and teachers during the visit, and also discussion groups with students and interviews with teachers before and after the museum visit.

The study by Archer et al. (2016) showed that the boys participating in this research enacted three performances of masculinity during their visit: (1) 'laddishness', typically involving behaviour of disengagement such as 'resisting doing school work, mucking about, macho behaviors, engaging in sexist/sexual banter' or 'finding ways to (appear to) resist doing any science work' (Archer et al., 2016, p. 454), (2) 'muscular intellect', involving 'displays of superior knowledge and intelligence' (ibid, p. 455), and (3) 'translocational masculinity'. The latter were rather sporadic moments where boys seemed to move beyond the previous two more stereotypical performances of masculinity and, instead, drew on 'their own varied cultural resources and experiences to establish links and points of commonality between their own lives, interests, and values and the museum context' (ibid, p. 457). Laddishness was by far the most commonly enacted masculine identity, with almost all boys performing it, followed by muscular intellect (fourteen boys). Translocational masculinity was noted on a small number of occasions, performed by twelve boys.

The Archer et al. (2016) study is the first one that examined the impact that laddish or muscular intellect performances (or other behaviours that are seen as disobedience or aggressive/abusive) have on excluding other students from engaging with the museum content, as far as we are aware. We think that it would be important to consider how certain groups (like the working-class boys in this study) can be supported to engage with the museum content through using their own cultural resources. Another issue that is worth considering is what culturally appropriate resources and contextual cues in the museum space could support more positive identities.

A return to the Colored Girls Museum

It is Saturday morning and Denise (a mother of two and full-time social worker who lives in Philadelphia) is on her way to the Colored Girls Museum with her daughter, Jeveane, who is ten years old, and Monna, eight years old, who is the daughter of a family friend. Monna's mum, who has a jewellery shop, works on Saturdays so, today, Denise offered to have Monna over for a playdate. Monna and Jeveane are very good friends and so are their mothers who grew up in the same neighbourhood and went to the same school. Denise and her family had been to the Fringe Festival at the FringeArts Building in July last year. She had heard about the Colored Girls Museum Festival from a friend who told her that Ian Friday, a global soul DJ whose work they both like, would organise a music and dance party. She had been really excited about the idea of having a Colored Girls Museum in Philadelphia. Denise and her family do not usually look to museums to be something of interest or to seek out, but this was different – it was about black women and that had hit a chord with her. She also wanted her daughter to see art produced by black people. 'This is not something our kids learn about at school', she had thought. Then, only last week she was listening to Ian Friday's programme on HouseFM.net. That reminded her of the Museum and she made the decision to take her daughter there on Saturday.

The Museum's involvement in the Fringe Festival and its collaboration with black artists known to the black community, relates well to Denise's self-concept. After all, one of the Museum's key aims is to present a range of experiences reflecting different ways of being a girl and going through different stages of adolescence and adulthood in the life of black women in the US. The title of the Museum also appeals to particular dimensions of black visitors' identity, while at the same time shaping both the pre-visit and in-gallery motivations of its visitors. The Museum embodies all the things that Denise, her family and her community value. It also embodies different possibilities for the growth of Denise's personal and cultural identity, as a black woman, mother and wife, and full-time social worker. This is consistent with theories of self, identity and agency coming from cultural psychology, anthropology and sociology which state that people have an array of self-concepts. These include both the 'me' and social 'us' concepts, both of which are activated by cues. These cues are situated and can be either negative (perceived as 'identity threats', for example) or positive, where identities are nurtured and people are able to contextualise and make sense of their personal, family and wider community experiences.

Earlier in the morning, Jeveane and Monna were really excited about spending the day together, but were not really sure that they would enjoy visiting a museum. They had both been to museums on school fieldtrips. Although some of them were 'ok', there was always something they had to do for school and it was not always interesting. Also there was never enough time to do the things they found interesting; field trips were always rushed. But her mum said that it was like no other museum she had ever been to and that it was something that she needed to see. 'It is about girls like you', she had said. As the group approaches the Museum, they are all surprised. It does not, indeed, look like any other museum they know. This looks like a normal house. As they come into the garden, they are greeted by a lady who takes them to the tool shed, which is full of pictures of black women. The pictures look old and that attracts the girls' attention. Their guide tells them that these women used to work in factories. She also shows them some needlework and tells them how it was made and how creative the black women who made them were. Denise tells Jeveane and Monna that these are like the tablecloths both of the girls' grandmothers used to make. That surprises both of them; they had never thought of their grandmothers' creative side, or of needlework as a creative activity. They are also surprised to find out that their mothers used to make their own embroidered badges when they were young. Jeveane and Monna would like to try it too and ask Denise to show them when they go back home. In line with sociocultural approaches to identity, the exhibition touches both on personal identity, through the use of personal objects collected by members of the community and exhibited in the intimate space of the home, and on collective identities, through the development of exhibits like the factory worker which reflect on the collective lived experience of black women. Furthermore, there is a clear link to Bourdieu's concept of cultural capital and how it can be used as a cultural asset. In this sense, both Jeveane and Monna already possess the habit of looking at and being able to associate with embroidery objects – among other familiar everyday objects – they can see in the Museum. They appreciate the fact that the objects they and members of their extended families have in their homes are 'museum-worthy'. This helps them relate these objects to the 'self' because they are part of their habitus.

As Denise and the girls go into the living room, the first thing the girls spot are some figurines placed on a crochet placemat on the fireplace and the portrait of a little black girl hanging above the fire place. They are all so beautiful and the little girl in the portrait looks around their age. Jeveane thinks that her mum was right; this museum is for girls like her and Monna. There is something in the atmosphere, just being in there. It is more personal and it is like hands-on as well. Meanwhile, Denise has exactly the same thoughts. The memories just come flooding back. She can really sense that she just zooms back into that time when she was a little girl. It is not so much the particular objects as the combination of it all: the colours, the patterns, the photographs, the smells, sounds and music. In particular, the music seems to be speaking to the girl inside her. It reminds her of the times when she did her Saturday morning chores, helping her mother as a little girl. She feels quite emotional and glad that she came and brought the girls. She cannot wait to tell Monna's mum and the rest of her family about it. They all need to see this. She takes her phone out, takes some pictures and shares them on Facebook.

The location and the interior and the fact that it is a house somebody lives in reinforces that fact that this is part of this family group's own world, part of their 'figured world'. A number of items, both tangible and intangible, reinforce their self-image, for example, how Denise sees herself through music or how the girls see their grandmothers as creative black women through the needlework.

As the group goes from room to room, they see more things that remind Denise of her own childhood and people in her family who had similar things when she visited their houses as a young girl, like, for example, the wooden ironing board her grandmother used to have. In all the rooms they are greeted by artists who talk to them about each room and what the idea behind each room is, and that all the artwork is made by black women artists. Denise can see the look on Jeveane's and Monna's faces, a hint of surprise mixed with immense pride. She feels proud too, but also happy and uplifted. She thinks she should try to do some art classes too, or perhaps make some jewellery like Monna's mum does. She makes a mental note to ask her friend about that. The use of art as a prism to look at familiar objects from the recent history of black women both at home and at work seems to have enabled Denise to construct new identities different to the ones traditionally ascribed to black women. Here Denise starts seeing herself as somebody who has new interests and learns how to make art. This is consistent with theories about learning identity and the agency of the individual to develop new interests, which is a way to become the person she wants to become. This example is also consistent with the positional nature of identity, put forward by sociocultural theories. In other words, how identity can change on the basis of participating in practices such as this museum visit practice.

Meanwhile, Jeveane and Monna enjoy going from one room to the next, especially when they go upstairs to the second floor and up a narrow staircase. 'What an exciting day it turned out to be, quite an adventure', Monna thinks. Her mum's friend, 'aunt Denise', was right when she said that it would not be like any other museum she had been to with school. Monna likes the art in particular. She also likes it being shown in an actual house and it reminds her of a theatre set. 'What was the last play she had been with her family called again?' She cannot remember, but she remembers that there was a fireplace and some figures on its sill just like the ones they saw in the living room as they came into the Museum. While Denise is talking to some other visitors and Museum staff, Monna starts talking to Jeveane about the figurines. They both want to see them again. There are some hand-made dolls there too. The adults keep talking and the girls become slightly bored. Jeveane's mum points at different objects now and tells the girls that their great-grandmothers and other black women of that generation had similar things. Jeveane appears to be attending to her mother reminiscing about everyday objects of her childhood like the old-fashioned steam iron. Her mother tells her that her grandmother, Jeveane's great-grandmother, had a similar one. She always worked hard and took in laundry to support her family. Jeveane and Monna start getting a bit restless now. They really want to go back to the room where they caught a glimpse of those wooden figurines. There was also that portrait of a little girl in a white dress placed above the fireplace. Monna keeps whispering to her, asking to go back to the room with the portraits, while her mother looks visibly emotional. Jeveane feels torn between her loyalty to her mother and her friend and considers different actions she can take. 'Oh, I know what', she thinks. She then asks her mother if Great-grandmother used to make crochet and offers to show her where she saw the placemat. The girl's action show her ability to manage her identities – as a daughter and member of a particular family unit as well as of the African American community, and as a friend. She also showed her agency by exploring different possible actions, chose one and engaged her mother and friend in this action (i.e., proposing to visit the room where the portraits and crochet placemat are).

Here Jeveane engages in a process of performing and negotiating between different identities, such as that of a daughter and a friend, and competing loyalties. In line with sociocultural approaches to learning, she draws on her understanding of her family history and what is of value to the black community (i.e., cultural resources and practices) in order to engage with the museum content, communicate what is important to her and to also engage with her group members.

As Denise, Jeveane and Monna trace their steps back down the staircase and back to the living room, Denise checks her phone and sees that many of her friends and family had 'liked' the pictured she shared on Facebook earlier. She smiles to herself…

Contextualising self and identity

Which type of identities do existing exhibitions or programmes in your museum represent? How do different types of groups respond to existing exhibitions or programmes and the way they represent identities? How do they perform their identities and how does the composition of the group and roles each visitor plays within the group shape their identities during the visit? How do particular performances of identity include or exclude other group members or other visitors? How do intentional and unintentional cues in the physical setting of the museum affect visitors' identity?

What do you know or can you find out about the cultural reference and practices of the people who do not currently visit your museum? What interests do they have and how do they pursue these interests? What do you know or can find out about the settings in which non-traditional audiences carry out their everyday and leisure time activities? How can you develop exhibitions and programme themes and interpretation that resonate with both actual and potential visitors? How can learning opportunities in your museum be connected to people's identities in a way that it is meaningful for them and their cultural practices? If you imagine your museum as a figured world, how would you enable different types of visitors visiting at different times and in different groups to relate to this figured world? Which aspect of the figured world of your museum do you have the ability to change/shape? How can you provide activities and resources that can be used by different visitors to figure their own world? What will the exhibition or programme narrative look like?

How can visitors use these narratives to understand themselves and perform their identity? How can you assess that based on the visitor's activities? How can you assess that based on activities of the other members of the group? What type of artefacts from your museum's collection could enable people to mediate their thoughts and feelings? What new role could audiences play (i.e., co-creators of the museum content)? What resources do you need to make available in order to change the way people engage with the content or the activities of an exhibition or event? How can you make people aware of possibilities of learning across contexts (rather than learning about similar content across contexts)? How is the content framed across different contexts and practices? For example, if you work in a social history museum what do you know about how people use objects in their everyday lives? How can you help them make the link between your museum's collection and equivalent everyday objects? How can you support families bridging the museum, home, school cultural practices and make the transition for their children smoother? What levels of help do you need to make available to non-visitors, first time or frequent visitors to your museums? How can the activities be designed to take your visitors through a learning journey, part of which may make them feel uncomfortable or require them to deal with material and questions that are unfamiliar or related to taboo subjects, like race, for example?

How can you use the concept of identity as an analytical category to study how it is manifested in your museum space? What analytical categories can you use in the study of identity? How you can utilise manifestations or enactments of identity – such as language, behaviour, choice of things to do or spaces to use/visit, who or which communities to associate with, what activities to engage with – in the development of these analytical categories? What types of grouping are associated with different sociocultural identities? Can your tools capture these?

Notes

1 This scenario was written by the authors using information available on the Colored Girls Museum website and blog, with the Museum's permission.
2 This chapter examines empirical research into how identity is enacted by visitors in museums, rather than how museums present identities. However, this research can inform the representation of identities in museum exhibitions or programmes, for example, as it can provide evidence on how these are perceived by visitors or highlight possible misconceptions or even reproduction of stereotypical views of the identity of particular groups of people.
3 In this chapter, we use the term cultural psychology to refer to the psychology of culture, since this is the most commonly used term in the literature.
4 Bourdieu (1990, p. 13) recognises that these dispositions are embodied, performed, but also transformed by individuals, 'by the agent's practice, his or her capacity for intervention and improvisation'. Furthermore, as Conde (2011, p. 7) notes, the concept of habitus is related to a whole '"system of dispositions", underlying the overall social influences on individuals'. This differentiation of dispositions combines not only structural and institutional factors, but also cross-cultural, 'conjunctural, events-based, situational or interactional' factors (ibid, p. 10).
5 For further discussion see Crooke (2007). We would also like to add that the research studies reviewed in this book take a rather positive approach to capital and how it can be developed as a way to combat the effects of disadvantage.
6 See also some of the early reports produced by the Smithsonian Office of Policy and Analysis (www.si.edu/OPANDA/exhibitions), such as Fronville, C.L. and Doering, Z.D. (1989). Visitor perspectives of tropical rainforests: A report based on the 1988 'Tropical rainforests: A disappearing treasure'.
7 In this chapter, we only focus on the elements of these studies that refer specifically to identity. More information about the studies can be found in Chapter 7.
8 There is an extensive literature focusing on dimensions of social identity such as gender and ethnicity which we cannot cover here. The reader is directed to the work of Hall (1990), Butler (1990) and also an overview of other relevant work in Archer et al. (2016, pp. 443–448).

References

Altschul, I., Oyserman, D., & Bybee, D. (2008). Racial-ethnic self-schemas and segmented assimilation: Identity and the academic achievement of hispanic youth. *Social Psychology Quarterly*, 71, 302–320.

Anderson, D. (2003). Visitors' long-term memories of World Expositions. *Curator: The Museum Journal*, 46, 401–421.

Anderson, D. & Shimizu, H. (2007). Factors shaping vividness of memory episodes: visitors' long-term memories of the 1970 Japan World Exposition. *Memory*, 15, 177–191.

Archer, L., Dawson, E., Seakins, A., DeWitt, J., Godec, S., & Whitby, C. (2016). 'I'm being a man here': Urban boys' performances of masculinity and engagement with science during a science museum visit. *Journal of the Learning Sciences*, 25, 3, 438–485.

Bauman, Z. (2000). *Liquid modernity*. Cambridge: Polity Press.

Bell P., Lewenstein B., Shouse A.W., & Feder M.A. (2009). *Learning science in informal environments: People, places and pursuits*. Washington, DC: The National Academies Press.

Bourdieu, P. (1977). *Outline of a theory of practice*. Cambridge: Cambridge University Press.

Bourdieu, P. (1984). *Distinction: A social critique of the judgment of taste*. Translated from French by R. Nice. London: Routledge.

Bourdieu, P. (1986). The forms of capital. In J. Richardson (Ed.), *Handbook of theory and research for the sociology of education* (pp. 241–258). New York: Greenwood.

Bourdieu, P. & Darbel, A. (1991). *The love of art: European art museums and their public*. Cambridge: Polity Press.

Bunting, C. (2007). Public value and the arts in England: Discussion and conclusions of the arts debate. www.artscouncil.org.uk/publication_archive/public-value-and-the-arts-in-england-discussion-and-conclusions-of-the-arts-debate/

Burns Owens Partnership (2005). New directions in social policy: Developing the evidence base for museums, libraries and archives in England. London: mla. (http://webarchive.nationalarchives.gov.uk/20111013135435/research.mla.gov.uk/evidence/documents/ndsp_developing_evidence_doc_6649.pdf

Carlone, H. & Johnson, A. (2007). Understanding the science experiences of women of color: Science identity as an analytic lens. *Journal of Research in Science Teaching*, 44(8), 1187–1218.

Clifford, J. (1994). Diasporas, *Cultural Anthropology*, 9, 302–338.

Cohen, R. (1996). Diasporas and the nation-state: from victims to challengers, *International Affairs*, 72, 507–520.

Côté, J.E. & Levine, C.G. (2002). *Identity formation, agency, and culture: A social-psychological synthesis*. Mahwah, NJ/London: Lawrence Erlbaum Associates.

Crooke, E. (2007). *Museums and community: Ideas, issues and challenges*. London: Routledge.

Davies, S. (1994). *By popular demand: A strategic analysis of the market potential for museums and art galleries in the UK*. London: Museums and Galleries Commission.

Davies, S. (2005). Still popular: Museums and their visitors 1994–2004. *Cultural Trends*, 14(1), 67–105.

Dawson, E. & Jensen, E. (2011). Towards a contextual turn in visitor studies: Evaluating visitor segmentation and identity-related motivations. *Visitor Studies*, 14(2), 127–140.

Doering, Z.D. & Pekarik, A.J. (1996). Questioning the entrance narrative. *Journal of Museum Education*, 21(3), 20–22.

Eriksen, T.H. & Nielsen, F.S. (2001). *A history of anthropology*. London: Pluto Press.

Erikson, E.H. (1959). *Identity and the life cycle: Selected papers, with a historical introduction by David Rapaport*. New York: International University Press.

Falk, J. & Dierking, L. (1992). *The museum experience*. Washington, DC: Whalesback Books.

Falk, J. & Storksdieck, M. (2005). Using the contextual model of learning to understand visitor learning from a science center exhibition. *Science Education*, 89, 744–778.

Falk, J.H. (2006). An identity-centered approach to understanding museum learning. *Curator*, 49(2), 151–166.

Falk, J.H. (2009). *Identity and the museum visitor experience*. Walnut Creek, CA: Left Coast Press.

Falk, J.H., Heimlich, J., & Bronnenkant, K. (2008). Using identity-related visit motivations as a tool for understanding adult zoo and aquarium visitors' meaning making, *Curator*, 51:1, pp. 55–80.

Fienberg, J. & Leinhardt, G. (2002). Looking through the glass: Reflections of identity in conversations as a history museum. In G. Leinhardt, K. Crowley, & K. Knutson (Eds.), *Learning conversations in museum* (pp. 167–212). Mahwah, NJ: Lawrence Erlbaum Associates.

Geertz, C. (1975). *The interpretation of culture*. London: Hutchinson.

Greenfield, P.M. (2000). Three approaches to the psychology of culture: Where do they come from? Where can they go? *Asian Journal of Social Psychology*, 3(3), 223–240.

Hall, S. (1990). Cultural identity and diaspora. In J. Rutherford (Ed.), *Identity, community, culture, difference* (pp. 222–237). London: Lawrence and Wishart.

Heider, F. (1958). *The psychology of interpersonal relations*. New York: Wiley.

Holland, D., Skinner, D., Lachiotte Jr, W., & Cain, C. (2001). *Identity and agency in cultural worlds*. Cambridge, MA: Harvard University Press.

Hooper-Greenhill, E. (2007). *Museums and education: Purpose, pedagogy, performance*. London/New York: Routledge.

House, J. (1977). The three faces of social psychology. *Sociometry*, 40(2), 161–177.

Hull, G.A. & Greeno, J.G. (2006). Identity and agency in nonschool and school worlds. In Z. Bekerman et al. (Eds.), *Learning in places: The informal education reader* (pp. 77–97). New York: Peter Lang Publishing.

Jenkins, R. (2000). Categorization: Identity, social process and epistemology, *Current Sociology*, 48, 3, 7–25.

Jenkins, R. (2008). *Social identity* (2nd edition). New York: Routledge.

Johnson, R. (1993). Towards a cultural theory of the nation: a British-Dutch dialogue. In A. Galena, B. Henkes, and H. te Velde (Eds.),

Images of the nation: Different meanings of Dutchness 1870–1940 (pp. 159–217). Amsterdam: Rodopi B.V.

Kelly, L.J. (2007). The interrelationships between adult museum visitors' learning identities and their museum experiences. Doctoral Thesis. Sydney University of Technology.

Kroger. J., Martinussen, M., & Marcia, J. (2010). Identity status change during adolescence and young adulthood: A meta-analysis. *Journal of Adolescence*, 33, 683–698.

Larraín, J. (2000). *Identity and modernity in Latin America.* Cambridge: Polity Press.

Latchem, J. (2006). How does education support the formation and establishment of individual identities? *International Journal of Art & Design education*, 25(1), 42–52.

Leinhardt, G., Crowley, K., & Knutson, K. (Eds.) (2002). *Learning conversations in museums*. New Jersey: Lawrence Erlbaum Associates.

Leinhardt, G. & Gregg, M. (2002). Burning buses, burning crosses: Pre-service teachers see civil rights. In G. Leinhardt, K. Crowley, & K. Knutson (Eds.), *Learning conversations in museums* (pp. 139–166). Mahwah, NJ: Lawrence Erlbaum Associates.

Leinhardt, G. & Knutson, K. (2004). *Listening in on museum conversations*. Walnut Creek, CA: Altamira Press.

Leurs, K. & Ponzanesi, S. (2011). Mediated crossroads: Youthful digital diasporas. *M/C – A Journal of Media and Culture*, 14(2).

Lindauer, M. (2005). What to ask and how to answer: A comparative analysis of methodologies and philosophies of summative exhibit evaluation. *Museum and Society*, 3(3), 137–152.

Lindholm, Charles (2001). *Culture and identity: The history, theory, and practice of psychological anthropology*. London: McGraw-Hill.

Macdonald, S. (2003). Museums, national, postnational and transcultural identities, *Museum and Society*, 1(1), 1–16.

Marcia, J.E. (1966). Development and validation of ego-identity status. *Journal of Personality and Social Psychology*, 3(5), 551.

Marcia, J.E. (1993). The status of the statuses: Research review. In J.E. Marcia, A.S. Waterman, D.R. Matteson, S.L. Archer, & J.L. Orlofsky (Eds.), *Ego identity: A handbook for psychosocial research* (pp. 22–41). New York: Springer-Verlag.

Markus, H.R. & Kitayama, S. (1991). Culture and the self: Implications for cognition, emotion, and motivation. *Psychological Review*, 98, 224–253.

Markus, H.R. & Kitayama, S. (2010). Cultures and selves: A cycle of mutual constitution. *Perspectives on Psychological Science*, 5(4), 420–430.

Matarasso F. (1997). *Use or ornament? The social impact of participation in the arts*. London: Comedia.

McLean, F. (2006). Introduction: Heritage and identity, *International Journal of Heritage Studies*, 12, 3–7.

Mcmanus, P. (1996). Frames of reference: Changes in evaluative attitudes to visitors. *The Journal of Museum Education*, 21(3), 3–5. Retrieved from www.jstor.org/stable/40479067

Mauss, M. (1979) [1950]. *Sociology and psychology: Essays*. London: Routledge & Kegan Paul.

Meeus, W. (2011). The study of adolescent identity formation 2000–2010: A review of longitudinal research. *Journal of Research on Adolescence*, 21, 75–94.

Miller, J.G. (2001). The cultural grounding of social psychological theory. In A. Tesser & N. Schwarz (Eds.), *Blackwell handbook of social psychology: Vol. 1. Intraindividual processes* (pp. 22–43). Oxford: Blackwell.

Newman, A. & McLean, F. (2004). Presumption, policy and practice: The use of museums and galleries as agents of social inclusion in Great Britain, *International Journal of Cultural Policy*, 10(2), 167–181.

Nonini, M.D. & Ong, A. (1997). Chinese transnationalism as an alternative modernity. In A. Ong and D.M. Nonini (Eds.), *Ungrounded empires: The cultural politics of modern Chinese transnationalism* (pp. 3–33). London: Routledge.

Oyserman, D., Elmore, K., & Smith, G. (2012). Self, self-concept, and identity. In M.R. Leary & J.P. Tangney (Eds.), *Handbook of self and identity* (2nd edition, pp. 69–104). New York/London: The Guilford Press.

Paris, S.G. & Mercer, M. (2002). Finding self in objects: Identity exploration in museums. In G. Leinhardt, K. Crowley, & K. Knutson (Eds.), *Learning conversations in museums* (pp. 401–423). Mahwah, NJ: Lawrence Erlbaum and Associates.

Rounds, J. (2006). Doing identity work in museums. *Curator: The Museum Journal*, 49(2), 133–150.

Sfard, A. & Prusak, A. (2005). Telling identities: In search of an analytic tool for investigating learning as a culturally shaped activity. *Educational Researcher*, 34(4), 14–22.

Simon, B. (2004). *Identity in modern society: A social psychological perspective*. Oxford: Wiley-Blackwell.

Sökefeld, M. (1999). Debating self, identity, and culture in anthropology. *Current Anthropology*, 40(4), 417–447.

Spencer, M.B., Harpalani, V., Fegley, S., Dell'Angelo, T., & Seaton, G. (2003). Identity, self, and peers in context: A culturally-sensitive, developmental framework for analysis. In R.M. Lerner, F. Jacobs, & D. Wertlieb (Eds.), *Handbook of applied developmental science: Promoting positive child, adolescent, and family development through research, policies, and programs* (Vol. 1, pp. 123–142). Thousand Oaks, CA: Sage.

Stainton, C. (2002). Voices and images: Making connections between identity and art. In G. Leinhardt, K. Crowley, & K. Knutson (Eds.), *Learning conversations in museums* (pp. 213–249). Mahwah, NJ: Lawrence Erlbaum and Associates.

Steele, C.M. (1997). A threat in the air: How stereotypes shape intellectual identity and performance. *American Psychologist*, 52, 613–629.

Steele, C.M. (2003). Stereotype threat and African American student achievement. In T. Perry, C.M. Steele, & A.G. Hilliard, III (Eds.), *Young, gifted and black: Promoting high achievement among African-American students* (pp. 109–130). Boston, MA: Beacon Press Books.

Steele, C.M. & Aronson, J. (1995). Stereotype threat and the intellectual test performance of African-Americans. *Journal of Personality and Social Psychology*, 69, 797–811.

Stylianou-Lambert, T. (2009). Perceiving the art museum. *Journal of Museum Management and Curatorship*, 24(2), 139–158.

Wagoner, B. & Jensen, E. (2010). Science learning at the zoo: Evaluating children's developing understanding of animals and their habitats. *Psychology & Society*, 3(1), 65–76.

Walker, K. (2006). Story structures: Building narrative trails in museums. In G. Dettori, T. Giannetti, A. Paiva, and A. Vaz (Eds.), *Technology-mediated narrative environments for learning* (pp. 103–114). Rotterdam: Sense Publishers.

Weigert, A.J., Teitge, J.S., & Teitge, D.W. (1986). *Society and identity: Toward a sociological psychology*. Cambridge: Cambridge University Press.

Wenger, E. (2000). *Communities of practice: Learning, meaning and identity*, Cambridge: Cambridge University Press.

Willis, P. (1977). *Learning to labour: How working class kids get working class jobs*. Farnborough: Saxon House.

9 Motivation: from visiting to devotion

Linking up museums and people through serious pursuits[1]

The Volunteer Inclusion Programme (VIP) run by the Museum of London Archaeological Archive has developed a model of volunteering that connects the motivations of diverse individuals and audiences with key elements of its mission. These include the management of collections and collections research, on the one hand, and outreach and public engagement, on the other; aims which directly link to the Museum's strategy to 'Stretch Thinking & Reach More People'. By engaging and sustaining the motivations of the VIP volunteers, the Archaeological Archive has managed to bring together these elements of work that are often conceptualised as separate realms in museums.

The Museum of London's Archaeological Archive is the world's largest (Guinness World Record 2012) and is part of the Museum of London's Archaeological Collections Department. Based at Mortimer Wheeler House in Hackney, East London, it cares for records concerning archaeological investigations of nearly 9,000 sites and holds over 3,500 detailed excavation archives collected over the past 100 years. Caring for such a large collection is a huge task, particularly because many archaeological finds need to be (re-)processed in order to meet current collections management standards introduced within the last ten to twenty years. The Arts Council for England funded VIP works with sites deposited prior to these guidelines being in place. The Archive has been experimenting with volunteer programmes that have focused on the care of its collections. For example, both the Minimum Standard Project (ran from 2002–2005) and the Archive Volunteer Learning Programme (ran from 2006–2007), which preceded VIP, involved volunteers in the collection care activities. Building on the knowledge gained from the Minimum Standard Project, the Heritage Lottery Fund funded Archive Volunteer Learning Programme particularly focused on enhancing the learning experience of its

Figure 9.1 VIP volunteers engaging visitors in the handling of animal bones. ©Museum of
London.

volunteers and providing them with transferable skills. It was
also the first programme that recruited volunteers who could be
defined as 'at risk of social exclusion'.

VIP has built on the ethos of these programmes as well as the
way they have been set up and run. In its early days, VIP was
conceptualised as a social inclusion programme, where those
at risk of social exclusion and the more traditional audience
of student and retiree volunteers came together. One of the key
elements of VIP is engaging with people's motivations and linking them to the real work of Archive curatorial staff as well as
to its vision. Key elements of the Archive that align with VIP
include fostering ownership of their archaeology and facilitating Archive users' development of knowledge about London.
Both of these elements relate directly to what motivates volunteers to join VIP, through their involvement in public engagement activities, VIP and its volunteers facilitate recognition of
'the importance of archaeology' among different audiences. The
public engagement element of VIP aligns with training needs
and motivations expressed by volunteers as well as responding to the expectations that potential audiences might have
when engaging with local archaeological activities. It needs to
be noted that in most cases these audiences are not specifically
coming for the archaeological object-handling events run by

VIP volunteers. The challenge for VIP volunteers is to enable different audiences to engage with archaeological objects in a meaningful way. This is one aspect of what motivates VIP volunteers to engage with public engagement activities.

The guiding principle of VIP is that the volunteers and collections are treated with equal importance. Volunteer motivation and expectations of their participation in VIP are the starting point for their recruitment. Typically, each VIP group consists of students, retirees and those seeking employment, or people recruited through charities such as those that support the homeless and individuals suffering from mental health challenges. Spread over a three-month period, an individual VIP project consists of a total of ten days of inclusive team work supervised by Archive staff. The tasks vary by visit and by project, but they all mirror tasks that Archive members of staff need to perform on a daily basis, including the care of the collection, its documentation and efficient and effective packaging. A lot of preparation work is involved before each project to ensure the schedules of tasks are varied so as to cater for the needs and various motivations of the volunteers. The tasks performed by volunteers closely relate to the two main divisions of the Archive's finds material: the general and the registered finds. Tasks associated with the registered finds (individual artefacts) are auditing the finds, and having their packaging checked and documentation updated; tasks associated with the general finds (bulk archaeological material) are repackaging and reboxing the finds. Varying this work on a daily basis is important so as to keep volunteers interested and motivated to work to a high standard. Also the authenticity of the tasks performed by VIP volunteers is seen as leading to quality of learning, social development and producing work to a high standard. The experience is designed to provide volunteers with new transferable skills or enhance existing ones, giving them greater opportunity in seeking further volunteering, work or studying opportunities.

A large part of the effectiveness and longevity of VIP is the continuous project evaluation, which helps to evolve projects so as to best cater to both the museum and volunteers' needs. Archive staff have evolved the VIP model and adapted it to accommodate community archaeology events. Volunteers who have already participated in VIP are recruited to deliver audience development and engagement programmes with the aim to promote archaeology in the outer London Boroughs. Volunteers better reflect the make-up of the different communities they engage with both in terms of their socio-economic and cultural background as well as the range of motivations they bring to engaging with archaeology in a social context. The programme extension also offers a form of sustainability of the VIP programme for its participants. A sign of the VIP model longevity is that it has been used and adapted by other organisations.

Most recently (2016), the Archive has combined this public participation approach with museum exhibition; 'Delivering the Past' featured a display of archaeology excavated in the 1970s and was supported by public-participation collections care work, object handling and archaeological walks, all centred on the same excavation archive. It was delivered by thirty-four volunteers over three months, donating over 1,500 hours of their time (equating to over £11,000 of added value for the Museum), five of whom went from visitor to volunteer, signing up to join the project's latter stages, having visited the event. Over 14,000 Museum visitors engaged with the project (12% of visitors) with 300 boxes of archaeology repacked in the process.

Introduction

The concept of motivation has been used to explain and account for human behaviour. It is a central concept in a number of subfields in psychology which have empirically studied human behaviour. Some of the most widely known motivation theories stem from very traditional and outdated approaches. For example, from the subfield of behavioural psychology, people's innate drives or operant learning (i.e., encouraging or discouraging certain behaviours by rewarding or punishing them accordingly) are seen as the cause of motivation (Skinner, 1969). Another rather overused (and rarely questioned) theory of motivation is Maslow's (1943) hierarchy of needs coming from a humanistic psychology perspective. The hierarchy of needs has been criticised extensively for its Western European cultural perspective (Hofstede, 1984) and the fact that, although it has been based on a very narrow and specific sample (i.e., the top 1% of the highest achieving university students or very well-known people at the top of their profession such as Einstein), it has been applied across different settings and with different types of people (Mittelman, 1991). Furthermore, it has been pointed out that there is not much empirical evidence that can support the claim regarding the hierarchical order and prioritisation of human needs (Wahba & Bridwell, 1976; Tay & Diener, 2011).

This chapter tries to examine what motivates people to use museums and engage with their content and practices. Use of and engagement with museums covers a range of practices from the more common museum visiting to volunteering. It can be argued that it covers museum practice itself as museum practitioners choose to work in museums for different reasons. Moreover, for many museum practitioners early museum experiences played a pivotal role in their decisions to pursue a museum career (Spock, 2000), while an increasingly large

UNIVERSITY OF WINCHESTER LIBRARY

number of museum professionals start their careers by volunteering in museums as suggested by the VIP programme in the scenario and relevant literature (Stebbins, 2007). More often than not, museum motivation research has focused on people who choose to visit museums in their leisure time. Volunteering as leisure and the motivation of volunteers to engage in their own recreation, while facilitating other people's leisure and/or engaging in museum practice has attracted very little attention in museum audience research. The same is true for non-visitors and for organised educational groups. For example, the reasons certain parts of the population (particularly people from non-white or working-class backgrounds, people with disabilities or LGBT communities) do not visit museums has attracted very little attention (for more discussion see Chapter 8). Very little attention has also been paid to the motivation of organised educational groups. The lack of motivation research with organised educational groups seems to be based on the assumption that these trips are driven by the curriculum which provides the context for that visit and shape the motivation of the group members. Some research exists that disputes this assumption (Osborne, Deneroff & Moussouri, 2005). The scenario we chose to present in this chapter highlights a number of gaps in theory and research around motivation, namely the narrow focus on (and conceptualisation of) what constitutes museum audiences which represent a small subset of the wider population.

When examining the existing museum motivation research, another issue that becomes obvious is that only a limited amount of work has focused on motivation to engage during the actual visit (for a discussion of what motivates people to engage see for Moussouri et al., in preparation). Yet, a lot of assumptions are made about what people are likely to do during their visit based on visit motivation. Although this is quite a major omission on the part of museum audience research on its own, the implications of this gap in research go beyond the lack of information or evidence about what motivates people to engage and carry on with their visit. The real issue is that motivation has been conceptualised as internal to the person or based on individual needs, and decontextualised. Yet, as sociocultural approaches to motivation show, motivation is a complex phenomenon which emerges as people engage in activity in a particular context. This approach is further discussed in 'Sociocultural approaches to motivation' below.

The assumptions made by conceptualising motivation this way are problematic for two main reasons. Firstly, the separation of motivation to visit from the setting (i.e., the particular museum located in a particular cultural context) and the activity of visiting itself fails to acknowledge the constructed nature of the museum visit experience (or any experience people have in the lived-in world) and its meaning. In other words, existing approaches to studying motivation in museums cannot account for how visitors make decisions about what to do next from all the (often conflicting) possibilities for activity, while maintaining the flow of activity. Secondly, there is an implied homogeneity in the level of identification with any museum and of engagement with its content. In fact, we know that only some groups of people choose to visit museums and, even among visitors, the level of engagement, identification and perceived importance of the museum in their lives varies considerably depending on frequency of visiting and visiting 'expertise' (Moussouri, 1997; 2003; 2007). As Holland et al. (1989) note 'unexamined assumptions of homogeneity are a problem [...] because they permit inattention to the social distribution of cultural knowledge and its role in power relations'. Sociocultural (and in particular situated) theories challenge decontextualised approaches to motivation, as discussed below (Lave, 1988; Holland et al., 1989; Hickey & Zuiker, 2005).

The discussion of motivation in the following section will identify and discuss key concepts behind a number of motivation theories developed in cultural psychology and sociology, followed by their application in museum research. It will also present relevant complementary theories that do not seem to have made the transition to museum audience research.

The basics of motivation

The Latin root of motive means 'to move' and early psychological research examined what moves people to act. Traditionally, motivation has been approached as an individual phenomenon and has focused on behaviour or cognition, both of which relate to innate characteristics of the individual or how the environment reinforces particular behaviours (Weiner, 1990). More recently, explanations of motivation have taken into account the wider social and cultural contexts in which people act and which give meaning to their experience. The focus here is on how different contexts (such as the home, the museum, the school) provide the resources people use to negotiate the goals and values that motivate them to act in particular ways (Sivan, 1986).

Of the individually oriented motivation theories, we will examine two theories, 'flow' and self-determination theories (SDT). Flow, a theory of intrinsic motivation developed by Csikszentmihalyi, refers to 'a state in which people are so involved in an activity that nothing else seems to matter; the experience is so enjoyable that people will continue to do it even at great cost, for the sheer sake of doing it' (Csikszentmihalyi, 1990, p. 4). Owing to their focus on intrinsic motivation, both flow and SDT can address one of the central questions about what motivates people to use and engage with museums. Both SDT and flow focus on well-being and effective functioning. Flow uses some of the key concepts developed by SDT but focuses more on the actual experience of flow. Furthermore, flow has been applied in both professional and leisure activities. The fact that flow has been applied in both professional and leisure activities makes the theory particularly relevant to museum motivation theory and research. It can shed light on aspects of the experience that engage people and drive them on; and it can be applied to museum visitors and volunteers.

Next, we will present one theory that comes out of sociology (leisure studies) – the serious leisure theory – which takes into account individual as well as social and cultural elements of motivation. Serious leisure is a theoretical perspective that has mainly been developed though the analysis of qualitative data (i.e., using a grounded theory methodological approach). But, it has also used concepts from other theories, such as flow theory, in an effort to ground individual experience of leisure activities in the wider social and cultural context in which they originate. Similar to flow theory, serious leisure has been examined with respect to both professional and leisure activities.

Self-determination theory (SDT)

SDT is an approach to motivation and human development that has been developed by Deci and Ryan (1985). It examines universal human needs that underlie intrinsic motivations and how these can be fostered and nurtured. Intrinsic motivation refers to engaging in activities that are inherently enjoyable or interesting. People are intrinsically motivated when they want to do something for its own sake, interest and enjoyment and when they get a feeling of satisfaction during rather than after an activity. The focus on intrinsic motivation comes from earlier work carried out by Deci (1971) who carried out experimental research using predominantly behavioural measures, called 'free choice' measures, where people were exposed to a range of tasks and then had a period of 'free choice' where they could decide whether they wanted to engage in some of the tasks/activities or not.

SDT is based on the assumption that people are genetically programmed to learn and develop, and that all behaviours are motivated by three psychological drives or needs: competence, autonomy and relatedness (Ryan & Deci, 2000). People experience a sense of autonomy and a feeling of freedom when they engage in voluntary, self-determined behaviours. A sense of competence comes from engagement in activities, the goals of which people feel capable of achieving. Finally, relatedness

refers to feeling a sense of belonging to a group or community within which certain activities and goals are important or
meaningful. Meeting the needs of competence, autonomy and
relatedness leads to greater self-determination and experiences
of happiness. It seems that the way that the VIP programme
has been designed meets all of the three needs identified by
SDT. Volunteers choose to engage in the activities the Archive
archaeologists do. The activities are challenging but at the right
level so that volunteers can complete them effectively through
guidance from Archive staff and peer support. This fosters a
feeling of ownership of their work and the development of their
knowledge about archaeology of London.

The aim of SDT is to examine conditions that facilitate or
undermine people's experience of competence, autonomy and
relatedness in different social settings. Settings that support
these needs, it is argued (Ryan & Deci, 2000), facilitate high-
quality types of motivation and engagement with resources and
activities and lead to enhanced performance and creativity, all
of which have a positive impact on happiness and well-being.
When settings undermine people's experience of competence,
autonomy and relatedness, there is a negative impact on well-
being. Referring to designed social learning settings, such as
schools (and, it could be argued, museum exhibitions, and
resources and activities that are part of programmes too), Ryan
and Deci (2000) argue that, for learning to be more self-determined – and hence intrinsically motivated – the learning environment needs to meet the three basic needs. In other words, it
needs to 'support the innate needs to feel connected, effective,
and agentic as one is exposed to new ideas and exercises new
skills' (Ryan & Deci, 2000, p. 65).

Flow theory

Similar to SDT, flow theory of motivation takes as its starting point that people are born with a desire to learn and
that this 'natural motive' is 'built into the central nervous
system', Csikszentmihalyi and Hermanson (1995, p. 35).
Csikszentmihalyi (1975; 1990) conducted his earlier work on
intrinsic motivation in a variety of settings and examined what
motivates people to pursue a wide range of activities, even in
the absence of any extrinsic rewards. The focus was on understanding the enjoyment of a range of intrinsically rewarding
activities, such as rock climbing or chess playing, as experienced
in the 'here and now'. The flow experience was seen as an integral part of the enjoyment of the activity, and was defined as
'the holistic sensation that people feel when they act with total
involvement' (Csikszentmihalyi, 1975, p. 36). Csikszentmihalyi
and Hermanson (1995) further elaborated on the term 'flow'

which was used to describe 'a state of mind that is spontaneous, almost automatic, like the flow of a strong current' (p. 70). When an individual is in flow he or she loses the sense of time and the sense of self.

Flow has been introduced to museums and also used in audience research, as discussed in the following section of this chapter. Indeed, Csikszentmihalyi and Hermanson (1995) attempted to understand how museums help people to learn through making 'intrinsic rewards part of the museum experience'. In this paper they explain flow theory, while at the same time adapting it for museum settings. They state that curiosity and interest are preconditions to what people select to do and see while they visit a museum. However, they state that positive engagement and development requires prolonged engagement with museum exhibits and activities, which need to be intrinsically rewarding. The flow state has been characterised as both being able to differentiate (i.e., fully express the self and developing individual uniqueness) and integrate (i.e., to feel connected with other entities, possibly identifying with processes in the world larger than oneself). Developments in differentiation and integration, as facilitated by flow states, can lead to growth in oneself. From this it follows that the 'dialectic between integration and differentiation is the process by which we learn' and that 'the key to "flow" activities is the growth of the self' (Csikszentmihalyi & Hermanson, 1995, p. 71).

Based on their previous research with flow activities across different settings, Csikszentmihalyi and Hermanson (1995, p. 70) have identified three universal characteristics of flow experiences. These include experiences that have 'clear goals and appropriate rules', 'immediate and unambiguous feedback' and 'opportunities for action in a situation are in balance with the person's abilities'.

Comparing SDT and flow

There are clear similarities between SDT and flow and the key concepts they use. SDT and flow are complementary and they rely on similar concepts such as competence, efficacy, autonomous behaviour and control. Furthermore, they both try to provide a 'proximal theory of motivation' (Csikszentmihalyi, Abuhamdeh, & Nakamura, 2005, p. 599) where the focus is on how mastery- and control-related behaviours have become rewarding for individuals and groups when they fully invest their attention in intrinsically motivating activities. Some differences can also be observed. SDT tries to understand the process of developing intrinsic motivation, whereas flow examines variations in enjoyment once intrinsic motivation for an activity has been established. Flow examines what people actually experience, focuses on the here and now of the experience, and examines experience with ongoing activities (Csikszentmihalyi et al., 2005). It tries to explain the *processes* involved when people engage in certain type of activities or actions, rather than the *outcomes*.

The VIP programme incorporates some of the key elements of SDT and flow theories. The activities participants are engaged in are varied, mirroring typical activities carried out by Archive staff. These elements make the activities meaningful and also allow participants to have control over the activities they engage with. They are also challenging activities that require deep concentration on the part of the participants. The goals of the activities are clearly set out and participants are supported by Archive staff and by other VIP participants, who give them immediate feedback and support them in developing the skills and capacity to complete them successfully.

Serious leisure theory

Serious leisure examines activities in which people engage in their free time. Once again the focus is on intrinsically motivated or 'un-coerced activity'[2] (Stebbins, 2001; 2005) that people choose to pursue in their leisure time because of its satisfying and/or fulfilling value. Stebbins views activity as a type of goal-oriented pursuit that people engage with – more often than not – both mentally and physically. According to Stebbins (2007, p. xiv) 'activities may be categorized as work, leisure, or non-work obligation' and they span across all areas of human activity and experience, and across a wide range of social and cultural contexts.

He has identified three forms of leisure which, although they are interrelated, are distinct from each other: serious leisure, casual leisure and project-based leisure. He defines serious leisure as 'the systematic pursuit of an amateur, hobbyist, or volunteer core activity that people find so substantial, interesting, and fulfilling that, in the typical case, they launch themselves on a (leisure) career centered on acquiring and expressing a combination of its special skills, knowledge, and experience' (Stebbins, 2007, p. 5). Casual leisure, although it is intrinsically rewarding too, is rather short-lived and does not require any particular training for participants to enjoy it. Finally, project-based leisure can be a one-off or occasional type of activity, which is fairly complicated, but also challenging and rewarding.

More recently, Stebbins introduced the concept of serious pursuits which incorporate serious leisure and devotee work (2012). Devotee work blends the boundaries between an amateur and an occupation activity, and refers to the type of activities 'in which participants feel a powerful devotion or strong, positive attachment; it is an occupation that they are proud to be in' (Stebbins, 2013, p. 15). What is particularly interesting about the serious leisure theory is that it covers the whole range of amateur-professional-participants in any type of human activity and professional practice. Stebbins (2014) has conceptualised different types of engagement in activities, including amateurism as well as hobbyist, volunteer, professional devotee and volunteer devotee work, as fulfilment careers (i.e., activities which are fulfilling in and of themselves and which are systematically pursued). And, it is exactly the fact that all these activities are powerfully attractive fulfilment careers that drives people to engage with them in different capacities or roles. These types of activities or fulfilment careers are characterised by high levels of personal investment and are associated with a wide range of rewards or benefits, both on a personal and social level.

Owing to the focus of the scenario used in this chapter on a serious leisure type of activity, it may be of interest to mention the qualities of this type of activity (Stebbins, 2010, pp. 19–20):

> One is the occasional need to persevere, such as in learning how to be a capable museum guide. Yet, it is clear that positive feelings about the activity come, to some extent, from sticking with it through thick and thin, from conquering adversity. A second quality is that of finding a career in the serious leisure role, shaped as it is by its own special contingencies, turning points and stages of achievement or involvement. Careers in serious leisure commonly rest on a third quality: significant personal effort based on specially acquired knowledge, training, experience, or skill, and, indeed, all four at times. Fourth, several durable benefits, or broad outcomes, of serious leisure have so far been identified, mostly from research on amateurs. They are self-development, self-enrichment, self-expression, regeneration or renewal of self, feelings of accomplishment, enhancement of self-image, social interaction and belongingness, and lasting physical products of the activity (e.g., a painting, scientific paper, piece of furniture). A further benefit is that of self-gratification, or the combination of superficial enjoyment and deep fulfilment. Of these benefits, self-fulfillment – realizing, or the fact of having realized, to the fullest one's gifts and character, one's potential – is the most powerful of all. A fifth quality of serious leisure is the unique ethos that grows up around each instance of it. A central component of this ethos is its special social world in which participants pursue their free-time interests [...] The sixth quality rests around the preceding five: participants in serious leisure tend to identify strongly with their chosen pursuits.

The wide range of qualities associated with serious leisure types of activities echoes the different motivations for engaging in the VIP programme presented at the beginning of this chapter. Among some of the things that motivate participants – from self-employed to unemployed, and from archaeology students who have already chosen a career in archaeology to those looking for a career change – to volunteer in the first place and then fully engage are: the social world or community spirit the VIP participants and coordinators co-create during their participation in the programme; and their engagement in real-life, challenging, meaningful and rewarding tasks which they can see through to completion, and share with other visitors.

Sociocultural approaches to motivation

This section examines how motivation has been approached by sociocultural and situated theories of learning and cognition. Although there are some differences, all of these approaches start with the premise that thinking, behaviour and practice are influenced by the context in which they occur. The focus on the social and cultural context of human activity makes these approaches to motivation, in some ways at least, compatible with the serious leisure theory of motivation. Work in this area is done across the fields of cultural psychology and anthropology (and their subfields) and a synthesis of some of this work has already been presented in the Chapters 4 and 5 so we will not go into a lot of detail here. What is of particular relevance in relation to this discussion of motivation is that it is conceptualised as the interplay between both personal and contextual factors that come into play when people act in any given situation/context. The possibilities for action in the moment (i.e., as people act in a setting) and the differences in motivation that different social and cultural environments afford and/or demand of people are focal elements of a sociocultural approach to motivation (Järvelä & Volet, 2004).

According to this perspective, the values that motivate people to act (and learn) originate in the sociocultural context, such as the home, the family, the museum or the work context (Sivan, 1986). Situated approaches to learning and cognition place an even greater emphasis on the role of context because they view knowledge as residing and distributed in elements of the context, that is in tools (such as language or objects/artefacts), in technologies (such as the Web or smart phones) and in social rituals (such as conversations or grocery shopping). This view of knowledge moves away from treating it as something that is owned by or resides in the individual's head (which is how knowledge is viewed by many cognitive approaches) and towards the social context within which knowledge is created and shared.

Both knowledge and meaning are constructed through collective experiences people have as they act in the world, using tools and as people interact and think in relation to others. Furthermore, the values people attach to activity are generated as they act in particular settings. The way this system of interrelations, values and available tools is configured differs across contexts. This creates possibilities for different knowledge to emerge in different situations. In this respect, 'motivation for activity thus appears to be a complex phenomenon deriving from constitutive order in relation with experience' (Lave, 1988, p. 184).

In the next couple of paragraphs, we will focus on one of the motivation theories that has been painstakingly developed and tested empirically across different contexts and areas of people's lives. This comes from the work that Daphna Oyserman and her colleagues (Oyserman, Bynee, & Terry 2006; Oyserman et al., 2012; Oyserman, 2015) have carried out over more than ten years. The theory they developed, called Identity-Based Motivation (IBM), bridges the concepts of self and identity, and motivation. So, self and identity are viewed as forces that motivate people to act. The name of the theory is remarkably similar to the identity-related museum motivation model recently coined by Falk (2009), but there is no reference to IBM there. We believe that, moving forward, the identity-related museum motivation model could really benefit from links to IBM theory. Because of the IBM link to self and identity, Oyserman and her colleagues' work is also mentioned in Chapter 8.

IBM is based on sociocultural theory – in particular, situated cognition – and focuses on the context and the person acting in that context (Oyserman et al., 2012; Oyserman, 2015). IBM is based on previous theoretical and empirical work that has shown that, for any given environment people find themselves in, they assess possibilities of action particular for that environment and in relation to a subset of their available knowledge that comes to mind in that moment. Furthermore, any particular environment also makes implicit demands about what aspects of it people should attend and respond to. For example, when processing archaeological finds a VIP volunteer needs to access their knowledge about object handling which is part of the VIP training, but the demands that an animal bone makes as compared to a Roman pot in relation to their handling are quite different. So the volunteer needs to access that particular knowledge responding to the implicit demands of the object but, at the same time, she uses those implicit demands of the situation at hand to make sense of what comes to mind. Oyserman (2015, p. 2) postulates that 'integrating these three features of situated reasoning, people act in ways that make sense in light of the interface between what comes to mind and what that seems to mean in context'.

Following on from the above, IBM theory focuses on 'how features of the environment influence what comes to mind when people consider who they are (the self) and the interplay of what comes to mind and features of the environment on the influence of accessible features of the self on motivation' (Oyserman, 2015, p. 2). The difficulty here is that it is hard to identify identity-to-behaviour links for a number of reasons associated with three foci: (1) the fact that the type of identities that come to mind and their meaning is context dependent and part of a dynamic construction process; (2) the identities that are available in a different context at any given time motivate action only if action is relevant to the situation in that particular moment; and (3) finally, the way people interpret difficulty, especially when they work towards a new or a possible identity, plays an important role since they may think that this identity is not possible for them in that moment. Having identified these three foci of identity-to-behaviour links, IBM theory allows us to address when and how identities matter for behaviour (Oyserman, 2007; 2009a; 2009b; 2015). More recently, Oyserman and Lewis (2017) have used IBM to examine differences in student performance and achievement among African Americans, Latinos, and Native Americans. Using IBM, they looked at racial-ethnic group membership and socioeconomic position (e.g., parental education, income) and the stigma associated with these memberships and positions, and how these create situations in which students have limited choice and control.

Using IBM as a guiding principle, we can re-examine the volunteers and what identities might come to mind during their VIP programme that might be relevant in the situation at hand and what kind of engagement behaviours they might trigger. The VIP programme creates possibilities for both personal and social identities to be experienced as volunteers work in a social setting, interacting both with archive staff and with other volunteers. For example, for a volunteer who is interested in a career change, being an amateur archaeologist is an important part of his personal and social identity and that motivates him to engage with the work of processing the finds and repackaging them. We will follow this amateur archaeologist's engagement with archaeological practice and how this activity becomes an identity-congruent behaviour for him in Contextualising motivation towards the end of this chapter.

Motivation in museums

Some of the early motivation research in museums used demographic and/or psychographic characteristics of visitors as a heuristic device in an effort to segment museum visitors and non-visitors, identify barriers to visiting and suggest appropriate learning provision targeted at diverse audiences and their needs (e.g., Hood, 1989). As research on 'flow' became widely known, how motivation is experienced became the focus of some rather limited museum research investigating what drives visitors during the visit (Cameron & Gatewood, 2000; Prentice et al., 1998). In museum practice, conditions of 'flow' developed in other settings were used to guide the development of intrinsically motivating or optimal learning experiences.

More recently, we have witnessed a conceptual cross-fertilisation between theories and methods developed by different disciplinary fields and accelerated by the use of new technology (Macdonald, 2002; Moussouri, 2003; Moussouri and Roussos 2013; Falk, 2006). This has affected all museum research, including research on motivation, and it has led to different conceptualisations and ways of studying visit motivation. Concepts from sociology, such as serious leisure, coupled with the possibilities that digital technology affords to accessing museum visiting experiences in real time have made it possible to examine motivation both to visit and to engage with the museum content and resources. For the first time, it has been possible to record 'how we do what we do', using video recordings and digital location trails that can be watched and interrogated by different researchers multiple times.

Visitor and non-visitor motivation: demographics and psychographics

Hood (1989) used a combination of personality traits, attitudes and lifestyles (known as psychographic characteristics) in order to examine why certain groups of people do not visit museums. She has not, however, provided any further theoretical explanation for her work. Hood's study showed that families value leisure time experiences that involve social interaction, active participation, and entertainment. The importance of the social aspect of the visit was also highlighted by other studies carried out in museums around the same time (McManus, 1992).

Using the above psychographic characteristics, one of the goals of the study was to help museums identify potential audience groups that are non-participants and remove the barriers to visiting that might exist. This study was also one of the first that linked motivation to visit to particular socio-economic and cultural characteristics such as education, age, cultural background, occupation and income, connectedness and engagement with community and leisure activities. Particular audience groups that shared those characteristics were identified, such as family groups, adults, school groups, senior citizens and

Motivation to visit relates to socio-economic and cultural characteristics young people. Since then, other studies have confirmed the link between motivation and socio-economic and cultural characteristics, but have also identified local variations in socio-economic and cultural characteristics typically associated with museum visitation and non-visitation (see Davies, 1994; 2005). For example, although general data on museum visitation suggest that more people from higher socio-economic groups visit museums in the UK, this does not apply to all museums across the country. Davies (2005) points out that particular types of museums and galleries such as social/local history museums and national museums appeared to attract people from working-class backgrounds (i.e., semi- and unskilled manual worker, and state pensioners, casual workers or unemployed). In fact, the ratio of visitors from working-class backgrounds to those from a middle-class background visiting varies, with the ratio for social/local history museums being 1:1 and for archaeology museums 1:4. Furthermore, although changing demographics may have altered the landscape of typical visitor characteristics that lead to visitation (or not), there is no doubt that these characteristics do play a role (for a discussion see Dawson & Jensen, 2011).

Particular types of museums and galleries are attractive to visitor profiles representative of a specific social class

Motivation and personal identity

Studies involving the role of the self and identity and how they shape visitor motivation have started appearing only in the past ten years (Falk & Storksdieck, 2005; Falk, 2006; Falk et al., 2008; Falk, 2009). Falk (2006) has argued that motivation to visit museums is influenced by visitors' identity on the day of the visit. Based on his reading of existing theory coming mainly from social psychology, Falk hypothesised that it would be possible to identify five clusters of identity-related motivations: the explorer, the facilitator, the professional/hobbyist, the experience seeker and rechargers (previously named spiritual pilgrim). Owing to the overlap between motivation and identity in this model, the identity theory that has influenced the development of this model is presented in Chapter 8 in more detail. In this chapter, we focus more on visitor motivation as these are expressed before or after their actual visit, according to Falk and his colleagues (Falk, 2006; Falk et al., 2008). The five clusters of museum visit motivations in which visitors were grouped are also based on leisure attributes that existing museum visitors ascribe to museums. This hypothesised model of what motivates existing visitors to visit museums was tested empirically, mainly based on self-report methods that captured pre- and post-visit data about visitors' reported intention to visit and some data related to their reflections of the visit (Heimlich et al., 2004).

As mentioned in Chapter 8, the result of this and subsequent studies (the vast majority of which have been conducted in science-related museums) refined the five clusters of identity-related motivations and matched people's entering-identities with types of visitors and types of experiences afforded by the museum to these types of entering-identities (Falk, 2005; 2009; Falk et al., 2008). These studies showed that, explorers are driven by curiosity and they visit museums because they value the intellectual experience these offer. They focus more on what they find interesting during the visit based on their personal interests. Facilitators correspond to socially motivated family visitors and focus their visit and memories of it on what others find interesting. Experience seekers correspond to tourists doing sightseeing and tend to reflect on 'the gestalt of the day' and their enjoyment of the visit (Falk et al., 2008, p. 72). Professional/hobbyists correspond to experts and have very-specific content-related interests which they pursue during the visit. Rechargers correspond to the spiritual aspect of the art lover category. Rechargers also focus on the gestalt of the day, like experience seekers, but, unlike experience seekers, they are more concerned with having a relaxing experience.

As alluded to above, at the heart of Falk's (2006) argument is the idea that personal identities of museum visitors are closely related to their entering motivations, and that they can be used to understand and predict long-term memory and learning outcomes of a museum visit. In other words, the individual's entering motivations create a basic trajectory for the visit, allowing us to predict how visitors will interact with the museum content and resources, as presented above (Falk, 2009; 2006). Falk (2009) argues that although the general patterns of a visit are predictable, the details of each visitor's experience are highly personalised and unique. According to Falk (2009, p. 160), the visitor's museum experience is satisfying if the marriage of perceived identity-related needs and museum affordances proves to be well-matched. Falk further argues that identity-related motivations are more predictive than visitor groupings based on traditional demographic variables, which are dismissed. The latter point contradicts findings from studies looking at the association of class (seen as economic and cultural) and gaze (Fyfe and Ross, 1996; see also the discussion by Dawson and Jensen, 2011). Another interesting point is that this model has been based on self-reported motivations to visit rather than an examination of visitors' motivation to engage with the museum content and how that is negotiated during the actual visit. In other words, this work sees motivation as an accountable product rather than as a dynamic process.

Other research focusing on identity seen from a sociocultural perspective has shown that identity is dynamically constructed

Satisfying museum visit experiences are those that meet perceived identity-related needs as people act in a particular context of social life (see for example research by Holland et al., 1998; Lave, 1988; Garfinkel, 1967). In fact, Falk et al. (2008, p. 57) go as far as acknowledging this same point:

> although (in theory) science center visitors could possess an infinite number of identity-related 'self-aspects', this did not appear to be the case. The reasons people gave for visiting each science center, and their post-visit descriptions of the experience, tended to cluster around just a few basic categories of reasons and descriptions, which in turn appeared to reflect how the public perceives what a science center visit affords.

Identity is dynamically constructed and research needs to focus on the person-acting-in-context; a focus on entering-identity cannot capture the person-in action aspect of identity

Despite the fact that Holland et al.'s (1998) work has been used in the development of this model, the authors did not examine the visitor in practice. Of course the work of these groups of researchers (Falk and his colleagues on the one hand, and Holland and her colleagues on the other) stand on different sides methodologically. Holland et al. (1998) have conducted a very detailed ethnographic study, while Falk and his colleagues (Falk et al., 2008) carried out large quantitative studies. The latter type of research does not tend to capture how identity motivates people to act, nor does it examine motivation as dynamically constructed and situated in particular contexts. A more detailed discussion and presentation of the criticism of identity-related motivations model is presented in Chapter 8.

Motivation as socially constituted in the world and shaped through experience

Other studies have been informed by sociocultural approaches or sociological concepts that take into account culture and its role in contextualising human behaviour. These have looked at visitor motivation in relation to the value museums have in people's lives more widely rather than in terms of measurable intended impact. Looking at a decade's worth of visitor research conducted in Smithsonian museums, Doering and her colleagues at the Institutional Studies Office (more recently renamed the Office of Policy and Analysis) of the Smithsonian Institution used 'entrance narratives' as a model to describe the type of roles museums play for their visitors (Doering & Pekarik, 1996; Doering, 1999; Pekarik et al., 1999). Doering (1999) was influenced by work carried out by Macdonald (1992) – which is presented below – where she found that visitors come to an exhibition with pre-existing key ideas or messages related to its theme. This is an idea common in the sociocultural literature (see, for example, the concept of narrative template in the work of Tulviste & Wertsch, 1994; Wertsch, 2002; cultural worlds in

Holland et al., 1989; and in sociology the concept of constitutive order in the work of Garfinkel, 1963; 1967). The entrance narrative model is presented in Chapter 5 so the discussion here will focus only on the aspects of the model that pertain to motivation.

Entrance narratives (i.e., prior experiences, knowledge and memories) compose the ways people perceive and interpret the world (basic framework), their knowledge of any given topic (that is shaped by the basic framework), and 'personal experience, emotions and memories that verify and support this understanding' (Doering & Pekarik, 1996, p. 20). Hence, according to this approach, more often than not, people visit exhibitions to confirm prior ideas about the world. Doering and Pekarik (1996) also point out that the level of formal education is a factor in predicting visitation patterns. Although there are variations across museums (Davis, 1994), this observation seems to be confirmed by studies conducted in museums of different types, sizes, and location (Moussouri, 1997, 2003, 2007; Hooper-Greenhill & Moussouri, 2001a; 2001b). Hence, although demographic characteristics alone may not be enough, they shape people whose motivations we are examining and may play a key role in determining people's position in the world and the types of organisations (including museums) they have access to and engage with. The concept of positionality is further discussed in Chapter 8.

Macdonald used the concept of 'cultural projects' to describe the role museums are perceived to play in visitors' social life and how that is culturally determined , very much like 'entrance narratives'. Specifically, Macdonald's research (1992, 1993, 1995; Macdonald & Silverstone, 1990, 1992) at the Science Museum, London, showed that visitors' motivation for visiting indicated the existence of 'a more general set of cultural projects about museums – about museums' perceived place in social life according to their visitors' (Macdonald, 1993, p. 12). Acknowledging the culture's influence on shaping motivation, Macdonald referred to motivations to visit museums as 'cultural itineraries':

> the idea of itineraries … make[s] it possible to think about motivations to visit the museum as both somehow slotting into wider sociocultural patterns – the idea of lists being somehow 'out there' being evident in visitors' own articulations – as well as giving ample space for considerations of visitors' own strategies for compiling their own individual lists or itineraries.

> (1995, p. 16)

The concept of cultural itineraries comes from Lave's (1988) work. In her book, *Cognition in Practice*, Lave examined the motivation and values that shape practice, taking grocery

Margin notes:

Visitors come to an exhibition with pre-existing key ideas or messages related to its theme

The level of visitors' formal education shapes visitation patterns

Motivations for visiting museums are shaped by the culture people live in shopping as an example of situated practice. She distinguished between wider values that shape the choices people make (in the case of grocery shopping they could concern healthy eating, or weight and its relation to beauty, etc.) and the particular shopping list that may include particular items as well as 'non-specific categories such as "treats" for children' (Lave, 1988, p. 155). Lave examined how both types of criteria of choice (i.e., wider values and the grocery lists) as well as the structuring resources of the supermarket are used by grocery shoppers to organise and sequence their decisions about grocery items.

In the case of the Science Museum, visitor cultural itineraries included the following: life cycle, place, family event and education. The educational itinerary was less important among the visitors, while family life cycle and place seemed to be more dominant. Macdonald (1993, p. 12) stated that 'for a museum to attract visitors, the more cultural itineraries on which it features – and the higher up on each it is – the better'. In other words, when the itineraries intersect, visitors' motivation for visiting is even stronger, while the dominant itinerary will probably shape the frequency of visiting. The latter point is supported by Merriman's (1991) study and our own research (Moussouri, 1997), which also has highlighted a close link between motivation and frequency of visiting.

> Visitors have more than one motivation for visiting a museum and that makes the wish to visit even stronger

Using Macdonald's concept of cultural itineraries to conceptualise motivation, Moussouri has conducted research – both independently and with other colleagues – in a large number of museums and with different types of visitor groups for over twenty years (Moussouri, 1997; 2003; 2004; 2007; Falk et al., 1998; Hooper-Greenhill & Moussouri, 2001a; 2001b; Moussouri & Johnsson, 2006; Osborne, Deneroff, & Moussouri, 2005; Moussouri & Roussos, 2013; Moussouri & Vomvyla, 2015). To date, Moussouri and her colleagues have identified ten distinct categories[3] of motivations related to visiting exhibitions (Table 9.1). These are: education/participation, place, social event, life cycle, entertainment, flow, biophilia,[4] introspection, political/participation and therapeutic. Some of these itineraries can be found in almost all types of museums, such as science museums, children's museums, art or archaeology museums, and are associated with characteristics that people value about all types of museums (Moussouri, 1997; Hooper-Greenhill & Moussouri, 2001a; 2001b). Itineraries that cut across different museum types include: education/participation, social event, life cycle, place and entertainment. The itineraries that seem to be associated with particular types of museums, owing to their subject matter, the type of the collections, and – to some extent – their location (e.g., being able to enjoy a natural resources in an urban environment) include: biophilia, flow, introspection and political/participation. For example,

> Biophilia, flow, introspection and political/participation itineraries are content or collection specific; the education/participation, social event, life cycle, place and entertainment itineraries are associated with all types of museums or collections

biophilia is more common in zoos, aquaria, parks and other nature centres (Moussouri & Roussos, 2013). Introspection is more likely to motivate visitors to museums or exhibitions with a history or social history focus (Moussouri & Johnsson, 2006). Flow tends to be mentioned by art museum visitors (Hooper-Greenhill & Moussouri, 2001b). Finally, political/participation is associated with museums or exhibitions of 'conscience', or those that have a social or political cause. Political/participation reflects an expressed wish to take action with the aim to affect the well-being of somebody's natural, social, and cultural environment or heritage (Moussouri & Johnsson, 2006; Moussouri & Roussos, 2013; Moussouri & Vomvyla, 2015). Such causes would include raising environmental awareness or fighting discrimination or exclusion. It would then come as no surprise that the political/participation itinerary has come up in a social history museum and a zoo. A common finding across all studies Moussouri and her colleagues have carried out is that people have multiple motivations for visiting. That is true for all types of visitor group, including family groups (Moussouri, 1997, 2003, 2004, 2007), adult visitors (Falk et al., 1998; Hooper-Greenhill & Moussouri, 2001a, 2001b; Moussouri & Johnsson, 2006) and school children and their teachers (Osborne et al., 2005). Furthermore, our research (Falk et al., 1998) has shown that visitors do not perceive these reasons (i.e., wanting to learn and have fun) to be conflicting, a finding supported by other studies (Packer, 2006; Packer & Ballantyne, 2002).

One of the earliest pieces of research Moussouri carried out (1997) demonstrated that, together with motivation, visit strategy is an important aspect of the flow and decision-making process during the visit. The term *visit strategy* refers both to a specific plan of what visitors might see or do in the museum, as expressed by visitors during interviews, and also to observable behaviour manifested by visitors' movements through the exhibition space, recorded through the collection of observation data (Moussouri, 1997). Visit strategy is close to what Lave (1988) refers to as lists, in the case of grocery shopping. Employing interview and observation data, this research identified three types of visit strategies: open, flexible and fixed. Visitors with an open visit strategy had typically not visited the museum before and were open to engaging with different exhibitions, activities or resources. Visitors with a flexible strategy were aware of museum/exhibition specifics which were on their list of things to do, but they were also open to other options. Finally, visitors with a fixed visit strategy had a clear list of things to do in the museum before they got there. Moussouri (1997) also found some evidence that cultural itineraries may shape their visit strategies. This was particularly salient in the case of frequent museum visitors.

All types of visitor groups have multiple motivations for visiting museums

The specific strategies for the visit play a key role in making decisions and maintaining the visit flow

Table 9.1. List of cultural itineraries found across visitor and museum types.

Cultural itineraries	Definition
Education / participation	Learning something in particular, more often just learning in general; exposing one's self or others (e.g., students, children) to the aesthetic, informational or cultural content of the museum and to the practice of the communities associated with that particular museum (e.g., zoology- or art-related community).
Biophilia	'The love of living things' – it is the innately emotional affiliation of human beings to other living organisms. It describes situations where one finds oneself relaxing and feeling a pleasant surge of energy.
Place	Museums seen as leisure/recreational/cultural destinations emblematic of a locale or region; it could include a destination or attraction; to see something specific such as a museum building or a specific type of exhibition related to the area (e.g., London) where the museum is located. Many people visit museums for this reason, including individuals on holiday or day trips or who have out-of-town guests.
Entertainment	Seeking fun, an enjoyable thing to do.
Flow	Losing one's self in the activity; losing the sense of time and sense of self; being immersed in the activity.
Life cycle	A repeated activity which takes place at certain phases in one's life; usually related to childhood.
Introspection	A category related to flow but separate; being 'transported' back in time and place: need to self-reflect, feel connected to and rediscover one's own personal/family/community history; often results in feeling a sense of (personal and collective) achievement and pride.
Therapeutic	Refers to reasons related to one's physiological condition. This describes the motivation of people who live with an illness or disability which seems to be at the front of their mind at the time of their visit. The visit is a way for them and their family to take their minds off things.
Political / participation	Some people view museum-going as a way of actively participating – individually and/or in groups – in events and institutions which promote the interests and well-being of one's community or the protection and preservation of the natural environment. There is an expressed intention on the part of the visitors to raise awareness and support for one's community or environment and to take action with the aim to bring about change.
Social event	A special social experience to be shared with family and/or friends, a chance to enjoy one's self separately and together.

Source: Moussouri & Roussos, 2013, p. 25.

The work by Moussouri (1997) provided a strong indication that certain types of motivation may be associated with particular museum visiting strategies. To further investigate this link, Moussouri and her colleagues set out to examine the relation between visitor motivation and visit strategies in more detail. In a study carried out at London Zoo, we interviewed visitors before their visit to capture their motivation for visiting (i.e., cultural itineraries). Visit strategies were captured by visitor detailed visit routes which were recorded using location-sensing technology on mobile phones (Moussouri & Roussos, 2013). The findings showed that particular types of motivation determined the type of places and activities families chose to engage with, and this choice was based on the function those places or activities play. Two types of activities were identified based on their function: an exhibit or a non-exhibit activity (i.e., playground, restaurant, café). Two visit strategies were identified that directly related to social groupings with distinct motivations: families with education/participation motivation actively sought to engage in exhibit-related activities, while families with a social event or entertainment motivation were likely to engage in at least one activity with a non-exhibit function during their visit. This finding strengthens previous evidence obtained through self-reporting techniques on the relation of motivation and visit strategy (Moussouri, 1997; Falk et al., 1998).

> Families with education/participation motivation choose to engage in exhibit-related activities, while families with a social event or entertainment motivation are likely to engage in at least one activity with a non-exhibit function during their visit

Building on Macdonald's (1995) research, the approach to motivation developed by Moussouri and her colleagues has contributed to our understanding of motivation as the interplay between cultural models (or cultural worlds, according to Holland et al. (1998); or the constitutive order, according to Garfinkel (1967)) and the values that exist within cultural models, on the one hand, and experience in everyday activity, on the other. This research has shed light into how culture affects the categories of motivation (i.e., cultural itineraries) people perceive to have and are able to account for. It has also shown how these culturally constructed motivations trigger action (i.e., to visit a museum on a particular day and shape the list-of-things-to-do on that particular day as expressed by visitors' self-reported and observable visit strategies), but also how they impart meaning to these actions and shape the way the visit is remembered. The concept of visit strategies that Moussouri's (1997) earlier research developed led to a closer examination of the visit strategies (Moussouri & Roussos, 2013). This work indicated that there is a close link between cultural itineraries and visit strategies, and how cultural itineraries play out or are enacted in the museum context. But this study also posed more questions than it was able to answer. The main question was 'How does motivation play out in real time in the museum context?' Moussouri and colleagues (Moussouri et al., under development) set out to examine how settings, visitors' acting and activity intersect, and impel visitors to engage with the museum content and activities, as discussed below.

Motivation to engage as constructed dynamically in context

So far, we have identified the gap in audience research examining how the activity of the visit is experienced and perceived during the visit itself, and how it impels action (i.e., engagement with the museum resources and the unfolding of the visit as people move from one exhibit to the next, for example). Csikszentmihalyi and his colleagues are probably an exception as they have carried out work in a museum context. As they point out, '[h]ow the person feels while acting tends to be ignored. Yet individuals constantly evaluate their quality of experience and often will decide to continue or terminate a given behavioral sequence based on their evaluations' (Csikszentmihalyi et al., 2005, p. 602). A situated view of motivation (i.e., Lave, 1988; Oyserman, 2015) would concur with this point as it views motivation for activity as deriving and developing together with becoming an actor in a particular setting and/or being able to draw on particular identities.

Using a situated approach to motivation, Moussouri set out to explore the relationship between self-reported pre-visit and emergent in-gallery motivations. In collaboration with Sara Price and Carey Jewitt, we have started exploring the interplay between the culturally defined pre-visit motivations and the in-gallery motivation which reflects how individuals make meaning in museum exhibitions (Price et al., under review). This idea was based on previous motivation research one of us (Moussouri, 1997) carried out, which used the concept of cultural itineraries and showed that cultural itineraries act as backdrops for action and meaning making. This earlier study also showed that the motivating force of cultural itineraries varies according to how salient the world of museums is to visitors and to their level of 'experience' with them (i.e., frequency of visiting).

> Motivations to visit act as the backdrop for action and meaning making

By combining research into pre-visit motivation and bodily interaction with exhibits during the visit, preliminary findings showed that pre-visit motivations play out in real time through micro interactions among visitors, exhibits (or exhibit elements) and contexts. Specifically, the most recent study (Price et al., under review) showed that families make meaning through touch-based sensory experiences that are mediated by other family members and other people around them, and by exhibits and other available resources situated in a particular context. It also showed that the meanings family members make are shaped by their pre-visit motivations as well as 'emergent motivations'.

> The making of meaning at touch-based interactives is mediated by other members of one's group or other visitors

Those emergent motivations develop as visitors act and navigate the museum space and engage with activities, resources and with each other. Patterns of visitor engagement reflected decisions about conflicting possibilities for activity, which led to different resolutions or decisions for different people and at different times. What visitors chose to attend to and engage with (the activity) showed what they value and, in turn, gave meaning to the visit itself (Moussouri et al., in preparation). The parameters of the social and physical context of the museum exhibition acted as a type of 'curriculum'. There was some indication that, owing to the open-ended nature of museum exhibitions, the 'curriculum' itself can become more complex every time visitors use the same exhibition. Once again, there seems to be a link between the complexity of engagement, on the one hand, and visitors' level of 'experience' with museums and frequency of visiting. This finding also speaks for the need to understand motivation in relation to the activity (people-in-action) in the exhibition setting. This is an ongoing piece of research which will be reported in future publications.

A return to the VIP programme

Marco is a self-employed architect in his early thirties. As far back as he can remember, he has always been interested in archaeology. One of his earliest memories as a child was watching Time Team, the TV programme where a team of archaeologists and other specialists would carry out an archaeological dig in three days. He loved that programme! He became obsessed with digging in their garden, or everywhere he went with his family after that. He just loved trying to dig up any old thing he could find and dreamed of digging up archaeological finds – maybe a Roman skull or some coins! He never found anything like that, of course. His most exciting find was a piece of pottery he found on the banks of river Thames in London. His dad said that it looked 'vaguely Victorian'. That sounded pretty old to Marco at the time. Gradually, his knowledge developed quite a bit and very soon he could identify his finds. He also used to lose himself in the activities of digging and cleaning the finds. This is consistent with self-determination and flow theories where people lose the sense of time and space and become immersed in activities that are challenging but one feels capable of doing. The activity gives people a sense of self-efficacy. It is also in line with the serious leisure theory where people engage, both mentally and physically, in a core activity that spans across time and across different contexts.

Digging and going to archaeology museums gradually became two of Marco's favourite activities as a young boy. His parents had always encouraged his interest in archaeology as a child. But then when the time came to choose a career between archaeology and architecture back at secondary school, they both encouraged him to go into architecture. He did enjoy his studies and, as student and then trainee architect, he was always drawn to projects related to historic buildings and conservation areas. These usually involved working in teams where archaeologists and conservators were involved too. It was during his work on the conservation of a Grade I listed building in London that he found out about the Archive from Martha, the buildings archaeologist he was working with. She told Marco that they have themed open days for the general public. He decided to look it up on-line in the evening. He was really excited by what he discovered on the Archive website. Not only did they run open days, they also ran a volunteer programme. Without putting much thought into it he applied for the next phase, September to December, right away. Then came an agonising wait and an email inviting him to an introductory tour of the Archive. The day of the tour he became convinced that this was what he always wanted to do. He wanted archaeology to be more than a hobby; he would like to devote more time to it. After completing some forms he was very soon recruited as a volunteer, adapted his work schedule and was soon involved in a number of activities, including caring for the Archive collection, documentation and packaging of archaeological finds. A couple of weeks into his volunteering job he seriously started thinking of changing careers. Marco's devotion to archaeology as a VIP volunteer is reminiscent of Stebbins' idea of devotee work blending the boundaries between an amateur and an occupation activity, an activity that Marco finds particularly attractive and fulfilling. He is willing to make sacrifices and invest a lot of his personal time.

For Marco, being an amateur archaeologist has become an important part of his personal and social identity. He is particularly motivated to engage with the work of processing archaeological finds and repackaging them. He finds the practice itself very motivating because it is in the context of the Archive. He knows that this is exactly what the Archive staff do as well and his interactions with them enable him to feel connected to the practice of archaeology. During his time at the Archive Marco's identity as a volunteer archaeologist becomes more important than his current work as a freelance architect. Having a community of like-minded people – his VIP community – with whom he can share this part of his identity reinforces his engagement and passion for archaeology. It is the atmosphere of the place and all the hints and clues that it provides that drive him on and help him become better at processing the archaeology finds. He can visualise the whole process in the way the space is organised and laid out. All the animal bones that his group needs to process today are out on the tables with the bags they need to be put in laid out next to them. The boxes where everything will be packaged sit on a table behind him. The room next door is where all the boxes are stored. He watches the other volunteers working together to categorise the finds using the identification sheet provided. The other day he heard Peter, their Archive manager, mention that the next public engagement event will be next month. He cannot wait to share his enthusiasm with other people in the community. The reference to the context of the Archive and how Marco is able to draw on different identities in this particular setting relates to sociocultural approaches to motivation. The reference to the practice of archaeology, the values that are embedded in it and how Marco, through the embodied activity in the Archive setting, makes meaning of his experience also makes direct links to sociocultural approaches to motivation (particularly reminiscent of Lave's ideas from a situated cognition perspective).

Contextualising motivation

Thinking about a new exhibition you are developing in your museum, what content, resources, activities, tangible and intangible objects can you use and how can you use them in a way that can challenge visitors' entrance narratives? How can the exhibition meet the motivations of different types of groups such as family, school or all-adult groups? What are some of the concerns visitors might have about the subject matter of the exhibition and how it relates to their social lives? For example, does it relate to environmental issues or to the well-being of their community?

Think about how you can highlight issues of particular concern to visitors in a way that they find interesting and motivates them to engage? Can you make links to similar content in other parts of the museum that will motivate visitors to explore? Seeing volunteers as one of your assets and resources, how can you involve them in scaffolding visitor experience and motivating them to have a deeper engagement with objects and other resources? Seeing volunteers as an audience themselves, how can you help them develop a feeling of ownership of their work and deepen their knowledge of the museum's collection?

How can you design the space of the exhibition in a way that supports the sequence of decisions visitors make during their visit and maintains the flow of the visit activity? Remember, people often come in groups; how can you support and facilitate group decision making, while providing many possibilities for activity? What resources will you provide to allow different types of audiences to draw on different identities available to them in a way that they will find the content/material engaging?

Notes

1 This scenario was contributed by Glynn Davis, the previous Archaeology Collections Manager, and Adam Corsini, the current Archaeology Collections Manager at the Museum of London Archaeological Archive. The information was provided in notes, interviews and a paper (Davies, 2014). It was then written by the authors and further edited by Glynn Davis, Adam Corsini and Roy Stephenson, Head of Archaeological Collections and Archive.
2 The term 'un-coerced' is intentionally used by Stebbins (2001 & 2005) instead of 'free choice' to indicate the various conditions that any choice is constrained by.
3 In all but one (Falk et al., 1998) of the studies we have conducted, information on visitor motivation is collected as part of an open-ended interview in which visitors are encouraged to express their motivation in their own terms, and while they respond to a series of questions not necessarily related to the purpose of their visit.
4 *Biophilia* is the term used by Edward O. Wilson (1984) to describe what he believes is our innate affinity for the natural world in his book, *Biophilia: The human bond with other species*.

References

Cameron, C. & Gatewood, J. (2000). Excursions into the un-remembered past: What people want from visits to historical sites. *The Public Historian*, 22(3), 107–127. doi:10.2307/3379582

Csikszentmihalyi, M. (1975). *Beyond boredom and anxiety*. San Francisco, CA: Jossey-Bass Publishers.

Csikszentmihalyi, M. (1990). *Flow: The psychology of optimal experience*. New York: Harper & Row.

Csikszentmihalyi, M. & Hermanson, K. (1995). Intrinsic motivation in museums: Why does one want to learn? In J. Falk & L. Dierking (Eds.), *Public institutions for personal learning: Establishing a research agenda* (pp. 68–74). Washington, DC: American Association of Museums.

Csikszentmihalyi, M., Abuhamdeh, S., & Nakamura, J. (2005). Flow. In Elliot, A., *Handbook of competence and motivation* (pp. 598–698). New York: The Guilford Press.

Davies, G. (2014). Opening up to archaeology – the VIP way. *The Museum Archaeologist*, 35, 47–61.

Davies, S. (1994). *By popular demand: A strategic analysis of the market potential for museums and art galleries in the UK*. London: Museums and Galleries Commission.

Davies, S. (2005). Still popular: Museums and their visitors 1994–2004. *Cultural Trends* 14(1), 67–105.

Dawson, E. & Jensen, E. (2011). Towards a contextual turn in visitor studies: Evaluating visitor segmentation and identity-related motivations. *Visitor Studies*, 14(2), 127–140.

Deci, E.L. (1971). Effects of externally mediated rewards on intrinsic motivation. *Journal of Personality and Social Psychology*, 18, 105–115.

Deci, E.L. & Ryan, R.M. (1985). *Intrinsic motivation and self-determination in human behavior*. New York: Plenum.

Demby, E. (1974). Psychographics and from whence it came. In W.D. Wells (Ed.), *Lifestyle and psychographics* (pp. 9–30). Chicago, IL: American Marketing Association.

Doering, Z.D. (1999). Strangers, guests, or clients? Visitor experiences in museums. *Curator: The Museum Journal*, 42, 74–87. doi:10.1111/j.2151–6952.1999.tb01132.x

Doering, Z.D. & Pekarik, A.J. (1996). Questioning the entrance narrative. *Journal of Museum Education*, 21(3), 20–22.

Falk, J. & Storksdieck, M. (2005). Using the contextual model of learning to understand visitor learning from a science center exhibition. *Science Education*, 89, 744–778.

Falk, J.H. (2006). An identity-centered approach to understanding museum learning. *Curator*, 49(2), 151–166.

Falk, J.H. (2009). *Identity and the museum visitor experience*. Walnut Creek, CA: Left Coast Press.

Falk, J.H., Heimlich, J., & Bronnenkant, K. (2008). Using identity-related visit motivations as a tool for understanding adult zoo and aquarium visitors' meaning making, *Curator*, 51(1), 55–80.

Falk, J., Moussouri, T., & Coulson, D. (1998). The effect of visitors' agenda on museum learning. *Curator: The Museum Journal*, 41(2), 106–120.

Fyfe, G. & Ross, M. (1995). Decoding the visitor's gaze: rethinking museum visiting. *The Sociological Review*, 43, 127–150. doi:10.1111/j.1467-954X.1995.tb03428.x

Garfinkel, H. (1963). A conception of, and experiments with, 'trust' as a condition of stable concerted actions. In O.J. Harvey (Ed.), *Motivation and social interaction: Cognitive determinants* (pp. 187–238). New York: Ronald Press.

Garfinkel, H. (1967). *Studies in ethnomethodology*. Englewood Cliffs, NJ: Prentice Hall.

Heimlich, J., Bronnenkant, K. Witgert, N., & Falk, J.H. (2004). *Measuring the learning outcomes of adult visitors to zoos and aquariums: Confirmatory study*. Technical report. Bethesda, MD: American Association of Zoos and Aquariums.

Hickey, D.T. & Zuiker, S.J. (2005). Engaged participation: A sociocultural model of motivation with implications for assessment. *Educational Assessment*, 10(3), 277–305.

Hofstede, G. (1984). The cultural relativity of the quality of life concept. *Academy of Management Review*, 9(3), 389–398.

Holland, D., Skinner, D., Lachiotte Jr, W., & Cain, C. (2001). *Identity and agency in cultural worlds*. Cambridge, MA: Harvard University Press.

Hood, M. (1989). Leisure criteria of family participation and non-participation in museums. In B. Butler & M. Sussman (Eds.), *Museum visits and activities for family life enrichment* (pp. 151–167). Philadelphia, PA: The Haworth Press.

Hooper-Greenhill, E. & Moussouri, T. (2001a). *Making meaning in art museums 1: Visitors' interpretive strategies at Wolverhampton Art Gallery* [West Midlands Regional Museums Council & Research Centre for Museums and Galleries report]. Leicester: University of Leicester.

Hooper-Greenhill, E. & Moussouri, T. (2001b). *Making meaning in art museums 2: Visitors' interpretive strategies at Nottingham Castle Museum & Gallery* [Research Centre for Museums and Galleries report]. Leicester: University of Leicester.

Järvelä, S. & Volet, S. (2004). Motivation in real-life, dynamic and interactive learning environments: Stretching constructs and methodologies, *European Psychologist*, 9(4), 193–197 (Special section: Motivation in real-life, dynamic, and interactive learning environments).

Lave, L. (1988). *Cognition in practice: Mind, mathematics, and culture in everyday life*. New York: Cambridge University Press.

Macdonald, S. (1992). Cultural imagining among museum visitors: A case study. *Museum Management and Curatorship*, 11, 401–409.

Macdonald, S. (1993). *Museum visiting* (Working Paper no. 1). Department of Sociology and Social Anthropology, Keele University, UK.

Macdonald, S. (2002). *Behind the scenes at the Science Museum*, Oxford: Berg.

Macdonald, S. & Silverstone, R. (1990). Rewriting the museums' fictions: Taxonomies, stories and readers. *Cultural Studies*, 4(2), 176–191.

Macdonald, S. & Silverston, R. (1992). Science on display: The representation of scientific controversy in museum exhibitions. *Public Understanding of Science*, 1, 69–87.

McManus, P. (1992). Topics in museums and science education. *Studies in Science Education*, 20, 157–182.

Maslow, A. (1943). A theory of human motivation. *Psychological Review*, 50(4), 370–396.

Merriman, N. (1991). *Beyond the glass case*. Leicester: Leicester University Press.

Mittelman, W. (1991). Maslow's study of self-actualization: A reinterpretation. *Journal of Humanistic Psychology*, 31(1), 114–135.

Moussouri, T. (1997). *Family agendas and family learning in hands-on museums*. Unpublished doctoral thesis. University of Leicester, UK.

Moussouri, T. (2003). Negotiated agendas: Families in science and technology museums. *International Journal for Technology Management*, 25(5), 477–489.

Moussouri, T. (2004). *Komodo dragons exhibit summative evaluation report*. Unpublished evaluation report.

Moussouri, T. (2007). Mediating the past: Museums and the family social life. In N. Galanidou & L.H. Dommasnes (Eds.), *Telling children about the past: An interdisciplinary perspective* (pp. 261–278). Ann Arbor, MI: International Monographs in Prehistory.

Moussouri, T. & Johnsson, E. (2006). *The West Indian front room research project: Engaging in conversations about home*. Unpublished research report.

Moussouri, T., Price, S., & Jewitt, C. (in preparation). Examining emergent motivation to engage with museum content during the visit activity.

Moussouri, T. & Roussos, G. (2013). Examining the effect of visitor motivation on observed visit strategies using mobile computing technologies, *Visitor Studies*, 16(1), 21–38.

Osborne, J., Daneroff, V., & Moussouri, T. (2005). *The challenge of materials: Theoretical and methodological approaches to examining learning in an informal science institution.* Paper presented at the Annual Conference of the National Association for Research in Science Teaching, Dallas, TX.

Oyserman, D. (2007). Social identity and self-regulation. In A. Kruglanski & T. Higgins (Eds.), *Handbook of social psychology* (2nd edition, pp. 432–453). New York: Guilford Press.

Oyserman, D. (2009a). Identity-based motivation: Implications for action-readiness, procedural-readiness, and consumer behavior. *Journal of Consumer Psychology*, 19, 250–260.

Oyserman, D. (2009b). Identity-based motivation and consumer behavior: Response to commentary *Journal of Consumer Psychology*, 19, 276–279.

Oyserman, D. (2015). Identity-based motivation. *Emerging trends in the social and behavioral sciences: An interdisciplinary, searchable, and linkable resource.* New York: John Wiley & Sons.

Oyserman, D., Bybee, D., & Terry, K. (2006). Possible selves and academic outcomes: How and when possible selves impel action. *Journal of Personality and Social Psychology*, 91, 188–204.

Oyserman, D., Elmore, K., & Smith, G. (2012). Self, self-concept, and identity. In M.R. Leary & J.P. Tangney (Eds.), *Handbook of self and identity* (2nd edition, pp. 69–104). New York/London: The Guilford Press.

Oyserman, D. & Lewis, N.A., Jr. (2017). Seeing the destination AND the path: Using identity-based motivation to understand and reduce racial disparities in academic achievement. *Social Issues and Policy Review*, 11(1), 159–194.

Packer, J. (2006). Learning for fun: The unique contribution of educational leisure experiences. *Curator: The Museum Journal*, 49(3), 329–344.

Packer, J. & Ballantyne, R. (2002). Motivational factors and the visitor experience: A comparison of three sites. *Curator: The Museum Journal*, 45(3), 183–198.

Pekarik, A.J., Doering, Z.D., & Karns, D.A. (1999). Exploring satisfying experiences in museums. *Curator: The Museum Journal*, 42, 152–173. doi:10.1111/j.2151–6952.1999.tb01137.x

Prentice, R., Witt, S., & Hamer, C. (1998). Tourism as experience: The case of heritage parks. *Annals of Tourism Research*, 25(1), 1–24.

Price, S., Jewitt, C., Moussouri, T., & Vomvyla, E. (forthcoming). The role of interactive digital exhibits in supporting scaffolded family interaction. *International Journal of Computer-Supported Collaborative Learning.*

Rounds, J. (2006). Doing identity work in museums. *Curator: The Museum Journal*, 49(2), 133–150.

Ryan, R.M. & Deci, E.L. (2000). Self-determination theory and the facilitation of intrinsic motivation, social development, and well-being. *American Psychologist*, 55, 68–78.

Sivan, E. (1986). Motivation in social constructivist theory. *Educational Psychologist*, 21(3/4), 290–233.

Skinner, B.F. (1969). *Contingencies of reinforcement: A theoretical analysis.* New York: Appleton-Century-Crofts.

Spock, M. (2000). 'When I grow up I'd like to work in a place like this': Museum professionals' narratives of early interest in museums. *Curator: The Museum Journal*. 43(1): 19–31.

Stebbins, R.A. (2001). Volunteering – mainstream and marginal: Preserving the leisure experience. In M. Graham & M. Foley (Eds.), *Volunteering in leisure: Marginal or inclusive?* (Vol. 75, pp. 1–10). Eastbourne: Leisure Studies Association.

Stebbins, R.A. (2005). Choice and experiential definitions of leisure. *Leisure Sciences*, 27, 349–352.

Stebbins, R.A. (2007). *Serious leisure: A perspective for our time.* New Brunswick, NJ: Transaction.

Stebbins, R.A. (2010). Addiction to leisure activities: Is it possible? *Leisure Studies Association Newsletter*, 86 (July), 19–20. Also available online: www.seriousleisure.net/uploads/8/3/3/8/8338986/reflections_24.pdf

Stebbins, R.A. (2012). *The idea of leisure: First principles.* New Brunswick, NJ: Transaction.

Stebbins, R.A. (2013). *Planning your time in retirement: How to cultivate a leisure lifestyle to suit your needs and interests.* Lanham, MD: Rowman & Littlefield.

Stebbins, R.A. (2014). *Careers in serious leisure: From dabbler to devotee in search of fulfilment.* London: Palgrave Macmillan UK.

Tay, L. & Diener, E. (2011). Needs and subjective well-being around the world. *Journal of Personality and Social Psychology*, 101(2), 354–365.

Tulviste, P. & Wertsch, J.V. (1994). Official and unofficial histories: The case of Estonia. *Journal of Narrative and Life History*, 4(4), 311–329.

Wahba, M. & Bridwell, L (1976). Maslow reconsidered: A review of research on the need hierarchy theory. *Organizational Behavior and Human Performance*, 15(2), 212–240.

Weiner, B. (1990). History of motivational research in education. *Journal of Educational Psychology*, 82, 616–622.

Wertsch, J.V. (2002). *Voices of collective remembering.* New York: Cambridge University Press.

Wilson, E.O. (1984). *Biophilia: The human bond with other species.* Cambridge, MA: Harvard University Press.

10 Questioning culture and power in museums

Aboriginal people and museums working together[1]

Time takes on a unique meaning in a museum. It's extremely rare for an artefact to be let go from a collection, so a never-ending duty of care exists. Traditionally, museum staff have worked from the assumption that the artefacts they are caring for will outlive the people caring for them. Objects are constantly treated for insect infestations; humidified and dehumidified; stored in stable temperatures with appropriate fittings, and so on. Still, the acquisition of an artefact by a museum corresponds with its removal from community circulation. Boomerangs will never be thrown again, cloaks never worn again. They are asleep, waiting to be woken by community engagement.

Historically, many Aboriginal people have had their cultural material exploited by museums but things are changing rapidly. Most museums are helping provide opportunities for Aboriginal people to connect to their artefacts in a real and practical way. In 1998, for instance, a group of Koori women entered the Melbourne Museum archive to view possum skin cloaks made by their ancestors (main image). By working there, these women ushered in a new wave of possum skin cloak making and in effect revived the tradition. This led to the establishment of the collective Banmirra Arts.

As well as conserving the physical objects in Indigenous collections, there is a new trend of employing staff to ensure that their emotional, cultural and spiritual aspects are safeguarded as well. Some museums are actively encouraging Aboriginal people to collaborate with staff on the care of the collection. At the Melbourne Museum, only female staff work on restricted women's artefacts, and only male staff work on restricted men's artefacts. These procedures were developed in conjunction with relevant Aboriginal communities, who have identified the objects for which these measures are applied. Community

Figure 10.1 Koori women Treahna Hamm (L) and Vicki Couzens wear 'Biaganga', traditional possum coats at the Melbourne Museum's Aboriginal Cultural Centre in Melbourne. Biganga, translates as 'keeping the tradition'. © EPA/ Julian Smith Australia and New Zealand OU.

access is prioritised and encouraged. Objects shift within the archive based on community advice and artefacts are loaned for ceremonial purposes.

In 2011 Maree Clarke, a Mutti Mutti/Yorta Yorta and Boon Wurrung/Wemba Wemba woman from north-east Victoria looked at the Melbourne Museum's collection of kopis (widow's caps). Kopis are gypsum caps worn to express an individual's mourning of a loved one or significant member of the clan. They were built up over time by layering gypsum on top of the head, with some weighing up to seven kilograms. After the period of mourning, the kopi would be placed upon the grave as a marker. Access to the archive provided the opportunity for Clarke to remake and revive the tradition of kopi making.

In 2012 Aunty Barb Egan, a Muthi Muthi elder from Robinvale entered the museum archive to review shields collected from her country. Viewing the line working on these shields gave Egan the opportunity to rework their designs and generate new contemporary art pieces that continue the link between Muthi Muthi cultural heritage and contemporary art practices.

In 2014, Wadawurrung mother and daughter Aunty Marlene and Deanne Gilson looked at South Eastern baskets and breast plates in the Victorian Aboriginal collection. They later put on the show Wadawurrung: Past, Present, Future, which used contemporary art to invite viewers to witness their connection to country forged through their ancestral objects.

Kimberley Moulton, a member of the Yorta Yorta and senior curator of the South Eastern Aboriginal Collections at Museum Victoria has movingly described the importance of this practice:

> Without connection to the community, our objects lay silent but our identity and culture are inherently linked to these objects that are very much alive. They are a tangible connection to our ancestors and embody the cultural connection we have to our history and to our living culture and without us being present with them, they stay asleep.

Sometimes there is a risk that an object could be damaged through community engagement. But what matters most is that indigenous collections can be seen as dynamic, living archives. It is hard to say what this means for the future of ethnography, but one thing is clear. The age of the museum as gatekeeper is coming to an end. Aboriginal people are reconnecting with cultural traditions through access to museum collections and that is a powerful thing.

Introduction

We view culture as situated in societies' power relationships. In this chapter we examine the role of culture, and hence power, in contextualising human behaviour. In the context of this book, this chapter examines why museums operate the way they do and what the role and purpose of museum education is. At the heart of this discussion are the questions: What type of relationships do museums want to foster with their audiences? How are those relationships enacted in exhibitions, programmes and other learning provisions? How does the representation of particular groups through museum exhibitions impact on how visitors interact with and respond to the exhibition narratives? Although calls for establishing new relationships between museums and their audiences go back to the late 1980s (Vergo, 1989), they were mainly perceived as a means for museums to provide greater access to its collections and other resources. In the museum sector, it took a few more years for the ethos and the language around the community–museum relationship to shift. For example, social inclusion in UK museums became a priority in 2004 with the publication of the *New Directions in Social Policy* document by Museums, Libraries and Archives Council (MLA) (Linley, 2004). This echoes similar sentiments from the sphere of museum practice in the US with the publication of the landmark report *Excellence and Equity: Education and the Public Dimensions of Museums* (Museum Education Task Force 1992). *New Directions in Social Policy* was the first policy document produced by the national development agency for museums, libraries and archives in the UK which recognised the contribution the sector can make to wider societal issues. Issues of fostering community pride, creating cohesive communities, empowering and engaging people from all backgrounds were put forward, while the role of social capital in community cohesion was identified (Linley, 2004). The new ethos and language of change in museum practice reflected developments and calls for change from within museums but it was also influenced by theoretical discussions in the sociological and education literature (among others) and debates for social action. For example, there are clear links to Bourdieu's (1977) work on social capital or the work of Freire (1970) and Giroux (1986) whose work connects education to the struggle for democracy, progressive civic action and thought. Their work has had a profound impact in the critical museum literature and practice. The relevant literature is rich in theoretical approaches that try to articulate the potential of public institutions to fulfil the aspirations of a democratic ethos and achieve social justice (Vergo, 1989; Merriman, 1991; Bennett, 1995; 1998; Hooper-Greenhill, 1992; 1999; Fyfe & Ross, 1996; Crooke, 2007; Sandell, 2002).

This vision of museums as democratic institutions and how the vision (Bennett, 1998; Witcomb, 2003; Hooper-Greenhill, 1999) might be applied in museum practice is situated against the backdrop of critiques of the historical nature of museums and collecting (Bennett, 1995; Hooper-Greenhill, 1992; Harrison, 2013). The tension between museums' colonial legacy, together with different views about the types of knowledge that is privileged by that legacy, and a democratic vision of museums is at the core of the discussion around the process of negotiation of power and knowledge in contemporary museums. The scenario presented in this chapter explores some of the contemporary approaches to negotiating power and knowledge between Australian museums and Indigenous communities, whose cultural heritage is in the museums' collections. Specifically, the way Indigenous heritage has been assembled, catalogued and presented as ethnographic collections has shaped the way their heritage was represented and knowledge about it was created. In this context, museums are seen as institutions enmeshed in the colonial infrastructure (Boast, 2011) through which the acquisition of collections from around the world facilitated the representation of culture as a readable hierarchy. One line of criticism about museums focuses on the way knowledge of other cultures has been constructed by imperial nations – where European culture was conceptually categorised as above all other cultures – is embedded in the way museum collections have been put together, categorised, classified, reassembled, and exhibited (Lidchi, 1997; Harrison, 2013). This is what, in the context of exhibiting other cultures, is often referred to as the *politics* of exhibiting (Lidchi, 1997, p. 153). Another line of critique uses a semiotic approach to analyse museum exhibition 'languages' (i.e., all the ways through which communication takes place in museums, both consciously and unconsciously, intended and unintended) to examine the way meaning is constructed and communicated in order to study how exhibitions represent other cultures. This is often referred to as the *poetics* of exhibiting (Lidchi, 1997, p. 153).

Other lines of critique focus on class, gender, and sexuality as well as how they often cross each other in order to show how stereotypical notions of those social constructs – such as femininity and masculinity, for example – have been naturalised and perpetuated in museums (Bourdieu, 1984; Bourdieu & Darbel, 1997; Hein, 2007; Levin, 2010; 2012). What is common in all these approaches is that the focus is on the type of knowledge chosen to be represented and the way knowledge is systematised and represented in museums, which is not generally made transparent in any way. For example, as seen in the scenario, the objects collected from Aboriginal communities in Australia had been cared for in terms of conservation needs and they became part of a museum collection that highlighted some aspects of their cultural significance, leaving out the emotional, spiritual and cultural aspects of the objects that also needed to be safeguarded. The way knowledge is systematised in museums creates a public–private division of knowledge which reinforces a conception of the public as passive consumers of content knowledge developed by experts behind the scenes (Hooper-Greenhill, 1992). It also makes museums less relevant and/or accessible to a large number of groups who do not normally visit.

The importance of all of the work presented above lies in the fact that it has helped us recognise how knowledge is constructed in a way that creates taxonomies such as 'civilised' and 'primitive' or 'upper classes' and 'lower classes'.[2] This has, in turn, demonstrated how education and educational institutions (including museums) have been involved in a 'socialisation' process of 'educating' the 'uncultured' and preparing them for social life (Hooper-Greenhill, 2000). In the museum context, where knowledge is developed by the experts and absorbed by the 'general public', there is a very clear divide between experts and non-experts, and structures of power, the legacy of which can still be seen across all museum functions even today. In this chapter, we examine the educational function or role of the museum in relation to those power structures. We discuss the social, political and cultural dimensions of education and, more specifically, the role that museums as cultural institutions with an educational and social value play or should play. We also examine what different critical theoretical approaches bring to bear on the debate about the role museums play in maintaining or challenging existing structures in society, and the degree to which they could or should be agents of social change and/or emancipation.

To do that, this chapter draws on literature coming from education philosophy and theory, sociology of education and curriculum studies, as they have been applied in museums, in order to provide a basic outline of key concepts and show how they relate to museums. As is the case with all the other chapters, the complex realities of museum learning practice do not reside in a single intellectual tradition. A large number of individuals and groups of researchers from diverse disciplinary fields and theoretical positions have contributed to this discussion, adding to the great complexity of this domain. Owing to the focus of this chapter on institutional structures of power and systems as a lens to conceptualise the museum–audience relationship (or lack thereof), we draw more heavily on sociological approaches (i.e., social critical theory) that view museums as social organisations. However, we also draw on cultural studies, social psychological and anthropological perspectives that investigate the human condition through an examination of the relationship between the individuals or groups of people and culture. In the sections below, we first examine definitions of culture – within which museums are located and interact – and power – as a key force in shaping cultural institutions such as museums. We then present some key theoretical perspectives which are followed by the discussion of relevant museum audience research.

The basics of culture and power

Defining culture

There has been little agreement on what the term 'culture' refers to across disciplines. White (1959), for example, points to the difficulty to define the term even in cultural or social anthropology where culture is the main focus of study. Attempts to define the term have produced dichotomies (White, 1959; Cole & Packer, 2011; Srivastava, 2013) such as: (1) culture is perceived either as learned behaviour or as an abstraction from behaviour; and (2) focusing either on the material, the man-made part of culture or on knowledge and beliefs. We will examine the first of the two dichotomies (i.e., culture as a learned behaviour versus culture as an abstraction from behaviour) by bringing into the discussion Vygotsky's (1978) views on this particular issue.

Vygotsky (1978), one of the key figures in cultural psychology, focused on particular aspects of culture – namely speech, writing and counting – and the meanings and concepts that exist in culture. He used these language-based tools to examine where culture and cognition meet and how they create each other. Vygotsky perceived individual development as embedded in the social and cultural context within which the individual lives. He argued that 'learning is a necessary and universal aspect of the process of developing culturally organised, specifically human psychological function' (1978, p. 90). According to Vygotsky (1978), at the beginning of life of an individual it is external mediators such as material objects and other people that help mediate psychological functions – our innermost thoughts – and only later these psychological functions are carried out through internal mediators (i.e., speech, number systems, writing systems). It is the role that language-based tools play in influencing the inner world of humans and in contributing to the development and progress of mankind and human culture that prompted Vygotsky to focus on these particular aspects of culture (van der Veer, 1996).

Cole (1985) notes another interesting aspect of Vygotsky's work, which focuses on the role social guidance plays in culturally organised activities in which young children or novices gradually adopt the role of adults. This 'shifting control within activities' is what Vygotsky called 'zone of proximal development' (Cole, 1985, p. 155). This interaction between adults and children or novices in the context of culturally organised activities leads to the acquisition of culturally appropriate behaviour. This lies at the heart of sociocultural theory where culture and cognition together are the focus of study. In this chapter, our focus tends towards his view of culture, in particular. Unlike cognitive approaches to learning and development, Vygotsky did not view the cultural context as a container surrounding the person. Instead he perceived cultural context as the weaving of objects, behaviours, relations among persons, activities and situations with the world (Vygotsky, 1978).

With regard to the second dichotomy mentioned above (i.e., the material, the man-made part of culture versus knowledge and beliefs), there has been an attempt by more recent interpretations of sociocultural theory to combine the beliefs versus material views of culture by bringing together the 'symbolic' ('received ideas and understandings … about persons, society, nature and the metaphysical realm of the divine') and 'behavioural inheritance of a cultural community' ('its routines or institutionalized family life, social, economic and political practices')

(Shweder et al., 2006, pp. 719–720). Weisner (2002) views cultural influences as located in activities and practices at the core of family life. In these culturally organised practices and activities the 'subjective and objective (are) intertwined', as individuals play an active role in shaping the activities they participate in. Cole and Packer (2011, p. 71), influenced by Vygotsky, 'think of the cultural medium as both material and mental'. We are surrounded by artefacts made by generations of people that extend back to the beginning of the species and that mediate between humans and the physical world as well as with each other. This view of culture highlights the tangled nature of human biology and culture, and the capacity of artefacts to express human ideas in a solid form. According to this analysis, culture incorporates both mental and material aspects (Cole & Packer, 2011).

In this chapter, we espouse both the material and the belief notions of culture. Culture consists of collections of artefacts that embody culturally organised practices and activities where the subjective and objective, and the material and the mental intertwine as individuals play an active role in shaping the activities they participate in and give meaning to them in interaction to others in any given context. This meaning-making process does not just incorporate concepts but also emotions, attitudes, feelings, and personal and social identities. This view of meaning making as a cultural process is further explored in Chapter 4.

The idea about how traditions, emotional, cultural and spiritual ideas are interweaved with and can be expressed through objects is at the centre of the scenario presented in the beginning of this chapter. Objects are not only seen as 'tangible connections' with the past but they also have the power to revive certain cultural practices or traditions when they are used as part of the practices of their communities. For example, the Koori women's experience with possum skin cloaks made by their ancestors (see Figure 10.1) at the Melbourne Museum started a new wave of possum skin cloak making through establishing the collective Banmirra Arts. In another example provided in the scenario, Maree Clarke – a Mutti Mutti/Yorta Yorta and Boon Wurrung/Wemba Wemba woman from northeast Victoria and practising artist – was able to revive the tradition of kopi making and reclaim this part of her heritage and to use her art to inspire others from her community.

Defining power

The role of power in culture has been explored by the anthropologist Eric Wolf (1984; 1999) who understood it to be an aspect of all human relations and social arrangements. He

UNIVERSITY OF WINCHESTER LIBRARY

argues that power is crucial in shaping the circumstances of cultural production through examining the relationship between ideas, power and culture. What is particularly relevant for the purposes of this chapter is his marrying of social structure, historical contingency and human agency. Wolf identified four forms of power that operate on an interpersonal, institutional and societal level: (1) *individual power* or *force of personality*[3] that describes the capabilities of individuals in the play of power; (2) *power imposed by one person on another*, which focuses on the form and direction of the play of power; (3) *tactical or organisational power*, which examines the social context or arena within which power is imposed; and (4) *structural power*, which is 'the power to control behaviour by governing access to natural and social resources' (Wolf 2001: 375). Wolf's idea of how structural power is engaged in the realm of symbols and ideas by conveying both control of resources (i.e., objects or collections) and symbolic construction (i.e., the way collections of objects are put together in order to privilege values and cultural attributes of certain ethnic groups, presenting such arrangements as the natural order of things) is particularly pertinent in the museum context. The notions of tactical or organisational power, and structural power are particularly useful to understand how Australian museums controlled and constrained the access of Indigenous people to objects from their culture, through the way they treated, cared for, researched and conserved them. The power they exert over these artefacts and their significance to the culture of the west-European settlers provided museums with their rationale and helped shape their organisational power, while at the same time it restricted access to those artefacts for the very people who produced them. As Wolf points out (2001, p. 375): 'The ability to define what things are is also the ability to define what things are to be had by whom, how, when, and where, with whom and against whom, and for what reasons'. For example, the scenario in this chapter discusses how ethnographic collections of objects from Indigenous communities were ordered, catalogued and cared for in a way that did not reflect key aspects that were significant to the Indigenous communities that produced them. What was made knowable excluded important emotional aspects of these objects. For example, *kopis* or widows' mourning caps are worn by some Indigenous Australian communities as a sign of mourning and are of great religious and social significance. Having access to kopis from the Melbourne Museum revived the tradition of kopi making.[4]

The next sections will discuss ideas introduced above about culture and power in the context of critical theories of education and learning.

Critical theory and transformative learning

According to Holland, et al. (1998, p. 34), the sociocultural 'school of psychology was the product of an earlier critical disruption' which began in Russia, post-revolution, with Vygotsky's work in the late 1920s and 1930s. In the US, the Progressive Education movement, starting in the early twentieth century with Dewey (1980 [1916]) as its key figure, coincided with a period of social conflict and political crisis following the economic depression of 1893 (Foley et al., 2015; Hein, 2012). This was followed by a similar critical turn in the 1970s originating in the theoretical work of the Frankfurt School of Critical Social Theory. Critical theory was developed in opposition to traditional theory (e.g., positivism), which was based on scientific activity and was seen as lacking any connection to the subjectivity of individuals, their experiences and to society (Horkheimer, 1975). This more recent critical turn can be seen in philosophy of education with Freire (1970); in sociology of education with Bourdieu (1977); and in education and curriculum studies with Giroux (1986) in the 1980s. The vast majority of this literature has focused on schooling and the role formal education plays in reproducing inequalities. The emphasis has largely been on how existing structures and institutions privilege particular types of behaviours, cultures and practices and present them as though they are the only ones. This view leads to ignoring or silencing those who lack privilege and power (Holland et al., 1998).

Following this line of thought, museums as cultural institutions enact social relations of power through modes of knowledge production and representation that are embedded in institutional structures and which, in turn, reflect power structures that exist in the wider community and society. Museums, it is argued, 'enact social relations of power' (Lindauer, 2007, p. 306) through the process of deciding 'how and in whose interests knowledge will be produced and disseminated'. As Hein (2012, p. 19) notes, '...education is inevitably political. Education is *for* something.'

In the context of education (both in formal and in informal learning settings), similar arguments have been made from a critical pedagogy perspective, with Freire and Giroux as its key figures. The question is, as Giroux notes (1986, p. 49), how 'students can be educated to take their places in society from a position of empowerment rather than from a position of ideological and economic subordination'. A very similar approach, known as 'critical consciousness', was developed by Freire (1995) where the aim is for the oppressed to develop a deeper understanding of the world and how disadvantage is constructed. This understanding, then, leads to taking action against oppression. What is common in both Giroux and Freire's work is that they view knowledge as cultural capital which makes it compatible with Bourdieu's theory of practice, which hinges on the concepts of cultural capital, field and habitus (also discussed in Chapter 8) (e.g., 1977; 1984; 2001).

The concepts of habitus (the internalisation of the social order in the human body), capital (the resources available to a person which can be economic, cultural, social, and symbolic) and field (social contexts) are closely related. People are able to acquire particular habitus through maximising the resources (which can be can be economic, cultural, social and symbolic capital) available to them (Bourdieu, 1986). For example, visiting art museums (*field*) was the preserve of the upper classes, members of which become disposed to art museum visiting and appreciating art from a very young age (Bourdieu & Darbel, 1990). These resources or types of capital represent what is seen as important in different fields (e.g., an art museum). Fields, then, are social spaces of competition and struggle. It is where individuals compete over occupying certain positions (being a member of a particular social class, for example) by controlling different types of capital that exist in different fields. Certain types of capital are deemed more important or are valued more within fields of struggle (such as art museums, where Bourdieu and Darbel (1990) carried out research) and these are reserved for the socially superior classes, as is the case with visiting art museums. So individuals' social positions in different fields are determined by the allocation of specific capital (Mahar et al., 1990).

All of the above theories identify and detail the mechanisms through which privilege and inequality are socially produced, and advocate taking action against oppression. Yet, resolving how this can be achieved has not been easy. Despite the divergent views on what avenues of action are possible and what they look like and the unresolved dilemmas that follow from areas of conceptual ambiguity, some concrete ideas about how to create viable space for reform have emerged. These can be placed on a continuum of possible actions that align to a more radical vision – where the emphasis is on overt political action – or to a progressive or reformist vision with an emphasis on gradual, progressive reform.

Culture and power in the museum context

In the museum context, the intellectual and moral merits of visiting museums, and their social and political significance started appearing in the museum literature by the late 1980s, with a movement that has become known as the new museology (Lumley, 1988; Vergo, 1989). This work tried to make the case for a museum education with a social purpose. As mentioned in the introduction, this shift in more critical approaches to studying museums and their audience was characterised by an increased call for reflexive museum practice and for critical approaches to research practices which acknowledge that the practitioner and practice or the knower and the known cannot be separated (Vergo, 1989). This early work examined museum education – its philosophy and practice – taking a predominantly institutional rather than an audience perspective – and making reference to a highly selective and wide-ranging literature, from educational philosophy and sociology or anthropology of education to learning sciences. For example, some work attempted to theorise museum education (or museum learning as it gradually became known) (Hooper-Greenhill, 1994; 1999; Hein, 1991; 1998). The predominant theoretical perspective used by these authors was constructivism – inspired by the work of Dewey and Piaget – with a focus on experiential and/or cognitive approaches to learning. The idea that visitors are actively making meaning that constructivism espouses is what resonated with these authors. In term of educational philosophy, Hooper-Greenhill's work made some reference to 'critical museum pedagogy' citing Giroux's approach – although reference to critical pedagogy as a distinct education philosophy was rather loose at this time – and to Bourdieu and Darbel's application of the concept of cultural capital in the art museum (Hooper-Greenhill, 1999). Hein's work has been inspired by the progressive education movement and, in particular, Dewey's writings (Hein, 1998; 2012). 'Museum education' in this early work was used in the wider sense of the term, that is adding a societal purpose and supporting democratic values. It is political and includes a larger moral aspect; it is education for social responsibility and democracy.

Sociocultural learning theory is another theoretical tradition that examines the cultural and historical basis of people's lives and the institutions they create and participate in. It examines 'the cultural nature of our lives' by focusing on human development, learning and education practices taking into account the social, cultural and historical context within which people live and operate (Rogoff, 2003). Some of this work makes direct reference to inequalities in opportunity in education as a result of lack of culturally specific 'repertoires of practice' (deep-seated cultural dispositions) a term similar to that of 'habitus' coined by Bourdieu (1977). According to Rogoff et al. (2007, pp. 504–505) 'people's repertoires of practice describe the formats they are likely to employ in upcoming situations, based on their own prior experience in similar settings. Repertoires of practice are highly constrained by people's opportunities and access to participate directly or vicariously in settings and activities where particular formats are employed.' This work connects participation in Western educational institutions – such as schools and museums – to specific cultural practices associated with middle-class approaches to organising life. It also advocates for a more culturally sensitive approach that takes into account the needs and the practices of practitioners, as they also use 'default' repertoires of practice.

Sociocultural learning theories were introduced in museums in the early 2000s (e.g., Schauble et al., 2000). Around the same time, reference to critical pedagogy, its principles and how they can be applied in museum learning began to appear in the museum literature (Lindauer, 2006). What constructivism, sociocultural learning theories and critical pedagogy share is an opposition to traditional didactic, expository learning approaches, the purpose of which is reinforcing the museum's authority and reputation as a holder of canonical knowledge and keeper of objects. They also perceive people as active learners, engaging with the world around them and making sense of it from within their own social contexts.

From the perspective of museum audiences, a number of researchers have explored the changing nature and social function of museums in the late twentieth century from a theoretical and ethical stance. Yet, from an audience research perspective, a relatively small number of published empirical studies have explicitly discussed the museum–visitor relationship taking into account the museum's social, political and cultural significance. There are many reasons for that clear division in research focus/approach, including the fact that many of the concepts and principles are hard to operationalise and study empirically or to be used to guide research practice. A review of the relevant literature indicates that the body of work that involves critical engagement with exhibitions or other types of museum provision tends to examine the institutional perspective. The focus of this work is on an analysis of an exhibition, for example, through a process of the researcher's own critical analysis of it rather than through audience research (see Vergo, 1989; Hooper-Greenhill, 1992; 1999; 2000; Bradburne, 1993; Witcomb, 2013; Lindauer, 2007); or through an examination of institutional intentions as they emerge during the development process (Roberts, 1997; Macdonald, 2002; Lindauer, 2006; Nomikou, 2013). Some audience research is also emerging within this area, particularly in science education and engagement, which offers analysis based on audience views (Dawson et al., 2015; Archer et al., 2016b). This is an emerging area of museum audience research where the focus is on engagement (or non-engagement) with museum content with an emphasis on social justice and equity. Theoretically these studies fall under sociocultural learning theories and critical theories. Methodologically, they primarily utilise qualitative research approaches, using mostly ethnography but also other participatory qualitative methodologies.

From a museum practice perspective, museum professionals have been actively experimenting with and trying to apply these concepts (e.g., Witcomb, 2003; Macdonald, 2003). Museum practitioners have sought to redress the power imbalance through engaging different groups or communities in museum practice (e.g., co-creating exhibitions) and in collections research. It has been argued that most of this work has largely focused on a rather gradual, progressive reform, representing a 'reorganising of existing categories to accommodate differing perspectives' (Harrison, 2013:12) rather than a radical challenge to institutional power. It has also been argued that museums seem to have an almost infinite capacity to adapt to their contemporary economic, socio-political and technological context, while, at the same time, retaining their authority (Andermann & Arnold-de Simine, 2012). However, alternative ways of framing museums and museum practices that 'work against a legacy of imperialism, patriarchal values, assumptions based on high culture and a privileging of institutional knowledge' have also been put forward (Witcomb, 2003, p. 12). It is important to support and highlight this type of conceptualisation and research and share it with museum practitioners. Indeed, it is often hard for museum professionals to imagine what a more radical reform might look like – in practical terms – in the context of museum practice. They seem to struggle, for example, with how a more radical reform could be portrayed and displayed in an exhibition and then viewed by different audiences. Likewise, how such a reform could be implemented in the current economic, political and funding climate with its emphasis on short-term economic impacts is problematic for museums (Moussouri, 2014).

The following section presents studies that examine audience engagement and encounters with elements of informal learning settings, taking an explicitly critical theoretical perspective. We decided to give this approach prominence in this chapter as it has not received the attention it deserves in the previous chapters. The first study reviewed below looks at how visitors and their experiences are imagined during the development process, which is then compared to self-reported visitor encounters. The author (Lindauer, 2006) advocates for the use of critical pedagogy as a guiding theoretical approach to exhibition development. The next few studies examine how visitors' and non-visitors' ethnicity, lifestyles, class, and differing geographical and social mobility shape the way they perceive museums and/ or afford different relationships with the museum content. The last – and most recently completed – study examines engagement with science among urban working-class pupils during a visit to a science museum, taking a gender perspective. This study is part of a larger research project, the Enterprising Science project,[5] which tries to understand young people's engagement with science and what support is needed to strengthen engagement with science post-sixteen. This project has mainly focused on secondary school children and their teachers in a school setting, with the aim of improving science teaching at school. We will first present the theoretical underpinnings of Enterprising Science followed by the presentation of a study of a fieldtrip to a science museum.

Developing exhibitions with the imagined visitor in mind

Margaret Lindauer's (2005; 2006; 2007) research has focused mainly on exhibition developers and the exhibition development process vis-à-vis the imagined visitor response and ideas to exhibition content and particular interpretative approaches. Lindauer combined critical pedagogy with critical museum theory (or new museology, as mentioned above) as a way to understand differences in opinions among team members during the development of exhibitions and to help the latter select compatible and coherent education and communication theories and methods that are best suited to foster the type of relationship a museum would like to develop with its visitors (Lindauer, 2006). Her work has also explored the possible application and implications of critical pedagogy when applied to exhibition development (Lindauer, 2006), taking the view that a coherent education and communication approach will encourage deeper intellectual engagement on the part of the visitor. Indeed, her research with visitors showed that the lack of coherent approach resulted in visitors having disconnected experiences, which led her to conclude that the exhibition mis-educated visitors.

The lack of coherent learning approach in the development of exhibitions creates disconnected experiences for visitors

Using Bourdieu's ideas to study visitors and non-visitors

Coming from a museum sociology perspective, Fyfe and Ross (1996) reported on one of the earliest studies informed by Bourdieu's work that was carried out with museum visitors. In particular, they explored how the concepts of habitus can be applied to local history museums. Fyfe and Ross (1996, p. 131) identified a need to investigate 'how different social groups and subjects "read" museums, according to the range of cultural experiences, needs and desires they bring with them is an aspect of cultural representation and reproduction'. This necessitated an in-depth investigation of topics such as social background, lifestyle and how museum visiting might fit in people's lives, community affiliations and locality; the subject of museum visiting was discussed only insofar as people themselves thought it was important in their lives and brought it up in the conversation. A total of fifteen interviews were carried out with all members of fifteen households (around thirty-five people in total), representing both working class and middle-class households. This particular paper (Fyfe & Ross, 1996) reports on three of those households, all of which were located in and around Stoke-on-Trent and Newcastle-under-Lyme in northwest England. This area is associated with pottery production and a now declined coal industry. The main finding of this study was that visitors' (and non-visitors' or lapsed visitors') lifestyles, social class and differing social and geographical mobility (related partly to migration) afford different relationships with their local area and its material culture (predominantly, physical sites and objects).

> Museums and their collections have different meanings for different social groups; lifestyles, social class and differing social and geographical mobility shape these differing meanings

Dicks (2016) used Bourdieu's concepts of habitus, field and symbolic capital as her theoretical framework in her study of visitors to an industrial heritage site, a disused coal mine, in Wales. The site uses audio-visual shows and live interpretation – ex-miners who act as guides and tell the story of Rhondda Valley miners, starting with the discovery of coal and all the way through to the 1950s and the nationalisation of the mining industry. Dicks (2016), who interviewed twenty-six visitors before and after their visit, found that the way visitors retold the miners' story appeared homogenous. It was a story 'of hardship and struggle, offset by the closeness of their community, and they all felt this struggle was justified' (Dicks, 2016, p. 56). This type of cultural framing corresponds to wider cultural narratives that exist in popular consciousness where working-class people are seen as 'heroes' who manage to overcome difficulties and prove themselves to be resilient in the face of adversity. This was a story of portraying working-class people (miners in this case) reflected both in the narrative of the site but also in the visitor's post-visit narrative,[6] regardless of their background (e.g., social-class, ethnicity, age, gender and so on). When applying Bourdieu's concept of habitus, Dicks (2016) was able to go beyond what she felt were superficially similar ways visitors voiced responses to the site. She examined the responses of three working-class families in more detail and discussed findings from two female members of different families who were interviewed. Dicks (2016) found that, although there were similarities in the habitus of the two women (both of whom were daughters of Welsh miners), they seemed to have appropriated the site differently. One of them perceived it as close to her sense of self-identity, while the other one distanced the site from her sense of self-identity but recognised that it had implications for the person she was. These experiences were different to those that middle-class visitors had at the site who did 'not recognize their own identities and

> Cultural narratives are powerful tools that organise meaning, i.e., how people make sense of and relate to the story of an exhibition

> Social class is not a fixed attribute of individuals, it is part of the individual habitus and as such open to improvisations. This means that members of the same social class will relate differently to the same exhibition

memories within the story and approach[ed] it as an object of knowledge', despite the fact that they appeared to have 'a clear emotional investment in it [the world of miners] and a sense of regret for its loss' (Dicks, 2016, p. 60). Dicks (2016, p. 60) clarified that the sense of loss that middle-class visitors experienced was not a sense of loss of self; it was 'the loss of a cultural ideal, a political vision'. Dicks states that, by closely relating visitor responses to their life experiences, she was able to gain a more nuanced insight into the interrelationships between the site and its visitors.

We now turn to a rare example of a non-visitor research study whose participants come from four low-income minority groups living in London in the UK (Dawson, 2014). These included members of a Somali, a Sierra Leonean, a Latin American and an Asian group. This exploratory study focused on the practices and perceptions of members of these groups; in particular, how they perceive exclusion from informal science education settings. Theoretically, the study was based on Bourdieu's concepts of habitus and cultural capital, while methodologically it took an ethnographic approach. This included participant observation in community group activities, focus group discussions, interviews and accompanied visits to a science-rich environment of the participants' choice. The vast majority of the participants had never been to an informal science education setting before and saw them as socially distant places and of little relevance to them and their families. Dawson pointed out the perceived mismatch between the participants' culture and practices and their 'notions of an imagined museum', which was 'implicitly classed and racialized by some participants' (2014, p. 990). The participants' habitus and lack of appropriate cultural capital shaped the way museums were perceived or imagined and how they perceived they should behave in a museum. Participants' perception that their culture, resources and practices would not be valued in a museum made some of them feel a sense of discomfort and led them to critique them, while others said that visiting museums is not something they would do. Dawson commented on the latter type of responses, where participants suggested that visiting museums was 'unthinkable', outside participants' worlds and practices, that it is an indication of 'how resilient habitus can be in guiding patterns of behaviour and practice' (2014, p. 991).

According to Dawson (2014), a key difficulty encountered by some participants was the exclusive use of English language (both in exhibit text and in communicating with staff) which was felt to be exclusive and problematic as it restricted their learning opportunities. This was despite the fact that they could all communicate in English. Participants' interactions with staff, when problematic or not helpful, impacted on their sense of comfort

[margin note:] Perceived notions about museums implicit in wider cultural discourses can make people from certain backgrounds feel that their culture and practices are not valued

[margin note:] The lack of certain types of capital (such as speaking English or understanding key concepts) essential for making sense of the visit seriously limits visitors' learning opportunities and decreases the likelihood of their visiting again

in the space or feeling welcome and valued as visitors by the institution. Despite the many issues, both perceived and experienced, during their visits to museums, in some cases participants were also able to have meaningful experiences with the museum content by drawing on their own cultural resources. Such occasions, in which the museum content resonated with them and with members of their family, 'enabled certain participants to suddenly recognize something of themselves in the [informal science education] institution, becoming in the instant closer to the "ideal visitor" who could relate to the exhibits, texts, and concepts presented by the museum, which were inaccessible for the majority of their visits' (Dawson, 2014, p. 998). Another positive connection participants made with the museum was that the visit enabled them to spend precious time with family and friends and share the experience.

> Exhibits, text, activities, content and staff provide scaffolding that allows visitors to draw on their cultural resources and can facilitate meaningful experiences for diverse visitor groups

Enterprising Science project – Ways of 'being a boy' and boys' engagement with science in a science museum

The 'science capital' concept – reminiscent of and influenced by Bourdieu's 'cultural capital' – was used in the Enterprising Science project to examine science engagement, with particular emphasis on social groups that are underrepresented in school STEM subjects and in science careers. Science capital refers to 'science-related knowledge, attitudes, experiences and resources that you acquire through life' (Archer et al., 2016a). Initial studies (Archer, 2015) showed that science capital was unevenly spread across pupils, while pupils' chances of having high, medium or low levels of science capital relates to their gender, ethnicity and cultural capital. Having identified that gender influences science capital, researchers used gender as a lens to study how different types of gender performance (i.e., ways of 'being a boy' or 'being a girl') affect engagement with science during a visit to a science museum. Below, we present key findings and concepts coming from the study that looked at performances of masculinity. Another study which examined girls' identity performances (Dawson et al., 2015 cited in Archer et al., 2016b) had not yet been published at the time we were writing this book.

This study focused on urban working-class boys' performance of masculinity in relation to their engagement with science and science identity, using Bourdieu's concept of *field* (Archer et al., 2016b). Archer et al. (2016b) used the concept of masculinity in order to understand gender performance and engagement with science within the socially constructed space of a science museum. Three types of performances of masculinity were identified. The most commonly enacted performances were laddishness and muscular intellect, and the third and less common one was translocational masculinity. The type of behaviours associated with laddishness included 'resisting doing school work, mucking about macho behaviors, engaging in sexist/sexual banter, becoming competitive, flirting, finding ways to (appear to) resist doing any science work and "having a laff"' (Archer et al., 2016b, p. 454). Muscular intellect performance was associated with behaviours that included 'assertive claims to scientific interest, confident demonstrations, and competitive verbal one-upmanship over scientific knowledge and assuming dominant role, telling other students what to do during the visit (in terms of both scientific content and the structure of activities)' (Archer et al., 2016b, p. 455). Finally, translocational masculinity is a term used to refer to performances where boys drew on their own varied cultural resources and experiences to establish links and points of commonality between their own lives, interests, and values and the museum context. These types of associations with cultural and cognitive resources available to visitors are often reported in other audience research, although not from the viewpoint of masculinity or this particular theoretical perspective.

> Boys performing the gender identity of translocational masculinity may help them find commonalities between the museum content and their own lives and values

This study (Archer et al., 2016b) showed how the science museum field privileged and normalised masculinity by foregrounding famous white men whose role in science and technology are prominent in the exhibitions, and by offering science activities that are competitive in nature. These included interactive exhibitions and games that the vast majority of boys participating in this study were engaged in. This, in turn, appeared to 'promote and normalize performances of hegemonic masculinity (which again also contributed to the recognition of the field as masculine)', such as laddishness and muscular intellect. The focus of this study was not just on a physical space or the physical environment of the museum but also on the actions of and relations between people in the physical space, both of which are the key elements of the field. This, for example, enabled the researchers to examine the impact that performances of masculinity on other pupils, notably girls and less dominant boys. The study showed that performance of both laddishness and muscular intellect resulted in excluding girls and less dominant boys who were less assertive and dominating. Dominant behaviours leading to the exclusion of less dominant students ranged from mocking, teasing and ridiculing to being shouted at or interrupted and, in some cases, pushed around physically. Another dimension of the actions and relations this study examined was the way the museum staff interacted with or supported particular performances of masculinity.

Examining those three types of performances of masculinity with the types of engagement with science they enabled, this study (Archer et al., 2016b) concluded that laddishness facilitated some engagement with stereotypically masculine topics (such as cars, aeroplanes or interactive exhibits that facilitated peer competition). On the other hand, this type of performance played a very limited role in promoting further science learning or a science identity, while it did reproduce an idea of science as being for boys, as the follow-up interviews suggested. At the same time, during the actual visit, performances of laddishness tended to exclude girls and non-dominant boys. This ranged from physical exclusion, at times, to rendering them 'invisible, to staff and other students, during the visit, which limited their opportunities to be recognized as performing science identities' (Archer et al., 2016b, p. 472). Similar patterns of reproducing exclusionary and masculine views of science were recorded in relation to performances of muscular intellect. These types of performances also promoted a view of science as authoritative and brainy. Having said that, performances of muscular intellect appeared to be congruent with identities of scientific expertise to the very limited number of boys. Finally, translocational performances of masculinity were congruent with science engagement and a science identity, which highlighted the importance of making links between science and the cultural backgrounds of the pupils. This is an example of how museums could build on the social capital of working-class pupils and redress the power relationships that often exist between visitors from certain backgrounds and museums. Nevertheless, the study reported that instances of these types of performances were isolated and, although they received positive feedback from peers and adults, they were not consciously supported by teachers and museum staff or facilitated by the museum environment.

> Boys' performance of laddishness and of muscular intellect can exclude girls and non-dominant boys from engaging with the museum content

A return to the museum – Aboriginal communities collaborations

Ian, a computer programmer in his mid-thirties, is visiting the Powerhouse Museum, while on a visit to meet family members from his paternal side who immigrated to Sydney in the 1960s. This is a trip that he had been planning to make with his father, when he suddenly passed away almost a year ago. His cousin told him about the Museum because he knew he would enjoy its focus on applied arts and sciences. He mentioned a new exhibition about Egyptian mummies where mummies are presented alongside their 3D CT scan visualisations. Ian downloaded the Museum map on his iPad in advance of his visit so he knew that the mummies exhibition is on the third level. As he enters the Museum, the details of a talk are announced; it is about how Aboriginal cultures and ancient Egyptians mourned their dead. This catches his attention and he decides to go to the talk first, as it is about to start. He takes a seat as somebody from the Museum introduces the speakers. The first speaker is an artist, and a member of the southeastern Australian Aboriginal community. She starts by acknowledging her ancestors and explains where she comes from and says a few words about her background. Ian realises how little he knows about Australian Aboriginal communities and that shakes his perception of the country; he is interested in finding out more. This sense of surprise at being welcomed in a museum by somebody from a non-Anglo background and his openness to address his assumptions is consistent with critical pedagogy which strives to challenge fixed assumptions about our own as well as other people's identities and heritage.

While those thoughts are going through Ian's head, the artist goes on to talk about *kopis*, which were mourning caps that a widow would wear after the death of her husband. After a period of mourning, the cap would be placed at the burial site. Meanwhile, a member of the Museum staff shows some images of kopis from the Yandilla area in northwestern New South Wales which is now in the Australian Museum collection. They explain that the cap was always white because white is associated with mourning in Aboriginal communities. The caps themselves are respected as much as human remains and that is why they are not displayed in museums any more. Ian finds the cap such a powerful object; he really feels connected to it. He thinks about how museums had used the heritage of Australian Aboriginal community so inappropriately before. This thought unsettles him but also makes him think about how contemporary museums deal with this issue. Maybe this talk is part of a healing process, bringing Australian Aboriginal communities and museums closer together. This makes him think about his own loss and mourning process. Here again we are reminded of critical pedagogy with its emphasis on affective ways of knowing and learning. It is also consistent with sociocultural learning that highlights the importance of making links between people's own cultural recourses, values and their lives.

The artist explains how and why the widow's caps were made and uses the mourning caps as a starting point to talk about grief and loss in Aboriginal Australian cultures. Although he is lost in his own thought for a moment, he realises that what the artist is now talking about is that the Australian Aboriginal communities are trying to come to terms with different types of grief and loss; the loss of their children, their land and their spirituality. Ian is now deeply moved to learn about traditional Aboriginal grieving practices. One can make a link between Ian's cultural capital and the way it acts as a bridge between his personal experience of loss and grief and the museum content. Links can also be made with critical pedagogy and the idea that objects and emotionally charged experiences can start a dialogue between visitors and their understanding of others or of events that happened in the past.

Contextualising culture and power

How can you use objects in an exhibition or a programme in a way that resonates with how people from different social groups understand and value them? How can the value people from different social groups attach to objects be shared through the exhibition text and/or other visual interpretation methods? What symbols can you use to help tell different stories that would resonate with different people? What support can you provide so that visitors from different social groups feel confident to use their own knowledge base and cultural resources?

How can you provide interpretation in different languages and enhance the experience of non-native speakers? Do members of gallery staff (front-of-house, guides, explainers) speak other languages; and if so, can they deliver on-gallery interpretation in other languages? Gallery staff can enhance the experience of audiences but they need to know how to approach and scaffold the experience of different groups and enable them to draw on their cultural resources, background or cultural capital. What training do you need to provide them with in order to be able to do that?

How can you utilise people's cultural capital in a way that acts as a bridge between their lived experiences and the museum content? What type of tools (such as objects and other interpretive media) and contexts (programmes, late events, outreach) can make them feel comfortable and want to engage? What types of spaces can be inviting and, at the same time, respect visitors' sociocultural background? How can you support affective experiences through the use of objects? What opportunities for meaningful inter- and intra-group social interactions and building of social capital can you create?

Notes

1 Text reprinted with the permission of its author. Russell Cook, M. (2016). How living museums are 'waking up' sleeping artefacts. [available online: http://theconversation.com/how-living-museums-are-waking-up-sleeping-artefacts-55950].
2 For a discussion of the link between the socialisation process, class and cognition and the role of cognitive science, in particular, in this process see Lave (1988, chapter 4).
3 Emphasis in the original.
4 This has also led to building a better understanding of grief from an Indigenous cultural perspective which kopi collections represent. Maree Clarke, who is also an artist, leads workshops for museums,

including the Powerhouse Museum (see: http://dfat.gov.au/people-to-people/public-diplomacy/programs-activities/pages/maree-clarke-ritual-and-ceremony.aspx and http://indigenousstory.com.au/works/image/maree-clarke-140/).

5 For more information about Enterprising Science see: www.kcl.ac.uk/sspp/departments/education/research/Research-Centres/cppr/Research/currentpro/Enterprising-Science/index.aspx; for application of the concept of 'science capital'. The author does not know how much longer this will be the address for this project – though at the time of submission this is correct. It refers to science-related qualifications. For interest, literacy and social contacts, in a museum context go to the Transforming Practice blog developed by the Science Museum: https://transformingpractice.wordpress.com/

6 Ideas about how museums and visitors construct narratives in exhibitions are discussed in Chapter 5 in more detail.

References

Andermann, J. & Arnold-de-Simine, S. (2012). Museums and the educational turn: History, memory, inclusivity. *Journal of Educational Media, Memory, and Society,* 4(2), 1–7.

Archer, L., Dawson, E., DeWitt, J., Godec, S., King, H., Mau, A., Nomikou, E., & Seakins, A. J. (2016a). *Science capital made clear.* London: King's College London. [https://kclpure.kcl.ac.uk/portal/files/49685107/Science_Capital_Made_Clear.pdf].

Archer, L., Dawson, E., DeWitt, J., Seakins, A. & Wong, B. (2015). 'Science capital': A conceptual, methodological, and empirical argument for extending Bourdieusian notions of capital beyond the arts. *Journal of Research in Science Teaching,* 52, 922–948.

Archer, L., Dawson, E., Seakins, A., DeWitt, J., Godec, S., & Whitby, C. (2016b). 'I'm being a man here': Urban boys' performances of masculinity and engagement with science during a science museum visit. *Journal of the Learning Sciences,* 25(3), 438–485.

Aronowitz, S. & Giroux, H.A. (1985). *Education under siege: The conservative, liberal and radical debate over schooling.* South Hadley, MA: Bergin & Garvey, Inc.

Bennett, T. (1995). *The birth of the museum.* London: Routledge.

Bennett, T. (1998). *Culture: A reformer's science.* Sydney: Allen and Unwin.

Black, L.A. (1990). Applying learning theory in the development of a museum learning environment, in ASTC, what research says about learning in science museums, Washington, DC, 23–25.

Blud, L.M. (1990). Social interaction and learning among family groups visiting a museum, *Museum Management and Curatorship,* 9, 43–51.

Boast, R. (2011). Neocolonial collaboration: museum as contact zone revisited. *Museum Anthropology,* 34(1), 56–70.

Bourdieu, P. (1984). *Distinction: A social critique of the judgment of taste.* Translated from French by R. Nice. London: Routledge.

Bourdieu, P. (1986). The social space and its transformations. In *Distinction – a social critique of the judgment of taste* (pp. 99–168). Translated from French by R. Nice. London: Routledge.

Bourdieu, P. (1990). *The logic of practice.* Translated from French by R. Nice. Stanford, CA: Stanford University Press.

Bourdieu, P., (1993). *The field of cultural production: Essays on art and literature,* New York: Columbia University Press.

Bourdieu, P. & Darbel, A. (with Schnapper, D.). (1997). *The love of art: European art museums and their public,* Cambridge: Polity Press.

Bradburne, J. (1993). Going public science museums, debate and democracy. In J. Bradburne & I. Janousek (Eds.), *Planning science museums for the new Europe: Seminar proceedings* (pp. 83–94). Prague: Narodni Technicke Muzeum.

Cole, M. (1985). The zone of proximal development: Where culture and cognition create each other. In J.V. Wertsch (Ed.), *Culture, communication, and cognition: Vygotskian perspectives* (pp. 146–161). New York: Cambridge University Press.

Cole, M. & Packer, M. (2011). Culture in development. In M.E. Lamp & M.H. Bornstein (Eds.), *Social and personality development: An advanced textbook.* New York: Psychology Press.

Dawson, E. (2014). 'Not designed for us': How science museums and science centers socially exclude low-income, minority ethnic groups. *Science Education, 98,* 981–1008. doi:10.1002/sce.21133

Dewey, J. (1980) [1916]. *Democracy and education.* Carbondale, IL: Southern Illinois University Press.

Diamond, J. (1986). The behaviour of family groups in science museums, *Curator,* 29(2), 139–154.

Dicks, B. (2016). The habitus of heritage: A discussion of Bourdieu's ideas for visitor studies in heritage and museums. *Museum & Society,* 14(1), 52–64.

Dierking, L.D. (1992). The family museum experience: Implications from research. In *Patterns in Practice* (pp. 215–221). Washington, DC: Museum Education Roundtable.

Falk, J. & Dierking, L.D. (1992). *The museum experience.* Washington, DC: Whalesback Books.

Foley, J.A., Morris, D. Gounari, R., & Agostinone-Wilson, F. (2015). Critical education, critical pedagogies, Marxist education in the United States. *Journal for Critical Education Policy Studies,* 13(3), 110–144.

Fyfe, G. & Ross, M. (1995). Decoding the visitor's gaze: rethinking museum visiting. *The Sociological Review,* 43(1), 127–150. doi:10.1111/j.1467-954X.1995.tb03428.x

Giroux, H. & McLaren, P. (1989). *Critical pedagogy, the state, and cultural struggle,* New York: SUNY Press.

Greenhalgh, P. (1989). Education, entertainment and politics: Lessons from the great international exhibitions. In Vergo, P. *The new museology,* London: Reaktion Books.

Gregory, R. (1989). Turning minds on to science by hands-on exploration: The nature and potential of the hands-on medium, in M. Quin (Ed). *Sharing science: Issues in the development of interactive science and technology centres* (pp. 1–9). London: Nuffield Foundation.

Harrison, R. (2013). Reassembling ethnographic museum collections, in R. Harrison, S. Byrne, & A. Clarke (Eds.), *Reassembling the collection: ethnographic museums and indigenous agency* (pp. 3–35). Santa Fe, NM: SAR Press.

Hein, G.E. (1991). The significance of constructivism for museum education. *Proceedings of ICOM CECA Annual Conference*, Jerusalem 1991, ICOM, pp. 89–94.

Hein, G.E. (1998). *Learning in the museum*. London: Routledge.

Hein, G.E. (2012). *Progressive museum practice: John Dewey and democracy*. Walnut Creek, CA: Left Coast Press.

Hein, H. (2007). Redressing the museum in feminist theory. *Museum Management and Curatorship*, 22(1), 29–42.

Hooper-Greenhill, E. (1991). *Museum and gallery education*, Leicester: Leicester University Press.

Hooper-Greenhill, E. (1992). *Museums and the shaping of knowledge*. London: Routledge.

Hooper-Greenhill, E. (1994). *The educational role of the museum* (1st edition). London: Routledge.

Hooper-Greenhill, E. (1999). Education, communication and interpretation: Towards a critical pedagogy in museums. In E. Hooper-Greenhill (Ed), *The educational role of the museum* (2nd edition, pp. 3–27). London: Routledge.

Levin, A.K. (2010). *Gender, sexuality and museums: A Routledge reader*. Oxford: Routledge.

Levin, A.K. (2012). Unpacking gender: Creating complex models for gender inclusivity in museums. In E. Nightingale & R. Sandell (Eds.), *Museums, equality, and social justice* (pp. 156–168). Oxford: Routledge.

Lidchi, H (1997). The poetics and the politics of exhibiting other cultures. In S. Hall (Ed.), *Representation* (pp. 151–222). London: Sage.

Lindauer, M. (2005). From salad bars to vivid stories: Four game plans for developing 'educationally successful' exhibitions. *Journal of Museum Management and Curatorship*, 20(1), 41–55.

Lindauer, M. (2006). Looking at museum education through the lens of curriculum theory. Introductory remarks for a special issue of the *Journal of Museum Education*, 31(2), 79–80.

Lindauer, M. (2007). Critical museum pedagogy and exhibition development. In S. Knell, S. Macleod, & S. Watson (Eds.), *Museum revolutions: How museums change and are changed* (pp. 303–314). Oxford: Routledge.

Macdonald, S. (2003). 'Museums, national, postnational and transcultural identities', *Museum and Society*, 1(1), 1–16.

Mahar, C., Harker, R., & Wilkes, C. (1990). The basic theoretical position. In R. Harker, C. Mahar, & C. Wilkes (Eds.), *An introduction to the work of Pierre Bourdieu: The practice of theory* (pp. 1–25). Basingstoke: MacMillan.

Museum Education Task Force. (1992). *Excellence and equity: Education and the public dimensions of museums*, Washington, DC: American Association of Museums.

Nomikou, E. (2013). *A museological approach to numismatic exhibitions: An ethnography of exhibition making in the Ashmolean Museum*. Unpublished doctoral thesis. University College London, UK.

Rogoff, B., Moore, L., Najafi, B., Dexter, A., Correa-Chávez, M., & Solís, J. (2007). Children's development of cultural repertoires through participation in everyday routines and practices. In J.

Grusec & P. Hastings (Eds.), *Handbook of socialization: Theory and research* (pp. 490–515). New York: The Guilford Press.

Sandell, R. (2002). Museums and the combating of social inequality: Roles, responsibilities and resistance. In R. Sandell (Ed.), *Museums, society, inequality* (pp. 3–23). London/New York: Routledge.

Shweder, R.A., Goodnow, J.J., Hatano, G., LeVine, R.A., Markus, H.R., & Miller P.J. (2006). The cultural psychology of development: One mind, many mentalities. In W. Damon & R. Lerner (Eds.), *Handbook of child psychology: Vol. 1. Theoretical models of human development* (6th edition, pp. 716–792). New York: Wiley.

Smith, L. (2006). *The uses of heritage*, London/New York: Routledge.

Smith, L. (2011). Affect and registers of engagement: Navigating emotional responses to dissonant heritage. In L. Smith, G. Cubitt, R. Wilson, & K. Fouseki (Ed.), *Representing enslavement and abolition in museums: Ambiguous engagements* (pp. 260–303). New York: Routledge.

Srivastava, A.R.V. (2013). *Essentials of cultural anthropology* (2nd edition). Delhi: PHI Learning.

Van der Veer, R. (1996). The concept of culture in Vygotsky's thinking, *Culture & Psychology*, 2, 247–263.

Weisner, T.S. (2002). Ecocultural understanding of children's developmental pathways. *Human Development*, 45(4), 275–281.

White, L.A. (1959). The concept of culture. *American Anthropologist*, 61(2), 227–251.

Williams, R. (1977). *Marxism and literature*. Oxford: Oxford University Press.

Wolf, E.R. (1984). Culture: Panacea or problem? *American Antiquity*, 49(2), 393–400.

Wolf, E.R. (1999). *Envisioning power: Ideologies of dominance and crisis*. Berkeley, CA: University of California Press.

Wolf, E.R. (2001). *Pathways of power: Building an anthropology of the modern world*. Berkeley, CA: University of California Press.

11 Conclusions

Any attempt to study museums inevitably transcends conventional disciplinary boundaries. So has this book, from the first couple of chapters where we examined the value of theory in the museum learning research and practice, and the methodologies and methods that have been applied in the studying of museum learning to the chapters that focus on particular topics that are the focus of debate in museum theory and practice. Each topic captures something of the intellectual problems that are of particular relevance to museum learning, what sets of questions different disciplines pose, and some of the tools (i.e., theories, concepts, methodologies and methods) that these different disciplines use for grappling with these intellectual problems. They all shed some light onto different aspects of the relationship between museums and society, and the value museums have in people's lives. For example, some of the intellectual problems of museum learning include the relationship between visitor agency and the social context of the museum; the role cultural values play in choosing to visit and engage with, or not visit museums; the role visitors' own cultural assets play in feeling at ease and being able to decode museum objects or content; the way that personal and collective memory interact to influence learning in museums; and how narratives interact with experience in learning situations, creating unique learning experiences.

We also want to highlight the overlap between topics here in this chapter. Whilst we have tried to signal through cross-referencing in the chapters where we think overlaps occur, there are undoubtedly areas of overlap that we did not think to mention, or for reasons of flow have not called attention to. For instance, there are multiple connections between identity and other topics, such as meaning making, narrative, memory, authenticity, etc. In addition, culture and power are relevant to each of the other topics of the book. In fact, some of the crossovers between topics may suggest fruitful avenues for further research. The question here, then, is how we can leverage the diverse theoretical and methodological resources researchers have used in researching these topics to address the intellectual and social problems with which the museum learning field engages. We believe that the answer to that can be found in practitioner–researcher collaborations for at least two reasons. Firstly, as the research presented in this book has demonstrated, the museum visit is a system of unimaginable complexity where each individual visitor's experience is situated within the experience of other members of her group, other museum visitors or groups and museum staff, all of which are located within a complex environment where an infinite number of interactions may take place. Secondly, the calls for carrying out research that takes into account wider dimensions of social relations and the context of the museum, rather than focusing on specific exhibitions, exhibits or programmes have become louder, and come both from within and outside the museum profession (Hooper-Greenhill, 2006; Tate Learning, 2011; Learning Research Agenda for Natural History Institutions, 2016; Dawson & Jensen, 2011). These are not issues that practitioners or researchers alone can begin to address.

There are already some collaboration models coming from science education (e.g., Bell, Lewenstein, Shouse, & Feder (2009) and children's museums (e.g., Sobel & Jipson, 2016) that examine learning in both formal and informal environments. These models demonstrate how it is possible to carry out audience research that can take into account both research and practice perspectives. In one of the chapters in the book edited by Sobel and Jipson, for example, Allen and Gutwill (2016, p. 193) present the model of jointly negotiated research (JNR), which incorporates four principles: '*negotiate problems of practice* that are of equal interest and importance to both researchers and practitioners; *advance both theory and practice*; *engage in collaborative design work* to explore and test new practices; and *build capacity to sustain change* beyond the immediate term of the research project'.[1] With some variations, all of the book chapters echo what Allen and Gutwill (2016) have identified as principles that characterise mutually beneficial practitioner–researcher collaborations (e.g., Hadani & Walker, 2016; Gaskins, 2016).

Each of the practitioner–researcher case studies in their book (Sobel & Jipson, 2016) is jointly authored by a practitioner and a researcher and offers rich examples of different models of partnership, its benefits, challenges, and outcomes and implications for research and practice. A number of reflection and analysis papers highlight the importance of 'getting more practice into research' and the need to 'identify a "persistent problem of practice" that both communities are invested in addressing' (Bevan, 2016, pp. 182, 183); and stress the need for practitioners and researchers 'to take their often separate missions and fuse them into a common culture, or at least, two cultures that can communicate' (Hirsch-Pasek & Golinkoff, 2016, p. 223). Gaskins (2016, p. 168) repeated that point in her paper, but focused more on the idea that the process of collaboration 'involves the coordination of two ways of viewing the world – two cultures [...]' and that 'the goal is not to collapse them into one [...]'. This idea of whether the museums and academic institutions – the two worlds practitioners and researchers inhabit – need to share a mission or a culture, or to 'develop new professional routines' (Bevan, 2016, p. 186), and the power dynamics involved in more traditional models of relationships between researchers and practitioners was debated in a number of chapters (see Hirsch-Pasek & Golinkoff, 2016; Bevan, 2016; Gaskins, 2016).

The models presented in the Sobel and Jipson (2016) book can, if adapted, be applied in different types of museums. When planning for a research collaboration, finding a partner who is willing to commit to it is very important. The other element of the collaboration is the focus of the research programme, which needs to focus on problems of practice. Problems of museum learning practice invariably are about audience (actual and potential) experience. Another element that needs to be taken into account is how the research collaboration will be funded. Finally, the focus of the research collaboration, in the cases of publicly funded museums in particular, will need to reflect policy priorities that directly affect museum practice and research around learning. Each of the above elements can be overwhelming and challenging in equal measure. What we will focus on here is how this book can help define and sharpen the focus of practitioner–researcher collaborations. So, taking the material presented in this book as a starting point, we (both museum learning researchers and practitioners) can begin to examine different methods, concepts, ideas, research and museum practices and how they intermingle; and acknowledge that there is an important body of knowledge that learning researchers and practitioners share and can capitalise on to further develop and improve their practice.

Generally speaking, museum learning practitioners aspire to create personally and socially meaningful experiences that will engage the body, mind and feelings, and that they will be powerful enough to be memorable and to transform people's lives. To achieve this 'ideal' visitor experience, practitioners have looked to their visitors for answers. But, although evaluation questions are relatively easy to come up with, it is much more of a challenge to ask research questions that have a theoretical motivation behind them. This book has identified many gaps in research and topics that can produce useful findings and identify issues that would be of interest to the museum sector. Here are some of the topics and questions:

What elements of the design and content of different spaces affect which identities (relevant to an exhibition of the museum themes) come to visitors' minds? What elements need to be incorporated in the design of a space to allow for engagement that expands visitors' world view and help them keep developing?

How do different spaces, programmes or mediated experiences enhance visitors' self-concept and encourage them to explore different future identities? What are the characteristics of those spaces? What role do other elements such as the type of social group visitors come with, their gender, ethnicity, social class play in changing visitors' self-concepts?

Visitors go to museums for many reasons, including seeing and doing things with others. But one of the least explored reasons is their wish to participate in the activities of the communities of practice that are associated with different museums. How can opportunities to meet and interact with members of staff from different departments shift visitors' identities and affiliations? What value can 'entering' the world of a curator or conservator for a short while during their visit bring to visitors' lives?

Likewise, no museum volunteer decides to engage with a museum without reason. Volunteers often have direct access to members of staff; sometimes the latter can be world experts in their field. Their interactions can relate to the task at hand, be of a social nature, or have a professional development element. To what extent do these interactions volunteers have with members of staff foster an interest in a field of study and develop volunteers' learning identity?

How can visitors' own resources and assets can be reflected in the museum's content and made relevant during their visit? What (conscious or pre-conscious) cues do visitors of different ages, gender, ethnicity, sexual orientation and social class pick up and how do these affect their visit? How do those cues shape the narratives that they construct about their visit, and how do these narratives feed into their identity building? What cultural resources do visitors draw from to develop their discourse in the museum context?

These are but a few possible topics/questions that research collaborations could examine. We realise that the focus on research topics/questions may give the impression of a power imbalance between the practitioner and the researcher. However, practitioners are the only ones who can ground these topics in their organisational context and the wider museum sector, and this is a very important element of effective collaborations. They also have access to existing evaluation studies which, as reported by many case studies of collaborative projects in the Sobel and

Jipson book (2016), are often the starting point for asking a fruitful research question. Evaluation studies, although different from research in nature, have the advantage of responding to a particular, situated issue within the museum. Despite the fact that a lot of the situated knowledge that is associated with evaluation studies is not made explicit, the practitioners who work there have a great deal of important tacit knowledge that makes the evaluation findings really meaningful. Researchers can bring to the table a deep understanding of theory and research methodology which can enrich the professional life of the practitioner. Research practice takes years to develop and establish and, more often than not, it involves apprenticeship learning. A long-term research collaboration could provide practitioners access to this type of apprenticeship learning and facilitate the development of their professional identity. In this way, familiarity with academic research and research methodology, on the one hand, and familiarity with the museum context and its mission and priorities, on the other, becomes a dialectic process; the relationship of practitioners and researchers is located in the museum and academic context.

Finally, since the visitor experience is always at the core of museum practice, this practitioner–researcher relation can also benefit visitors (and possibly non-visitors). By grounding their practice theoretically, practitioners can enable visitors – through exhibitions, programmes and other resources – to ask deeper and more meaningful questions about museum content and collections such as 'what is the meaning of art or science in my life and the life of my family?'

Note

1 Emphasis in the original text.

References

Allen, S. & Gutwill, J. (2016). Exploring models of research–practice partnership within a single institution. In D.M. Sobel & J.L. Jipson (Eds.), *Cognitive development in museum settings: Relating research and practice* (pp. 190–208). New York: Routledge.

Bell, P., Lewenstein, B., Shouse, A., & Feder, M. (Eds.) (2009). *Learning science in informal environments: People, places, and pursuits.* Report published by the National Research Council, Washington, DC: National Academies Press.

Bevan, B. (2016). Wanted: A new cultural model for the relationship between research and practice. In D.M. Sobel & J.L. Jipson (Eds.), *Cognitive development in museum settings: Relating research and practice* (pp. 181–189). New York: Routledge.

Dawson, E. and Jensen, E. (2011). Towards a contextual turn in visitor studies: Evaluating visitor segmentation and identity-related motivations. *Visitor Studies*, 14(2), 127–140.

Gaskins, S. (2016). Collaboration is a two-way street. In D.M. Sobel & J.L. Jipson (Eds.), *Cognitive development in museum settings: Relating research and practice* (pp. 151–170). New York: Routledge.

Hadani, H. & Walker, C. (2016). Research and museum partnerships: Key components of successful collaborations. In D.M. Sobel & J.L. Jipson (Eds.), *Cognitive development in museum settings: Relating research and practice* (pp. 171–180). New York: Routledge.

Hirsch-Pasek, K. & Golinkoff, R.M. (2016). Two missions in search of a shared culture. In D.M. Sobel & J.L. Jipson (Eds.), *Cognitive development in museum settings: Relating research and practice* (pp. 222–230). New York: Routledge.

Hooper-Greenhill, E. (2006). *Studying visitors*. In S. Macdonald (Ed.), *Companion to museum studies* (pp. 362–376). Oxford: Blackwell Publishing.

Knutson, K. & Crowley, K. (2005). Museum as learning laboratory: Developing and using a practical theory of informal learning. *Hand to Hand*, 18, 4–5.

Learning Research Agenda for Natural History Institutions, (2016). www.nhm.ac.uk/content/dam/nhmwww/about-us/learning-research-agenda/A%20Learning%20Research%20Agenda%20for%20Natural%20History%20Institutions.pdf

Leinhardt, G. & Crowley, K. (1998). Museum learning as conversational elaboration: A proposal to capture, code, and analyze talk in museums. Learning Research & Development Center University of Pittsburgh. Museum Learning Collaborative Technical Report # MLC-01 Available at http://mlc.lrdc.pitt.edu/mlc

Sobel, D.M. & Jipson, J.L. (Eds.) (2016). *Cognitive development in museum settings: Relating research and practice*. New York: Routledge.

Tate Learning. (2011). *Transforming Tate Learning*. [Accessed on 27 February 2017: www.tate.org.uk/download/file/fid/30243].

Glossary

A

Accommodation, the mental process of changing an existing concept in order to fit a new piece of information that does not fit with this concept.

Agency, the capacity of an individual to act in the world.

Analogy (and relational analogy), the use of comparison between objects or events to understand other properties about a less familiar object or event. When items share multiple properties, knowing something about one of the items can allow the learner to infer information about the other. For example, people may be able to guess that a cat they have only just learned about will have similar interior properties to other cats, eat similar food to other cats, and have some of the same behaviours as other cats they know about.

Argument, a series of statements that constitute a reasoned set of ideas about a particular topic. The elements of an argument include a claim, a warrant or backing, and a conclusion.

Assimilation, the mental process of adding a new instance of a concept to the list of items that can be categorised within that concept.

Authentication process, according to Frisvoll (2013, p. 273) 'authentication' is a 'social process involving a complex range of elements [...] which are linked to discourses outside the consumed tourism product'.

Autobiographical memories, some episodic memories are purely about the self and as such, can be considered a special form of episodic memory.

B

Backing, this element of an argument, also known as a warrant, connects the claim to the data.

Basic framework, ways people perceive and interpret the world. See also mental model. Both concepts focus on the existence of a cognitive model of an external reality and one's own possible actions/interactions with it and make sense of it.

C

Capital, all the resources available to a person which can be economic, cultural, social and symbolic.

Claim, element of an argument that denotes the substantive statement that may be supported with the data provided.

Collectivistic concept of identity, defining the self as embedded in contexts and relationships; see also social concept of identity.

Collective memory, the shared history of communities. Collective memory helps to form community identity. Individuals within a community tend to all have a sense of an event that has occurred or a way of doing something that is shared by the rest of the members.

Communities of Practice (CoP), the ways that groups of people participate in practices that are culturally bound, which are passed on to new members of the group through apprenticeships and 'informal' training. Term original coined by Lave and Wenger.

Conclusion, this evaluation of an argument follows from the data, claim and warrant (or backing). When the main elements of an argument are judged to be worthwhile or valid, the conclusion can be to accept the argument's claim as true.

Constitutive order, creating social order through 'constituted rules'; concept close to cultural worlds, figured worlds and cultural models.

Cooperative talk, this type of talk can be contrasted with disputational and exploratory talk. Whereas disputational talk largely consists of disagreements or arguments, cooperative talk contains primarily agreements that build upon each other in a non-critical way. Exploratory talk involves thoughtful consideration of the other person's statements in order to help each other to grow conceptually. These types of talk stem from the Thinking Together programme.

Critical pedagogy, an approach to education that advocates for the questioning of traditional methods of teaching because of their association with the oppression of those with less power in society.

Cultural production, refers to major transformations in the modes of production as cultures evolve from kin-based to tributary and then to capitalist production modes.

Cultural tools, Vygotskian notion that people rely on tools (such as language) to communicate with each other. Tools are socially agreed upon (conventional) and allow the conveyance of ideas.

D

Declarative memory, this is the sub-set of memory that people are usually able to explicitly name or recall. It is made up of semantic and episodic memories.

Deindustrialisation, the reduction of industrial activity in a region or country.

Discourse, the negotiation, between speakers, between readers and writers, or interlocutors of other types, whereby people come to find meaning in interactions.

Discoursal identity, the process of developing one's identity through telling stories about one's past, present and future self. The identity development process is seen as dialogic and it includes tension and simultaneity as well as agreement and reconciliation with other discourses present in the society.

E

Embodied experience, the lived experiences of people. It focuses on the physical aspect of perception, the body's interaction with environment, thought, self and external world.

Enquiry, an approach to instruction which entails allowing learners, with the help of knowledgeable others, to direct their experience by coming up with a problem to solve and seeking ways to solve it.

Equilibrium, a learner's drive for a sense of balance between what they sense and what they understand (an imbalance resulting in a state of confusion).

Episodic memory, part of declarative memory referring to memories relevant to particular events, like 'the first time I went to London it was raining'.

Epistemology, the process of obtaining knowledge, and what type of knowledge is seen as valid.

Experimental method, a method of study usually associated with science (natural or physical) but sometimes applied to social sciences. It involves the control of variables such that manipulating one independent variable can result in measurable effects (or lack thereof) on a dependent variable.

F

Field, social spaces of competition and struggle, where individuals compete over occupying certain positions (being a member of a particular social class, for example) by controlling different types of capital that exist in different fields.

Flow, a state of complete immersion in an enjoyable and fulfilling activity where an individual loses the sense of time and space, and where nothing else seems to matter.

G

Gaze, ways of viewing, of seeing and being seen; in the museum context it refers to the visitor–object relationship. Originally the term described the anxious state that comes with the awareness that one can be viewed.

Generalisability, the ability to make judgements about situations that are similar to those which have been studied, despite the lack of direct study. Evaluation of the applicability of findings beyond the sample to a wider population.

Grounded theory, the development of theory based or grounded on data systematically generated through basic research.

H

Habitus, the internalisation of subconscious habits in the human body; ways of moving, speaking, postures of the body and general conduct are a core part to habitus. It refers to the habitual way in which the body relates to the environment, and which is learnt through the everyday interaction with certain cultures or subcultures.

Hegemonic, the dominance and subordination of particular groups of people by members of another group who assume dominant roles and engage in behaviours that demonstrate power.

Hypothesis, specific prediction that can be generated from a theory.

I

Individualistic concept of identity, perceiving the self as separate from contexts and relationships.

Inferential statistics, quantitative means of using information from a sample (data) that has been measured to make judgements about the wider population, which has not been directly measured (generalisation).

Initiate-Respond-Feedback, type of discourse pattern which is prevalent in schools (together with Initiate-Respond-Evaluate). Teachers tend to initiate the communication by asking a question (for which there is often an expected correct answer). This is followed by the students providing a response, at which point the teacher provides some feedback about the response (e.g., 'Good!' or 'That's not what we usually think of when we define the Victorian period').

Intentionality, with reference to narrative theory, intentionality relates to the interpretation of others' motives.

Interpersonal, Vygotskian concept referring to the way that learners gain information first from other people in a social situation. This is sometimes referred to as 'interpsychological'.

Intrapersonal, Vygotskian notion (also called 'intrapsychological') to denote how concepts exist on a personal plane. These have generally been converted from the interpersonal through habitual use or repetition. Concepts become intrapersonal following a process of internalisation.

Intrinsic motivation, engaging in activities that are inherently enjoyable or interesting. People are intrinsically motivated when they want to do something for its own sake, interest and enjoyment and when they get a feeling of satisfaction during rather than after an activity.

L

Latent, a quality that is hidden or unobservable. In some research, inferences are made about latent qualities by pooling together information and surmising, through either qualitative or quantitative analyses, something about underlying properties of people or situations.

Laws, describe occurrences in the natural world without providing a broader explanation for their existence.

Likert scale, this is a response pattern used in questionnaires. It denotes a range of opinion potentials, usually from 1 to 5 or 1 to 7, with the extremes of the scale suggesting strong agreement or disagreement.

Long-term memory, an area in the mind where people store memories that can be held for a relatively short time (a few minutes) up to a lifetime.

M

Mediation, the process of using a tool to help understand or communicate about an idea. The use of language as a tool to help communicate, through symbols, is an example of the way that meaning can be mediated between people.

Member checks, in qualitative research it is often the case that a participant of a study looks over transcripts or analysis to ensure that the researcher has framed his or her ideas in a way that was intended.

Mental model, focusing on the existence of a cognitive model of an external reality and one's own possible actions/interactions with it and making sense of it; see also basic model.

Metacognition, the act of thinking about thinking. See also self-regulated learning.

Models, researchers (or others) may construct a diagram of how a phenomenon or process takes place. A model, in and of itself, is not a theory. But a model that includes explanatory proposals can constitute part of a theory.

Multiple-choice, a type of response for a questionnaire (or test) in which there is a limited number of possible choices.

N

Naïve theory, a set of ideas put forward about core knowledge by some researchers in developmental psychology; it is not a theory about learning, but rather an attribution to children that they have a theory.

Narrative, a type of story that is told, either intentionally or unintentionally, to create a coherent pattern of understandings about events, identities, and ideas. Narratives tend to be transmitted culturally in conventional ways and, as such, are passed down through generations.

Nativism, a theory suggesting that children are born with an innate predisposition to learn language (or other skills) because of a structure in the mind or brain.

Non-declarative memory, a type of involuntary memory, which is often triggered non-cognitively. Non-declarative memory stores are primarily things that people are not conscious of. This may include skill-based memories, such as how to ride a bicycle.

Numinous experience, responses to objects or places which have strong affective – real or imagined – associations.

O

Object-based discourse, the way in which objects are experienced by visitors from different cultural and social backgrounds.

Object-based epistemology, refers to all that is known about the natural world, through collecting and classifying specimens. Within this approach to knowledge, things exist as objects and are separate from the knower.

Ontology, in reference to approaches to the conduct of research, refers to the way that reality is construed.

P

Place-Based Education, an approach to education inspired by Dewey's ideas, which advocates motivating pupils to engage with the local environment while participating in learning that is experiential in nature.

Positive psychology, the study of positive human development. Positive psychologists are concerned with four topics: (1) positive experiences; (2) enduring psychological traits; (3) positive relationships; and (4) positive institutions. The term was coined by Maslow. Positive psychology has roots in the humanistic psychology of the twentieth century, which focused heavily on happiness and fulfilment.

Preconscious process, a process in thought or cognition relating to concepts that are not available to a person's conscious understanding. Sensory memory is an example of this because it has not yet come to a person's awareness (unless focused upon).

Problem-based learning, an approach to teaching in which pupils work toward a goal and in doing so must make use of a variety of learning concepts and tools, utilises the learner's own initiatives for projects to help them to go from current understandings to build new ones.

Psychographic characteristics, certain values, attitudes, desires, opinions, lifestyle and personality characteristics of consumers of products.

Psychology of culture, a number of disciplines including cultural psychology (sometimes known as psychological anthropology), cross-cultural psychology, and indigenous psychology.

R

Rehearsal, the repetition of information, verbally or otherwise, which helps to keep information in working memory and possibly transfer it to long-term memory.

Referentiality, the element of a narrative that helps the receiver of information interpret it. It provides grounding for a story.

Reliability, the believability in results of a study (particularly quantitative) in that the findings will be repeatable. A person who uses the same measures or means of collecting data should be able to get the same results as those published in research reports.

Representative sample, the concept of drawing participants that are like the wider population in ways that are relevant to the study. For example, if one is interested in all four-year-olds in the UK, sampling only four-year-olds in London, or four-year-olds from highly educated families would not be representative of all four-year-olds.

S

Saturation, within some qualitative research, the stage when, after a certain amount of data have been collected, no further insights are deemed to be gleaned.

Scaffolding, a concept coined by Bruner referring to the adult–child (or teacher–student) interaction that aims to facilitate an individual's learning. The interaction forms the 'scaffold' for learners to develop their understanding within. It is related to the zone of proximal development concept (see below).

Scripts, understandings or expectations that people have about events. In encountering an event that is (relatively) familiar, a person can refer to the script to fill in the information about what to expect. A classic example is the restaurant script in which people enter the building, are greeted by a host, who takes them to a table. At this point there is a menu, a server takes everyone's order, then brings the food; people eat; they ask for the bill before paying and then they leave.

Self-efficacy, the concept that people can judge their ability to perform in a particular situation.

Self-regulated learning, learning that is guided by metacognition. There are multiple elements of self-regulated learning, including planning, monitoring, and evaluating progress.

Semantic, part of declarative memory referring to information that is known generally, such as facts or explanatory relations between concepts (e.g., 'The capital of the United Kingdom is London').

Serious leisure, the systematic pursuit of a voluntary activity that the participant finds interesting and fulfilling.

Sensory memory, the type of memory that takes in all information in a relatively 'unfiltered' way through the senses, not discriminating for any particular type of information.

Short-term memory, also known as working memory (see working memory).

Situated learning, this concept derives from the communities of practice theoretical perspective. It relates to the idea that people learn best in the situation in which they will use the information.

Situated memory, memories that are formed through and therefore influenced or triggered by particular social circumstances.

Social concept of identity, seeing the self as embedded in contexts and relationships; see also collectivistic concept of identity.

Social constructivism, theoretical perspective that is based on both elements of sociocultural theory, which emphasises the interaction of groups, and constructivism, which focuses on the learning of individuals through their own agentive actions.

Socio-cognitive, closely related to social constructivism. This perspective on learning focuses even more on cognitive elements of learning and the mechanisms involved in learning, but also proposes a strong influence of the social situation.

Structure–agency debate, the relative importance of agency – i.e., whether people are capable of intentional (agentic) behaviour/actions – over structure – i.e., whether human behaviour is constrained by social structures (such as family, religion, education, media, law, politics, and economy).

Systemic-functional linguistics, approach to linguistics developed by Halliday, which considers language to be a function of a social semiotic system. It is more interested in the function of language than the structure.

T
Theory, a 'comprehensive explanation of some aspect of nature that is supported by a vast body of evidence' (Ayala et al., 2008, p. 11).

Transcription, the writing of speech for later analysis of language and/or narrative.

Transferability, a sense of the types of context for which similar patterns might be expected to be obtained.

Triangulation of data/theory/investigator, the use of multiple means to arrive at a conclusion in research. This may involve using alternative types of data collection to gain greater sense of a useful insight to the situation or having multiple investigators conduct the study or using multiple theoretical frameworks for analysis.

V

Validity, the idea that quantitatively measured concepts measure what they purport to measure.

W

Warrant, element of an argument that connects the data with the claim (see Backing).

Wh-question, a question that asks something to do with Who, What, Where, How or Why of an object, concept or event.

Working memory, the part of memory where the main work of 'thinking' happens. It is also known as short-term memory. Attention is focused on some precepts or concepts for the purposes of maintaining the idea or generating new understanding.

Z

Zone of proximal development, Vygotskian concept referring to the potential a person has for learning about a particular thing at any given point in time. This can be measured by examining what the person is capable of doing on his or her own in comparison with what he or she can do with the aid of some more advanced person.

References

Ayala, F. et al. (2008). *Science, evolution, and creationism.* Washington, DC: National Academies Press.

Frisvoll, S. (2013). Conceptualising Authentication of Ruralness. *Annals of Tourism Research*, 43, 272–296.

Index

References to figures are shown in *italics*. References to tables are shown in **bold**. References to endnotes consist of the page number followed by the letter 'n' and the number of the note.

UNIVERSITY OF WINCHESTER LIBRARY